The Girls' Guide To Off Grid Living

Author, imagining herself as a sailor despite the pants being outgrown floods.
Photographed by her fellow tomboy sidekick in this first self-directed photo shoot.

Amanda Kovattana is the author of *Diamonds In My Pocket: Tales of a Childhood in
Asia*. Her essays appear in the following anthologies: Everyday Mutinies: Funding
Lesbian Activism edited by Esther D Rothblum, Nanette K Gartrell, *The Lesbian
Polyamory Reader: Open Relationships, Non-Monogamy, and Casual Sex* edited by
Marcia Munson, Judith Stelboum, *On My Honor: Lesbians Reflect On Their Scouting
Experience* edited by Nancy Manahan, *Dyke Life: From Growing Up To Growing Old,
A Celebration Of The Lesbian Experience* edited by Karla Jay, *Encountering Cultures:
Reading And Writing In A Changing World* edited by Richard Holeton.

The Girls' Guide To Off Grid Living

A Memoir

Amanda Kovattana

Tiny Red Desk
Publishing

Contents

Introduction

So You're The One

Why would a maturing woman want to live a life that required a composting toilet? That was the unasked question that hovered over my off grid life. Was it enough to write a book about? Certainly I could interest people in other aspects of my experiments in sustainable living, but no, this was the topic around which all the other design aspects of my self styled life revolved. So I'm sticking with it.

Writing my first book had been one of the most satisfying things I had accomplished. It helped me understand my own heritage better than a decade of psychotherapy. But my family was not happy with my book *Diamonds In My Pocket* which was dismaying. I had written it as a love letter to my childhood in Thailand, describing each of my relatives and how their unique personalities had contributed to raising me. But alas, I had given away too many secrets and it was unseemly of me as a member of a high profile family to write a book that wasn't a fabulous fiction filled with accomplishments and cast in reverential tones, much as one would write a memorial book for a recently departed relative, as was part of our custom.

This peculiarly Western act of self reflection and investigation into possibly unpleasant memories, unseemly thoughts and long buried secrets, was foreign to them. The purpose of telling one's family story, at all, was to embroider the past, elide the unpleasantness, the carefully guarded family skeletons and set yourself and your family up as deserving and heroic, almost martyred in our efforts to better ourselves for noble reasons. That was the proper thing to do. After all if you were from old money, you had a reputation to uphold, especially if the fortune was largely lost. There I go again telling secrets.

Coming of age, as I did, in the confessional atmosphere of American psychotherapy, particularly California in the 70's, I had no intention of glossing over the dirt, the grit and juicy bits that flesh out a life. I told my stories of my unique childhood informed by the stories my mother told to me, of her cross cultural experience coming to Thailand as a young English woman. She carried the history for our family and told it to my eager ears to show what she had gone through and how she had done the best she could. She was very proud of my book and sold copies to all her friends. My father didn't live long enough to see it published, but he too, seemed proud of my storytelling when he heard me read a story on the radio about his grandfather's funeral, in a special program my memoir class put on with five of our best writers. My father was a teller of secrets too, sometimes maliciously out of frustration at how things had turned out. The rest of my Thai family were curiously uninterested in telling stories of the past and largely filled my ears with instruction on how to comport myself as a proper member of high society. The task of civilizing me in the hopes of returning me to Bangkok occupied my grandmother for many years.

Ironically I didn't even consider returning to Bangkok in my 20s, because I realized I was gay. I didn't know how Thai families accepted their gay children and that there was already a rich tradition of lesbians in Thailand especially butch lesbians. I was already invested in the emerging gay movement in the States and thought any hope I had of finding a girlfriend lay in staying put. My grandmother did tell me that I didn't need to marry as a woman, but I never gave her a chance to introduce me to the lesbians emerging within our family circle. In retrospect I would not have put it past her. My father, upon meeting a Thai lesbian in his travels, sought to introduce us immediately. He just didn't say what he saw. Keeping the kids from dropping out of their class was more the concern.

When the family heard that I had enrolled in a construction class, my relatives were all abuzz. "Amanda wants to become a carpenter" they said to each other, shaking their heads in disbelief. This was somehow the lowliest occupation I could possibly engage in. Something only a newly arrived peasant would do when they came to Bangkok. I did not bother to correct them that I did not have in mind the life of a laborer, but I was amused that they were so shocked. They were happier when I worked indoors with clients as an organizing consultant.

I put thoughts of another book aside, but I had kept a blog of the unusual life I was living. A life that would puzzle my relatives no end. When a favorite teacher near my home in California, decided to hold a women's memoir writing class, I was eager to join it for the camaraderie of sharing our stories. I didn't know if I would write a book. I thought to write a pamphlet about how to build and use a composting toilet like one I had made from common items. But the popularity of youtube videos, in this do-it-yourself department, had overtaken any need for books. Once I was again writing memoir, I realized, it would be much more interesting to write about how I used this composting toilet in my life, and furthermore, why I even wanted to. No one else in the tiny house community had any desire to dwell on this distasteful necessity. But I soon found that such a line of inquiry was a rich vein I could mine that would reveal, not only what my values had become, but if I even had a purpose in doing what I was doing.

Where my first book had been written to honor the country I loved and the family that raised me, this book would have no such pretentions. It would be just for me. The characters that came forth in my stories were not ones I necessarily wanted to honor. In fact they were more likely to have annoyed me in some way. But happily there were some stalwart friends who emerged too.

The accounts of jobs I was doing at the time were part of a technology that is gone now and it pleased me to describe those experiences for posterity. When I realized that a lot of what I had witnessed and participated in had historical value, especially concerning those heady years of the emerging gay community, I went back to my journals from those times and matched up pivotal dates with my real time accounts of those events.

The more I read of those journals, the more it reminded me of the insight about siblings. How they have such different memories from each other, that they might as well have lived in different families. My journals often did not make any mention of the memories that most stick in my mind. While I had painstakingly recorded, word for word, important conversations, with key people in my life, that I don't remember at all. And some events I only vaguely remembered, but had diligently recorded as part of my triumphant celebrating. I had, after all, written things down in order not to have to keep them in my head. When it came to piecing together the trajectory of my life, these accounts became invaluable and added a layer of detail I had long forgotten.

My story begins in the recent past, in Silicon Valley, where I sought to join the discussions percolating about how to live more sustainably. In Palo Alto in the fireside room of the Unitarian Church I went to see a movie about food waste. Hosted by the local chapter of Transition Town a discussion followed, which was the whole point for this solution-seeking group. A woman stood up to describe the wonders of her Bokashi composting endeavors as an efficient means of processing food waste. It was far more effective, she said, than even the much-loved backyard composting system.

My attention leapt at the utterance of this Japanese word Bokashi. This fermenting technology was a key part of composting my own human waste. As soon as the discussion was over I clambered through the rows of stackable chairs to get to this speaker to tell her of my practice of this innovation.

"Oh so you're the one," she said looking at me in somewhat of a covert fashion. "My husband found your blog" she explained and went on to tell me how, in preparation for their trip to Oregon for the total eclipse, he had been researching a portable composting toilet system. They would be parking their van in a field with hundreds of others who would likely overwhelm whatever Porta Potties were there. "It worked," she said though I could tell it wasn't exactly an operation she had enjoyed. I was so struck by the coincidence of talking to someone who had actually read my blog for instructions to put into immediate personal use that I forgot to ask her what tips she had for composting food waste.

I mean, what were the chances of me meeting a person who had searched for information that could have come from anywhere? But I had become a person compelled to share such stories of off grid living, on the internet, that beast of a grid, that had nearly everyone in its grip. Everyone, save those who were really off-grid, who wouldn't even bother about being an influencer on such a time wasting phenomenon of group think. But this was Silicon Valley, where innovation was the water we swam in. So it was not so much of a coincidence to meet someone else with an early adopter mind looking for an untried solution to implement.

The Palo Alto chapter was full of people who felt they could solve problems by putting into practice solutions on an individual basis. We were after all in the birthplace of innovation that came out of tinkering in suburban garages. The actual HP garage had been preserved for posterity as a museum. I was not so different from these lone tinkerers. I was a child of an electrical engineer who, fearing he would be made obsolete by the onset of computers, had built his own from a Heathkit set, working night after night for a year soldering resisters onto circuit boards just so he could learn what a computer was from the very wiring of it.

Transition Town used community meetings to choose local projects that were within reach for citizens to make more sustainable. This idea had came out of Totnes, England as a response to diminishing global resources particularly oil. Such change revolved around developing community The end goal being to come up with local alternatives to centralized systems that would be vulnerable to diminishing global resources particularly oil. Systems such as an electrical grid so huge that a branch falling on a wire could cause the entire eastern seaboard to go dark in the middle of a winter storm.

The Bay Area was also the birthplace of the tiny house on wheels as conceived by architect Jay Shafer in Sonoma County just north of San Francisco. I was now known among my circle as one who had successfully managed to outfit and live in a tiny house. To many, the tiny house seemed like a good solution in the midst of a housing crisis of such proportions that the road to Google headquarters was lined with late model RVs parked nose to tail as far as the eye could see. It was something people asked me about in the hopes that it would prove to be a viable alternative housing. A sort of Sony Walkman of housing. (The Sony Walkman had reduced an entire hi-fi set to a box you could clip onto your belt.)

A man I knew as my permaculture discussion group facilitator approached me with a question.

"I have a friend who wants to live in a tiny house," he said. "Would you be willing to talk to her about how she might get one?" he asked. I sighed inwardly at this false hope.

"Tell her it's not really about the tiny house. It's about who you are, who your community is and what resources you bring to the project. And whether you're willing to live semi-illegally as far as parking it anywhere because no town wants you." He let me rant on a bit more. "If this town really wanted to solve the housing crisis and find a place for all the RVs roaming around town switching places every 72 hours it would. But no it's all bogged down in safety issues like having the right security lights and facilities," I said. I could see by the look on his face that his friend was not the kind of woman who was up to the parameters of a semi-legal existence in a hostile environment.

People come to the idea hoping to stuff as much of their middle class expectations of a dream home as possible into a tiny house with the goal to simply be able to afford a house they could call their own. The tiny house trend had become a distraction from the problem our society had created by not providing sufficient low income housing in the first place. I couldn't afford to live here either, but that wasn't why I lived tiny.

I came to tiny house living as a sailor would to an ocean voyage having so admired, in sixth grade, the 16 year old boy who sailed around the world solo on a 24 foot yacht and whose bare torso harnessed to the railing of his boat graced the cover of National Geographic magazine. Like him I had set sail on an adventure into unknown territory. I wanted to find out what living tiny had to teach me about living, about how much basic resources one actually needed to live. And at what point was a small abode too small? Indeed at 6ft wide, 13ft long my tiny house felt more like our family sailboat in its truncated narrowness than the tiny houses twice the size that now populated cable TV.

The more I understood that I was different from other tiny house dwellers of the House Beautiful variety, the more I wondered what it was about me that I had brought to this venture. What drove me to want to live this way? Why would a modern woman aspire to live a life designed around a composting toilet, a feature endemic to tiny houses as it was near impossible to incorporate a flush toilet into one given that it was on wheels and severed from any connection to the ground to connect to a centralized sewer system. Yet this was the feature that most fascinated me.

Being off the ground a tiny house was essentially on stilts much like a Thai house. Thailand had such a deep impact on my core sensibilities around day to day living, that I had intentionally incorporated some of those features in the outfitting of my tiny. The story of my off grid life must then revisit my childhood growing up on the family compound in Bangkok. But was it just Thailand that had imbued me with these lifestyle choices?

Why didn't I simply adapt and assimilate to an American style of living when I moved here at the age of ten, an age that lent itself to such flexible adaptations. Not to mention a built in cultural inclination to do so that made assimilation a feature of our model minority Asian profile. Thailand it turned out had informed my physical and sentient memories, but my inner narrative had already been captured by another Western culture even before I set foot on these shores. The culture of my mother and my mother tongue — the Queen's English.

The English that had embodied in its children's books a close relationship to the English landscape, to magical realms of the imagination and fairy tales, to the right to roam freely in a truly free range manner that encompassed daily adventures walking through fields on exploratory expeditions with butterfly nets and mason jars, riding old bicycles with wicker baskets, messing about in boats sailing the lake country and riding ponies with English saddles, while across one's body a brown leather school satchel was slung full of bread and cheese, cold meats and a corked glass bottle of water. This England peopled my world with characters from these much loved books whether they came in animal form wearing formal Edwardian outfits or in human form wearing ordinary clothes with sensible buckled on Mary Jane style t-strap sandals much like my mother had on in her school photos. The England of the war years that had informed my mother's morality, frugality and sensible British parenting.

But there was yet another element that informed my early life despite already being so full of Englishness as I was. And that was a period so dark in my mind I had refused to even look at it until now for it had a mean flavor to it and a voice that was arrogant and cocky in its cynicism. I kept brushing these memories aside. I mean what had this failure of the imagination to do with my later optimism and vision? Surely it was an aberration, a detour into sullenness and escapism.

In retrospect it might have just been the '70s with its cultural load of emerging feminism and lesbian separatism that had briefly captured me as I struggled to see my future through the murkiness of diminishing possibilities. My sexuality having cut me off from any sort of a mainstream path. Carving out a way to survive seemed to be the best approach I could adapt for myself.

Yet the '70s also contained within it the human potential movement that had had such an impact on the emergence of Silicon Valley and on California culture. The idea that the mind had the capacity to reprogram its entire perspective which would then allow you to recreate yourself apart from your past and entertain new neural pathways that could heal and grow a new self actualized life for yourself, were concepts carried on for several enlightening decades. Such ideas along with the cultural influences of my birthright made me not entirely a rebel unto my own causes, but a product of my time.

In the end, whether I fell off the grid of expectations or intentionally bypassed it, this girls' guide to off grid living is offered as a recollection of living a life on one's own terms.

PART I. THE GIRL

AMANDA KOVATTANA

Chapter One

A Walk Home

Bangkok 1965. My mother sat in the chair at the hairdressers, the one I had just vacated. My freshly cut hair was an easy pixie cut that would take little time to maintain and would save us both time. My mother had her own fully accessorized outfit and hair to perfect every morning for her marketing job across town at Grant Advertising.

Mummy looked up at me from the hairdresser's chair and asked me if I thought I could walk home alone since it would take some time for her to have her hair colored and set. I welcomed this invitation. This was a chance to be a Big Girl in the English sense. An independent and solo agent of my own existence just like the girl heroine in my *Milly Molly Mandy* books. Such independent adventures were unheard of by my Thai relatives. No-one went anywhere alone at any age. My grandmother— my Khun Ya (as I called her)—especially would think it unseemly.

The streets of Bangkok were considered dangerous for a girl of my class background as being seen on the streets alone might be an invitation for a kidnapping. A kidnapping had been reported recently. But the kidnapper hadn't done the deed at all and had just put some child on the telephone to pretend they had been kidnapped, while the anxious parents waited to hear the ransom demands.

I heard about it on the TV news at Khun Ya's house where I would go after eating dinner with my parents, a maid having come from the kitchen, walking across the driveway carrying a large tray of whatever was on the menu that day. At the Big House so full of life, my Khun Ya and my aunts discussing whatever was the news of the day, while my parents sequestered themselves in their air conditioned living room sealed off with expensive window glass.

Upon hearing this kidnapping story my Auntie Sakorn turned to me and told me that if I were ever kidnapped I was to speak English on the phone so the family would know it was really me. Everyone chimed in their opinion that this was a good idea. This was my secret weapon they all agreed. It would be one of the advantages of my being a mixed race, bilingual child. I was proud of this secret skill.

The one time one of my English classmates did wander away from school and outside onto the street, he was brought back by a nice Thai man who had bought him an ice cream and watched him eat it while practicing his English on him. The man persuaded the boy to tell him the name of his school—Mrs. Clayton's school. And so he was returned to us. This cross cultural story was celebrated with a certain subversive joy by my school mates and teachers for it confirmed for us a trust in the good nature of Thai people and of the benign nature of the world. Such as one would enjoy in a civilized country like England.

For every story of fear there was always a story of good luck to balance things out. You could choose which kind of story you liked. And having already made my acquaintance with the benign cosmos one afternoon at school after everyone else was gone, I trusted that I would be held by this force. Some would call it God. Some would call it luck. It was just a knowing that came to me as I sat on my heels amusing myself with some chalk on a chalkboard sitting on the ground resting against the two room school of Mrs. Clayton's British school for children of expats.

I had looked up from the chalkboard as though summoned and turned my head towards the sunny patch of playground. Seeing the light I felt the information pouring into me of this benign invisible helping force and was assured that it would always be at hand. I only needed to call on it, though I didn't know yet how. I just knew to trust it. My mother too seemed to live in this trust despite having been bombed nightly during the London Blitz. The streets of Bangkok did not look so scary to her, compared to the bombed out streets she had played in.

The hairdresser was on the main thoroughfare only a block from our lane. No streets needed to be crossed. So I set off for home noticing everything with new eyes. The shopkeeper sweeping the sidewalk in front of her shop. The men carrying heavy pieces of wood into the furniture making shop. The post office with its red pillar box out on the sidewalk. All of this only I would witness at just this moment in time. And no one took any notice of me, a girl alone wearing a cotton dress and buckled on sandals. This privacy of observation allowed me to become aware that I had my own sense of things. That I could observe the world and make note of it without anyone else having to see it with me. I carried this special mission to notice everything all the way down our quiet lane until I got to the fenced in compound of our family homestead and entered the driveway through the open gate. Then the spell was broken. I was once again back in my rightful place playing in the garden. To be watched by Khun Ya when she was home and the house staff as they went about their chores when everyone was at work.

I also had a job in Khun Ya's world. It also involved walking, but not alone. For two years running I had participated in fashion shows held at the palace across the street. Children from my kindergarten showed up in new outfits sewn by local seamstresses for the occasion. Our teachers instructed us on how to walk down the runway that had been constructed to rise above and in and around the many tables of the garden party. A party that would be attended by members of high society. These were well born people of the Thai upper class. Scores of them sitting at round tables with white tablecloths. Since it was my job to walk this runway I had no fear. Being admired by family and friends was how we were introduced as the emerging generation. And after we were done, there would likely be ice cream.

The first year we were dispatched down the runway in pairs. I wore a pink checked dress with white ruffles running down the front. My runway partner wore a crop top and capris decorated with a design at the hems. Very Audrey Hepburn. We were also photographed for a full color photo in the Sunday magazine of the paper. Nearly all girls, only two boys. One boy wearing a matching sailor outfit with his sister. And another in a beach outfit with swim trunks and a terrycloth jacket.

The second year I was pleased that we would each walk the runway solo and were instructed to make two turns at the corners of the runway pausing to show off the outfit with pointed toe. I had on yet another pink dress of a finer more grown up chiffon. Khun Ya having determined that pink was my day of the week color since it was Tuesday in Thailand by the time I was born. Each day of the week had a different color. It was something we all learned in kindergarten.

The rehearsal went off without a hitch. That evening my hair was curled and piled on my head. I looked forward to my walk. Then at the last minute Khun Ya was by my side with a woman and two little girls I did not know in matching outfits of a modern design that made my dress look provincial. Modern because the pinafore was made of a red vinyl worn over long sleeve ruffled white blouses.

They were the daughters of the ambassador to France. In the brief introduction I could see that this was a very important family that Khun Ya wanted very much to introduce me to. She told me that I was to take the eldest girl with me on the runway walk. I did not want to. After all this girl had not been at the rehearsal and did not know the exacting manner of the pause and turn. The precise pause to show off the dress before completing the turn. Not to mention that our outfits clashed—the red vinyl did not go with the pink chiffon. But it was my job to accommodate those who outranked me and the little girl was clearly thrilled to be accompanying me. As we were standing there a press photographer took our picture with me holding the hands of each of the girls. I am not quite smiling. Dutifully I walked the runway with my charge and at each turn she ran around me as if we were playing a game of crack the whip. I'm sure it was quite adorable this running in circles. I did not think so, but what could I do. I did not begrudge this little girl her fun. She too would come to know her job in due time. How beautiful and dignified she would have to look. I would see for myself decades later on Facebook.

The life that Khun Ya envisioned for me was filled with such events as she attempted to insert me into society. She got me a position in a ballet company performance for the queen doing nothing at all except holding a flag while the dance company twirled around me. For my costume I had a tall military style hat covered in gold paper with a sequined sash I wore over my ordinary black leotard and ballet flats. A reporter interviewed me which resulted in a photograph and a brief paragraph about what I said and how serious I was about my role as the youngest performer. The journalist talked of his surprise when I wrote my name in English for him. It became the point of his story. What to make of this difference? I wondered.

We were a diplomatic family in the sense that it was our duty to welcome visiting dignitaries just as Khun Ya would welcome Queen Elizabeth a few years later along with an entourage of Thai ladies in traditional Thai silk sarongs and jackets bowing as she passed. An 8 1/2 by 11 press photograph of the event in a gold frame sat on her buffet in the dining room as a testament to this royal event. This visitation from British royalty impressing me greatly and even more so with each passing year the further I drifted from my aristocratic roots.

But I was not really interested in pursuing this life of fraternizing with royalty. There was just too much waiting around when royalty was expected. So I did not miss it at all when my mother intervened and sent me to Mrs. Clayton's school which would end my runway career. And the yearly addition of a pink dress to my wardrobe. For I would now wear the more soothing pale blue cotton required of our uniform.

There was not a lot of variety to choose from for children in those days. When it came to clothes I liked pockets and told my mother so. She found me long pants in blue twill (we didn't have denim in

Thailand) with pockets topstitched with white thread and the initial "A" embroidered on one of the pockets in white. We were both thrilled with this find.

"A" for Amanda," my mother said.

Pants (or trousers as the British would call them) were what I could wear at home. One day a seamstress in the family made me an outfit that perfectly suited me. A paisley button up shirt in purple with purple shorts. I wore it immediately on a trip to the beach town of Hua Hin with Khun Ya for a ceremonial occasion involving lots of flowers that the staff who accompanied us spent the evening stringing together into wreaths. I was not required to attend, so Sarmta the driver entertained me by driving me around the bustling town that evening full of people and bright lights as it was.

My public life required dresses as a marker of my sex. I did not mind this because being a girl was clearly a high status position in my family and also in Thai society. My favorite dress had a nautical theme and three patch pockets in navy blue marching across the white bodice. I paired them with my favorite shoes. American saddle shoes Mummy found for me at the thrift shop at the American embassy, where I found a Cub Scout manual. I persuaded her to buy it for me as well because, as I showed her, it was filled with craft projects. She recognized the value of such crafts; she who had also been a Girl Guide in England.

I loved the paper models my mother found for me that I could cut out and build—castles and houses as well as Easter baskets, woven pot holders and paper dolls. But the first time I made something that did not come in a ready made kit was a turning point. This adventure was inspired by a corrugated box I had come upon in the servants' quarters. It was big enough for me to get inside it. No one else had claimed it so I took it to my room and after my mother put me to bed and turned out the lights I crept in it and fell asleep. My mother, not finding me in my bed when she checked on me later, discovered me inside my box and woke me to put me back into bed. I sleepily wondered why? I had been perfectly comfortable in the box.

"You can't sleep in there," she told me.

The next day I decided that if I was too big to live in the box then it was just the right size for Oedipus our Siamese cat. I took the box into the lanai area of the house and got a sharp knife from the kitchen. With a pencil I drew windows on the side of the box and carefully cut them out so they were shutters that could open and close. Satisfied I got out my paintbox and painted flowers up the side of the walls. I arranged the flaps of the box so they would look like doors and painted a roofline across the top. I was so pleased with my creation and its beautiful flowers along the walls that I forgot all about the cat. He didn't seem in the least bit interested in the box anyway and was nowhere in sight.

But I did have to tell someone about the house I had created. It was too grand to just leave alone, being the largest thing I had ever made. So I ran into the servants quarters to boast that I had made a house for the cat. My nanny was busy, but she assured me she would come and look at it later. She suggested that I visit Khun Ya up in her bedroom. I climbed up the stairs to the top floor of her house, the highest point on the compound. I found her putting papers away and told her about the house I had built for my cat. She seemed intrigued and she told me she would come down to see it.

I returned to our house and soon enough Khun Ya descended from her room and came into the house looking for me.

"Show me this house for the cat," she said as she came in the door. So seldom did she pay a visit that I felt honored to be the cause of her entry. My creation sat on a bench where I had been working on it and she came over and sat down next to it. I didn't know how she would react to my art piece. I knew from the still life paintings that hung on her wall in her dining room that Khun Ya was an artist and had trained at her convent school to make these paintings. She regarded my creation with a gentle curiosity and I demonstrated how the windows worked and showed her the flowers.

"Don't you think the flowers are pretty?" I asked her proudly.

"Yes they are quite nice," she said. And she sat awhile longer admiring it and the view of the garden outside the glass doors. Then she went back to her room. And that was enough to deem my efforts worthy. I grew a passion for making things from ordinary materials, designing what had not existed before from what I found on my travels. I cut an outfit from old newspaper; a little vest and an A-line skirt. I stapled the pieces onto my body and attempted to walk around without tearing it apart. Encouraged, I folded a hat as my nanny had taught me to do and set it on my head. Then had my mother photograph me in my paper dress in the garden, posing as I had seen in fashion magazines admiring a flowering shrub.

When I was eight I asked if I could go to England—the source of the children's books in which girls found things to do. My mother seemed delighted and agreed to send me there for the summer on my own chaperoned on the flight by two businessmen she knew.

For my trip to England my mother packed my red suitcase and another one full of my many dresses, a few pair of shoes and the long pants and shirts that I would wear playing in the neighborhood. Khun Ya gave me a white leather purse in which I carried that very precious document called a passport. The whole family came to see me off as if I were a state official, an ambassador. And for this special role my mother had the dressmaker sew up for me a copy of the Chanel suit in shocking pink. This alone impressed upon my English grandparents that I was no ordinary little girl, which was perhaps my mother's intention.

I carried with me a little case full of tiny toys including a pack of tiny playing cards. I taught my business companions to play all the card games I had learned from the old nanny who sat in the kitchen in the servants quarters with coins in her ears. I was so excited I made these poor men get off at every stop we made along the way even when we didn't have to.

They were glad to be relieved of their duties once we arrived and did not accept an invitation to tea when my grandparents came to fetch me. My grandma helped me settle into the room that had been my mother's which had a huge bed I climbed into every night with some difficulty. Grandma assured me that the room was just the same as when my mother lived there. It didn't really look like a child's room with its floral carpet, vanity table and lace curtains, but I came to enjoy sitting up in bed reading in such a cosy room. The days were so long that I rarely experienced the night since it was still light when I went to bed.

Across the hall was the little blue and white kitchen which seemed so contained and clean after the open air one in the servant's quarters back in Bangkok. No mosquitoes would bite me here; nor large frogs gather. Within these painted walls everything was put tidily away in cabinets. It was in the kitchen that I learned the most about English customs. At the stainless steel sink, Grandma taught me how to wash the dishes in a dishpan and dry them with a hand towel. She had a method and an order about what to wash first. I was entranced by the fact that there was a right way to do dishes. But she mostly let me sit on the stool so I could tell her stories about my home while she did the dishes.

I would have many outings to stately homes with my grandparents who loved a walk in a well manicured garden. I would make friends with the neighbor kids from India and accompany them to the park to wade in the stream in Wellington boots. There were so many adventures to have in this quiet suburban neighborhood.

Half way through my stay Grandpa took me aside and gave me a little talk about how the rich needed to be taxed so that the poor could be taken care of. This seemed eminently sensible. There were lots of poor people on the streets of Bangkok and beggars, especially maimed and sightless beggars. Taxes sounded like a good idea. It was the only conversation I had with my Grandpa that I remembered in full. He had a tendency to talk to me as if I were an adult, a pint size adult. It gave me a head start on thinking about systems and society.

Later I would wonder what compelled my Grandpa to speak to an eight year old about taxes and social justice concerns. Perhaps it was my suitcase full of tailor made dresses or my stories of living with servants and a chauffeur. For theirs was the first house I'd been in that didn't have servants. I enjoyed the self-sufficiency of it. The little bit of cooking, cleaning and gardening that went into such a life. I walked to the grocery store too with my grandma and her little cart on wheels to buy the things I saw in the pantry.

Grandpa had given nearly everything of value he owned to the war effort — radio, binoculars, a camera. And after the war he saw the national health service instated and this was a very good thing that even I could take advantage of with a good teeth cleaning every time I came to visit. England was a model to me of sensible things. Like public libraries. I would accompany my grandpa on errands that sometimes required that he leave me for an hour or so at a public library. I couldn't have been happier finding the latest books in the Milly Molly Mandy series that I so loved. Now there was an only child who did sensible simple things like learn to plant watercress or ride a bicycle or going to the seaside. Simple events but still worthy of a story with illustrations.

And so it was on such a summer day on holiday at the seaside with my grandparents that I decided to walk by myself on the pebble beach while everybody was inside watching TV. It was the moon landing and the first walk on the moon by Neil Armstrong. My grandparents had gone to a neighbor's house to watch it on their TV. I clearly wasn't impressed enough with this American event to give it viewing time indoors on such a lovely afternoon. I still remember my walk. It was not recorded for posterity. But it was full of my own thoughts.

Chapter 2

A Deception

In 1968 we immigrated to the U.S.. It was my mother's idea; she chose California after a business trip with my father, wowed by the natural beauty and the friendly, casual culture. My father told his mother he was leaving Thailand in order to save his marriage, but the move also expanded the engineering projects he could work on, once at the home office of the American company he had been working for, Stanford Research Institute (now SRI International).

On our way to our new home in the U.S. we flew to England to visit my grandparents and our English friends. As we drove a rented car down the country road looking for our destination I shouted out at seeing my best friend Pippa waving at us from a tree.

"There they are," I said alerting my parents. Pippa climbed down from the large tree followed by her brother Rupert. On the grass Nickolas now a toddler was walking about beneath the tree. The children had been sent to wait for us at the corner where we would have likely missed the turn to the farm. They had been there for over an hour maybe even two. We had telephoned of course, but no one expected us to keep to any deadline so we hadn't stopped to find a call box as we neared Cambridge.

Pippa's family had known us in Bangkok where Pippa's father had been an interim university professor and Pippa and I were at Bangkok Patana school together. Her father was now at Cambridge and the family lived in one side of a semi detached two story house they rented from a farm family. The now elderly farm couple lived in the other side.

I was so excited to be in England the land of my favorite children's books *Milly Molly Mandy* and *The Famous Five* with its tomboy character who called herself George. But as an only child I couldn't get up to any adventures. Now with my best friend and her brothers I was ignited into action. Having presented myself in a nice dress to Pippa's mother, I was free to put on my trousers and a borrowed sweater. My white t-strap shoes were too nice to get muddy so Pippa said I could wear her brother Rupert's Wellington boots standing with hers at the back door. I was thrilled with them and they fit perfectly. Real black rubber boots just like George often wore. Rupert was fine with wearing his red t-strap sandals as it was quite dry out.

Pippa and Rupert showed me all their favorite places—the stacks of hay in the barn that we could climb as if it were a pyramid, the tractor was another climbing spot and the mysterious and slightly scary tunnel used for a farm chore I couldn't quite visualize. Pippa showed me how if you stood at one end and looked into it you couldn't see a thing. Then she took me inside the barn and had me look through it so we could see daylight. She had Rupert stand in front of the daylight end so we could see him in silhouette. This was all tremendously interesting to me. I had three days to enjoy it all. I loved the idea of farm life.

My father came out to take a picture of us. I had just discovered a pitchfork which I'd only seen in photos. I pressed the business end into the ground with my Wellington booted foot resting on one of the sides as I looked up from my "farm work." My hair was short so I was confident I looked like a boy. A boy who knew how to use a pitchfork though I'd never seen one before. Rupert stood beside me holding a cracker and Pippa was behind me holding baby Nickolas. We all looked at the camera.

On my last day Pippa's mother told us that we were to have another visitor, a family from America with a girl our age. We were naturally expected to entertain her and I did not like the idea one bit. This was my England with my English friends and I didn't want to share it with an American girl. But I had to be a good host now that I had become a member of Pippa's family and knew all the fun secrets of the farm. Pippa too didn't want to share our time with this American girl. We were solid in our shared history having been fast friends in Bangkok. We had also been three legged champs at all the races we entered. She was just that much taller than me that she could comfortably tuck me under her arm as we linked our bodies together as one champion running unit.

Though our school prided itself in how many nationalities we represented there were few Americans as they mostly went to the American International School. Americans set themselves apart already. They were different. Their toys were different, more sophisticated with lots of parts and ready made themes. They were distinctively adult like Barbie with her stiletto heels and scary bust line in the zebra swimsuit. The boys had cars that you could make crash with parts that were made to look like a crumpled fender. The American families I visited in Bangkok had rooms littered with these toys.

At first the toys didn't look like any fun and I ignored them, but the family with the Barbies and crashed auto with the auto repair garage were so full of life, wanting to show me their treasures that I got sucked into the excess. It was so much fun to have them bring their toys to life especially the boy who took special care to impress me. I would get overexcited and high on the excess then crash on the way home becoming so moody and disappointed my mother stopped taking me to see them.

Pippa had fewer toys than I did. We adopted pet rocks we discovered by the pool at her apartment complex; round smooth ones the size of guinea pigs. We tied red ribbons around them, carried them around and had them play with each other. It was a whole world of make-believe we shared. This American girl we were expected to entertain I feared would not think anything like that would be cool. I was sure of it. Would she even think it was cool to look through a long black tunnel to the light at the end big enough for Rupert to stand in? I didn't even want to know. She likely wouldn't understand how we were tomboys and not interested in dolls or dress-up.

So I hatched a plan to entertain ourselves at her expense. I told Pippa we could pretend that I was one of twins. First she would introduce me as a boy named Simon. (This was the boy name my mother had chosen.) And then as she was showing the girl the farm I would run inside and change clothes so they would then find me in the bedroom as the girl twin. I was confident that I would pass as a boy. Two summers ago when I was in England visiting my grandparents I had gone to the public pool and into the changing room alone while my grandmother sat in the bleachers waiting to watch me swim. On my return to the changing room a mother challenged me.

"The boys changing room is across the hall," she said to me in a firm bossy way, standing with her daughter who was about my age. I had come in wet with a towel around me. I said nothing. To tell her I was a girl would be to show her she'd made a mistake, and that would put her in the wrong. Then what? I wished to spare her as any polite Thai person would. I continued past her to change. She would realize her error soon enough if she thought about it. I had after all already been into the dressing room once already and my clothes were there in a locker. She saw me again when I was dressed standing in front of the mirror combing my hair. I had a dress on then.

"Why didn't you tell me you were a girl?" she asked me no more friendly than the first time. Again I said nothing. Why should I have to account for her mistake? I thought. I just continued to comb my hair looking at myself in the mirror until she left. No Thai had ever mistaken me for a boy. I had a pixie cut like Twiggy; this was the latest style my mother had promised. Thai boys had their hair cropped up their necks and they never had bangs. The British though had the Beatles and since I was not blond I was more Beatle than Twiggy.

Pippa agreed to my plan and Rupert was in on it too. When I was introduced as Simon I was in the barn sitting on a bale of hay. As soon as I was identified as Simon I said hello and proceeded to climb to the next bale talking in a knowing boy way as though I knew my way around. My voice slightly lower, my stride longer. It felt good to be a boy as if I'd earned a new rank. When Pippa and the American girl left I ran inside, up the flight of stairs into Pippa's bedroom and changed into my best dress then sat on the bed waiting feeling slightly passive looking pretty as though I didn't ever go outside and climb bales of hay. A few minutes later Pippa and the girl came into the room and I was introduced as Amanda. The girl exclaimed in surprise.

"They look so much alike," she said so loudly in her American accent that Pippa's mum Pam came in to see what was going on. "She looks just like her brother" said the girl to Pam. Pam looked at her puzzled then at me and said "That's Amanda. She doesn't have a brother." I was watching the girl's face as she registered that she'd been had. It was a look of hurt more than anger at having been excluded from the joke. Her long brown hair framing a pale face looking at us a little sadly too. I had somehow betrayed her, a girl in the universal club of girls. She wasn't so different from me, an only child trusting in her ability to make friends. I felt bad. No one said anything.

"Go downstairs all of you and have your tea" Pam said and we hurried past her. We behaved ourselves after that and played a board game with the American girl for the rest of the evening with no further thought of ill intentions. But I remained stricken by my deception and being called out by Pippa's mum. How long had I thought we would carry on with the charade? We hadn't thought about how we would end it. I hadn't committed to being a boy full time. I didn't know if I wanted to be one of the boys, join their club and prove myself among them. I just wanted my own world of being a boy just as my Aunty Ah Pahdt had declared when she told me I had a boy spirit (from my having been a man in a previous life). If I was going to be a boy again, it would have to be my secret.

Chapter 3

Meet Me After School

The rest of our holiday we would spend camping through Europe. I helped my father put up the tent; it weighed about fifty pounds. I got good at connecting all the heavy metal poles to make the frame which included extra leg sections that boosted the roof line over our head. The cumbersome canvas had to go over that roofline and for this my father needed my help raising it over our heads and pushing it over the tent frame. Then hammering down all the tent pegs. It was a very handsome orange tent with a blue roof, a zip open door to a foyer inside and an inner tent that just fit the three of us in our sleeping bags. I hardly knew my parents at such close quarters, but I never tired of this strange nomadic adventure of making our home every night at campsites where other families were doing the same.

We had flown to Stuttgart, Germany from England where we went to pick up a pearl white Mercedes at the factory; my father had special ordered it for use in California. A beautiful chariot with forest green interior and the distinctive boxy shape of the '60s. I was so proud I had the immediate impulse to want to wash it and keep it clean for good. As a travel game my father asked me to spot the difference between our Mercedes and the German ones on the road. This mostly had to do with configurations of the lights. I also liked looking for the white oval stickers on the back of cars that would tell me what countries the families inside them came from—D for Deutsch, A for Austria, GB for Great Britain. That way I would know if I could speak to them or just play with their kids in the universal gestures of mime.

We bought all our camping equipment in one fell swoop the day after we got the car then headed to Italy. The campsites often had a playground and sometimes more elaborate gaming facilities and even a grocery store. My mother sent me to get a head of lettuce at one. I came back with a cabbage. She had no more idea what to do with it than I did. We would make other such mistakes once we got to the United States, but we were bonded now as a family.

At the end of our camping holiday we put everything in the trunk of the car and drove it to a port in Holland where we sat at a coffee shop and watched as it was loaded onto a boat. Then we flew to New York where a five hour layover gave my father a chance to show all the paperwork we needed to be admitted into this humongous country. In San Francisco our nomadic life was not quite over. We spent another month living in a motel near my father's new job at Stanford Research Institute in Menlo Park. I was enrolled in a school nearby.

Once we bought our California home, I changed schools to one within walking distance where I would be a newcomer to the fifth grade class. The school day had already begun when I was brought to the door of the classroom and given over to my new teacher. The silver-haired teacher looked on me kindly and introduced me to the class. I was possibly the only Asian child in the entire school, not that this concerned me. I was used to it from being in England. There were also four Hispanic kids in my class. When a plump, friendly white girl offered to show me around at recess all seemed fine.

It was still fine when the day ended even though a rather tough looking girl had come up to me at recess and said, "Meet me after school. I'm going to beat you up." She did not say why. I looked at her curiously. She was challenging me to a fight, but not to kill me. More as a game to see who would be tougher. I did not want to play this kind of game especially in a dress. And I had never had such a fight before. I invoked a higher authority.

"My mother doesn't want me to fight," I said. This turned out to be a good choice of words. My answer implied that I was indeed capable of fighting and had been so good at it that my mother had to specifically tell me not to do it again. The girl gave me a look to determine if this was true and walked away. I was glad when a couple of boys who had taken an interest in me offered to walk me home.

I fully expected the girl to find me after school and I kept an eye out for her, but I didn't see her at all. Somehow instinct and having a good handle on the English language with my English accent had saved me from getting my clothes messed up. And maybe all those afternoons I had spent watching kung fu movies from Hong Kong that the Thai TV stations would broadcast on school holidays had helped too. There was always a girl fighter in them. Girl fighters who never got their beautiful long silk trousers and embroidered tunics messed up.

School children in American schools did not wear uniforms as they did in Thailand. In 1968 girls were still required to wear dresses though change was in the air and later that year there would be a protest by school-age girls. I had not made any friends to venture an opinion on the matter. I wasn't worried about friends. I was used to being alone and had long relied on the company of books. English books that allowed me to continue living in an England whose school children wore uniforms with distinguished school blazers.

In my fifth grade class, the smartest girl took the challenge to wear pants to school on the prescribed day of protest. I understood the concept of protesting, but it didn't interest me. I was a good girl, what people called a teacher's pet in fact. I did what I was told and preferred it that way. Khun Ya would have been proud. She who welcomed international guests hosted by the Thai government had taught me how to greet royalty and what was proper dress for any specified event of importance. I expected I would always be informed of what to wear. At home I could wear what I wanted, but I knew I was expected to wear dresses to places where I was to interact with grown-ups. This made me feel I was getting the protocol correct.

Just remembering all the correct greetings in English and all the correct honorifics in Thai plus all the taboos with feet and body positions was enough for most of us.

Nothing happened to the girl who wore pants to school on the day of protest in my American 5th grade class, but she didn't wear them after that one day. Girls continued to wear dresses at least for the rest of the year. When I chose to wear a dress to the dentist he complemented me on it. I was pleased with this.

I told my mother on the drive home, "I like wearing dresses because people tell me how nice I look" I waited for her approval. I thought she would be pleased that I was getting it about being a grown-up.

"You shouldn't wear a dress because of what others will say. You should wear what pleases you," she told me slightly annoyed that I had already picked up the message that girls were supposed to please others. I said nothing for I also knew that my mother liked me to wear dresses. She always had a say in how I dressed and I usually complied to her wishes. No one had ever told me I had to like what protocol was required of me. But here she was saying I should wear what pleased me. Well in that case I would damn well wear pants. Pants with pockets just as she had found for me when I was eight with the letter 'A' on the. pocket. I don't think she realized she had just blown her own authority over how I should dress. This tension would grow fiercer as I veered away from her own stylish ideas of what I should wear. My mother prided herself in being a fashion plate.

I remained a traditionalist. I liked uniforms and the regimen of rules over the dilemma of too much choice. School uniforms created a class of people whose job it was to learn. It distinguished us and gave us a place in society just as the saffron robes of the monks distinguished who they were. Plus it saved me from having to decide what to wear and by the same token who I was or what it was I belonged to.

Chapter 4

My Secret Life As A Boy

I wanted to join the Girl Scouts. I could belong to something and wear a uniform too. My mother had told me so many stories of the Girl Guides troop she had belonged to in England just after the war. Her scout leader, a young woman not much older than the scouts themselves, had taken them on hikes and camping trips where they learned to make their own gear and cook outdoors.

My Great Aunty Jessie in England sent me a reprint of the original Girl Guide handbook written by Lord Baden Powell himself—a small book with a white cover with red and black type. The book offered lots of instruction to girls on how to look after their own health, use a compass, draw a map, make a cooking fire, and build a shelter. Lord Baden Powell clearly thought girls were capable of such skills. The text was extensive and he explained all sorts of survival skills and reasons for being a useful member of society. It was his confidence in girls that earned my loyalty. I read everything I could find about this fine man who as a boy had given a lot of thought to contingencies and had attempted to play the piano with his feet in case he lost the use of his hands. One could always find a way to make do.

A girl who belonged to the local troop took me to the church near the school where the Girl Scouts met in what looked like a converted garage. It was a very disappointing endeavor. We glued macaroni to cigar boxes and spray painted them gold. Someone chose a ridiculously long silly fantasy name for their patrol which annoyed me because it had nothing to do with nature.

And the Girl Scout handbook offended me more as it had illustrated instructions on how to get out of a car by swiveling the legs out held together so we didn't flash our underwear. I did not see anything in this handbook that seemed useful. I got my green uniform and sewed on all the patches as instructed. The only point of the uniform seemed to be to sell cookies, for we rarely wore it otherwise. And why did we have to sell cookies when we could just do a chore for money like the scouts did in England on their bob-a-job fundraising week? I stayed long enough to make it to the first campout which was in a park next to the zoo in San Francisco. Equally disappointing was that a bunch of fathers came with us to put up the tents and we didn't even get to watch them do it diverted as we were by some game activity. And here I had helped my father put up our very heavy canvas tent all over Europe. So much for learning scouting skills. I ran around the park with the overexcited girls who clearly were not camping material. I was a snob already.

I turned to the Boy Scout Handbook. In the introduction was the Norman Rockwell painting "Tomorrow's Leader" of a Boy Scout holding a compass and looking into the distance as if into the future. That was the spirit I was looking for. I studied the handbook thoroughly and told my next door neighbor Shelley that I wanted to become a Boy Scout even if I wasn't allowed to join. Shelley, who was fourteen and seemed very grown up to me, had introduced herself as soon as we settled into our new house telling me how she and her mother had peeked into our mailbox to see what our names were. She was so nice I went to see her all the time and thought of her as a big sister. I asked her important questions such as what was the difference between the word "darn" and "damn" and was "frick" a really bad word or just a minor one.

Her brother Mike was an Eagle Scout. This impressed me, but he wasn't around much and I had no interest in talking to him. I didn't want a real Boy Scout showing me up. This was my secret life as a boy. One I indulged by reading Boy's Life magazine from the library and imagining myself going to camporees and whittling scrap wood. For my birthday I asked for a pocket knife.

I asked Shelley to test me on my tenderfoot requirements. I passed easily having memorized the scout oath, learned all about the flag and what was a good citizen, and how to be a conservationist of the wilderness. That last was a new concept for me. I liked learning these rules about my new country.

Everything about the scouts had a story referencing history. The flag being folded into a triangle to imitate the tricorn hats of the colonialists for instance. Now that was an interesting hat. I folded my all purpose black felt hat into a tricornered one so I could enjoy this design. I was very fond of books on making costumes. Having learned of the usefulness of a felt hat I promptly found such a hat when I accompanied my parents to visit a friend my mother had met at work. The hat was in a goodwill bag at the door and the friend told me I could have it.

My mother did not discourage me in my Boy Scout pursuits because she too had seen how poorly the Girl Scout manual compared and was glad that I was learning skills like knot tying and first aid. My mother had been a tomboy, too, she told me. Girls who had been tomboys clearly had an edge.

The library had all the merit badge books the Boy Scouts had to offer. In my handbook I noted the ones I wanted to earn: camping, citizenship, nature conservation and first aid. The pictures of different kinds of wounds and how to splint a broken leg with a tree branch fascinated me. The slim volumes that were the merit badge books made these grown up skills and activities seem manageable. The one on money management laid down skills I would use throughout my life starting with recording every penny I spent, which later helped me to budget for projects.

The library also offered books about another entity that was all about uniforms and skill building. Large coffee table books full of pictures showed how regular citizens were groomed into smart uniformed members of the armed forces. I loved this transformation process, the sense of purpose and the adventure of it. The uniforms for women were pretty dorky with their restrictive skirts and hats that didn't have proper brims, but that didn't put me off because I had no interest in becoming a woman when I could so easily imagine myself into a smartly uniformed male body. The books covered each of the armed forces separately and after careful study of the offerings of each one I decided the Navy was the most versatile. I liked being on the water. And you could still be a pilot for the navy with their ocean going aircraft carriers. Being under water in a submarine sleeping in a hammock and climbing in and out of hatches that had to be sealed with a wheel device was cool. *Twenty Thousand Leagues Under the Sea* had been a very exciting movie for me. Not to mention the decor of nautical Victorian excess.

I soon found out that another neighbor had been in the Navy because sometimes he wore a sailor's hat when he was tinkering in the garage. I so admired his sailor hat that he gave me one of his extras. I loved how the brim once folded up transformed the bucket hat into the iconic sailor shape.

Seeing my interest in sailors, my mother told me about her favorite childhood series called *Swallows And Amazons* published in the 1930s—a British favorite for several generations. Those were at the library too. I loved that they were British and that it was about camping on an island the children would sail to alone. Their father, who was away at sea, captured in a couple of sentences of a telegram the entire spirit of what would later be called the free range child movement.

"If not duffers won't drown. Better drowned than duffers." This was his answer to his four children having written their separate letters to him to ask if they could camp on Wild Cat Island by themselves while mother stayed home to take care of the baby. It did not strike me as unusual that these children were allowed to roam all over the lake country by themselves. Other British children's books also had children going exploring without adult supervision.

I would soon have someone to share these books with. I met Annette through her sister Helen who was in my grade at school. When I came to play at Helen's house, her little sister Annette was the tomboy to Helen's mothering persona. They had parents from Denmark and I immediately recognized a kinship with these fellow immigrants who had similar frugal values as we did and also left their children to look after themselves while both parents worked. Mostly the three of us hung out together cycling to nearby destinations or playing in their very large front yard. For in this yard was a Viking ship that had been built for a parade float. The adult Danes could dress up as Vikings and celebrate their solidarity at the town's 4th of July parade with much drinking in public from horns while on the float.

Annette and I gorged ourselves on the *Swallows And Amazons* series and any other books with girls who liked adventures. We hung onto make-believe games and pretended we were explorers alone in a foreign land or sailors or shipwrecked survivors. There was one game I remember with amusement for it was my idea. I called it Inspection. Annette was to be a soldier in boot camp while I played the Sergeant. We were at my house in my room so first I messed up the bed and threw notebooks and papers all over the floor. Then I stood outside the closed door while she raced to put the room to rights. At the end of the prescribed time of a minute I called out "inspection" and opened the door to check the room for orderliness. Then she got to mess up the room and I took the role of the soldier. We both passed inspection so there was no point in playing it again. We preferred wrestling with each other which we did on her vast lawn. We also pitched my brand new pup tent on it one summer. With Annette's companionship I could delay the end of my boyhood well into high school.

There was also to be another venue for my boy self—the Children's Theatre.

My mother took me to the Children's Theater in Palo Alto to audition for *The Wizard of Oz*. The directors had laughed when they asked me to walk as the Scarecrow and I did a hurky jerky walk across the stage. I was encouraged. Here it didn't matter too much if you were a girl playing a boy. The theater had a long tradition of cross dressing that were exempt from laws against cross-dressing on the street. I didn't get a part so I joined the stage crew.

"What's your name?" the set director asked me.

"Amanda," I said.

"Do you go by anything shorter?" he asked.

"Andy," I said. Andy was the name I had chosen for myself at camp the year after 5th grade when all the girls decided to go by boys names. I forget why.

"Ok Andy. We'll be building sets everyday after school," said the director. And just like that I was in. One of the boys. For it was mostly boys. Helping to pull out flats, hammering them together and becoming part of the crew when the play was ready for performance. The girls tended to help in the costume department in the basement which was also cool. The walls were lined with labeled boxes neatly arranged on shelves. "Hats, gloves, animal noses. Feather boas, riding boots and crowns." They had everything.

I got a part in the next play which had a huge Greek chorus for it was a Greek play—Aristophanes *The Birds*. I was a seagull. Most of the birds came in pairs, but I was a single. I could have been Jonathan Living Seagull people said. The book was everywhere spouting its little wisdoms. We had a dance coach who told us to go to the duck pond and watch how the birds walked and took off and landed. Then she choreographed our entrances. We had lines like "peck their eyes out" and "let them wear hats."

None of us younger ones understood the play. Something about taxation by the bird people on any earthly communications to the gods. We just looked up to the handsome fellow who played the lead wearing a short tunic that looked a bit like a dress. And then a beautiful blond woman wearing a tiara descended from the heavens in a chariot shaped like a cloud. The play was supposed to be a political allegory. It wouldn't have mattered what it was about. It was great fun.

I was smitten with the theater bug. With acting and being somebody else—a character—an empress, a woodsman, one of the ugly sisters.

How magic was that? The idea of embodying a role not yourself was in itself a subversive act of shape shifting I had not before experienced.

The theater offered all kinds of practical hand skills to create environments, illusion, costume. I learned to make boxed pleats for a Shakespearean doublet, paper mache noses for *The Wind In The Willows* animal masks, apply make-up, hammer together wooden frames, paint sets and walk silently in the dark while back stage. The adult community theater was next door and the shop behind it was my first experience with a workshop or maker space as we might call it now.

The multiple theaters in town provided both social collaboration and storytelling in the context of a pre high tech Palo Alto. It transcended time and expectations as a young director experimented with *Midsummer Night's Dream* performed in a Kabuki style with Puck played by a black girl in white Noe make-up. It crossed racial boundaries, boundaries of biological sex, and national boundaries. Every school with an auditorium and a stage was loaned out to the Children's Theater in the summer. I returned to it year after year until the necessity of a full time job cut into my theater schedule, but I kept in mind the thought of the theater as a possible adult profession.

I was going to a private school a few blocks from the theater which made it easy. Annette stayed with the public school system so I did not see her every day during the school year and had to make friends with girls of my own age. I was beginning to feel the difference between how the girls behaved and how the boys behaved. I sat with the boys at lunch though they paid me no attention at all. But I didn't want to sit with the girls because the conversation was too pointedly personal being about how we looked, who was developing breasts, who had their period and all the boy/girl gossip of would be romances. At the boys table just one boy seemed to do all the talking. He told stories with phrases like "the large red-eyed No-No." I was so entertained by this phrase I used it as a prompt several days running just to get him going again.

I thought boys actually knew how to do things, but when I asked an eighth grade boy if he could help me fix my bicycle I soon realized that he knew less than I did about bicycles. The girls having seen me talk to him were then asking if I liked him. He thought I liked him too, by the way he smiled at me. I stopped sitting with the boys then.

But I was even more determined to get to the bottom of this dividing of the sexes. In class one day I challenged the young female teacher of my seventh grade class about the division in status between men and women.

"Everything a woman can do, a man gets to do better as a professional," I declared. "Woman can cook, but a man gets to be a chef. A woman sews, but a man gets to be a tailor. Men are waiters but a woman is a waitress. A man gets to be an actor, but a woman is an actress." My teacher, who I thought was the nicest most hip teacher I ever had, began to look aggravated and dismayed at the same time. I was counting on her to see my rationale. Maybe even concede that I could go right ahead and be a boy. She half rose from her seat.

"A woman can have a baby," she said pointing her finger at me, "and don't you ever forget that." It was not the answer I was hoping for. It was a dumb answer, I thought because I was talking about professions not reproduction. I did after all know how babies were made. But I could see that I had crossed a line. I didn't want to push her any farther. Perhaps she too felt trapped inside the limitations placed on women. But she was also right about the baby thing. I said no more and that was the end of that conversation.

The whole feminist paradigm was hovering waiting to land on my shoulders, but I wasn't letting it. I would still do the boys exercise reps in the Canadian Air Force Exercise pamphlet that my parents brought home. I would help my dad with all the boy chores, do yard work, paint the fence or fix the car. My mother still expected me to clean the bathroom and make the beds in the morning. I couldn't complain since we no longer had servants and someone had to do it. Both my parents could use a sewing machine. My dad sewed because he couldn't find tennis shorts to fit him so he had deconstructed a pair from France and copied each piece with his drafting tools. My mother did because dressmaking helped her stay a fashion plate. I used the machine to sew my Daniel Boone costume for Halloween from an old sheet I had dyed in coffee per instructions from a library book. A friend's father loaned me an antique gun nearly as tall as I was to carry trick or treating.

Thailand had been a better place for women I remembered. My mother had her picture in the paper for the market research she did; women ran businesses, were account execs and were respected as owners of property. They could be the boss and were respected. Respect was sorely missing in American society especially for women. Men said things to and about women that were downright unfair I observed. And the women took it and sassed them back, but didn't correct them.

But women didn't want to be called girls anymore by men. On a ski trip my mother had some younger women friends along. They were discussing what women should be called. I was listening in, trying to be invisible. Suddenly one turned to me.

"What would you rather be called. A girl or a woman?" she asked me. I did not like these choices.

"Female," I said falling back on a science category. I wanted to depersonalize my sex to the least derogatory term possible. Female had a slightly science fiction vibe to it in a future where we would all wear skintight jumpsuits.

In the summer of my fourteenth year just before I was to go to an all girl's high school, Annette and I went on a backpacking trip with the Sierra Club. We outfitted ourselves in second hand work boots I found at the thrift store and bottom-of-the-line canvas back packs and canteens. The leaders were volunteers and the camping areas seemed a bit makeshift, but they did know the trail. We were crossing the Santa Cruz mountains from a state park not far from home and making our way to the Pacific Ocean. Midway through the trip my respect grew for the young man who led our little coed group of backpackers. At the end of the third day I saw him take out a pocket knife so he could cut through the twine around the hidden cache of freeze dried food that had been left for us.

"Did you belong to the Boy Scouts?" I asked in admiration and recognition of his knife.

"I would never belong to such a paramilitary organization," he replied evoking all the fervor of the anti-war demonstrations going on during much of my American life so far. Vietnam was a war that involved Thailand in military support of the Americans in Southeast Asia. American soldiers had visibly been a part of my childhood terrain. My father had been involved in that military relationship as an officer in the Thai Air Force. But I had long been absorbing the message of the young protestors that the U.S. had no business being in this war. My trail guide was reminding me that I was a part of these global conflicts. World events bigger than my interior life. I felt a glimmer of adult thoughts at his response.

The words paramilitary was a container of such disdain for the armed forces that my whole fantasy world of uniforms, neatly organized mess kits, signal flags and military maneuvers collapsed in on itself. I knew that my sense of justice was with the anti-war movement. I understood how destructive war was from the bombing of London that my mother lived through. My parents discussed Vietnam at home. My father on the side of strategy and my mother on the side of peace. I sat listening to them at the dinner table, but I could no more make out what it was about or where the moral ground was than I could from the TV. It was true that Lord Baden Powell had started the scouts as a response to aid in the war effort. But this American war did not strike me as being about self defense. I was being called home to myself. To speaking out and questioning authority.

The word paramilitary held out a bigger concept that evoked an alternative—that there was a non-military way of going about things. It did not necessarily have rules and protocol, but demanded more of me. There was a romance to the military to be sure from all the movies. Of belonging, of having an intense purpose and moving as one unit. A place where I could prove my loyalty and bravery just by participating. But I also knew I could never bring myself to take orders from a chain of command. One that did not include the consideration of other nations, other peoples, or even me. It was expected of a soldier to get in harms way without question. A small country was being torn up for this. Was it really necessary? I didn't find it to be. I had to admit I was, in the end, a pacifist.

And here was a man with scouting skills who did not love even the concept of the scouts because it reminded him of the military. And he had not said anything disparaging about girls. We had all carried our own packs, girls and boys alike, slept on the ground, and bonded over our sore feet and our blisters. After one long and hard 15 mile day we were all tired. We weren't into making it a competition. Finishing was enough. I made it all the way to the ocean carrying my own pack even when others happily threw theirs in the pick-up truck that came to meet us a few miles to the end. And because I had said I was going all the way with my pack two other guys decided to too. That night me and my two guy companions slept on the beach side by side hoping the tide wouldn't come in and soak us, satisfied that we had accomplished something.

I didn't give up on the scouts altogether. I joined the Cadette Girl Scouts for older girls with a pair of real wilderness type leaders, a husband and wife who took us on hikes rain or shine, and on a snow camping trip. But the military uniforms, the shiny shoes, military barracks, tents, and gigantic ships vibrating with machine noise and all the particulars of rank and chain of command I tucked into a back closet of my mind. Much later I would find that in the privacy of my fantasy life I was so comfortable in this military closet that it provided me with numerous volumes of sexual fantasies of men in uniform and ranks to be transgressed by desire. The success of these fantasies assured me I would always have a place for my imagination and my boy body. I would come to see that this was just one in a series of acts of imagination that would be the key to getting off the grid of conventional thinking. Indeed the expansion of the human experience had everything to do with acts of imagination.

Chapter 5

The Woman Network

"I told your Aunty Chong that you have your period so she'll know to look after you," My Aunty Ah Pahdt told me before she left for the office. I was only slightly mortified at this announcement and I nodded my acceptance of it. I had already given my privacy over to my family when my period started for I had no means to buy supplies. I was in Bangkok for my first visit home since I was ten; now at 15, all the confidence of being ten having left me. At best I could be goofy to amuse my American peers, but in Thailand that would be corrected as undignified. And now after a two months hiatus I had to bear the humiliation of not having it together for this period thing. I had only started bleeding the year before. My mother had bought me a beginners boxed kit of sanitary napkins in anticipation. It came with a belt made from dressmaking elastic with metal grips to hold the napkin in place. And two safety pins in case I wanted to pin it to my underwear. I chose that option.

"Later you can learn to use a Tampax," my mother said. That would be a welcome minimization of this bulky thing; I appreciated her saying I could use them. Some mothers forbid the use of tampons to preserve one's hymen a strange new word to reference virginal tissues like a seal to show you hadn't been tampered with. This proof of virginity the girls in my 8th grade class had discussed.

I didn't even know the words to ask for what I needed in Thai. I was grateful that I had just the day before heard my nanny Samarn say she had bought several boxes of Kotex because they were on sale. So I told her I was in need of the Kotex and she was happy to offer me her find. And she thought nothing of telling my Ah Pahdt who asked me without fanfare how I was doing. My mother never asked me anything about my cycle. I don't think we ever spoke of it after I was obliged to tell her since that was the thing to do. Tell your mum so she could make a note of it for your medical file. I told my Ah Pahdt that I had not menstruated for two months so had not brought supplies for my six week stay. I had secretly hoped it had abandoned me for awhile.

"Perhaps all that water skiing brought it on," she said conversationally referring to our excursion to the beach over the weekend. I began to relax into this normalization of our shared bodily function. My Aunty Chong was now scheduled to take me shopping and I was looking forward to this outing with my two cousins Neung and Nor. Close in age to me we had grown up together and they were like sisters. Ah Neung the big sister and Nor the adorable younger one we played with. They took me to Central the one department store nearby. We were there as the doors opened and all the sales girls and security guards were lined up to greet us with the traditional Thai wai, the hands in prayer position with a slight bow. Aunty Chong was fun to be with. She said what she was thinking in plain language. She scoffed at the line up and did not return their greetings, just gave a nod.

We visited a few departments then Ah Neung wanted to shop in another part of town. It was a fun day until I realized my flow was more than I had anticipated and I was glad to be heading home.

"Would you like to go out to dinner with us? Your Uncle Whit would love to see you." Aunty Chong invited. Oh yes I would love nothing better than to visit with Khun Ya's little brother for he was a man who delighted in everything. But I couldn't say yes. I was in distress.

"I'd like to go home," I said in a small voice from the back seat of the car.

"Do you have cramps?" she asked realizing I had gone silent.

"Maybe she doesn't have a Kotex," said Ah Neung in her big sister way.

"Oh yes right," Aunty Chong said. This conversation was getting more excruciating by the minute and I stayed silent next to Nor who had gone equally silent knowing she was out of her depth.

"Do you need a Kotex?" Aunty Chong asked.

"Yes," I said meekly.

"Where do we buy them I wonder?" she said.

"I don't know," said Ah Neung, "I usually send the maid to buy them." Now our little shopping tour had become a campaign in search of a landmark. A hole-in-the-wall store among an entire street of hole-in-the-wall storefronts. One that sold feminine products. Would that be a pharmacy? Or a dry goods store? I had no idea. Luckily an appropriate store was soon spotted and Ah Neung hopped out of the car to make the purchase. But that wasn't the end of my plight for we were nowhere near home and would meet Uncle at the restaurant near his work.

"I know. Let's go to this hair salon place I used to go to," said Ah Neung who was 17 and had already put lots of hours into the latest fashions and hairstyles. We pulled up in front of another hole-in-the-wall storefront and the four of us trooped in across the painted cement floor. Aunty Chong explained our entire dilemma and asked if I could use the bathroom. I just stood there looking at the floor, listening, relieved that I did not have to negotiate this mission with my broken Thai. The lady proprietor said of course and smiled at me beckoning me to go to the back of her store.

Ah Neung gave me the paper bag with the goods and I made my way to the bathroom conscious that I was on stage as I climbed a few tiled stairs to the door. I knew that my walking gingerly with little steps telegraphed that my predicament had reached the leaking onto pants part. But the ladies just chatted not paying me any unwanted attention as I listened and tended to the task at hand. I was relieved that I could handle this part.

"All good?" Aunty Chong asked as I reappeared by her side. I nodded and made my way outside still taking small steps. They followed after me as we walked to the car. "Can you see any blood?" Aunty Chong asked Ah Neung who paused to look.

"No can't see any blood at all," she reported. I was good. I could proceed through the evening bolstered by an entire box of Kotex. I was so grateful for this network of women who understood this most base of our bodily expressions and had strategized on my behalf to shepherd me through this so awkward learning stage. Not even a learning stage for there would always be situations of leakage and overflow. But I had learned that women would help you. Perfect strangers even, bonded by this common dilemma of our body.

My mother had not been able to talk about it because her mother hardly knew the facts of life. So prudish was the Edwardian English about sex. And so no stories were passed along, each generation held in isolation from the next. She was pleased to be able to hand me a pamphlet for teens from the doctors office acquainting us with our developing bodies and describing the "facts of life" with nice anatomically correct cross sections of sex organs.

Aunty Chong did not mention a single detail of my trials to my Uncle. This was not a subject to be discussed in front of men, as much as Thai people loved to tell stories on themselves and each other. I was assured that they would not betray my discomfort by saying anything and we had a lovely time at dinner with Uncle Whit. And I was delivered safely home with my extra box of Kotex.

Throughout the week Ah Pahdt would wait for me when we went out with family and privately ask if everything was alright after I made visits to the bathroom. My confidence was growing as I assured her all was well. I stacked my Kotex boxes in a big pink pyramid in the bathroom so comfortable had I become until Samarn suggested that I put them away in my room because company was coming and there would be men on the premises.

How comforting to know that this network of women had my back. Though I would not feel quite as confident that such a network existed in the West, just to have been held for that awkward time in Thailand during my adolescence planted in me a longing for the women's community I could see was still strong in my home country.

My mother had not complied with the custom of the Thais to segregate themselves by sex at dinner parties and public gatherings. Always there would be the table for men and another table for women. Or the circles of chairs. Photos of my mother at parties showed her sitting with the men in such a circle. She scoffed at the women's circles. She did not find their stories to be compelling. Those funny stories; the anecdotes of things that happened to them. Self deprecating stories allowing them to share their predicaments with other women. She didn't seem to realize that the men only welcomed her because she was a foreigner and they wanted to practice their English. She did mention that she had defied this custom implying that she was a modern woman. A woman who could handle being in a male world as she clearly was at her advertising job.

She did not tell me where she found her support. She did have friends she talked to one on one, but it was not this collective idea of a woman network. That was too foreign for her. She didn't like being talked about one bit. She had felt shamed when her mother talked about her to other mothers. And her father was full of religious shaming. So there was not really a collective bone in her body. The very concept I would learn was unique to Asian culture. It was what made a woman network possible. The concept that we were all in this together.

Chapter 6

It's Just Rain

It was dry where I was sitting on the stairs of what we called the sunken patio just outside of the school library at my girls school. It did look like it might rain, but I wasn't worried. I had a sailors uniform top on over my school uniform. I was very proud of this find from the thrift store. An actual U.S. Navy issue dark blue pullover trimmed with white braid and two stars in the corners of the collar. I thought it went well with the blue skirts of our school uniforms, especially since our midi blouses had the same kind of sailor collar.

My friend Veronica saw me as she was walking by and greeted me. We had been friends since sixth grade and prided ourselves in our comradeship given that we were the only non-white students in our class at the time. We had been friends outside of school too, going to the ice rink on weekends. Her parents would drop her off at my house and my dad would drive us to the rink. Skating was what we had done together since junior high. She lived in the black neighborhood in East Palo Alto where we never seemed to go.

We no longer ran in quite the same circles in these later years of high school for I had been pushed into the smart girl classes. This just encumbered me with existential intellectual questions while raising my stress level and lowering my GPA.

I never got past the first line of *Anna Karenina*. "Happy families are all alike; every unhappy family is unhappy in its own way." I had to think about that. It had the promise of being an absolute, a principle by which I could live my life. But was it true? I was happy in Thailand. Did that mean it wasn't worth writing about? That must have been all I needed from that tome, for I had no interest in reading about Anna's unhappy life. I was relieved when our teacher said we wouldn't be discussing it because it was the summer reading. So on we went to Dostoyevsky and I faced the first exam question of the class.

"What was the theme of *Crime and Punishment*?" I had no idea. I had never in my life been asked such a question. I thought I knew what a theme was. For instance if you wanted to have a Hawaiian luau party or a casino game theme party you would decorate appropriately. How could a story have a theme? Somehow some deeper knowledge was involved to penetrate this question and I wasn't getting it. I was dumb that way.

My mind could not grasp it. I was used to being smart and now I had reached my high water mark for smart. Thank goodness for Virginia Woolf. I could totally understand a stream of conscious narrative and reading *Mrs. Dalloway* had me on the edge of my seat. Was she in love with Sally Seton? Would she actually admit it? There was that kiss between them after all. My papers came back with Bs and a single comment, something like "good start, but you have not yet touched on the theme at all." It never occurred to me to ask what she meant by theme—that things could actually be explained so I could understand it. I accepted my fate that I was never going to get an A in this class.

She did explain that the title of Edward Albee's play. Tiny Alice was a slang term meaning Tight Ass which stood for homosexual, but she didn't explain why this was so and I knew not to ask. It was one of those depth markers we weren't allowed to swim beyond. Homosexuality only allowed in the deep end and we'd be in over our heads for sure, possibly expelled if we so much as asked such a question. My very smart friend Judy might know from her extracurricular reading. She sat next to me holding hands with another girl. They were not lovers.

I knew that because I could ask Judy anything. We had been lovers or close to it. A little physical contact went a long way then, especially at fourteen. Our friendship was so different, so curiously intimate the way it had evolved. We met as Freshman new to the school. She had on a handmade button that said "This button is an attempt to communicate" which served as an icebreaker one lunch time when I found her sitting alone on a bench eating a sandwich. Something about our covert conversation led to more daring revelations in secluded moments. Little hints of sexual innuendo even and finally Judy's revelation that she was bisexual. And I was too I realized; she had just put a name to it. We escalated to a sleepover at her house. That night had felt even more intimate as we ate ice cream together and laughed at each other's way with words. I was so charged up by this exchange that as we lay on the floor of her bedroom in our sleeping bags, I was completely focused on my desire to hold her hand, and somehow I knew she felt the same way. An hour must have gone by as I studied the situation. Her hand lay outside of her sleeping bag above her head. Suddenly I reached out and grabbed it squeezing hard. In a split second she squeezed back and we squeezed as hard as we could before releasing our grip. My emotions were released too and we fell asleep still holding hands.

Our relationship was rarely public because we were so different. There was nothing we shared in our public lives. Nor were we exclusive in our feelings for each other. We had crushes on different girls for different reasons sharing this information with each other in private. We read each other's journals on occasion. Ours was more a bond of the exploration of our interior mind, of ourselves as writers behind the scenes constructing different lives for ourselves. I was the athletic one in gym class while she hid behind the oak tree when the class was asked to jog around the Circle—the huge circular lawn that formed the center of the school. The giant oak tree at the perimeter. She kept up with the latest music and counter culture books.

Judy was the smartest girl in our class; she wrote her essays in the bathtub while I sweated through an entire Sunday trying to wrestle something onto the page. She found Edward Albee quite amusing as if she was in on the joke; she did tell me that tight ass was a reference to anal sex which was too unfamiliar a concept for me to take seriously. I favored the existential and the absurd. I loved *Waiting For Godot*. It tickled me that waiting in itself was a topic and the characters had no more idea than I did what we were all waiting for.

I asked Judy what was going on with the handholding in English class. I didn't know this other girl very well. She struck me as conventional and was not smart enough or neurotic enough to attract my attention. She was a boarding student which implied a troubled past or absent parents. Judy explained that they were just holding hands for mutual support and it seemed to put our teacher on edge; this appealed to their rebelliousness. Our AP English class was a strange beast that way. It required thoughts that put into question the very goals we were supposed to be embracing to ensure our future. Literature will do that to you. It was subversive, paying attention to details normal people couldn't be bothered with and was likely written by misfits of their peer group.

Meanwhile Veronica kept her focus on what her grades would mean for her future.

"Why," she had asked her English teacher, "don't I get an A? I did the work?" Mr. Hadley couldn't offer an answer. I knew his hands were tied. He was required to grade us on a Bell curve that forced us to constantly compete with the brightest girls in the class. Mr. Hadley with his too long hair resting at his collar and his Earth shoes had done his best to bring us subjects to alleviate the relentless academic workload.

His film appreciation class had taught me an analysis of cinematic language that gave me a lifelong interest in movies. And it was in his creative writing class that I felt his kindness, for he never put down the romanticisms of our interior lives that tainted our writing efforts.

It would never have occurred to me to challenge a grade. I resented the girls who by their very existence rendered me merely average; an assessment, created by this highly competitive school, that would form my opinion of myself for most of my adult life. I succumbed to the crushing workload and accepted my middling B average. Veronica seemed to have a much firmer grip on how the overall system was unfair in its culling method.

Having greeted me on that not quite rainy day, Veronica came to join me and sat down next to me. I was just watching people go by, so she did too. Then the first tiny drops of rain began to fall into her afro and onto my Navy pullover. I wasn't feeling the rain through the thick wool so I made no move to get up and run for cover. And she didn't either. We just watched as people ran for cover with such urgency you'd think the rain would melt them.

"It's just rain," Veronica said after a moment. Her voice holding a tone of revelation. I agreed enjoying showing my friend how to ignore conventional expectations. Just then a classmate walked by and yelled across to us from the shelter of the covered walkway.

"Hey Veronica what are you doing sitting in the rain?"

"Note she didn't ask me," I said to Veronica. "Everyone knows I'm crazy already," I added. She didn't disagree and I smiled to myself at my own witty insight. No one was going to question why I was sitting out in the rain. They already figured I was a lost cause. Veronica got up and walked to cover while I stayed sitting in the rain until all the pavement was wet and I could feel the moisture. I wanted a tangible reason before moving for cover.

There are moments when you realize you are never going to be normal. That was the one that stuck in my mind. I knew that the whole school saw me as slightly off kilter, eccentric in the British sense. I had based my reputation on doing the unexpected largely for the sake of creative rebellion. It had started with the dress code. I studied it looking for loopholes. It said nothing about forbidding the wearing of suspenders with our skirts. So I got out my red suspenders from my ski pants and clipped them to my skirt. The red stood out in that sea of blue skirts and white shirts. Soon I got a notice asking me to report to the Dean in her office. She asked me why I was wearing red suspenders.

I explained about the rules not saying anything about suspenders.

"I can see you are a rebel," she said. "So how come you don't just break the rules then?" she asked.

"Well I'm a conservative rebel," I said. She burst out laughing and said she would remember that, as if it was the funniest thing she'd heard all year. Breaking the rules would be dumb I thought. I didn't want to get expelled. I loved this school. The teachers and the girls here were my family; the extended family in a compound just like my life in Thailand that I so missed.

Pushing to the boundaries of the rules was more fun. I left off the suspenders and focused on neckwear. There was nothing in the list of uniform violations that forbid wearing a bandana tied around the neck, or floppy bows or, best of all, bow ties. Those dapper retro bits of silk that showed up in thrift stores on occasion.

The school strived to be conservative, clinging to tradition and history in the hopes of being in the same league as their more established East coast counterparts. Very little of the outside world permeated our cloistered community. What did seep in came through my young mother who was getting her degree at San Francisco State. Her MFCC— marriage, family and child counselor degree. (A discipline that was to be the yardstick by which my mother would judge family dynamics, including ours. A discipline against which I would learn to defend myself in the currency of its jargon and concepts.) My mother, who went by Pat, short for Patricia, noted the pieces of mail my school sent out to her were addressed to her using my father's name—Mrs. Termpoon Kovattana. Wasn't this a bit antiquated in this day of women's lib? she asked me. I picked up on her sense of irony and decided to write a letter to the school newspaper challenging this custom of using our fathers names as if our mothers didn't have their own names. What kind of an example was this setting for a school that aimed to make leaders of girls? No one responded. Controversy was not on the menu.

The librarian told me my letter made a good point and many of my teachers thought so too. So I figured the most conservative driving force behind the school decorum must be the parents. To express this I wrote for creative writing class a satirical letter of indignation from an imagined parent threatening to remove her daughter from the school if the administration did not immediately stop the "barbaric" practice of forcing her child to swim in freezing conditions as part of some competitive torture ritual shared with other schools. It wasn't really funny enough, but I thought it was devious in that it implied that such a vexed parent was clueless to competitive sports and modern life. Plus I hated swimming when it was cold.

I submitted the piece to the creative writing magazine along with a short story of an incident from my childhood in Thailand; an incident where I am being asked to translate an insult from a lonely American kid to my Thai playmate. The way I wrote the story in the third person left me with a creepy feeling. Given the context of the disembodied English language it read like Kipling in that it implied a caste system rendering the Thais as inferior by default. I had resented his book *Kim* for the same reason. This made me resentful of the whole premise of fiction, but mostly it put me off being a writer. Literature was after all crafted works of fiction, stirring together a mosaic of observations into made up characters and plots—especially plots.

I'd heard the old adage to write about what you knew, but it couldn't just be memoir. Who was allowed to do that, except maybe Anne Frank? I continued to write fiction for creative writing assignments, but eventually I would be my own character in my own story. It was Mr. Hadley who offered salient advice for character building that would guide me. He read to us a short story told in the first person and then proceeded to point out how this unlikeable character lured the reader into his point of view through the use of detail and an ongoing commentary of how he felt when these details frustrated him and bore down on him. It didn't make me like the character any better, but it did engage me in his story.

I was saved by drama class. In my junior year I had a role so suited to my personality I never really shrugged it off. That was the year I played the Artful Dodger in *Oliver*. And the school watched as I stepped into my boy persona in public. An act that in itself felt subversive all the more because it was allowed under the guise of acting in the school play. And allowed because it was a girls' school. We borrowed a few boys from the nearby boys' school to play the men, but they didn't intrude much into our world of girls being in power. And they didn't rank at all in our girls' school universe. Our school had the higher academic standard and we prided ourselves in our level of scholarly achievement. We knew we were clearly superior to the pimply faced specimens sent over from the boys' school. In this female centered school I no longer resented the fact that a boy could take something away from me just because of his sex. As long as I demonstrated my worth.

During the play my grades dipped the lowest they had ever been when a C in math punched a hole in my line-up of Bs. My parents came in to talk to the principal worried that I might need to repeat the year. I knew my low grades in math were from my failure to check my work. Had there been a dollar sign in front of the numbers I might have cared more. I clearly was never going to rank academically, but more subversively than that, I didn't really care. There was something suspect about this that I couldn't quite put my finger on. What was the point of all this competition and effort? And how much more was I willing to work? Not that much I knew. I would simply accept that I was a slacker. I did what made sense to me. I joined the yearbook committee to help preserve the memories of this girls' school life. I was already nostalgic for the mystique of it, just as I had been by the stories my mother had passed along to me of going to a girls' school in England.

In my senior year I was appointed yearbook editor and held in my mind the whole narrative of our collective stories, overseeing the images that would represent us and fighting with my team for the cover design I wanted. It was my proudest moment to stand up in front of the school holding that yearbook as the entire student body burst into applause and cheered loudly.

As the year came to a close I pulled myself together enough to fend off my chronic procrastination and get my term paper finished, though it was already past the deadline as it was. I wrote my paper on individualism supported by such literary works as *The Fountainhead* and *Steppenwolf.* The topic suited me. And maybe I was finally getting a hang of what was meant by a theme.

As a final parting note I bent the rules one last time. We were required to wear white floor length formal dresses for the graduation ceremony. We were lectured on how the sleeves could be capped but not sleeveless and the neckline could be neither too low to reveal cleavage nor too high and Victorian which would break the sightline of our lovely necks. I planned to wear my signature white bowtie with my dress. I told no one of my plans because I had already been written up for wearing this bowtie in the school panorama photo just a few weeks prior. I chose a dress pattern with a scoop neck to show off the tie and my mother sewed it for me. There would be faculty guards posted at the doors to the chapel as we filed in holding our bouquet of red roses. So I had the tie hidden in my white gloved hand and put it on once we were safely seated in the pews inside. I duly climbed up to the stage to receive my diploma and as I turned I caused my parents and teachers to gasp when they saw that bowtie standing so crisply on my neck. With this last bit of sleight of hand I had gotten past the adults monitoring us and cracked the orderly perfection of the schools image by throwing my signature gender bending gesture into the mix. I grinned in triumph. What could they do to me? Write me up for detention?

Once out from under the schools authoritarian image control I had no real idea of who I was. With nothing to rebel against there were no goals I had to achieve. No one telling me what to do.

Veronica on the other hand would sail through life as confident as she had been in school, despite a college pregnancy that put her into the workforce earlier than expected. Her father had told her sternly that she wasn't going to get any help from him and he would expect her to do good by her daughter, raise her in a proper home, send her to a private school and then to college. And that's exactly what she did, working her way to the top of her employable range at a local tech giant with an eye towards shouldering whatever responsibility was offered and becoming the office manager.

I saw her briefly during this phase of her life. She was giving me a ride somewhere and told me she needed to pick up her daughter from nursery school on the way. When the daughter appeared from the schoolroom Veronica spoke so sweetly to her it was as if they shared a private world. It was far from what I had been offered by my mother with whom I shared that strange British coolness between us. Veronica introduced me to her daughter and told her how we used to go ice skating. She had clearly made single motherhood into something special and would later descend on her daughter's private school campus to defend her whenever she thought she was being academically short changed by being put into the slow kids class.

When her daughter went off to college to pursue a degree in psychology, Veronica could finally take the career path she wanted for herself. She took a course in interior design. She did so well she got the attention of the teacher who gave her leads to jobs. At that point we met again at a class reunion and she hired me to hang pictures for one of her clients as I was, at the time, free lancing as a handyman.

When I arrived at the modest house in a gentrifying neighborhood at the appointed time, Veronica walked me through the house from the hand carved custom front door she had chosen, to the shower she had designed with handmade mosaic tile—a striking mix of dark blue and a bit of gold and green Italian glass. She spoke as if she had been choosing such things for years. The client clearly trusted her.

While I was on the job we told stories on each other in front of her client family. I reminded her that she had once wanted to be a dentist.

"Really? I don't remember that," she said.

"You said you wanted to make people's teeth look nice," I explained. She in turn told the family I was from a very prestigious and wealthy family in Thailand.

"Well not exactly," I protested. I was after all wearing my working class outfit—white painter's pants and a blue work shirt.

"No really she is," Veronica insisted, milking the privilege out of my class background which would in turn bolster hers. I mean that was the whole point of us going to such an exclusive private girls school wasn't it? She had told me how just saying the name of the school in a job interview was a door opener. As in "You went to Hogwarts? Oh right you're a wizard. Right this way then." I couldn't figure my way out of this one for I was loath to being called a snob behind my back for such name dropping.

The teenage son seeing an interesting ironic angle to my life said "Did you come to the U.S. so you could build houses?" I gave up.

"Oh all right," I said, "it's true my relatives were horrified that I wanted to be a carpenter so I had to come to America in order to have any fun in life." That was as good a way as any to explain my convoluted life. And it made the son smile to have gotten it right.

And when the client mom took us out to lunch Veronica boasted of how I was related to the Thai royal family.

"I am not," I said embarrassed. "I just have a friend who's a member of the royal family." A cycling buddy who was a special friend from our time spent together while she was in the U.S. for college. It was bad enough that I was even mentioning her royal status.

"Well why can't you just say you are?" Veronica asked seeing a social advantage by association.

"There are rules about that." I insisted. Clearly rules that a royalty-free, self-made American thought were immaterial. The client looked bemused. She and her contractor husband had built their wealth from careful investment in real estate. We were, to her, as exotic as hot house flowers. With my English accent and my exacting way of expressing myself there was no way to pretend I was from more humble roots. My class privilege was spilling out all over my painter's pants and blue work shirt.

I wasn't sure what to make of Veronica's lesson in social mobility. She had so clearly made a success of herself by pure gumption and her father's expectation that she would do it. I was just a dabbler doing lots of things passably well and outfitting myself in the uniform of the working class so I could pretend I had bootstrapped my way up from a humble background. People seemed to expect such an immigrant story just from looking at my Asian face at a time of mass migration of refugees from the Vietnam war. (Or as I came to think of it, the American war for imperial interests in Vietnam.)

Veronica couldn't figure out why I didn't make more of myself. She, who had the confidence of the Black middle class and a family history of upward mobility, saw no advantage in playing down any assets one might have. But I wasn't ready for that kind of responsibility to perform. She on the other hand couldn't wait to show what she could do.

Veronica understood that the system was biased and she made it work for her. I believed that the system was so broken it was going to do us all in; much like the Roman Empire with its lead pipes and overextended army. Our history teacher had told us we would like the Romans because they were a lot like Americans. This intrigued me and offered me a clue. The fall of the Roman Empire was my marker for my search. But it would take me a lot longer to figure out why I thought our system was broken and create a reality that would offer an alternate path.

Chapter 7

Enter Unicycling

UC Santa Cruz, my college of choice, turned out to be the perfect campus for a unicycle. It was too hilly for a bicycle and the pedestrian pathways were easily navigated by unicycle, but I hadn't thought about this perfect pairing until I arrived at the school. A unicycle just happened to be part of my bag of tricks following a theme of alternative solutions that was becoming a part of my out-of-the-box approach. I had become interested in riding one in my senior year of high school when I saw the unicycle drill team from the town of Concord riding in the Fourth of July parade in Redwood City. I loved this parade—the pageantry of it and the smartly uniformed marching bands. Not to mention the campy Americana of it; plus it was free.

Annette and I would make sure to get there early so we could sit right on the curb. We could easily ride our bicycles there since it was in the next town. The unicycle drill team consisted of a large group of boys and girls riding in formation all dressed in khaki chinos and white shirts. They made this mode of transportation seem perfectly normal while at the same time its gyroscopic upright nature transported it to a parallel universe of movement and mobility. It was all the fun of a bicycle with half the volume. I took one look at this unique mode of transportation and I had to have one. I'm not sure what it was about it; the minimalism of it or the association with the circus—a childhood favorite for adventure stories.

My parents wouldn't buy me one because they saw it as a passing fancy, and said I would abandon it once I'd mastered it. More likely my mother, who worried about my regressing back into childhood, just didn't think it was a pursuit fitting a maturing girl. So I saved up the fifty dollars to buy one myself and my father took me to the one bicycle store that had one in stock. Schwin was the only brand that made unicycles. And the library had the one book that covered the topic of riding one. It was the hardest thing I had yet attempted to do, but I was by now obsessed with it. A block of wood behind the wheel kept it stationary just long enough to jump on the second pedal. I kept at it all day for the three days of a Memorial Day weekend until finally I could mount it long enough to ride down the driveway.

I was not the only kid who had decided to ride such a thing. There was another girl at school who had gotten one so we practiced together, but I was the first one to master it well enough to ride it down the aisle for Monday morning assembly. I had already learned how to juggle for the Christmas pageant so this seemed like a logical follow-up. I didn't quite make it all the way down the aisle because the carpet made the wheel twist in an unexpected way and I had to jump off to save myself, but I had made my point. The point I was always trying to make in this high pressure school; that life needed levity and an element of surprise.

My choice of college was pretty much limited to something local and affordable. I didn't have the grades for Stanford which would have also required a scholarship, so I applied to the UC system and chose the Santa Cruz campus for its rural beauty and proximity to home. It had colleges within the school which gave it a British feel and felt more manageable in its intimacy. I chose College V, the arts college. I knew nothing about the hippie culture of UC Santa Cruz or its reputation as somewhat avant garde in that no grades were given. Not having grades scared off those more ambitious in a social climbing sense, but gave me a sense of relief.

It was a Saturday when my parents drove me over the Santa Cruz mountains in the family station wagon with my one trunk, navy blue with a cheap brass colored lock and two large latches. I had already picked my roommate. We had gone to high school together, so I didn't feel entirely out of it even though everyone had already been in school a week. I was delayed because we had gone to England late in the summer to take advantage of the lower airfares after Labor Day. I found my way to the three story L shaped building known as B Dorm. My hall mates were curious who was this missing person and were looking forward to meeting me. A couple of the guys on the hall offered to help me with my stuff. They carried the trunk between them and as they stood there in the middle of my shared room, one asked.

"Where shall we put it?"

"Oh drop it anywhere," I said in an effort to sound casual and laid back. And so they did, dropping it right where they stood with a thud on the hard cement floor which was covered with the thinest of industrial carpeting. I looked at them somewhat shocked.

"You did say drop it anywhere," said the one who had asked. I knew I had been warned. This was not a group that cared about being helpful. They cared about being smart asses. My mother didn't notice and left me to put my things away. At dinner time, people gathered in the hall outside of my door so I did too. A woman came down from the next hall smoking a cigarette and speaking in a fake aristocratic British accent.

"Shall we go down to dinner then?" She asked. She didn't know yet that I had a British accent and was chagrined, later berating her mates for not warning her, but we became fast friends. Ann was one of the few women who was literary—a writer, plus she was a character, a conscious construction of a personality which always counted for something in my book. I already felt odd so it was good to have company.

The next time I was home I came back with my unicycle. It made me feel safer than walking through the woods at night. Santa Cruz was at the time the rape capital of the country. It seemed highly unlikely that a rapist would attack a woman on a unicycle. The very idea made me laugh. Riding a unicycle was also a great ice breaker. It also helped overcome the usual assumptions people had of an Asian girl, especially at this largely white school. Still my hall mates ran me through all the usual projections of what an Asian girl was or could be to them especially in the exotic sexual proclivities department. The unicycle with its own set of associations with the circus, paired with my exotic presentation popped people right out of their projections. It was a magic tool in that sense; one that would grant me protection and power.

I found I could take it downtown on the bus where I could ride it on my errands. Santa Cruz was an entertainment town so a unicycle didn't seem all that unusual. I wore a red blazer I had found at a thrift store. It reminded me of school blazers in England. I also wore the exact same shoes that my mother wore when she was in school. I knew from her school photos what they looked like and they were still being made by the same Start-Rite shoe company—Mary Jane style sandals in a brick red with a pattern of tiny diamond shaped perforations in the toe. Boys wore that pattern too. They were quintessentially British, and were around for another decade before the marketing of the American athletic shoe as a technical advantage took over. I had bought them on my trip to England that summer and wore them so much they needed resoling. So I popped downtown to a shoe store I had seen. A giant harrachi sandal was hanging outside the door with a sign that said "Ken's Shoe Store." Ken himself came out from behind the counter to have a look at me.

"You look like a Tarot card," he said taking me in from head to toe.

"What's a Tarot card?" I asked. Oh to be so new to the world.

"It's a bunch of cards with people on it dressed like you," he said. This did not intrigue me enough to look into it. It would be several more years before I would make my acquaintance with the Tarot and a few more before I would study it in earnest. Looking back through this lens of being a Tarot card I was of course The Fool card. The court jester stepping intrepidly into space as I embarked on my journey carrying my little bag of tricks. Ken was able to resole my shoes and I had a new friend. I stopped by to ride into his store every time I was downtown, just to say hi.

Chapter 8

The Transvestite Revenge Squad

In my first week at College V, I met the college drag queen in the coffee house. He was in his normal boy clothes at the time, so I didn't think anything of it when I was introduced to him. He was sitting with his girlfriend who was one of my hall mates, so Ann and I joined them. Mark was his name. He had long blond hair tied back in a ponytail, an oval face and a languid quality about his voice. He was wearing a tweed blazer over a t-shirt which he had silk screened himself as part of his own business silk screening t-shirts for local shops. His degree had been in art and this was how he had applied his degree in this practical entrepreneurial way. Being entrepreneurial was very much a Thai thing too. Mark selling t-shirts made perfect sense to me as a livelihood, but it was not the topic I chose to bond with him about.

I asked him about the scar I noticed on his eyebrow that was similar to a scar I had, and he told me about the childhood mishap that had resulted in the scar. He was so frank in answering I found it refreshing. None of my hall mates offered a straight answer to anything. When we left the coffee shop, Ann asked me if I knew his story. I didn't. He was a hermaphrodite she said. What we would later understand as intersex or DSD—a disorder of sexual development. He was identified as a girl when he was born, but later discovered to have an undescended male genitals so was given hormones to bring out his boy parts. Because, as Ann said, the male doctors naturally assumed if he had a penis he would want to use it. On occasion he would dress as a woman. I was of course intrigued.

"Why would he talk to me?" I asked Ann when she told me this background. Why would someone who had such an unusual story bother to talk to me, a mere freshman, was what I was asking because Mark had already graduated from UC Santa Cruz.

"Because you're beautiful," Ann replied as if this was my lot, my privilege in life. I took this privilege to mean that I had permission to proceed with my association with Mark. That I would be considered a peer.

When I asked Mark about how this discovery was made about his true sex, he said he had been kidnapped as a young girl because his family was wealthy and worth a ransom. Much like my family, I thought, nodding. When he was returned he was taken for a medical examination to determine if he'd been violated. His doctor then discovered that he had a penis that had not yet dropped into view. His parents were advised to correct the mistake that had occurred at his birth. Being well to-do they had the means to move to another town where Mark was introduced as a boy. He was a woozy boy at first he said, but he got used to it. His parents did not know of the drag queen part. They would have expected him to be gay he said, but not to wear women's clothes.

He would soon grace us with his female presence which was impressive given that he was over six feet tall. We had a party on our hall and he made his appearance wearing a '50s style auburn wig with a vintage frock. Half way through the party he changed into another outfit as was his custom. This time in a blond wig wearing riding jodhpurs in tribute to Faye Dunaway in a scene from *Chinatown*. He carried a riding crop to set off the outfit, which was a fine prop for flirting because you could touch someone without actually touching them. I also loved the idea of having a wardrobe change mid party and would look for it so I would know the half way point of any given party.

At a later meeting when he was back in his boy clothes he told me about the Transvestite Revenge Squad. He had a t-shirt for it, showing a woman in stiletto heels drawn in classic 50's pulp comic style. The premise of it was that since cross dressing was illegal (except on Halloween) to dress in the clothes of the opposite sex was a form of protest and social defiance. He told me the details of this law, how he had to have at least one article of men's clothing on in order not to be arrested; in some states it was three. The ordinances varied from town to town and remained on the books as late as 2011 in Oakland.

Cross dressing historians have pointed out that laws against cross dressing go back to Joan of Arc who was burned for being a heretic on five counts of cross dressing. Joan of Arc was conjectured to be following a pagan tradition of spirit mediums. Though made a saint she was not Catholic at all, but like most country folk of the time still following the earth based pagan traditions. The voices she was hearing instructed her specifically to wear men's clothes. Joan of Arc was a girl icon for me from childhood. I knew her story from a strip of slides that came with the toy projector my mother got me. The part about hearing voices was the whole point of this slide and I accepted this as I accepted the psychics that Thai people consulted regularly to know what the future held. Cross dressing spirit mediums were also a presence in Thailand and Burma, and are still in existence today.

I could easily understand that in order to step into her power, Joan of Arc had to put on the clothing of power, but there was also something about being able to do that that was magic in a way that couldn't happen if you wore the clothes meant for your sex. Power was infused into you because of the wearing of the clothes of the opposite sex. As if it was a ritual signal that you were ready to receive such transmission. The reason there had to be laws against cross dressing in Europe was to suppress the return of the old pagan religions and the power it had over the people.

The reasons for these laws in the United States was in part to keep women from running away to join the army, to keep men from committing fraud, to curb prostitution and public delinquency and above all to protect social morality. (Morality often being about who was allowed to wield power.) It varied from state to state. The message was clear. Cross dressing was a social taboo, but like many taboos had deep roots into undisclosed territory much like homosexuality. To break these taboos was to be an outlaw. But the way Mark was framing it there was a purpose to this outlaw status and that was to change society. This appealed to me too.

Mark always kept a bag in his car with his boy clothes in case he had to escape a bad situation. This practical tip appealed to my "be prepared" training from the Boy Scouts. I had also noted that Nancy Drew kept an overnight bag ready for impromptu travel.

Women were automatically a member of the Transvestite Revenge Squad Mark explained. Because women wore men's clothes all the time. I was pleased that I as a women was automatically accepted into his club. He was right about women being exempt since they now wore pants and it wasn't seen as anything unusual. There were certain boundaries to this lenience though. I had already figured that out.

My father was fond of custom made shirts in assorted bright colors with French cuffs so he could show off his cuff links and the precious stones set into them. He had the shirts tailored in Thailand when he went to visit his mother. Attracted by so many alluring colors of the shirts I would open his closet and gaze at them all. Ten I counted. There was an orange one I decided was perfect for Halloween so I put it on with cufflinks and chose a black tie to go with it tucking the shirt into my jeans. Pleased with my Halloween colors I went out to show my mother who happened to be entertaining a friend.

"Look this is my Halloween costume," I said triumphantly. After a short pause my mother said to her friend.

"Amanda is a transvestite." Stung by this label I turned on my heels and retreated to the bedroom to return the shirt to my father's side of the closet. Halloween was sacrosanct. Halloween was when you could dress in a persona not your own. I had just wanted to try on this color which happened to be a man's shirt, but my mother had chosen to put a label on it. That's what psychologists did and I was becoming an embarrassment to her, so she had to pigeonhole me before her friend could. I would never forgive the discipline of Western psychology being so full of itself thinking it had everyone pegged and every society figured out. Her friend though was more forgiving and told me later at our annual New Year's Eve party that she was bisexual. I just smiled.

The label did not stop me though even if it was a warning that I was in danger of being seen as a social deviant. I just became more attuned to that line I wasn't supposed to cross; aware of where it was at all times. I did bring some of my father's white shirts to school, a silk one from Hong Kong and another with Chinese characters monogrammed onto the pocket. I wore the monogrammed one for a photo of myself recreating the cover of Patti Smith's recent album *Horses*. Her rendition of the song *Gloria* so defiantly declaring her attraction for another woman became my gay anthem immediately. I played the album on repeat to the annoyance of my hall mates. Her androgyny made mine ok, too. The iconic black and white photo of Patti with a skinny black tie and a blazer thrown over her shoulder taken by Robert Maplethorpe brought out a defiance in me just in imitating her.

But Mark was already inspiring me in a different direction. I began to see vintage dresses through his eyes and looked for them at my favorite thrift store. I found one I wanted to give him that seemed big enough. It was a black satin brocade with a pale pink lining over the breasts. The dress had drop sleeves and a neckline that fell off the shoulders into spiky petals circling the bodice that appeared to be falling open to reveal the antique pale pink brocade inside. The dress itself was a black sheath. It was a stunning creation so I tried it on myself. The effect was at least as amazing as Mark in drag. It was me in drag. This appealed to my theatrical side. That you could step into a role to navigate social situations that otherwise left me vulnerable to what others wanted to project on me.

I assessed the construction of the dress and saw that I could take it in by several inches with a single seam up the back, for the zipper was on the side seam. I could then wear it myself to our upcoming party. I found a pair of black silk stiletto heels and long black gloves plus a little black hat with a veil. And in emulating the '50s style that was Mark's signature I got a garter belt and a pair of sheer black stockings to complete the drag queen effect of this outfit.

It was to be an initiation party for Peter one of Ann's gay friends who lived in A dorm. To be initiated into the Transvestite Revenge Squad Peter had to appear in public in drag. Mark would dress Peter from his own capacious wardrobe of vintage dresses. He owned so many dresses he had two rods in his closet one behind the other to handle the load. He must have coopted the closet of the adjoining bedroom. I had been to his house where he proudly showed me drawers full of neatly arranged long gloves with their pearl buttons. Another drawer for costume jewelry. His many wigs on wig stands on top of his closet in a line-up of heads all with the same 50s perm style just in different colors. His stiletto size 11 heels in neat rows at the bottom of the closet. It was an amazing feat of organization this room. He had also built his own bed frame. Each post of the bed supported built in book shelves enclosing the bed in walls of his vintage paperback collection of pulp novels. He showed me some of the lesbian ones with their covers showing pairs of women in stiletto heels and sheath dresses looking at each other suggestively. We all loved this campiness as much as he did.

Mark also loved Porsches, owned six or seven vintage ones and worked on them himself. He seemed to recognize me as a fellow tinkerer for he showed me a pair of Porsche pistons so I could see for myself how smoothly they slid in an out of their casings. He was the first adult I had met who demonstrated what being in control of one's own life might look like. He even owned his own house and rented rooms to ladies of the night. He too plied the trade and would offer his female persona to johns with an ad in the San Francisco Bay Guardian. Sometimes he would come and see us after, still dressed up and tell us just a few lines about how it went and if the John was nice or not.

On the night of the party I watched Peter arrive wearing a white dress with a full skirt walking pretty confidently in his heels. He was clearly enjoying himself and was greeted with affection by his women friends. Mark followed wearing something shimmering and gold. When he found me in my newly acquired outfit he understood exactly what I was doing in the drag sense. We leaned over the balcony railing together and he talked to me in a wistful poetic fashion.

"Never forget me," he said in that husky diva voice.

"How could I possibly forget you," I assured him. Later in the evening he found me again in the lounge. I was leaning against the wall with a drink in my hand and he got on his knees in front of me.

"I want you to grow a big cock right now," he said looking up at me. I just smiled at him. "Can't you do that?" he pleaded. I had no words. I knew he wasn't asking me to bed. He was recognizing me as a peer, initiating me with this complement of his desire and admiration. And ever the gentleman he never touched me or groped me.

My wardrobe would never be the same after I met Mark. Having taught me how to be a boy in drag, I too now had a set of boys clothes with my 501 boot cut Levis, and a red blazer over a t-shirt, just as he had his everyday blazer over a custom silk screened t-shirt and his two pairs of the exact same men's shoes. The rest of my closet was dress up.

I had always loved costume. From childhood I had a much loved booklet about historical costumes my mother had given me. I studied the history of fashion to understand Western culture for it was only in the West that clothing was an expression of the individual rather than a marker of a person's status in society. Western fashions came to the East as a form of status. Fashion was also a driver for capitalism as it was the original vehicle of "dynamic obsolescence" with the advent of fall and winter collections that rendered last season's fashion out of style. But as much as we are commodified by fashion it continued to be a tool of resistance and solidarity. Fashion had helped with the emancipation of women with bloomers that had popularized cycling. My favorite black and white childhood saddle shoes that had spoken to me of the flashy aesthetics of the U.S. even had a history. They were created to show solidarity of white allies with the civil rights movement. Thus fashion could carry a message.

I came to understand that clothing and fashion were a vehicle for occupying space and changing it at the same time. Mark used it to enchant and intrigue with the visual discrepancy of being a man in a glamorous expression of femaleness. It changed the way people responded to him and allowed him to express himself more fully. I later learned that the term glamour is borrowed from witchcraft as it is used to enhance a spell or create an illusion by enchanting the viewer with the glamoured appearance of the witch herself.

It was important to me to be fashionable enough to hold my own in the class I was raised to live in, especially at high school reunions given by my fancy pants prep school, and to go to dinner with my relatives in Thailand at high end hotels. I also wanted to adhere to my frugal values which would later become eco values. I was learning to solve these challenges by designing my own outfits combining used clothing, salvaged fabrics, indigenous garments and renaissance costume patterns.

Mark moved to Seattle to buy a property where he could park all of his vintage Porches right on the grounds. I never saw him again, but as promised I have never forgotten him.

Chapter 9

I've Come For You

My hall mates hung out in the hall late into the night. They sat on the floor lounging about, taunting passersby and each other with provocative lewd statements. They were like puppies tugging at pant legs with their teeth—in their own eyes they were rough and mean, but in memory more soft and playful. We did have a lounge with actual couches, but the lounge did not offer the opportunity of mixing it up with strangers unless to hang over the balcony during the day.

Late one night I heard a group just outside my door and came out to join them. Caesar (not his real name) was sitting with his arm around a woman who had a single room at the end of he hall. She was a dancer, short, blond with an enigmatic face and the startling name of Cindy Sunshine. It was not a hippie name, but a German name pronounced Sunsheen. But we pronounced it the way we read it and were endlessly entertained by it. Caesar who was a theater major was just learning to play the ukulele; he worked her name into a song. Then he strung all of our names first and last together to the tune of *Frére Jacque*. And we sang it with him learning everyone's name along with it. My name being the longest was the only one that would fit the middle line which made me sound like the hall linchpin. His songs livened up our little group along with his cheesy jokes.

That pivotal evening as I joined them on the floor Caesar pointed his beer bottle at me and said "I think you should fuck Cindy here. She'd really like that." I looked at her face trying to read it for clues, but the expression on her enigmatic face was noncommittal though slightly demure. I never knew when these boys were pulling my leg and I wasn't going to react. Did they even know I was bi identified? I just smiled.

"I'd be open to that," I said. She happened to be my type—her face not classically beautiful almost verging on homely except that she had a beguiling way of presenting it.

"I never know who's kidding around here," I said locking eyes with her engagingly.

'Well yeah, that's the thing," she said her voice slightly nasal. No one made a move so after a few more minutes of this empty promise I went to bed and soon the group dispersed.

I slept nude and was under the covers when I heard a quiet but definite knock. I slipped on my dad's white monogrammed shirt which was long enough to cover what needed covering. My roommate was fast asleep and didn't budge. I opened the door just enough to find Cindy standing quite close to me still dressed.

"I've come for you," she said. At which point I took her in my arms and kissed her, so bold I was in this atmosphere of permissiveness and open sexuality. And so delicious was this kissing after all those years of guarded longing furtively looking around in case someone were to see me a little too close, too intimate, staring too silently into the faces of the girls who won my affection in high school. Too delicious this pressing together of breasts floating freely in the embrace. I closed the door gently behind me and followed her down the hall holding her hand. She slept on the floor in her tiny single room and wasted no time stripping off her clothes and rolling into it with me.

I explored her body, soon finding my way and we mirrored each other with our hands until we were breathing in tandem with each other and climaxed together. Wow. Sex had never been quite like this with men. For there had been men. I made sure of that the summer before, aware that my virginity would be a liability here at college in the sense of feeling too green, too innocent in the company of men. Some things you just have to have experienced in order to make an informed decision. Losing my virginity had been perfectly fine with this particular traveling hippie man with his seamless suntan and drawstring pants selling flutes out of his VW Square back. He was a friend of the director of a play I was in that summer. I met him at a cast party. I was more attracted to the dark haired girlfriend he was with that day. Then he came to a rehearsal alone and Hank, the director, said to go to his house and wait for him and he took me with him. We were having a little party while we waited for him but Hank never showed up. So my seamless suntan man entertained me by showing me how to juggle in tandem with him passing the balls between us.

"Want to see something neat?" he said and picked me up and taking me to Hank's bedroom so he could lower me on the waterbed.

"My parent's have a waterbed," I said. Jeesh, it wasn't like I'd never seen a waterbed before. I was unaware that it was a ruse to get me in the bedroom. He offered to give me a massage and of course one thing led to another. He claimed afterward that he hadn't planned it. And I allowed it to happen as if it were perfectly natural. I took the pain of first penetration as a form of connection and passage to the knowing I sought. We even saw each other again. He suggested dinner so I showed up at dinner time at another house party he invited me to, but dinner was never offered so I left. If there wasn't going to be free food I wasn't sticking around. I walked home hungry.

Men, I decided were all about owning you. The way they put their arms around your shoulders walking down the street in public as if you belonged to them. I was selling myself pretty cheap considering that all I wanted was a meal. At the next cast party I slept with Hank who was short and stocky with a neanderthal face that got him lots of Shakespearean character parts. I even slept with him again because I actually liked his broad beefy body and the effortless directness of his approach. There was no come on. I just ended up with him. I did get better at this sex thing, but my heart wasn't in it.

But women I could actually connect with, look into their souls and entice them, with nothing but my charm. Daring them to cross the line. The line between what was approved by society and what was not. To cross the line for love I took as proof of their attraction and their feelings for me though I sensed it wouldn't last unless they also embraced the life of a sexual outlaw.

The lesbians at UCSC didn't seem to recognize me as one of them with my long hair and my ethnicity. There were no visible lesbians of color at the time. (In fact there were few anyones of color so white was the UC Santa Cruz student body.) I also refused to wear the lesbian uniform—the plaid flannel shirt and overalls. There was a separatist movement sweeping the community with women only spaces springing up in urban areas—coffee shops and bookstores mostly. I considered the separatist label for a week or so as I explored these spaces and households.

Polyamorous bisexual more suited my identity depending on what I was reading or listening to—Patti Smith or Chris Williamson, Anais Nin or *Rubyfruit Jungle*. Patti won out. Her anger and defiance matched my guarded defense. I couldn't handle Chris Williamson's earnest, swelling declarations of her feelings for women surrounded, as I was by the sarcasm of my hall mates. I wanted to question the disconnect of the women who wanted to create women-only space and I borrowed their male sarcasm to do it with. Androgyny was the style, since the butch femme personas of the 1950s was now considered too patriarchal by feminist standards, and androgyny was neither. I questioned one woman who was still butch.

"Why do you dress like a man if you want to create safe space for women?"

"Because men have the power," she said. I understood what she was saying from my secret life as a boy. Wearing women's clothes I could see was mostly about commanding the attention of a man with sexiness and glamour. But the wearing of pantyhose, heals and dresses was so severely restricting it limited movement and put you in a class that was considered second to men. But being a boy didn't get me power. It was more the absence of powerlessness. And the opportunity to be more fully myself.

I soon hung up my separatist identity after visiting an all-woman household in town with a dyke buddy. The host proudly boasted that even their dog was female. This struck me as slightly absurd to include the pets in what I felt was basically a political act. The separatists had to go to some lengths to create women only spaces; they were defiant about it, but seemed to occupy the space more with the air of shell shocked victims than angry rebels.

I didn't really understand the politics even after reading *The Dialectic of Sex* by Shulamith Firestone, the feminist manifesto of the day with its undertow of Marxism. I had no political training to attempt to parse out a meaningful analysis. Why did politics have anything to do with lesbianism? Where was the glamour that sparked sexual attraction? The lesbians here did not show the least bit of interest in me, let alone want to date me. I wasn't real to them, dressing up in all my various costumes. As an Asian woman I was more recognizable as a fetish of white men in some Kama Sutra fantasy. I knew this because I was fielding these projections in comments from men associating me with the exotic femme fatale persona which was all anyone knew about Asian women from the movies.

I did befriend a lesbian who lived across the quad in A dorm. A kind mature woman who was far removed from the acidity of my hall culture. She suffered from constant back pain so spent a good deal of time lying down and had arranged her ground floor room to accommodate a mattress on the floor. During a long car ride to the city when I kept her company lying in the back of her friends hatchback she willingly told me her story of first love. It was a story so filled with internalized homophobia it was painful to dwell on. I was glad I hadn't been raised in this close minded Christian culture.

My idea of a lesbian was more Marlene Dietrich in top hat and tails singing in a cabaret act in the movie *Morocco*. Or riding on a train with her Asian side kick in *Lady From Shanghai* and a trunk full of outfits to die for. Where was the gay life of Paris and Berlin in the 1930s that I'd glimpsed in books or the subversive lesbian of the 50s played so handsomely by Candace Bergen in the movie *The Group*. My high school lover Judy and I had howled at the campiness of this portrayal. There was a glamour and fluidity of women finding sexual power with each other which the men couldn't touch. A humor in this mocking of heterosexual norms. I didn't want to be separate; I wanted to infiltrate hetero-space and render it powerless. So I had found love within my own hall with Cindy. It was not exactly a collegiate atmosphere of students supporting each other in a common endeavor. More a gulag of acerbic tongue lashings. But it was home.

I learned early what kind of gulag it was when I introduced my teddy bear Rupert to those who came to visit in my room when I first arrived. I had removed the childhood pajamas my mother had made for Rupert at my request as a child when I was old enough to realize he was naked and told her he needed to have clothes. In high school with Rupert again naked I had given him a black velvet bowtie which I thought gave him a more adult appearance. He was thus reintroduced as my mascot in my last year of high school. Such a childhood object was still ok within the girls school culture. Having an emotional life was valued and showed heart as we stepped into the leadership of being seniors. So vigilantly did I have to keep a lid on my feelings in order not to betray my homosexuality that I needed such a marker, a way to show a softer side of me. I didn't want people to think I was cold and unfeeling. And no one shamed me for having a teddy bear. Alas how my prep school education had failed to prepare me for the ravages of College V.

Ann thought he was cute and this allowed us an immediate bond in that first week of our friendship, along with her endearing faking of a British accent, but the final condemnation went to Caesar who would use words of criticism to frame my character on this new art college turf.

"You really are sentimental aren't you?" said Caesar who had seated his lanky self on my desk. He gave me his goofy sardonic smile. He wasn't casting a judgement per se, but I knew that in the art world he espoused, being sentimental was the kiss of death. He might have even been glad that I had feelings that he couldn't show himself, but his words managed to hit at some core part of me. Caesar had taken something I treasured and challenged it from an artistic perspective. I stood my ground and put my bear gently back on the shelf, but the damage was done. Something in me slammed shut.

My girl's school sensibilities with all its cranked up emotional girl drama expressing the trials of the heart had also allowed the tentative expression of my emerging creative writing with very little criticism. In a week this was all summarily squelched to make room for the daily dose of micro hazing in this atmosphere of brutalist concrete architecture whose most vocal members wielded a sardonic wit in search of topics to skewer as an appetizer before dinner. My hall mates who lounged in the hall outside my door; the cool kids who became my group of identity ran a constant commentary of sarcastic insults at every expression of humanity and art that attempted to emerge. Nobody was spared.

In the hall where we hung out most evenings there was an atmosphere of public performance; we were a captive audience for each other. One night as we were waiting to go to dinner, the ring leader of our hall, Julius (not his real name) with his Mick Jagger hair and large sexy lips, announced that he was going to make mad, passionate love to me. Then he turned towards me and pressed my body up against the wall with his body making humping movements while fondling my breast with one hand. I played along in an aloof sort of way because it was funny at first and because I thought it meant that I was part of the in-crowd and that this would be a one time joke. But it didn't stop there; the more it became clear to him that I was not interested in his body, the more he wanted to claim ownership of mine. Once he had performed this faux humping act he took the opportunity to fondle my breast as sort of an evening aperitif. I had thought we were friends, but he crossed a line with this joke. And I was somehow without a good reason to object. After all I had agreed to it. I didn't have the wherewithal to tell him to stop. I knew it wouldn't earn me any points.

In the aftermath of the '60s decade of Free Love I prided myself in being open minded about sex and nudity. My father had a subscription to *Playboy* magazine which my mother also claimed to read because it had well written interesting articles. I just read the cartoons which were risqué and informative. As a young child in Thailand I discovered the stash of magazines in a cupboard in the kitchen which shared a wall with my bedroom. I heard my father rummaging through them one night. His fingernails were scratching the shared wall and woke me up. I froze terrified. I thought this scratching noise must be an animal. That there was a rat inside the kitchen. I was so relieved to realize it was my father when I heard him move about and my body relaxed noticeably as the tension of fear drained from my muscles. The next day I went to investigate what he kept in there and spent some time admiring the statuesque ladies laid out in the centerfold. They were so beautiful and their poses struck me as goddess like. I was used to looking at art as depiction of deities. Thai temples were adorned with half naked women who were mythical creatures. Why wouldn't women be photographed in this way too? Playboy being still tasteful at the time, being free of genital shots, I did not see anything degrading about it.

In high school the Broadway play *Hair* caused a sensation for having the actors half naked in some scenes. My mother's friends talked about it and weighed in on how this was no big deal though it so clearly hadn't been done before as there was a news segment about it on the Six o'clock news. Being ok with nudity and sexuality was the emerging context of the time.

When my body developed I could see that I was going to have a very fine form myself. One that would serve me better naked than with clothes on. For clothing required fashion sense and I was not yet confident in this arena nor did I have money to buy clothes. Plus I felt I was too short to carry if off. I was still wearing my tomboy clothes when I was first offered a chance to skinny dip by friends of my mother. She and I were invited to the house of a friend for an impromptu swim in the pool after an event. And as none of us had planned on a swim party the hostess invited us to skinny dip or borrow one of her swimsuits.

My mother headed for the bedroom to don a suit and was horrified that I was going to choose to skinny dip because there were a few men present. She tried to stop me, but given that the hostess had said it was ok I was already halfway to the pool in my birthday suit. So my mother had to deal with it. It was the first time I had openly defied her wishes, but I had turned 18 and figured I had the right. Once in the pool she was ok with it since everyone else was ok with it. And one of the men had discreetly slipped into the pool bare assed before everyone else arrived. When she discovered that he too was unclothed that seemed to make it all ok and even hip for me to be showing off my body. For my mother It all seemed to be about what the men thought.

The English, I learned from Margaret Mead in a pamphlet she wrote to guide the American GI's, were all about men setting boundaries for sexual flirtations while in the U.S. it was up to the women to keep the men from taking advantage. So the American GI's thought the English girls were sluts. And the pamphlet helped. My mother however was no help to me about keeping men's hands to themselves. Or about giving myself to men. I more thought of it as allowing men access. In my hip idea of myself I gave the men on my hall a slew of mixed messages. On the one hand I seemed precocious about seeming to want sex. I had read Erica Jong and talked about the benefits of the zipless fuck as if I knew a thing about it.

Though I had made it plain to Julius that I was not interested in being romantic with him he did ask me to sleep with Caesar who hadn't seen any action in ages, he said. I agreed to this favor he was asking of me because I liked Caesar despite his comment about me being sentimental. Caesar hung out with Julius and emulated his sardonic wit, but his style lacked the sting that Julius would impart. While Julius was intentionally mean, Caesar was prone to the absurd and had a boyish pranksterish delivery.

"Here check out my giant Australian sand worm," he said to me as I passed by the hall group. He was holding out his pants pocket for me to put my hand into. I looked at the expectant faces of the others and declined. Then he confided that there was a hole in the bottom of his pocket which implied that he wasn't wearing any underwear. He was so clearly pleased with his silly humor it endeared me to him.

So Julius told Caesar to go to my room at a certain hour of the evening and I met him there for the agreed upon fuck. He had the slimmest penis I'd encountered so was easily accommodated which was a relief. He didn't have any hang ups about it though it slipped out twice; it was more like we were kids playing. Nor did it take long and he didn't expect any romantic affection on my part. It was my version of the zipless fuck. I thought we might at least be closer as friends, but neither of us nurtured it. Unaccustomed as I was to confiding in men.

Caesar did write a song about me that was part put down, part celebratory. It was about my sexuality. He used my whole name which we had already discovered was the musical linchpin of all the names on the hall. The name is what made it sound celebratory. Then there was the one liner meat of it. How "She plays Patti Smith every goddamn day, but she can't decide if she's straight or gay." He was pointing out that it was clear I was gay which was mostly ok with me. It saved me having to come out though it put a spotlight on me every time he sang it in public. One I got used to and in the end celebrated with him. He sang it with affection mixed with truth telling. One that was racy for the day being as it was about homosexuality. I resonated with this subversive affectionate truth telling. The song was popular and I heard that he sang it long after I'd gone from UC Santa Cruz and no one knew who this Amanda was.

Julius also wanted to put me down for my sexuality, but his intent was much more about humiliation by telling lies about me. At lunch one Saturday with maybe four of my hall mates in a sparsely populated dining hall he suddenly said "I'm going to announce that Amanda lost her virginity last night."

"No," I said loudly, but he was already standing up tapping his water glass with a fork, the sound ringing as people looked his way. I jumped up and made an attempt to pull him back into his chair by his belt. This did nothing except show everyone who he was talking about. He made the announcement in a disinterested monotone as if announcing that the library would be closed for renovations. Then we both sat down. And people went back to eating. It was clear to me that he'd done no damage to me, just to himself in showing what a prick he liked to be. I was sure that given his reputation for being a jerk no one believed him or cared. But I hated feeling defenseless in the face of a false narrative.

There were other women who did care how Julius treated them and I heard later that nearly every woman on the hall had been in the counselor's office complaining about the hostile environment he was creating. By going along with it I too contributed to this hostile environment. It made me want to distance myself from those memories later, ashamed of the person I had become. It was the price I paid for acceptance into the in-crowd; a status that also gave me some fame and immunity. Enough to keep me hanging out with them. Because that's where the party was happening. Everything was fodder for their jokes and no one told them or us otherwise. If there even was a them or us in this homogenous school.

"Wanna Thai one on," Caesar had asked when he learned that I was from Thailand. The Thais loved play on words and I thought this clever and funny so I laughed. A remark like this would likely be considered racist now, but at the time I understood racism to mean actual discrimination as in being barred from a place and I certainly wasn't being barred from UC Santa Cruz. There was only one other non-white student at College V, an Asian man in the grad student wing. (UC Santa Cruz had 8 colleges at the time; they got names once a big donor sponsored one.) The Asian man interacted with me too on my travels, but not as aggressively. The axis of power was definitely along sexist lines; one I had little experience in navigating though I could feel the denigration behind it; the disrespect for one's person which was anathema to a Thai where protocol was so formal just to touch someone of the opposite sex was considered disrespectful.

Most obvious to me was the overt sexism of judging women who did not meet the men's criteria for attractiveness. Julius demonstrated this when a pair of binoculars appeared and we were all participating in a bit of *Rear Window* ogling of occupants in the rooms of 'A' Dorm across the quad from our third floor vantage point hanging off the balcony of the lounge. After I had a peep and quickly realized I was invading someone's privacy, I gave Julius back the binoculars and he narrated his usual witty patter which soon turned dark as he found a first floor room occupied by a lesbian couple.

"Oh look at them. They are so fat how can they even find each other's clit?" he asked. I heard others laugh. The comment was so visceral it made me wonder for a moment if this might actually be an issue. But I did not defend them. The lesbian community at the college seemed suspicious of me so I didn't feel I had to defend them. And in my loyalty to my hall I would not find fault with anyone on it. Indeed it never occurred to me that I could complain about Julian or any of the other students. Even when someone scratched into my door the words "Fuck Dyke Cunts". What coward would do that? I wondered and let it be. I hated the C word. It was so harsh and obscene. There was no male equivalent that implied quite that level of cutting nastiness. Dickhead was too nice, more a comment on clueless bad behavior than embodiment of vicious, intentional, directed nastiness. I could never bring myself to use it.

I sassed back by claiming to own a castration kit. When the guys demanded to see it, I pulled out my high school biology dissection kit that I had brought from home one weekend especially to illustrate my claim. They turned away snorting to themselves and made no further comment. A few days later I told them I had teeth in my vagina. This seemed to be enough to erect a visual barrier against casual entry.

I was trying hard to develop a persona that would fend off the male bravado while simultaneously trying on the contempt of the bullies, practicing to see if I could make it my own.

I presented myself one afternoon at one of the many art openings for student work in a newly acquired vintage black cocktail dress which came with a little bolero jacket to top the slim profile of the sheath dress. A little black hat with a veil offered me the mystique of Candace Bergen and a very long cigarette holder which was so very Audrey Hepburn in *Breakfast At Tiffany's*. None of my hall comrades were with me as I sallied forth to this art exhibit. The artist was clearly not one of the cool kids with his long curly hair falling to his shoulder. He had a gentle demeanor and offered a bemused smile at my entrance.

"How nauseating," I said loudly at the framed art work as I struck a pose in front of one. All were self-portraits, rows and rows of screen prints in different tones and gradations, somewhat Andy Warhol like in spirit.

"How narcissistic," I pronounced. The artist and other viewers stared at me in disbelief. I soon had to leave. I could hardly bear my own company as I spoke my false witticisms in such an arch voice. It was just not me.

One afternoon I was in Julius's room asking about a school assignment as he sat at his desk. He answered my question then reached up and stroked my nipple through my tank top. I wasn't wearing a bra; we didn't then. My nipple hardened.

"See you can respond to a man," he said. I was unimpressed and said nothing. He went on, "All the women at College V tell me how charming you are," he said, "but to me you're just a bitch." I smiled for I didn't know that the women were talking about me and was pleased with this debonair vision of me charming the ladies. If Julius thought I was a bitch it was of no consequence to me.

"It's a matter of interest," I said. My interest in woman. My complete disinterest in men. I think that's what made him continue to taunt me. I turned on my heels pleased with this news about women's thoughts about me and left his room.

Julius continued to grope my breast when he felt like it. It wasn't until the next year that I fought back. On this evening we were dressing up for a Halloween party in Paul's room snorting lines of coke. Paul was our big man on the art campus. He had a job doing graphics for the college, thus money to buy cocaine which he shared so he'd have an instant party. He was dressing up as David Bowie and applying make-up. I had on a black satin shirt and Julius was dressed in a purple velvet jacket applying purple eye make-up.

As usual he announced that he had to say hello to my tit. I had grown tired of this routine so I slapped his hand away as soon as he made contact. Wearing a costume somehow gave me confidence. He immediately put his hand back on my breast and I slapped it down again so he slapped back at me and we were about to go at it cat fight style when Paul said, "Quit it you guys," in a tone that meant business. He was after all the hall R.A., the resident assistant, which was why he had a double room to himself.

I had more wished he had told Julius off for his ongoing groping and been a witness to my suffering, but it would have to suffice. And that was the end of it. Julius didn't reach for me again. Nor did he participate in the group encounter that came after this party as six of us got naked in Paul's double room with the two single beds tied together. Julius had his limits I realized, surprised. His groping was all for show.

The next semester the college made him an R.A. as an end run around to divert his disruptive behavior. Once given this power and responsibility it took the bite out of his bad behavior just as the college hoped it would. This just demonstrated to me how men were rewarded with responsibility for their aggressive bad behavior. A gambit that never forced them to really develop their leadership skills. It was just a manipulation of power dynamics to refocus their energies. There were women R.A.s but not anywhere near me. These examples of male behavior I took for granted though other men would take pains to tell me these were aberrations. That my entire college experience was made an aberration by this hostile environment. Never would I experience the camaraderie that would create that warm spot in my memories of my college education. On the contrary it made me seek my own counsel and question what was learned in school from the start. I wanted off this academic grid.

Chapter 10

A Journal Stolen

Cindy and I were seen together regularly so were known to be an item. No one made any comments. I gave her my heart freely and became attached to being with her though I knew she was not mine alone. Monogamy was not a strong core value of the times. Nor was it for me. After all my father boasted of his grandfather having had 13 wives and his father having had two—my Khun Ya and my Auntie Sakorn were both highly significant to my life on the family compound.

Cindy and I took to dressing alike. We both owned a pair of 13 button U.S. navy blue wool pants which we wore with a white button up man's shirt. This furthered our image as a couple.

Our fey gay friend from the next hall saw us as performers for a project he was working on. He had both a boy's name—John and a girl's name—Lauren. He wrote a long piece of poetry in two voices that he wanted to be performed by two women so he asked us to do the reading that would debut this work. We dressed in shimmering black dance skirts and black turtlenecks. John/Lauren had gathered an attentive audience in the college lounge after dinner one night. The poem was a tribute to Gertrude Stein, but all I remember of it was that as I finished reading each page I dropped the page on the floor behind me while Cindy carefully turned to lay each one on the stone hearth of the giant fireplace behind her. Watching the pages fall to the floor gave a sense of suspense said one viewer. This performance of obscure meaning fulfilled our fantasies of ourselves as avant garde performing art students.

Caesar also cast us in a scene he was working on for his directors class and had us play the lead roles in a scene from *Rosencrantz And Guildenstern Are Dead*. We rehearsed nightly in the college studio space and performed for his class. We applied ourselves with all due seriousness. He also photographed us in the costumes we wore — black bowlers and white silk shirts with red suspenders on our thirteen button pants. We posed as men, but in one I had an arm around Cindy claiming her with a look of ownership while she gave her expressionless dancer's face with her chin in the air.

We had a little gallery showing of the matted 8 x10 photos. It didn't require a gallery space. We simply pinned them to the wall of the hall, put up a flyer to give it a name and announced a gallery opening. On the designated evening we opened a bottle of champagne with our hall mates. That this collaboration claimed space for two cross-dressing women to be seen together required no permission. That was the beauty of it. We left the show up for a couple of weeks. By the end of it Cindy and I were history. There was a journal involved that I had let her read, but it so annoyed her boyfriend that the two of them refused to return it. I followed her around asking for it every time I saw her.

"I'm so confused," she would say when I confronted her; then she would float away wearing that vacuous expression. My frustration grew and one night I demanded that she give it back to me. She said no her boyfriend wouldn't let her.

One night my friend Ann encouraged me to call the proctor for his help getting it back. The proctor said for stolen property such as this we needed the help of the police. As a written document it could be considered a class project he said. Listening to his words, my journaling was suddenly elevated to student work. Summoning the police made it worthy of defending.

I put on my black trench coat over my black turtleneck. The outfit had scared her when she first saw me. She said I looked like a Weatherman. I had never heard of them, but learned that they were a terrorist group. I put on my black fedora and we went to meet the proctor outside by the entry to the college. The squad car rolled up the circular driveway and the proctor and I got in the back seat to explain the situation. Then the two policemen, who towered over me, accompanied me back into B dorm up to the third floor to knock on Cindy's door. By the time we arrived on the hall people were popping their heads out their doors to see what was going on. I stood between these two tall men in blue enjoying what a commanding presence we presented. They knocked on Cindy's door. It opened slowly. Cindy looked small and frightened when she saw these imposing police at her door.

"I believe you have a notebook belonging to this student," said one of the policeman.

"I don't have it," she said in a quiet voice. "It's at my boyfriend's house and he lives off campus."

"Could you let him know he needs to return it?" He said. She agreed to pass along the message. They bid her good night and she closed her door. The officer then turned to me and said they couldn't do anything as long as the property was off campus. I would have to contact the Santa Cruz police if I wanted to pursue it. I didn't want to take it that far just for one spiral bound notebook, but the very act of being able to bring a pair of policemen to Cindy's door gave me a legitimacy that spoke volumes about the value of my writing and my right to document my life in such fashion despite the words of her boyfriend telling me I was mentally unsound to spend my time so obsessively recording. He said I often got things wrong and misheard things. He made me feel odd for recording my life so obsessively.

I didn't know then about Samuel Pepys, the London diarist who provided detailed accounts of life in 16th century England, including evidence of the first cup of tea being drunk in the kingdom; this being the only known record of this famously English beverage having been imbibed at that time; coffee being the preferred stimulant until then. And it would be several more decades before I would be able to enjoy through the popular BBC series *Gentleman Jack*, the delightful discovery of Anne Lister's diary and the first lesbian of England. Lacking these British forerunners I could only promise myself that I would not stop recording my life in journals no matter what anyone said, though I would take care to be more accurate and double check things I might have misheard. And I would be a bit more careful about revealing the fact that I kept a journal at all.

The journals became my lifeline in my journey through these uncharted waters of being. Swimming as I was in foreign seas—a biracial, lesbian still attached to a British identity, but being perceived as an Asian woman and something of a fetish for white men. I couldn't make them not see me that way, but I could at least see myself. Writing established the very ground under my feet and what I knew to be true. At first my college journaling was painfully pretentious affecting a sarcasm I thought would make me sound sophisticated. I wrote about my latest targets of love, describing the women I was trying to charm and what happened along the way to garnering their attentions. I came to rely on my journals to know my own mind and to use this writing practice to sort out whatever dilemma presented itself.

Over time I noticed that the journal had a wisdom of its own and was able to offer me its counsel. When I wrote all the details out, the narrative created an arch that showed movement, and so pointed to solutions. I could see through this act of storytelling, what might be the logical next step and the consequences of my desires. Through my writing I created a world that included me when the world around me did not. This went a long way to preserving my mental health.

I did try to enroll in a writing class. On the day of orientation for the class the professor read a story he felt worthy of attention. The paragraph he read described the thoughts of a male physics student who, while doing his homework, had decided to alleviate his boredom by masturbating. What got this attention was that the piece was written by a woman.

"Now how would a woman know how a man thinks?" he said clearly taken by this revelation. Perhaps he thought it was a piece we could relate to, but the message was clear—women writing students were to be praised for getting it right about men. Class admission was granted upon review of a piece of writing. I submitted my now childishly story from high school. I had been so proud of it for I had captured myself as a boy character meeting the girl of my affection in a dream sequence full of piano music. I thought it was the height of romance. It did not win me a seat in this class. Just as well I thought. To seek the approval of such a teacher would be a twisted power dynamic that I knew, instinctively, would be detrimental to my soul. Instead I took a playwriting class. A man was teaching that class too. He would have the other students read our work like a play. A man in the class who read a piece I wrote about my father, imposed upon him a British accent. This was just never going to work, I thought. I longed to write about lesbian characters, but couldn't bring myself to submit such material. It would be several more decades before I signed up for a writing class again.

Chapter 11

Visit To The Circus

That summer I returned to working on plays at TheatreWorks though it paid nothing and I needed an income, having used up all my savings buying a chocolate chip cookie every night at the coffee shop. This was an unexpected expense I discovered per my habit of recording all my expenses as I had learned from the Boy Scout merit badge booklet on personal finance. I was also expected to buy all my own text books. But summer jobs were scarce. 1977 was a recession year so deep the usual bookstores did not want to hire students who would abandon them come fall and I didn't have it in me to lie.

I took the only job available pumping gas at a discount gas station where frequent turnaround was expected. They were willing to hire girls because they were more compliant than boys and when paired with guys kept these errant men from getting into mischief. The job came with a uniform and a change dispenser to attach to my belt. The company even washed the uniform which was a perk because they stunk so much of gasoline I didn't want to bring them into the house. I came home and changed in the garage. My hands were sore at the end of the day from pumping, but I didn't mind the job so much. This traditionally male, working class job appealed to my appetite for life experience more than being a sales girl did. I was at least outdoors and customers were decent and sometimes charmed by the novelty of a girl attendant. I wore my hair in two braids and as my arms turned brown from the sun I'm sure some mistook me for Native American. As I was sent to different stations the scenery shifted from the high end residential town of Los Altos to the industrial section of San Mateo. I was also asked to be available for both day shifts and night shifts which meant I had to give up the job I had been assigned working the spotlight for the play at TheatreWorks. Sacrifices had to be made in the real world I reckoned.

I was indecisive about returning to College V. My parents' divorce had made them less of a force to confront now that I could approach them as single entities. My father had no patience with my indecisiveness; he told me to stop taking "Mickey Mouse" courses and get credentials stating that I could do something—even writing since that's what I did best he said.

"I don't mind if you become a book writer," he said, "as long as you write." I was surprised that he would support the idea of being an author, but I knew he meant writing as a paying job. But my heart was in theatre. I had been taking drama classes and dance. He saw no career options for these pursuits. He was probably right, but at least in college I had a serious chance of participating in the school's drama productions.

I told him about my stolen journal and was surprised to learn that he had kept a journal during his college years too, but the notebooks had been stolen from the trunk of his car along with all the rest of his belongings.

"You must get it back," he urged, "It is your life there on paper," I assured him that it was just one notebook, not all my journals. I was intrigued that he valued the idea of capturing one's personal life on paper. This introspective pursuit was counter to the man I saw perpetually immersed in computer circuit boards and car repair. I told him how I had talked to the police and they had filed a report. He said if this person gave me anymore trouble he knew the chief of police at Stanford who knew all the police in all the districts in Northern California. My father was big on knowing inside people; a very Thai way of wielding power. I replied that I didn't really want to call the cops on Cindy and hoped to negotiate with her in a civilized manner.

"You can't be civilized with people who are close to you," he said. This was what wisdom he had to impart from his last years of marriage. He was not exactly skilled in the communication department ,so I took his statement with a grain of salt.

My mother had all but promised me that I would find my passion in college as she had when she discovered the field of psychology. I did take a psych class, but I already knew so much from listening to my mother that it didn't draw me in. I was losing ground in my academic standing. I had used up my advance placement college credit to keep up. I had dropped some classes due to incomplete homework. I couldn't bring myself to write papers. I had once cranked them out on a regular basis in high school, hating every minute of it if I wasn't interested in the topic. The only topic I had been interested in was film history. My favorite subject—creative writing—having proved to be a bust. And now the papers required more words just when I had less to say. I had aimed to be a lit major, but the books were tomes of boredom immersed as they were in philosophical meanderings and there simply wasn't time to read them properly. Stendhal's *The Red And The Black* for instance took weeks to read. I took a Western Philosophy class because the professor came highly recommended. But when I learned that Kant had declared that mind must be separated from body I was filled with disdain.

"No wonder," I thought to myself, "that is clearly what's wrong with Western Civilization." There was no Eastern philosophy mentioned even for contrast. I remained disdainful and just as lost. There was no where to hang my own experience; no words for what I would later realize was a Buddhist informed perspective.

An academic education I could see was a good way to destroy all interest in a topic. You took on information that didn't necessarily interest you, but was part of a class curriculum. In the end you basically became an agent of the institution that imparted this carefully chosen information. You were authorized by it to go out in the world and perform your profession simply because you had learned all the rules.

There had to be another kind of education, I thought. I searched for inspiration as I always had at the public library. I found a book for students looking for unusual summer jobs. It was an encyclopedia of every possible odd job from scuba diving for lost golf balls to amusement park attendant to camp counselor. One entry caught my eye —joining the circus. The Ringling Brothers Barnum and Bailey circus, the book promised, hired young people to sell concessions. And best of all the entire circus traveled by train, two of the largest privately owned trains in the world.

My favorite childhood stories had been about traveling circus caravans perhaps because the children in them spoke several languages and were adept at going from town to town with all their belongings in a house on wheels. I wanted to be a trapeze artist. After all I already had circus skills in unicycling and juggling. Breaking into the business selling concessions seemed like a good way to get in.

While hitching a ride into town from campus I met a woman who drove a VW bug that was painted on every panel with a cartoon character. Well known ones like Donald Duck and Goofy. I asked her if she had painted the car herself.

"No," she said, "I worked for a while with a carny." Carny meaning a traveling carnival.

"What was that like?" I asked, "did they accept you being an outsider?" She told me how they left her alone at first, but when they got to know her they were very friendly and affectionate as well as generous in offering of their artistic skills. I was intrigued by this vision of camaraderie and artistic exchange. I'd think about the circus and the train to while away the time at the gas station especially at one station that was near the train tracks. I'd picture myself running alongside the tracks and jumping on a freight train like a depression era hobo.

Only the young are so romantic. I could not have embraced a vision so opposite of what was my birthright—of my level of privilege and class up-bringing. It would have been more fitting to look for work being a steward on the Norwegian cruise ship waiting tables, as the brother of one of my high school mates had done. But even that seemed too tame. I could easily imagine the kinds of kids from clean middle class families like my friends signing up. The circus offered not just travel, but performers, circus animals and something of the unknown in terms of people—freaks as they were once known. What kind of people flaunt their most socially unacceptable features.

As the fall termed loomed I felt I had to check out this vision. I couldn't shake off wanting to run away to the circus. Then the gas station fired me for coming up short on a shift. It was the one time I had a shift with the only other girl hired that summer. They blamed me for making incorrect change or miscounting because I wore gloves. My father's old flannel lined leather gloves from his college days in England. I always took them off when I handled money so I didn't think that was the case at all. I did not suspect the other girl of stealing any more than I would. It was too late in the summer to get another job.

I borrowed my dad's station wagon to drive up to Daily City to watch the circus parade that was promised in the paper for the show that was coming to the Cow Palace. I was thinking of the scene from *The Greatest Show On Earth* with stars in sequins riding on elephants going down Main Street. There wasn't much of a parade it turned out. Only unadorned elephants being hurriedly walked up the side of the busy road like cattle going to market. It was a short distance from the train yard to their quarters at the Cow Palace. The other performers including what looked like the show girls were dressed in town clothes and were headed for a day off in San Francisco. I heard them saying good bye to those staying behind.

Walking around the yard I admired the air-brushed tigers on the side of a black van, but I did not see any tigers behind bars of a train car. I went to the Cow Palace, but the doors into the auditorium were locked. In the hallway I did see a dwarf walking by looking purposeful and that gave me a tiny bit of a thrill that confirmed I was indeed at the circus. A young man who seemed to belong to the show chatted with me. He had on a beaded suede fringed vest with a cowboy hat to match. His nickname was Elvis "because I sing like him" he said. He claimed he had been brought up in London and his stepfather was in the movies. He told me he had ridden horses in rodeos and had a "57 Chevy. He had only been with the circus for five weeks. But when he learned why I was there, he said he could get me a job with concessions. I thought this boast might have some merit and I let on that I was interested. He asked me what kind of concessions I wanted to sell.

"Cotton candy," I told him because it was the most visually arresting thing I could think of.

"Those aren't popular, " he said, "I sell licorice. You make more money with licorice." This surprised me. I contemplated these practicalities of choosing a concession that made money.

"You think if I got you a job you'd be my girlfriend?" he asked wasting no time. He seemed harmless enough with a sleight build and brown hair though his face was unshaven. I didn't know how to say no to such a frank question from a man promising to do me a favor.

"Maybe," I said and thought I should end this relationship right there. I tried to walk away, but he followed me. I went back to the train yard and wandered among the empty freight cars thinking to practice jumping on one. I found an empty one I could climb into. A slant of sunshine lit up the dusty floor boards just as I had imagined them to look. But then Elvis climbed in with me and I realized it was not such a good idea to be alone in it, secluded from sight with this Elvis. I jumped out again and walked away.

"Why did you jump out," he asked following me.

"I have to leave now," I said and he let me go. I walked back to the Cow Palace and went into the arena where the circus hands were setting up. I found a seat next to an older man who looked like he had authority. He was watching the proceedings and I chatted him up. He was the circus veterinarian it turned out. I told him I was applying for a job and mentioned that I could ride a unicycle.

"We got chimpanzees that can ride a unicycle," he said in an informative way, not making fun of me, but this fact did put me in my place. How could I top a unicycle riding chimp. It made me feel somehow pedestrian. There was nothing else to see. I stood about in the empty hallway then decided to go home.

At home I pondered why I didn't just join the circus right then. I wrote down a detailed account of my visit in my journal wrestling with my feelings. My dream had been tarnished somewhat by my disappointment at the lack of theater in the promised parade, by the emptiness of the train yard and my encounter with "Elvis", but I still yearned for this adventure that I had conjured up in my mind. I was torn. I knew I was free to go, emotionally uninvolved with anyone; that there would likely not be another time I would be this unattached. But I couldn't do it, not just yet. I just didn't have the guts I admitted to myself.

"One day I will wish I had," I wrote summing up my lack of courage and ambiguity about my decision.

Chapter 12
The Domes Of Oz

I did return to College V and moved into a top floor room across the quad in A Dorm away from my old hall. A friend and I decided to room together. I was the most out lesbian in the dorm and Robina was the most out straight girl in the sense of being perceived as promiscuous. The simpatico of these labels gave us a bond in a shared bad girl fame.

We got along quite well once I stopped rearranging the furniture and settled on having my bed high above the fray in a makeshift loft I put together. This included much measuring and drawing and thinking to figure out, for I was fond of graph paper and floor plans. I brought from home a hollow core door that was left in the garage after my dad replaced the closet doors with sliding mirrored ones. I used the door to straddle the furniture we were issued in our dorm rooms; two modular units. One with a built in mirror and drawers which had bookshelves on the back. The other a closet unit. Both of the same height. With my door on top of these units, it created my loft bed and a dressing room in the space underneath. Doors would become my favorite item for repurposing in future projects and I would fondly remember this loft.

I made a ladder by I cutting up a thick dowel into four pieces, tying the dowel rungs at appropriate long-legged intervals with a length of nylon rope. One of the advantages of living on the top floor was the 15 foot high ceilings that sloped down towards the windows following the roofline. Lofts had been a tradition at College V until the fire marshal put a stop to them because they were built over the door and if they collapsed in a fire would block the exit. But nobody questioned mine. It didn't straddle the door and no building and hammering had been observed so nothing was mentioned to anyone.

I attached my ladder by tying it to the closet pole where it was partitioned for long dresses. The rungs were thus supported by one side of the closet and the partition. The rope stretched a bit when I first put my weight on it, but I was able to climb this precarious rig up to my door platform where I had laid my mattress. And somehow the geometry of it was stable enough that the whole thing didn't fall forward with my weight.

My minimalist loft was the first "home nest" I made for myself. (Not counting the blanket hanging over the knee hole of the discarded office desk which furnished my childhood room.) I further made myself at home in my perch by building a little bedside organizer unit from scrap wall paneling offered to me for $5 by a helpful sales clerk at the lumberyard. I hammered it together with tools my father gave me. I thought a tool kit would be an appropriate gift for him to fund upon my leaving home for college so he gave me money for it. I bought the tools myself from Sears—a hammer, two Philips screwdrivers and two slot ones and a pair of pliers. Having made my bedside organizer I put in it those things I needed to keep close—my journal, a pen and Rupert Bear.

I would not give up Rupert to be cool. He had too much power now that I had stood by him at the risk of being deemed sentimental. He had after all been with me my entire life, having been a gift from my English grandmother when I was born. I had then traveled with him strapped into my airplane seat when we flew to Thailand. And so perhaps it was not completely a design coincidence that I should build a nest for myself high above the fray where Rupert would be safe from comment though he was still in view for the few who looked up. This perch gave me a new outlook on my college experience.

A woman I had stalked for weeks and still could not discern if she might be remotely interested in kissing women lived on the second floor of A dorm. I often walked by her room on the off chance I could flirt with her. On this night of my rounds I heard a man's voice I recognized coming from the bathroom and realized he was showering with someone.

It was Paul, our golden boy on campus. As an art student his acrylic abstract paintings were so avant gardé none of us could find anything snide to say about them except that they were priced by the yard. He had been my roommate's boyfriend earlier that year, but they had ended it, by the time he got around to me. I slept with him just because he asked and he was friendly and casual about it. "I know you don't love me," he said, "but it'll be fun."

In this post free love hippie era of sexuality and pre AIDS, sex was a playground of zipless fucks. A way to get to know people and experiment for the fun of it.

I followed the sound of Paul's voice until I was in the foyer of a shower cubicle and saw he was with with "S" the object of my flirtations. When they greeted me with pleasant surprise I stepped into the shower itself fully clothed letting the water rain down on me, which made them laugh.

Paul asked S if they should invite me to partake with them. She didn't object, so he suggested I take my wet clothes off and soon we were in her room. By all appearances this was a one night stand and S was keeping a cool emotional distance. So I did too, keeping Paul between us. Then I slipped onto his smooth thin back as he was penetrating her which titillated me more as a concept than as an actual intimacy—that I was fucking her by proxy as it were.

Women's sexuality was to be celebrated I felt, but it did not escape me that women also bore the greater risk in this game. I realized at one point that every woman I knew had had an abortion, at one time except me. We all knew our options, but things happen, risks are taken. When I would hear about one woman or another going for an abortion we wouldn't discuss why; we didn't want to know why because there was no escaping being pregnant once it happened so no point in discussing it. We'd all been there. Because of this fact of our bodies I felt a solidarity with all women. It was the one thing that held us together as a sex and the one thing that separated us from men who did not share this burden on such a visceral level.

I saw a woman come home after an abortion one afternoon. I could see it wasn't a procedure undertaken lightly. There was something so fragile about the whole ordeal. I had feared being pregnant just once, but just those two week's waiting until I got my period was enough to instill in me the feelings of being trapped by the biological fact of my sex and I got on the pill as soon as I arrived on campus as a Freshman. The influx of hormones giving me morning sickness for a few days. I stayed with it even when it became clear that I was mainly interested in women.

I had an ongoing list of women I was interested in traveling further afield to other colleges across campus. Spring quarter came, and with it new blood to peruse. A new girl appeared, simultaneously unsophisticated in a small town sense yet quite worldly for having been raised on a commune known as OZ. She was a breath of fresh air to our sordid sensibilities. Her hippie parents had named her Panda, the cuddliest creature they could think of. Panda bore her name with pride and a boldness that kept the harshness of any teasing at bay. Her outsider status in the hippie subculture somehow aligned with my outsider status as a foreigner. We became fast friends. "Pandamanda" people called out when we showed up.

Panda's sexuality was broader and more sophisticated than most of us had experienced owing to her commune experience being considerably less uptight and conventional than our suburban families. Nudity was the rule and sexuality more freely expressed and talked about among the adults. Eventually the commune disbanded because the children roamed the land in a gang and the parents felt they were losing touch with their own children. When one of the kids asked who Jesus was his parents woke up to the gaps in their home school education and decided to move away. By the time Panda left home only a few of the commune members were left.

"Come visit my home. My parents would love you," Panda invited me one weekend. She said this with an intonation I couldn't quite read. "How would I be of interest to hippies?", I wondered. In the experimental way of the times Panda and I were lovers briefly. Enough to give her bragging rights to her friends back home.

I had plans to go hang-gliding with my father, but he told me not to come because he had loaned the station wagon to my mother, who was moving out of the house. There were also two movies I wanted to see and a dance being hosted by Gayla our campus gay club. But Panda was so insistent that this would be a fun getaway that I agreed to go.

She drove us the incredibly long distance to Point Arena in Mendocino. Pointless Arena, she and her pals called it, the Western most point on the West Coast. Otherwise a tiny town populated by hippies and rural locals. We picked up her brother's girlfriend on the way and made a party of it.

It was quite dark when we arrived that evening so Panda drove us straight to the family homestead. Getting out of the car I was vaguely aware of the sounds of a river. Her father and her two younger siblings were there to greet us having just crossed the river by canoe. Her father handed me a paddle and invited me to step into the bow of their canoe waiting to see how I would do. I was only slightly surprised that one was required to cross by boat to get to their home. I was after all from Bangkok where so many could be seen living on the water in houses on stilts. I addressed the paddle with workmanlike attitude and was glad I had earned my Red Cross canoeing license during my stint in the Cadette Girl Scouts in high school. Soon we made it to the landing on the other side. Before us lay the double domes shingled in redwood; classic hippie constructions of Buckminster Fuller's famous design.

Her parents, with their chosen hippie names, Redwood and Savitri welcomed me warmly. It was Savitri's family money that had bought the land. Redwood had been a college professor when they met.

Panda and I bedded down in her childhood bed curtained off in a corner of the larger dome. Her brother and sister having their own niches one in the loft, while the kitchen and dining room table took up most of the rest of this dome.

The next morning I took in the expansive view of the surrounding meadows and walked around the domes in awe taking in the details of the craftsmanship, the handmade door, the plank floors, the rough paneled walls of real wood. The kitchen was a massive clutter of jars on varnished wood counters and open shelving that hid nothing. A large wood stove in the center heated the domes. I noted too, the anachronistic element of a child's cartoon baseball poster against the rough hewn wood walls and the simple cotton curtains screening off the beds offering but a thin wall of privacy.

Panda's parent's dome connected to the kitchen dome with a short covered section that was the front entrance of the house. The front door had repurposed glass from a store set into its center. It still had the remains of lettering indicating open hours. I loved this timeless touch— signifying the reuse of materials. Her parent's dome was the charming part of the house with its old roll top desk, wood and leather captain chairs and big bed with custom built headboard containing space for books. It was in this headboard that Redwood directed my attention to a tiny lamp which he proudly told me was powered by their newly installed micro windmill. He pointed out the window and I could indeed see the windmill spinning away, all to power a single source of electric light. I was impressed by this, by how you could do things one piece at a time. They used oil lamps everywhere else.

Panda's family liked to play Bridge and Mastermind and several games were going on as we talked. My attention was directed to the quality of sound within the dome, how it amplified voices so easily. I heard a little about how the windows had once been glass but had to be replaced with plexiglass, plus there was the problem of leakage. A problem inherent in domes that Buckminster Fuller hadn't anticipated, as he had envisioned them as factory made, not put together by DIY crews of largely inexperienced young people. One large triangular shaped pane had a crack in it that was duct taped. I loved too, the outdoor shower which to me was deliciously daring. Oddly enough I have no recollection of the toilet so it was probably a regular flush toilet.

Panda told her parents that weekend that she was bisexual and I was proof. They seem to take it in stride for I hardly noticed a reaction. This further elevated their coolness in my mind. Her parents liked me and didn't mind my wandering around taking pictures of their home. Savitri spoke to me like a peer as we shared that we both kept journals. I was pleased to have an adult see the value of this practice. The cynicism of my College V persona evaporated and gave way to an awe and appreciation for what a community could do when people were open to experimentation.

Across the meadow there was a community house which was not a dome, but a more traditional rectangular building with high ceilings. In it there was a large kitchen. This was the domain of Lani Ka'ahumanu a woman who had been the cook for the commune who would later become the spokesperson of the emerging bisexual community in San Francisco. (It was at Oz that she would fall in love with a man while still identified as a lesbian.) Off the kitchen was the only bathroom with a tub which was in full view of a large window. Nudity was part of the culture of OZ. Lots of cute photographs attested to this.

Next to the communal house was a very steep hill. If any disputes came up a meeting would be called to discuss the issue, but participants were required to meet at the top of this hill. That way all the energy that propelled people's anger would be used up by the time they reached the summit. Panda expressed her amusement at this physically mitigating solution to a human conflict.

She told me stories of her childhood growing up on this intentional commune full of other hippie parents whose eight children ran together in one big pack. After being home schooled for their first few years the older kids went to the local public school where they were well ahead of their age group which was why Panda was only 17 when she showed up at College V at UC Santa Cruz. They also took over the school government as they were the ones with initiative and leadership skills. Indeed Panda conducted her life as one big opportunity for leadership. I envied her ability to learn; she was somehow able to pick out what was fun and easy in subjects I found arduous. Languages came easily to her and she read Dickens as one would a graphic novel.

In the winter they moved to an old bakery because canoeing across the river in school clothes when it was cold made getting to school a family ordeal. We stopped in at the bakery building too and Panda showed me the office and the deprivation tank that was installed in one of the rooms. It was used by the adults to experience another kind of high, so interested were they in all manner of human potential experiences. I looked under the cover. It was dark inside and filled with warm water to create the sensation of floating. I imagined lying there for eight hours. It opened my mind to a lifetime of interest in what the human mind could do. She told me how once there was an air leak that released a bubble at regular intervals and the man who happened to be in the tank at that time experienced an orgasm just in anticipation of that next bubble brushing past his feet. Such stores of concentration and anticipation turning into sexual expression was the stuff of hippie legends.

In the end the commune didn't last. It took a lot of energy to manage. Boundaries were very loose and had to be reckoned with again and again. People moved away and Panda's family envisioned a new project. They opened a summer camp for kids and marketed it to the adults following the human potential movement at places like the Esalen Institute. People there were delighted to have a place to send their kids. I tucked this example of American entrepreneurship into my mind. How one could launch into something that played to what talents and assets you had and make money off it. This was something I had only seen in Thailand. Panda spent her summers helping supervise and direct activities at Camp OZ and showed me the printed materials with their playful illustrations. She and her siblings made movies of the play the kids did as if it were the easiest thing to shoot footage, get it developed and edit it with a hand splicer. "It really felt like I was making a movie when I was editing it," she said.

All this history gave me a sense of the challenges of trying to create a working community in an isolated rural area where the local farm families and their conventional culture were in stark contrast to the interests of the expansive minds of the human potential movement. Panda's family embodied these values as had those they had invited to visit and share their lives with them.

We spent the three day weekend exploring the different shelters people had built, rough hewn cabins and smaller domes. I met two young boys, brothers, one named Carrot and the other named Radish. Names they had chosen themselves. I wondered what would become of their sense of identity later on. I saw the gardens and the big outdoor hot tub we would soak in that was heated up with a wood stove. Panda claimed her upper body strength came from chopping all the wood required to heat the tub. Her broad shoulders were proof of this.

Nearby there was a big barn full of books, games, and puzzles. I chose a puzzle and spent a day putting it together, enjoying the long emptiness of the day. The next day I felt a need for more stimulation. Browsing the library in the barn I took down a Danielle Steel novel and devoured it. After three days of amusing ourselves and breathing the country air and feasting my eyes on rolling meadows my head felt so pure and empty that I had become quite hungry for entertainment even of the most commercial kind. I clearly wouldn't last in such a rural setting as fascinating and lovely as it was here. I had grown up in cities less than an hours drive from an international airport. This fact made me feel connected to my home in Thailand. Living a days drive away from such an airport made me uneasy.

I was too shy to ask questions so it wasn't until years later when OZ was sold and I visited Panda's parents in their San Francisco Victorian home that I asked Savitri how the commune came to be. She said once they bought the land it was so beautiful they wanted all their friends to see it so it started with a campout. And things evolved from there in the way that things do in California. Savitri was game to try all the prevailing human potential trends and Redwood just as happy to manifest it and organize the structure of those early commune days.

Panda and I were inseparable friends for the rest of the quarter. I left UC Santa Cruz at the end of that year. After my parents' divorce my father told me that I would have to find a way to make a living without a college degree because he wouldn't be able to pay my school fees now that he owed my mother half of his pension which he did not yet have. In truth I was not sorry to have an excuse to leave College V and to sever my obligations to my parents. I did not like the conventional path that a college education represented. In my mind it seemed to diminish possibilities rather than expand them squeezing you into ever narrower channels of knowledge. And then at the end of it you had to work at what would likely be an equally narrow job.

"Work is not supposed to be fun," my father said.

"Well you like your work," I pointed out. He did in fact seem to think it was fun to solve engineering problems that no one else could. While my mother also found satisfaction in training autistic children after she got her family therapists license. Parents called her the Miracle Worker because she gave them programs that kept their child's behavior in control. At least enough so that they didn't have to be sent away to a home. But I had no passions that seemed to lead to a possible career.

Chapter 15

A Tiger Will Eat You

Upon returning home from college, my father seeing me at loose ends, suggested I spend the summer in Thailand at the family compound. Khun Ya had offered to pay my fare so I wouldn't have to work a summer job. I recognized the generosity of the offer and once in Bangkok under her ever watchful eye, I gave in to her dictating my every move. She got me invitations to social events with my Bangkok peers; college kids who were also attending school in the states. My summer unfolded in the company of this band. We traveled in two vans provided by a friend of Khun Ya's, the mother of three boys in the group. She owned a five star hotel and knew where all the popular tourist attractions were. We went parasailing at the beach and took a boat to an outlying island. Another weekend we went to the mountains where I could show off my swimming skills against a current in a river only the guys were attempting. This got me the admiration of an older girl I had admired all summer; the heir to a well known whiskey brewery in Thailand.

"What do you want to do in life?" she asked me in Thai.

"I want to act in films," I said.

"I could introduce you to someone who makes movies," she said. That was how things were done in Thailand, but somehow it didn't sound compelling. Acting in films was not something I sensed my relatives would approve of anyway. And asking the favor of a friend to take me in did not appeal to me. I had already been rebuffed at *The Nation* one of Bangkok's two English language newspapers. Ah Pahdt had a friend there who was an editor and had told her I wanted to work as a journalist. But I could see that I was being treated as a problem—a young person in need of favors. There were no "summer" jobs in Thailand I was told. I looked skeptical about this offer to meet someone in Thai films and said nothing.

One night after dinner, with the family assembled in the living room of my grandmother's house, their faces powdered white having had their evening baths and wearing their pajamas, I told them that I wanted to join the circus. Like a Greek chorus they all spoke at once horrified voicing their disapproval. It was clear to them that selling cotton candy at the circus was something only a street urchin would do.

Suddenly like many things in Thailand my aspiration had become a class issue.

"If you want to have adventures you should join the Rotary Club," said my grandfather who was a member. I couldn't think what kind of adventures a club of old men could offer.

"Besides a tiger will eat you," said Ah Pahdt teasing me. It was hopeless. It was not in the Thai culture to understand my search for adventure, for a unique experience of the self discovery that seemed to fill all the books I read—English and American books. I felt even less understood by my family, but I knew it wasn't personal. Everything in their lives was planned and had a program. Programs designed to keep them and me from entering into anything unknown. They were longing to offer me every connection they had that might interest me, but these family connections were to me uninspiring limitations that fell short of what I was seeking.

There still remained one thing I could do that would pass my relatives approval. I decided to have clothes tailored. My cousins Neung and Nor took me to their dressmaker. I chose some plain broadcloths of a solid maroon and another in a dark teal. Shades similar to my father's many shirts. Neung explained to the dressmaker that I could draw my own designs, so I drew two shirts. One had an asymmetrical closure going down the front on a diagonal with pointed shoulder epaulets inspired by the costume of Thai dancers. Once made, it was more reminiscent of a uniform for Star Trek, but I was quite happy with it and when I got home I finished it with pearl button snaps meant for cowboy shirts. The other shirt I drew was a Han Solo shirt. I had just seen Star Wars with my father at the local cineplex back at home. He had heard the buzz about it from his engineering colleagues and had taken me as soon as I returned from school. I was not overly impressed by the comic book plot and the two leads. Luke was too earnest and Princess Leia sassy, but give me a break with the dress already. But I recognized in Han Solo the cynicism and devil may care attitude of an outsider that felt familiar and through him the series grew on me. My shirt though was disappointing. It did not work in maroon; the maroon made it look like hospital scrubs. But my relatives were happy that I was upgrading my wardrobe.

My grandmother, having seen me looking hungrily at all the boots in the window at Tony's Bootery, gave me money to have a pair of boots made. Standing in his show room filled with the heavy scent of leather I admired the many variations of cowboy boots. The cowboy was another icon of the outsider that attracted me. A loner with a job to do. I didn't have enough money to have a pair of cowboy boots made, but seeing my appreciation Tony assured me he could get me a very nice very red leather to make me a pair of boots for the price I could afford. He duly noted that I wanted the fancy cut at the vamp similar to his cowboy boots. I ordered a stacked three inch heel which was the highest I could tolerate and a tall boot, taller than the cowboy boots. When they were ready for pick-up Khun Ya went with me to get them. I tried them on in the show room. They were splendid, fitting me like a glove all the way up my calf; boots suitable for a superhero.

"Are you sure they're wearing red boots in California?" she asked dubiously when she saw how red they were.

"Oh yes," I said, quite sure that I would be the only person wearing such splendid red boots.

My father wrote to me near the end of my trip suggesting I stay in Bangkok and find a job since I did not have any clear plans, but the thought of being so closely watched by my grandmother made me feel claustrophobic. His suggestion galvanized my sense of preservation and I wrote him a curt letter back that I did have plans. I was going to join the circus. It was my only original thought and I continued to cling to it like a "get out of jail free" card.

When I returned from Thailand my father asked me when I was going to leave for the circus. I figured I could go that Friday. The circus train had already come through San Francisco by then so I had to catch up with it in Fresno. My friend Tim offered to drive me. He had had his own running away dream in his desire to get out of his home town of Rochester, New York. He had tested out of high school early and left home in his van to become a ski instructor so he could train as a downhill racer. In the end no one would hire him with his long hair and his fast skiing scared the ski patrol. So he washed dishes the whole winter and slept in a basement full of ski bums, their sleeping quarters partitioned out with hanging sheets. This I could see was an adventure; one that did not unfold as planned, but it had still allowed Tim to achieve his goal of skiing, just not in quite the style he had aspired to. After that he figured it would be easier to go to college.

He had lived in B Dorm in a single room at the end of my hall with a loft bed he built over his drum set. I had ended up in this loft bed with him twice. He had courted me with a bottle of wine one night and I had given him the one night stand benefit. We all understood the meaning of a one night stand—the zipless fuck of it. But two had to mean something more he concluded. I just enjoyed talking to him. He would keep me up for hours analyzing our every experience, putting questions to me that I continued to answer as his questions helped me to define myself and my curiously unWestern Thai perspective. I thought our talks might evoke more feelings in me, but they hadn't. Tim struggled with his feelings for me and decided to be my best friend. He still had his van. We had gone skiing in it once, sleeping inside in the parking lot of the ski resort at Squaw Valley. And now he would help me to achieve my dream.

Before I left I saw my mother over dinner in her studio apartment. A fun little adobe house near Stanford that a friend had offered so she would have somewhere to go after leaving my father.

"Whatever you do don't run away to the circus," she said as we parted. I said nothing.

"Would you really go," she asked.

"I would if I could," I said. My parents were being cautious with me around this. I was eighteen. There was nothing they could do to stop me doing anything I set my mind to, and I had been talking about the circus ever since my earlier visit that first summer after college, long enough that they could see it wasn't a passing fancy. I had the support of my friends too.

I was looking forward to Tim sharing this adventure of me applying for a job at the circus. He liked to talk to people and had reams of questions that could reveal everything there was to know about a place as long as the person had the patience. As we drove south and over the highway known as Pacheco Pass the van lost power and would go no more. We had to pull over to the side of the road and decide what to do next. We ended up spending the night under Tim's drop cloth (from summer jobs as a house painter) listening to semis barrel past on the two lane highway. The highway patrol checked us out in the middle of the night and said he'd call a tow truck. In the morning we were just finishing our breakfast when a tow truck came by to haul us to the nearest truck stop. I sat there while Tim contemplated what he would have to take apart to fix his van.

I decided to leave him to it and catch a ride with a trucker pulling out of the rest stop. The trucker said he wasn't supposed to stop for passengers, but seeing as he was technically not pulling over for me he let me on board. It took some effort on my part to climb up the high chrome steps, but soon we were underway. He told me about a girl he picked up once who crossed the country with him and even slept in the bunk with him, but there was no question about her wanting to mess around. She wouldn't have none of that. Besides he was married and had two kids. I looked behind and saw that there was a bunk in this cab.

He pulled into Los Banos which was as far as he was going, and I got a ride with another trucker. This one was half Irish, half Native American. When I told him I was going to Fresno to apply for a job with the circus, he was delighted. He thought it was a great idea because there sure was nothing happening in Fresno in his trucker's view on his town. He dropped me off at the convention center where the circus was booked and I soon found the concessions stand. The first person I asked told me to look for Bob Johnson and pointed me in the right direction. When I found him I stood by him and tentatively said "Hello," waiting for him to look up. He had on a white shirt and tie and was focused on his clipboard. He seemed accustomed to these walk-up applicants and didn't look up.

"I'm looking for a job with concessions," I said.

"We've got no beds," he said looking over his glasses at me. "Try Charlie at the snow cones stand. I think he's hiring." Feeling crushed already I walked around to find Charlie who told me he could hire me for the day, but there was still no beds. No bunks left on the train so I would have to follow the circus in a car and I wouldn't earn enough to pay the gas plus food. I could see his point. I also learned that the girls who worked with the circus have small private compartments while all the guys lived in open compartments sleeping in bunks. That's why it was harder to accommodate girls. I asked if my chances would be better at the beginning of the season. "Ten times better," he said.

"It's hard work," he warned me. At the concessions stands you only got $7.50 a show for standing there and you really had to hustle to make $50 to $300 a week in commissions. I took this in and mentioned that I had never actually seen the circus perform and he let me in through a back curtain for the second half of the show. There were dozens of concessions vendors all hustling energetically. They were very young I noted and very clean cut in an all American way and all were white. The show itself didn't impress me as it was very much a conservative family variety show and over the top in glitter. It was getting late, and I knew I should not stay for the next show.

As I left, a fellow who had pointed me in the direction of the concessions stand asked if I had found what I wanted. I said yes and asked him about the winter quarters in Florida where the circus lived. He gave me the address and told me to write to Bob Johnson and then call him and ask him for a bunk before I took the trouble to go all the way to Florida. I thanked him for his good advice and headed back to the highway to find another semi going my way.

I ran four blocks to catch up with one waiting at a crossing for a freight train to pass. I jumped on the step to his cab and looked inside. I could see by the quilted red paneling and girlie decorations that he was the hot rodder of truckers, but he was only going to Sacramento so I hopped off. I tried another and he was only going a short way too. I could have taken the ride and found another ride beyond that, but I was losing my confidence with the setting sun. The truckers might not be such gentleman at night if they didn't have wives to go home to.

Snapping back into a more mundane reality, I walked to the greyhound bus station to catch the bus headed for San Jose and sat next to a young man about my age who looked like he wouldn't mind company. He was excited to be on his way to UCSC to live at Kresge College right next door to College V. I considered the irony of this meeting sending me back into the college milieu of my class destiny. He was full of talk about natural foods. I could see he would fit right into the Santa Cruz scene. We chatted the whole way. He had a friend waiting to pick him up in San Jose. An East Indian man with a gentle accent who gave me a ride all the way home to Menlo Park while he talked catching up with his young friend. When I asked if he wanted gas money he said I could go inside and ask my rich daddy for $40, but when he saw the look on my face he said he was kidding. Were we actually rich I wondered? But it was clear he didn't care about gas money. I was awed by this generosity as well as relieved. The little bit of serendipity with these two strangers was enough to feed my passion for chance meetings and restore my confidence in matters of adventure.

I also had that number with which to call Bob Johnson. I did write him and then called every week obsessively, but every time I called he gave the same answer. There were no job openings with the circus. At least not for me, perhaps by some predetermination on his part that I wasn't a good fit. I hadn't exactly felt like a good fit with the straight looking group of young people I had seen in Fresno.

Or maybe my better judgement was kicking in. I'd seen enough to realize that the traveling I would be doing would be in the industrial backyards of all the big cities where the circus performed. There were no picturesque gypsy caravans as in my childhood books, but somehow there had been something of what I was looking for I thought—an international collection of free spirits. But like the kids in Fresno the people I would meet would likely be working class, much like those I had gotten to know at the gas station. There, an older man who had driven a truck for a living, had commended me for going to college and clearly felt this was the only way to a life of greater opportunities. I could feel his regrets for himself.

There was something more that both attracted me and made me cautious. Something edgier and more dangerous in the way the circus was always leaving town. A criminal element hinted at in circus history that went beyond stealing clothes from a washing line. Still I hung onto my obsession and worked it into all my thoughts about my future, making decisions not to accept other opportunities because what if I was offered a job at the circus? I still wanted to be free to go.

I had been so attached to the idea of joining the circus that I didn't allow myself to take in the reality of it and have a dialog about whether it would suit me. It had felt like a calling as obsessions often do. It had become a rip cord for bailing out of a life that disagreed with me, a symbol of something else—an illusion of control over one's destiny. Women ran away from their lives all the time, but usually by marrying the first man who was passing through; an option I would not entertain.

Many years later I would have a friend a bit older than me who had managed to run away to the circus for real. He lasted two weeks, he said. He left because it felt dangerous to him. The men he encountered working for the circus tended to be low on impulse control and when drunk would pull out firearms and threaten to shoot someone—anyone who crossed them. I shuddered thinking if he, a man, felt it was dangerous, just think of what it would have been like for me.

Part II. THE GIRL GUIDED

Chapter 16

For You It's Just A Game

I poured over the classified ads, briefly entertaining the idea of being an "exotic dancer" before I found a job busing tables, pleased that it was at the British Bankers Club. This was a tony new restaurant in an impressive historic corner building in Menlo Park with a bank like facade of white columns two stories high. It actually had been a bank, then administrative offices and a police station. Now it had an old lighted sign that said London Central Bank with a clock in it that actually kept time. Locals called it the BBC for short.

The women who waited tables there, wore the same dark pants, white shirt and striped tie as the men, but we were only allowed to work during the day. Women having only just been hired to work at the BBC which was possibly why there was an enamel vintage sign over the door to the kitchen that said "men only." It was meant as a decoration along with all the other enamel signs to evoke historical gravitas and the air of a men's club. The owners were antique collectors before they opened the restaurant. They had a tiny store in the same building where they sold antique pocket watches before the restaurant was created. Every time I read the "men only" sign I walked through those doors with impunity.

As a busboy I didn't wear the tie, just the white shirt and white apron. All the other floor staff were white and patrons took me for an immigrant bootstrapping my way into the American dream. Once an elderly woman with her women's group looked up at me, pronounced me adorable, and then asked me very sweetly if I spoke English.

"Yes I do," I said turning up the crisp pronunciation of my British accent a notch; she turned away as though struck. I felt bad and at the same time triumphant. Another day a man intercepted me as I speed walked across the dining room and thrust a $20 bill into my hand.

"I so admire what you are doing," he said. I thanked him looking puzzled. What was it I was doing I wondered to myself. One of the waitresses whose husband also worked as a waiter explained to me why I was not quite one of them, even though I worked hard and did what I was asked.

"For you it's just a game. You'll go back to school" she said, "for us it's a real job," This puzzled me even more. Why couldn't they go to school too? A state school or junior college was still affordable then.

The brown people worked in the kitchen for a white chef—a foreigner. One day the Mexican sous chef made me a nice meal to eat before my shift and served it to me in the upstairs dining room before we opened.

"He probably wants to ask you out," the waitress said to me. I frowned annoyed; being kitchen staff I felt he was beneath me, but I ate the food anyway.

"You can't fault him for asking," she said. No I couldn't. I wasn't really out to the staff, but I didn't want to be a target for men either. I contemplated what I should say. Finally it came to me so when he did ask as he stopped me in front of the row of freezers I told him "Only if you wear high heels and a dress." He rolled his eyes exasperated and went to complain to the Mexican dishwasher.

After I had some experience under my belt working upstairs in the mezzanine, I was sent downstairs to work with a waiter I didn't particularly like. He had an exacting style that demanded an attentive busboy; one who would know to take the order slip from him while he was still at the customer's table and deliver it to the kitchen to show how efficient we were. He had made me cry once with a reprimand, though I was loath to let him see my tears. How was I supposed to know what he wanted? I did not know how to respond to his reprimand. Tears of frustration sprung to my eyes and I quickly turned away. At the end of that shift he had the nerve to imply that I had used tears to manipulate him. Just like a woman. I stared at him. Now I was angry. I had no words. I felt my fists ball up and a line from a Patti Smith song sprung to my lips. I sung it to him as an anthem of my resilience.

"We shall live again," I sang it low and threatening. I didn't even know what the song itself meant, but the overall tone of it was right. I just had that line to stake out my existence in plural as though I were a people. Then I walked to the kitchen wondering what I even meant by it. He didn't give me any trouble after that.

I was working the lunch shift with him on the infamous day that Dan White shot Harvey Milk and Mayor Moscone at City Hall in San Francisco on November 27, 1978. He was the one who told me the news and I stood there for a moment taking it in and thinking about it as I cleared away dishes. I knew that Harvey Milk was the first openly gay supervisor and that this would mean something to the gay community. How much it would mean was revealed later on the TV that night as my father and I watched the news. I saw that there was a candle night vigil going on and I wanted to jump in the station wagon and drive up to the city to join it, but I couldn't get past having to ask my father if I could use the car.

I did not know much about Harvey Milk, but I did make note of his message that if he were assassinated we should not mourn with a huge funeral, but come out in his name. Not that his murder made one want to. I followed the trial that would acquit Dan White with the lame Twinkie defense. His light sentence of manslaughter six months after his death enraged the gay community. That was the night my father and I watched the riots on the TV news and saw police cars being torched, three of them at least. I watched riveted.

"That's the end of the gays," my father said, "they will be run out of town." He did know I was gay. He had figured it out for himself from things my mother told him about how I was obsessed with one girl at school or another and only talked about girls. Never boys. He told her that maybe I just liked girls. She saw it immediately once he'd said it and blamed him for not treating me like a girl. What would that have looked like I wondered?

I think what my mother meant was that he didn't treat me like his little princess. He spoke to me as an extension of his own thoughts saying whatever he happened to be thinking about that he wanted to tell me. This seldom included what might be going on in my life. It was I who more read his mind so we could actually have a conversation. I didn't take it personally when he said it was the end of the gays. I knew he didn't mean me. I stayed silent. I did not think it would be the end. It felt more like a beginning. Much like the riots that had boosted the Black civil rights movement, the gay community was tighter than ever and galvanized now.

No one talked about it at work once the news had broken, not even to speculate why the double murder happened. They didn't relate to what was going on in San Francisco. We were just the quiet upscale suburbs. I was used to living in a world apart from others, mostly due to being a foreigner, but now I was gay too. I felt further distanced, caught between the class hierarchy of the restaurant and the maleness of it.

A boy I knew from the private elementary school I went to came in and applied for a job. He was a little younger than me. He recognized me and we spent a few minutes reminiscing and talking about what became of our school mates. He got a job busing tables too, but not for very long. He was soon working the bar and then was promoted to manager which gave him the right to send me on errands for the bar. I watched his ascent angry that he was so quickly promoted. I was vaguely conscious that he was working a system that favored him as a white male.

"You're my only real friend here," he confided to me once in a conspiratorial tone. What ever did he mean? I didn't trust him now he was elevated over me. We had been friends, but now he was focused on being pals with the owners offering them discount car repair at his father's auto store. I did not fraternize with the owners. They made me wary the way they treated people and talked about them. I recognized the same competitive meanness of putting people down as I had seen with the men at College V. At least now I knew to avoid engaging with such meanness.

I really wanted to reconnect with one of the many community theaters I had worked with, but I didn't audition for any plays thinking that I'd be gone to the circus by the time the show opened. So I spent my free evenings going to the movies. It was there that an enticing opportunity opened up to me.

The Biograph was a little hole-in-the-wall movie theatre in Palo Alto that showed second run movies for a discount price. I was there often enough that I started talking to the theater manager about the films. Jack was an aspiring screen writer and movie buff, personable and handsome enough in a sea captain sort of way. He had also been a pilot with the navy which sparked my interest. He asked me to a matinee of *Comes A Horseman* with Jane Fonda. I didn't see the harm in accepting and I loved the movie; loved seeing such a tough independent woman cowboy. But he must have got to wondering why he couldn't charm me any further and he hit on an answer, but first he tried to get me to offer the information.

'If there's anything about yourself that you would want to tell people, just say it, right now," he said. But I couldn't. I was paralyzed. It was the perfect opening, but I couldn't say straight out that I was gay. And I didn't really know why.

"It came to me while I was sweeping out the theater that you might be gay," he said. Finally I could cop to it and confirm his guess. But we still acted like we were dating and even made out a couple of times at his apartment. It was the price of being friends with a man I thought. He also gave me a job as a projectionist. That was the real prize. He wanted to go away for the holidays and needed someone who could run the theater while he was gone. Someone responsible, but also mechanically inclined who could handle fire. So he showed me how to operate the projectors and handle the running of the theatre.

The twin projectors at the Biograph were already vintage, using the old technology of carbon arc lamps to generate a light bright enough to project the movie onto the big screen. This meant setting up two metal rods in moveable clamps on a track inside the projector. The clamps were moved with wheeled handles outside of the closed compartment. To ignite the carbons the projectionist would turn on the power, then twist the handle so that one stick of carbon would touch the other and then back out again. The voltage would leap across the rods and ignite into a flame so bright it would blind you. You could also roast hot dogs on it, so I was told as part of old timer lore.

Meanwhile the film was already moving through the head of the projector and around the sound drum. So part of the job was to thread the projector beforehand which had to be done with just the right size loops or the sound would be out of sync. And too much tension at any point and the film would break which meant getting out the cast iron splicer and piecing it together again with specially designed tape with matching sprocket holes. Worse if the film got stuck in a sprocket somehow, the heat of the lamp would burn a hole in the film and create that spectacular effect of melting into a bigger and bigger hole until it disappeared leaving a white screen. A white screen was the most public display of projectionist negligence. I was eager to learn. It looked easy, being all there for my eye to see yet just challenging enough to be worth doing.

The true test of the projectionist was not to be lulled into a false sense of security once the film started, and you were hanging out in the lobby eating popcorn and reading a book. Because every five or ten minutes the carbon rods were getting further apart as they burned down, so they had to be adjusted or the picture wouldn't be bright enough. Then at exactly a certain point an hour or so into the film you had to be waiting in the booth as the power switched to the second projector because by that time the carbons were all burned down. And most movies had another hour to go. So the second projector would start automatically cued by magnetic tape and you had to be there to strike the carbons in that second projector to fire up the lamp. This task was so exciting it made me feel very accomplished to execute such a changeover. But that wasn't all.

The Biograph was so small that the projectionist was also required to sell tickets and concessions as well. It was a one man show except on weekends when an assistant came in to help with the concessions. I was thrilled to be the manager. It was just the right amount of responsibility and tension to keep me on point. And there was a certain unpredictability about it that made every night an adventure. People came in off the street wanting to talk. One was so drunk he walked right into the theater; I ran in after him to retrieve him. Sometimes a film might break requiring an emergency splice. Once in a while a customer wanted their money back because they didn't like a film or someone steals a candy bar while you're in the booth. But my favorite thing was having customers ask me what the film was about before they bought a ticket. Summing up the movie in a few short sentences gave me the authority of an ad hoc movie critic.

It was, if I paused to think about it, a three ring circus of a job. Plus I loved movies. I loved movies more than I had the idea of traveling with a circus. I could simply travel through movies, sell concessions to customers and have the thrill of a live audience. Working at night felt slightly subversive as if I had escaped the 9 to 5 paradigm. As if I had run away from it. And I didn't even need to leave town. I stopped calling the circus for job openings.

I covered for Jack the week he was gone and then worked the two nights he was off. And when Jack recommended me to the manager at the Palo Alto Square Theater I got a few shifts at their concessions counter. During my stint at this theater they opened *The China Syndrome* with Jane Fonda as a reporter for a meltdown at a nuclear plant. Two weeks later Three Mile Island had a partial meltdown at their plant and we were swamped selling out every show. How uncanny we all thought. Plus I was already a fan of Jane Fonda.

I now had enough work to quit my shifts at the BBC. The restaurant owners did not seem at all dismayed to see me go when I gave my two weeks notice. I noted in my journal that it was often that way with me and jobs. The boss would be thrilled that I was interested in such a lowly service job and pleased that I could do it so competently, but then after a while I would make them uncomfortable and they weren't sorry to see me go. This was as true of this job at the BBC as it had been at the gas station job before it. Perhaps the waitress had been right. For me it was just a game and people sensed that.

I made my final entrance to the BBC on New Year's Eve. I showed up at the restaurant shortly before midnight wearing my vintage three piece man's suit from the 1940s. What an amazing find that suit was. I found it at the thrift store during my College V days. It was eery that it fit me even to the pant length which were cuffed and had buttons on the waist for button on suspenders. The vest had a watch pocket. You could still buy a Westclox cheaply at the five and dime so I got one to wear with the suit.

When I walked in the front door of the BBC that night the tall blond waitress ran up to me and kissed me, then took me over to join a table of her friends and to my surprise sat in my lap. I soon realized she wasn't flirting with me, she was just showing me off. That night all sorts of people wanted to kiss me, men, women even the lady chef. I was happy with my appearance. Then I slipped out the back door of the kitchen before anyone could ask for more.

Chapter 17

Movie Nights & Motorcycles

The job of running a movie theater completely absorbed me. And now that my days were free I started thinking about going back to school for the fun of it. I liked being around students and enjoyed riding my bike onto the Stanford campus when school was in session. I was infected by the excitement in the air when the fall term began and every time I went into the bookstore the book titles would excite me enough to think of actually reading them though that would be taking things too far. But I knew I wasn't like the old guy at the gas station who had been defeated by school and went to work as a long haul truck driver. I was able to complete classwork and genuinely liked learning. I just didn't want to be crushed by it.

It was easy enough to enroll at Foothill junior college, pay my own way and just take the classes I wanted to take—in jazz dance, French and piano. But nothing that would require writing. That would be asking too much. Too much of my soul. So I just maintained this quasi adult making-a-living thing without thinking about it too much.

When I turned twenty-one the importance of this milestone birthday brought this illusion crashing down on me. There was no denying it. I had no real plan of what I was going to do with my life. I was happy day to day going to my classes. My "finishing school" classes I called them. I could just about breathe into myself if I didn't attempt to take the long view of what would become of me. Others in my peer group from high school and UC Santa Cruz were completing their degrees. The smart ones as   lawyers and therapists. The creative ones, the writers, were finishing degrees that would lead to editing jobs or to teaching school.

I had invited my UC Santa Cruz friends to my birthday party which I promised would be worthy of the ones given at College V. And I had invited my mother to come too, forcing my divorced parents to make an appearance together for me. It made a nice photograph. I stood between them wearing my custom made red boots peeking out under my Sasson jeans and a tight fitting black t-shirt with some kind of glitter logo on it.

I hosted a fine party for my friends that weekend, but on Monday I rolled out of bed depressed and lay about the house all day. By afternoon I felt the need to confess my failure. I got on my bicycle and rode to the place where I was sure to find someone I knew. The Menlo Park library where I had held an after school job as a library page. I locked my bike up and went into the library. I spotted a familiar face at the children's desk—a cheerful elderly woman who had long been the children's librarian. She smiled at me. I walked over and flung myself into the chair next to her desk and addressed her with my despondency.

"I just turned 21 and I haven't made anything of myself," I announced dramatically, wearing my despair on my sleeve. She looked at me to see if I was serious and then she just laughed and laughed. And I looked at her and her very white hair and I laughed too. For it flashed before me that her considerable age made meaningless such a melodramatic self assessment at the age of twenty-one. I was barely of age. I would have plenty of time to sort it all out.

I could make up for it with style. Those Sasson jeans. Such a great fit. And my red boots. I could go a long way on style. I just needed a little something more.

Next door to the Biograph was the Cafe Morocco which served its Moroccan fare to you as you sat on cushions on the floor at a low table. A waiter would pour hot tea into your cup from standing height which was a feat in itself, but the featured entertainment was a live belly dancer. Her name was Johanna and she loved an appreciative audience Jack told me. So I slipped through the shared bathroom between us and the restaurant, into their kitchen and peeked through the curtain when I heard her finger cymbals going. Jack had already introduced us when she came over after her show one night. So when she saw me she came up to me and gave me a special serenade with a couple of salutes with her hips, her scarf held across her dark eyes, her curly dark hair large behind her.

I was naturally smitten and for weeks after would hang out in the parking lot on my days off hoping to catch her coming out of the restaurant. And while she warmed up her little Opel GT two seater sports car she talked to me. She had last lived in Greenwich Village. Had I known how gay this neighborhood was I might not have been so tongue tied, but she gave no indication of her sexuality, and I felt paralyzed to come out with mine. Finally I told her about my adventures at College V and she didn't flinch and continued to be affectionate. One night after our customary hug I ran my hand down her arm to her hand and grabbed it and she returned the grab until I dropped her hand not knowing how to go further. She looked at her hand as if it had failed her, but made no move of her own. She knew I was interested, but she wasn't giving me any help at all. A little more experience with such non-committal woman and a little more confidence and I would have attempted more.

I just wasn't gay enough yet. I had a better time of it if I thought of myself as bisexual. Jack thought I just needed to have a good sexual experience with men in order to be won over to men as well. This just exasperated me. Men's bodies were attractive to me, but they didn't hook me emotionally. My thoughts were all about being in love with women.

"Maybe," I wrote in my journal, "my body was straight and my head was gay."

I set to investigating what being gay might mean. I had begun to explore the city the summer I worked at the gas station. On my days off I drove my father's station wagon the 30 miles to the city and began to explore the neighborhoods beginning with the Mission because it had promised a cross cultural feel and of course Chinatown where I hoped to feel the Asian culture I still missed so deeply. Eventually I ventured up to Polk street because I had heard that was the gay neighborhood.

Being a quiet weekday morning there wasn't anything happening and I ducked into the first bookstore I came to. Nobody bothered me or asked to help me and I was overcome by a liberating feeling of something close to joy. No one on this street would presume I was straight! Which meant they could equally well allow me to be gay. No need to tell anybody. No questions hanging in the air one way or the other. I was so giddy with this realization I stood in the front of the store looking at the photo books on display. All the books seemed to suggest identities intertwined with alternative sexualities. But I was too frugal to buy anything so I went back out into the street. Further along there was a leather store full of motorcycle jackets and chaps that somehow was gay too. The name of the store might have given me a clue—Hard On Leather.

I looked in the store window, but I didn't go in. It was enough to just walk this street. On later visits I would discover the free newspaper published by the gay community The Bay Area Reporter, BAR for short. It was really the only way to find out what was going on. That and the flyers on telephone poles and the occasional bulletin board.

Eventually Jack moved to another state when the Biograph was sold to a tech magnate who founded Apple; one of the Steves, but not Jobs. It was clearly just a toy for this Steve to own a movie theater. And when he lost interest and closed the theater I got a job at the two theaters on the street behind us—the Aquarius and Bijou. I soon worked my way up to learn the more modern Italian projectors at these theaters. These Italian beauties didn't burn carbons, but had a giant xenon bulb so the whole movie could be shown on one huge three foot reel. We just pushed a button and the familiar clack clack of the gears turning and the sprockets aligning with film started at the same time as the bulb came on.

I escaped my loneliness by spending all my nights off at the movies which I could see for free as part of the courtesy exchange between theaters for theater employees. The movies about lost alienated rebel characters salved my own alienation. I would embody them, inhabit these characters for weeks at a time. One week it was the young boy who finds a mentor in *My Bodyguard*. How easily I could feel him under my skin.

I found myself striding down University Avenue in my movie high, observing the people in the street when I caught myself looking at reality as if it was a movie. As if I was sitting in the theater watching it.

"Reality." I said to myself with a sense of discovery and irony "was a movie you could walk in." I caught myself. It was perhaps a little too escapist. Too much like a drug addict. Might it be time to create my own character in my own life?

I set to crafting a new outfit for my gay persona. I wanted a black jacket fitted to me. I really wanted a leather motorcycle jacket, but that was beyond my budget. At the yardage store black satin used for linings was cheap so that was alright. There being no pattern for my vision I drew my own. It was fitted like a fencing jacket, had a quilted lining and was double breasted with a zipper off to one side running up to the stand up collar. When it was finished I was impressed. It was exactly what I had in mind. It looked very Emma Peel zipped up. And half zipped it created the wide signature lapels of a motorcycle jacket .

I wore it with my Levi bootcut 501 jeans. But I didn't wear boots. I wanted black leather sneakers with the distinctive Adidas white stripes. Another expense way out of my budget even if I could find them in my size, but I had noticed that Adidas soccer shoes were black leather and they were always showing up at thrift stores. So I found a pair in my size and had them resoled with running shoe treads for not a lot of money. Now I had my black leather sneakers. Worn with a black t-shirt Jack had given me with the American Film Conservatory logo on it I had this persona down. I was a pint size, Asian girl replica of a gay man such as I had seen in the Castro. The uniforms of the gay community from preppie (jeans and a polo shirt) to leather men (jeans and leather chaps and motorcycle jackets) were standard.

Tim joined me on my adventures. He had also dropped out of UCSC because he was so behind. He had left each class with a trail of in-completes having not learned how to bang out his assignments. His perfectionism paralyzing him. He hadn't intended to move so close to me at my dad's house, but the converted garage he had found to rent was less than a mile away.

I helped him design his decor. The wall behind his drum set he covered with egg carton flats to deaden the sound. We painted the back walls black. The kitchen we painted silver and the corner with his bed bright red to match his red chenille bedspread. Tim insisted all the surfaces be glossy so he could wipe them clean easily in his fastidiousness. We were very pleased with our night club styling all paid for by the landlord who never for a minute thought anyone would paint a wall black.

One night we went to the DeLuxe bar, a small gay bar in the Haight-Ashbury neighborhood. It sported the chrome emblem of a '50s Chevy classic car as a logo. A huge mural size black and white photo of the car in a black frame covered one wall. This was the height of the chrome gay male styling. I wanted one of their t-shirts because the logo was so cool. A muscle t-shirt that hugged the body with white type on black. As Tim and I walked up to the door a man popped out. He stood looking us over.

"This ain't no candy ass bar," he said. We looked at each other and walked in.

"And we ain't no candy asses," I said to Tim.

"I guess he thought we were straight," I added. We weren't that. Tim now identified as bisexual owing to an encounter with a gay man I introduced him to (a friend of a friend from my photography class) and I was most definitely not Tim's girlfriend. American men with Asian women weren't all that common then. I wore the DeLuxe shirt, its body hugging form clinging to my every curve under my satin jacket.

All I needed was a motorcycle. I could only borrow my father's station wagon when he wasn't driving it to work so I was riding my bicycle everywhere and it was just a little too far to ride to Foothill College especially uphill. It made me very hungry and I wasn't very good at feeding myself yet.

My father had had a motorcycle in his college years and ridden it all through Spain on holiday so I felt it was a family tradition and it was frugal on gas. With Tim's help I found one to buy that was just the right size, not too intimidating, but not a moped either. It was a royal blue Honda with a 175 cc motor. Small enough so I could straddle it easily and yet it had the weight and feel of a real bike. I was immediately overwhelmed by the purchase and kept it a secret from my father hiding it at Tim's place while I read a book from the library about how to own a motorcycle. Tim learned to ride it first and then we took it to an empty parking lot where he could teach me.

I was determined not to die on it as my parents feared. I was super careful about riding protocol and followed speed limits. I read accident reports to find out all the ways a bike could go down. Every time I got on the bike and put on my helmet I repeated a mantra to myself. "Look alive. Stay alive." The bike became my daily transportation in all weather. I loved pulling up to the front of the theater, turning into the street and backing it up to the curb to park it. I had arrived Brando style, but with a touch of Emma Peel as I pulled off my helmet and let loose my long hair.

Not long after I started working at the Aquarius and Bijou I met a woman named Angel. She was a tall attractive Latina with dark hair in a Joan Jet shag. She was very shy so didn't stick around to chat. But one day I noticed that she had penciled in two linked women symbols next to her initials on the timesheet. She was a lesbian! I waited for a shift with her to talk to her and we started hanging out together especially once she traded in her moped for a real motorcycle. We loved the effect of us both riding our bikes together driving the two blocks to the Aquarius and parking our bikes simultaneously at the curb. This always got a few looks from passersby.

I made friends with the other women at the theaters and also hired a woman Tim and I met. She was going to the same movies we were seeing. The second time we saw her we offered her a ride home and got her story. Elly had come from New York to the ballet dance school in town. But she wasn't able to dance when we met her due to an injury. She wore the same outfit every day; a beige tent dress over pants. Every day the same beige dress as though her body was under renovation. She was a wit and a cynic suffering from culture shock in California, but she liked movies and I wanted to talk movies with her. Now that I had a group to hang out with we would stay after our shifts and show ourselves whatever the new movie was.

One night we had a conflict. My manager John who played in a band wanted to use the larger Bijou theater after hours for band practice the same night we were going to show the movie to ourselves. I would not have my plans foiled. Surely there was a way to have my private movie night. It came to me. I would show the new movie at the Aquarius after the show got out there. John did not object. So with the help of my crew I pulled the 3 foot reel of film off the projector and carried it out to the sidewalk. But it was so heavy, far too heavy to carry two blocks so I suggested we set it on its edge and roll it down the sidewalk to the Aquarius. The brilliance of my workaround so amused me as we rolled our movie down the street that I felt on top of my game in a way that I would come to recognize as my signature problem solving mode. If circumstances were too limited to allow me what I wanted, I would figure out a way.

Chapter 18

Birthday At the Aquarius

The last day of my 21st year I rode my motorcycle to the beach to clear my head. My complex romantic life was more than I could sort out so I went alone. It was a warm late Spring day, but not so warm that I was willing to disrobe from my black leathers.

I enjoyed the effect of my black leather outfit as I parked the bike and walked down the path to the beach with my helmet still on. I didn't want the wind to mess up my hair. There were enough others there on the beach to give me the sense of being an anomaly in my full leather suit. When I got to the sand I lay down on it face up looking at the sky, my head cradled in the helmet and my body fully cocooned in my suit like an astronaut.

"I am the man who fell to Earth" I thought to myself thinking of David Bowie in the movie of that name. I am an alien unable to communicate in fully human terms. I took off my heavy black gloves, letting my hands fall at my side so I could feel the warm sand and sift it through my fingers. Nobody paid me any attention. I thought about how I had traded my loneliness for the attention of women, as many as I could interest. It was no secret that everyone who worked at the two theaters were flirting with each other.

But it had all become too much. I felt suffocated by my girlfriend Glenda. Glenda had made a habit of coming by the theater whenever I worked which made me feel trapped since I couldn't leave. I didn't actually feel I had much in common with Glenda. She was a research biologist at Stanford. I had met her through the Stanford Gay People's Union at a costume party on Halloween. She had been dressed in a cowgirl outfit and I was dressed as a space alien in my turquoise ski pants, a shiny shirt and a pair of antennas on my head. She called her car Trigger she told me and at the end of the evening asked me to come home with her so I followed her big tan American car on my motorcycle to her studio apartment. She towered over me at 5" 11'.

"Isn't she a little tall for you?" One of the women in our lesbian group asked me when she saw us dancing together at The Answer, the local gay disco bar.

"Not lying down," I quipped. Glenda loved sex. She was seven years older than me, but since she didn't lose her virginity (to a man) until seven years after me, I told her we were sexually the same age. She pursued our relationship aggressively marking it with sappy cards for our one week anniversary then one month. Now it was two. She wanted to be close to me. Too close. And she did not really get it about movies.

On the day Alfred Hitchcock died it was Glenda who gave me the news as she drove us in her car; I remember the intersection we were driving through as we made a left turn towards the Guild Theater.

I loved his movies with their beautiful blond heroines—*Rear Window*, *North By Northwest*, *To Catch A Thief*, *Lifeboat*. And who could forget *Psycho* or *The Birds*. Hitchcock was a master director, the way he had all his shots storyboarded. It was so organized and efficient. I admired this frugality of time and film stock saved in his film making. *Notorious* with Ingrid Bergman couldn't be more perfect a film. Every shot had meaning. I had studied the film in my high school film class.

I did not have a tv or radio so hadn't heard until Glenda told me.

"Oh, Alfred Hitchcock died," she said as casually as if telling me there would be a storm coming and I should be careful on my motorcycle.

"He died?" I said stunned. I had thought he was somehow invincible. I felt suddenly bereft. No one close to me had died yet in my young life. I thought of all the potential films that would never be made. Glenda looked at me in my speechless solemnity. She laughed a bit at my reaction.

"If I'd known he was a family member I would have broken it to you more gently," she said not hiding her laugh. And I swallowed my feelings knowing she would never understand.

When it came to women I held my cards close. With men even more so. In fact I did not deal in the currency of feelings at all. I was so overwhelmed by any chance of people understanding them. Feelings were the sort of things that cropped up at the juxtaposition between one culture and another in my experience. Usually when one culture's set of circumstances ran full tilt into the cultural framing of the other culture thus causing an emotion that I couldn't explain to members of either one.

It only took a few months for Glenda to realize that I wasn't going to open up to her either. No matter how many Kenny Loggins songs she tried to inspire me into it. My preference was for the divas anyway— Patsy Cline introduced to me in the movie *Coal Miner's Daughter* which we showed for 8 weeks solid. Aretha Franklin because of *The Blues Brothers* which we had for 10 weeks, the longest a movie had ever played at one of our theaters. Bette Midler since *The Rose* and of course Barbara Streisand going back to *Funny Girl* in high school. And Liza Minelli as Sally Bowles in *Cabaret* the first movie I saw with a homosexual subplot. I emulated Sally Bowles' casual attitude towards relationships. Always looking for the next passion that might take me somewhere new. I painted my nails a shimmering green like hers. "Devine decadence," she said explaining this indulgence in her opening line.

Glenda I knew was not doing it for me. She already had her life all planned up. There was no room for decadence divine or otherwise. No room for crazy artistic inspiration.

"All that matters is that you care about me and want to be with me," she said when I pointed out the difference in our levels of maturity. "Do you?" She demanded.

I answered her with silence. It seemed weak to say I just lost interest. "Well I guess I don't," I said finally through my gritted teeth.

"I wish you hadn't said 'I guess'," she responded in that rational mature way she had being so much more articulate about naming her feelings. "I don't want to close the door on you because I still feel something for you ," she said. "What do I have to do?" I thought, "Be completely cold?" I just wanted things to stay light and affectionate and she was making it heavy and commitment intense. What more could I say? I was too frustrated to find words that wouldn't sound blunt and hurtful.

"Maybe I can get used to seeing you once or twice a week," she concluded.

"It's not worth it" I said.

"I'll be the one to judge that," she parried. No winning with this kind of tenacity.

I wanted to tell her I had my eyes on Elly who didn't know if she wanted me close or not. Elly spoke in riddles so as not to reveal too much. She was prone to cynicism, but then would do something cute like bring me a chocolate Easter bunny. She was remarkably able to read my moods which kept me interested. She herself was often depressed and talked of feeling dead. I flirted with her as much as I could get away with.

Now both Elly and Glenda were annoyed with me for not telling them what I wanted. I had tried to break if it off with Glenda, but she kept coming back to make sure I meant it. Then Elly was annoyed if my time was monopolized by Glenda. It was a mess. I was glad I had come to the beach alone. The warm sand supported me and let my mind roam with the wind and the blue sky. My black suit would soon be too warm so I got up, made my way to my bike and rode back over the Santa Cruz mountains.

My mother too wanted to give her input having heard from my father that I was coming and going from the house like a non-communicative space alien. She came down to the theater to speak to me about it. We went to a nearby bar where she accused me of being out of touch with reality. A popular refrain. I defended my grasp of reality with practical examples.

"And if I can't relate to people it's not exactly my fault, " I finished

"Well I should have spent more time with you when you were little," she conceded, "but we were just kids ourselves. We didn't really have it together enough to give what was needed to a baby," she explained. This was true enough and we let a truce bandage up this wound,

Tim also came by the theater to give me his analysis of my psychological state. Having himself been smitten by me, he had befriended Glenda and sought to ease her distress. He wanted to know why I kept chasing after women and then backing off from having a relationship. After cross examining me he concluded in Freudian terms that I was trying to win my mother's affection while still trying to separate from my parents. He asked me to imagine how many women I would have to interest in a year to get over this need to win over every woman I was attracted to.

'Maybe ten," I said playing along.

"So that would be 300 women in 30 years," he calculated. I laughed. He asked me to imagine them all lined up at once so I could kiss each of them in turn. This amused me; the idea of it. It did not however do anything for me. There was no emotional logic to it.

I was painfully aware that I couldn't seem to articulate my feelings and would go silent in frustration. How had I become so cut off from my feelings? I had been fine in Thailand when I visited at 15 and again at 20. Recently I made a call to my Auntie Ah Pahdt at the behest of my college friend Panda who was going on a trip to Thailand.

"What's up?" She asked in Thai. I told her about Panda's upcoming trip and how she wanted to visit our family home.

"Why does she want to do that?" She asked. Just the sound of her voice taking care of my request made me feel whole.

"To see where I grew up" I told her. That was all she needed to know to understand the nature of my request.

"Ah you young people," she said, "Mai Pen Rai—never mind— I will figure something out." I was so thankful she understood the importance of my request. For a friend who wanted to verify my story and my existence in another culture. I was so happy to have successfully delivered this message that I felt fully connected to my feelings of gratitude.

Ah Pahdt had always been able to read the slightest nuance of my facial expressions as had other family members on my Thai side. That was all that was required to register my feelings. Here in America facial expressions were not enough even if people could read mine. Inscrutable was what people told me my Asian face looked to them. I heard it so often I began to believe this stereotype myself; that I did not in fact have feelings or they were buried so deep I might as well not have had them. So they invited me to tell them what I was feeling, but when I told people the truth of how I felt they reacted in combative ways. They just couldn't accept my words at face value. It was as though the things I said just opened up a boxing ring for them to box their truth into me. To insist on their view of things. There were no free feelings to be had in this land. I couldn't just feel what I wanted.

No one in Thailand would expect statements of unguarded feelings except possibly between childhood friends. In order to articulate a feeling I had to take into consideration, not only the feelings of the recipient, but societies expectations and homophobia and internalized homophobia if any. So feelings were best left alone. It was a risk to express them. It would be a long time before I understood that though Americans were all about saying what was real, what was the truth, they couldn't really handle it coming back at them. Not from someone with such a hugely different perspective as I seemed to embody to them. I hardly understood myself how different my perspective was—this mixture of Buddhist fatalism, karma and luck overriding Western notions of individual autonomy and self determination.

In time I learned that by listening carefully to their reference points I could glean enough to understand where they were coming from. That allowed me to figure out what kind of truth they would be able to hear. Every one had their own story about how the world worked and many refused to hear another viewpoint. Thus truth to me became an ever shifting context of reference points. And I got tired of explaining myself.

Having cleared my head at the beach I decided the best thing to do was to plan a birthday party for myself. This way everyone would be assembled in one room and I would be the one who could move freely among them. I put the word out to all my work buddies and friends

The following week on a quiet Monday night I smuggled into the Aquarius theater four bottles of champagne. Luckily my manager wasn't there. Then I went to our sister theater two blocks away to get ice, riding my unicycle as was my habit. (It was easier and faster than lugging a five gallon bucket on foot.) I carried the bucket in my arms close to my body like a big baby. This kept the center of gravity over the wheel and it was easier to mount the unicycle this way.

When I came back there were balloons and crepe paper all over the place. Elly had brought it all and had got the other staff members on duty that night to help her decorate. She even had funny hats for us. Customers were asking what the occasion was and were wishing me a happy birthday. We got the six o'lock showing on. We were showing *Caligula* that awful spectacle produced by the owner of *Penthouse* magazine. It was full of famous British actors with some *Penthouse* lesbian porn spliced into the middle of it. It was also three hours long so gave us lots of time between shows.

My friends started to come by. Angel gave me a rhinestone bedecked cigarette holder. I didn't smoke, but I needed such a prop for my Audrey Hepburn costume. Just as I was reading the card, a sweet letter about how we should be friends again, Elly came out of the theater with a cake all lit up with candles. We crowded around it. It was an odd square cake — with white frosting and a strange centerpiece.

"You have to guess what it is," she said. It took me two seconds to recognize it. It was the alien baby bursting out of the chest. We all stared at it in amazement. It was such a masterpiece. A bakery might have made it. I looked at Elly with new eyes. She must like me a little I thought. She handed me a card with a picture from Rocky Horror Picture show of the conventionalists standing all in a line. "The party starts with you" it read and she signed it Allienne—a play on her name Elly-Anne. She had truly outdone herself.

We poured champagne with strawberries in the glasses and set to demolishing the cake. More friends came by and my mother who slipped in to see *Caligula* then came out to tell us how bad it was. Then went in to watch some more. Glenda showed up with a cake of the kind we used to eat together, but so many people were there she couldn't get a word in. Judy my high school girlfriend put an arm around her and took her off to the couch to console her. They had become friends too, as Glenda had sought out anyone who knew me trying to figure out how to reach me.

I found a present under my motorcycle helmet from an employee who had worked her first shift under my management. It was a pair of toy hand cuffs; an accessory for my black leather jacket. I loved that kind of detail. People whirled around me in six different conversations. I said silly things and went around hugging everyone, freely enjoying the affection, thrilled with how we had pulled this off. Then the show let out and most of the guests left. Two went to see *Caligula* to properly celebrate my birthday they said. And I laughed sitting in the ticket booth basking in the afterglow.

Chapter 19

Pride and Leather

The gay male culture fascinated me with its hedonistic sensibilities and interest in young people to the point of attempting to lower the age of consent. That was the agenda of NAMBLA, the North American Man Boy Love Association. At the gay liberation rally I attended in San Francisco following the annual march I was curious to see who these people were. I went to their booth where I stood to one side so I could watch undetected. I saw a full grown hunky young blond man amidst middle aged men in their tight t-shirts and jeans. Their black leather jackets slung on chairs. The idea that these older men would mentor young men who often were kicked out of their homes seemed fitting. Who else would raise these kids?

And it was erotic to me as a young person in the same way that discrepancies in status and power could be erotic, in the sense that a person of lesser status could have a visceral affect on a person of higher status. There was power in having such an effect. (In later years I would learn from others and from my own experience with power imbalances how much having more wealth, age, and experience controlled the lives of the partner with fewer resources.) Beyond the eroticism of my fantasies lay the fear of homelessness for these youth, a fact that would become more prevalent in later decades.

This theme of older and younger men persisted in gay culture even after NAMBLA was ousted from the Pride events under pressure from the lesbian community. Lesbians did not want to work for a movement dedicated to lowering the age of consent. They were in the midst of trying to persuade the men that the sexist oppression that women suffered was also behind the oppression of gay men. And because both of the sexes were interested in advancing the acceptance of homosexuality by society they were eager to quell accusations of pedophilia and NAMBLA was mothballed (although it still remains an organization).

As a movement that celebrated sexuality the gay community would chronically attract the most transgressive sexual behavior from pedophilia, to leather fetishes, to the infamous golden showers signaled by a yellow bandana tucked in a back pocket. The bandana code alone was a visual indicator of all the sexual tastes being celebrated by the men. Pocket size cards were available from leather stores (as a marketing tool) to clue you in on all the variations; bandanas were displayed in their storefronts. Eventually the opposing sentiment of just wanting to be held made its appearance with tiny teddy bears that would fit in a back pocket. This was just too cute and the tiny teddies were popular as gifts for a beloved. Then the teddy bear was claimed by the leather stores and soon they were displaying in their storefronts full size teddy bears wearing black leather vests and caps. I really wanted one. It was all part of the edgy scene of hyper realized sexuality and identity.

For a while the men seemed to acquiesce to the lesbian feminist position, but the celebration of male sexuality, heady with new liberation and the macho image being cultivated to eclipse the stereotype of gay men as limp wrist-ed nellie queens, was too compelling. And I too was attracted to this raw erotic power, collecting catalogs from leather stores and eyeing the motorcycle hats with their shiny brims and chrome chain trim.

It was all very much in keeping with the gay discos and independent movie houses Tim and I frequented in our explorations. The only place remotely alternative like that in Menlo Park was Kepler's book store with its plywood bookshelves and display tables, well graffitied bathrooms and posters of rock stars covering the walls. I browsed there for hours feeling subversive while reading *The Child's Garden Of Grass* (a book on how to grow marijuana) and looking through the alluring oversize books of photos by Helmut Newton depicting men in black leather and a woman on all fours wearing a saddle on her back and nothing else but a pair of tight jodhpurs and shiny black riding boots. That was as close as I could get to queer iconography in my home territory. Kepler's was my go-to hang out especially on holidays when the library was closed.

The Bay Area was positively sterile in terms of gay culture. Life was so heteronormative that everywhere I looked, every billboard, every storefront display, every person walking down the street insisted to me that happiness lay in being heterosexual. I called the steady drip, drip drip of these reminders "heterosexual water torture." This phrase amused Tim who had also enjoyed the diversity of Santa Cruz, the open sexuality and the free flowing counter culture ideas and conversation that went with it. We did not find any of this in the colleges here. Certainly not at Stanford and not much chance of it at Foothill College either. But there was a hold out for a Gay People's Union (the GPU) which was housed in the old firehouse just off White Plaza at Stanford. It hosted a women's coffeehouse and I decided to check it out on the prescribed Tuesday night.

Dressed in my satin jacket, jeans and black leather sneakers I rode my bicycle to the campus and ventured in carrying my bicycle pump so it wouldn't be stolen. The GPU was on the second floor with other clubs on the first. I had already checked it out during the day. It was empty at the time, so gave me a chance to take in the place without having to talk to anyone—the old couches, easy chairs and book shelves. I read the titles of the books, found nothing new and turned to the bulletin boards. That was when I saw the flyer for the women's coffee house night and a yellowing article I recognized from the San Francisco Chronicle's Sunday magazine with its cover photo of the gay parade in San Francisco that I had caught the tail end of two years ago.

The photo showed men holding up poster size black and white photographs on wooden stakes. One was of Anita Bryant the singer and former beauty queen who appeared regularly on TV as the spokesperson for Florida orange juice. "A day without orange juice is a day without sunshine," she cheerfully proclaimed. The other photos were of Hitler, Stalin, and Idi Amin, and another of burning crosses. I thought it was a bit harsh and over the top to put an American woman, an entertainer, among such male despots, but it was also ballsy. So much had Anita Bryant made herself an enemy of the Gay community, by seeking to repeal gay rights with her Save Our Children campaign, that I could see that a point was being made.

"A day without human rights is a day without sunshine," mimicked back the Gay community on a handmade sign. All the gay bars were boycotting Florida orange juice en masse. So successful was this boycott that the Florida Citrus commission allowed Ms. Bryant's contract to lapse two years later and her career went down the tubes.

The boycott was my first taste of political agency; that what individuals did as a group could stop an enemy. The enemy being so vocal and righteous it gave us something concrete to rail against; the very unChristian hypocrisy of it overriding our own internal homophobia that had kept so many quiet before. Anita Bryant gave a face to that enemy, a face that spoke of suburban moms and angry fathers. Christians I knew were fond of claiming a place for us in hell. Luckily I didn't believe in a hell, being Buddhist, but their persecution added a certain danger to my American life that made me ever vigilant. They could pop up anywhere these Christians and challenge my "lifestyle."

One had already—the mother of a high school love interest who had gone through my backpack and read my journal while I was visiting her daughter in the pool house of their apartment complex. This mother had long suspected my affections for her daughter. But now that I was in my first year of college and I was out my journal thus proved my depravity and she came down to the pool house to have it out with me just as her daughter was admitting her recent boyfriend could not hold a candle to the intensity of what she had felt for me.

My Christian persecutor burst through the door announcing that we could be arrested sitting here like this. We looked up startled as she took a chair and began a tirade about how I was sinning against God. She railed on for a good hour as I stood my ground defending my homosexuality while her daughter tried to calm her mother down. She told me how she would shoot me if she ever caught me with her daughter and all the ways I was a sinner. When she began to wind down she asked me what we would do if we were homosexuals; would we go into the corner and make out? Now I was disgusted.

"It's about love,' I said.

"That's not love," she said adamantly. It was telling I thought, this curiosity about what lesbians did. I reflected later how it might be erotic for her this forbidden sin. She continued to dress me down. Finally I declared I was leaving and walked to the door. I asked to get my things, but she told me I couldn't go back into the apartment; she would drop off my backpack at my house the next day. I realized I was cornered and in the seconds I stood barefoot at the door with my back to her I decided to give her what she wanted—the renunciation of my sins.

"Alright," I said gritting my teeth, "I promise."

"Promise what?" she asked taking the bait eagerly.

"Promise I won't be a lesbian anymore," I said.

"Come here," she said and told me to kneel down before her and she had me swear to it, repeating after her that I was not going to live as a lesbian anymore and I would think of my friend as a sister. I smiled at this line and looked at my friend. If she thought that this bit of play acting would so easily change my stripes she was really deluded, but she got her scene of renunciation. Then she wanted me to hug her which I did trying to make it sincere. She clearly wanted to be the savior in this renunciation play. Thus mollified she allowed me to return to the apartment with her daughter while she sat in the pool house savoring whatever it was she had extracted from me.

"Can you believe I did that?" I said. My friend acknowledged it was crazy and I collected my stuff, grabbed my journal, and fled in my father's station wagon back to Santa Cruz tensely navigating the windy mountain road. I was shaken by the experience, but also glad that I had not really conceded anything in this confrontation with my own Anita Bryant by proxy. A woman who had read my journal and been so shocked by it that she had thrown it down on the couch and poured a powdery substance on it (flour from the kitchen perhaps) as if to douse my words of their power.

Christians thus became my mortal enemy. Mothers were suspect too. I avoided both. Mostly I was angry that my life options had been cut short because homosexuals were viewed as deviants, that I essentially had no legitimate future if I were out, only a shadowy closeted one. I did not want such a life spent guarding information and keeping my love life secret. I steered clear of professions that exacted this price—teacher topped the list. I had seen teachers at the first gay parade I marched in at Santa Cruz wearing paper bags over their heads to attend the march because they knew they would be fired if their gay identity was revealed. The eye holes cut in the paper bag brought home to me their fear. I added to my list any profession that might serve the public or be in the company of children cutting out an entire class of respected professions. Working nights at a movie theater perfectly suited my shadowy illegitimate lifestyle.

There was a caveat to being so openly hated. Even though this persecution terrified me in a personal way, it galvanized my right to exist. After all this was America and I had freedom of speech. Marching down the street so openly in that first small parade in Santa Cruz shouting for our rights made me feel I was part of an American experience and I wanted more. So I had taken the day off from my gas station job the following year to attend the San Francisco gay liberation rally. I too had kept that Parade cover article from the Sunday paper. Seeing it on the wall of the Stanford GPU connected me with this outpost of the gay community.

The night of the Stanford women's coffee house I strode into the old firehouse as if it were my rightful place, a gay embassy in a heterosexual nation. I walked up to the second floor and into the main room. Some folding tables and chairs had been set up and a comfortable number of women were sitting amiably at the tables. They looked up at me as I entered, my shiny black satin jacket zipped up to my neck; all 5' 3" of me ready to take on any challengers. My black bike pump in my hand looked like a billy club. No one said anything.

"Hi," I managed to say as I glanced at all the faces in the room. They said "hi" back. They looked friendly enough, but I couldn't just sit down and get comfortable as though it were a bridge club, for lesbians were not my people either. They didn't always see me as one of them, I had discovered at Santa Cruz. How would they feel about me here in this neck of the woods? An Asian woman with long hair dressed like a gay man or at least not like a lesbian. They seemed friendly enough so far. All were white women, but that was not surprising. And not all had short hair. A few sported long hippie hair. They were inconspicuously dressed; a bit on the preppie side.

I stalked around the perimeter away from the group pretending to look at the book shelf as though I had come here just to find a journal. As I completed my inspection of the room, no one called out to me or asked me why I had come as someone had when I went to the first lesbian group I found at Santa Cruz on campus. The women here continued talking paying me no mind so I figured I was safe and sat down in the empty chair at the end of the table facing the door. The woman immediately to my left made room for me, shifting her chair. She offered a friendly smile.

"I'm Stacy," she said introducing herself.

"I'm Diana," said the woman across from her and I told them my name.

"We were just talking about socks," Stacy continued. Socks were safe, not an intimidating subject at all which put me at ease. I nodded and told them there was a sock table at the Hodge Podge a little seconds store my mother had taken me to. Diana said she would check it out. I listened to the rest of the women for a bit then asked if they were all Stanford students. Only two in the room were. This surprised me. This was a good sign. It meant that I wasn't the only outsider; that the group was open to all lesbians in the community. I had a legitimate right to be here on a campus where I didn't attend classes. Stacy said she attended Foothill College so I told her I was enrolled there too. I hung out until the end of the event then walked out with the remaining women.

Outside, standing by my bike, I showed Stacy that my club was actually a bicycle pump and not a night stick as she had thought. I put it back into its clip on my bike and asked her what days she was at Foothill. We agreed to meet again on campus seeing as we didn't know any other gay people there. It seemed timely to begin a community. Soon I introduced her to Tim and the two of us invited her nearly everywhere we went.

One of the outings was a viewing of the movie *Alien*, the first installment in 1979. It was my favorite movie at the time because of Sigourney Weaver, of course, and her dyke icon role as Ripley the tough talking crew member who ended up facing the bad ass alien in her underwear and blasting it into space. We went to see it at one of the Cinedomes in San Jose with its amazing wrap around screen. Stacy spent a good deal of it with her hands over her eyes. I knew every scene by heart, had read all the fan magazines, the Mad Magazine take off and the graphic illustrated comix. I bought a pair of canvas high tops that were the same color as Ripley's space station boots. I was still looking for the right olive drab jumpsuit though I did find a digital watch just like the one she wore, only it didn't have two faces. I was pleased with the find, though I thought digital watches were obsessive compulsive, insisting that you tell time to the exact minute. Really who needed such precision? Only Tim ever wanted to know.

When I got my new motorcycle I rode to Stanford to see Stacy who worked as a security guard in a parking lot there. I pretended I was going to run her over.

"Can I see your I.D. please," she said backing up in alarm before she realized it was me.

Eventually there was an opening at the theaters and I persuaded her to take the job so she too could be part of my girl gang—three lesbians and a gregarious straight girl named Dana. On our days off we planned outings. On a two day break, we packed a huge watermelon and a ton of food to spend the night on the beach. Angel wanted to make what she said was a watermelon suck which required hollowing out part of the watermelon and pouring vodka into it. Then she made holes in the side and we each got a straw to suck the brew from inside the melon. It made us drunk enough to play Truth or Dare, skipping the dares and just asking what we wanted to know as we tucked into our sleeping bags. The three lesbians told of our first time making love to a woman. We found out that Dana had never entertained the possibility of kissing a woman. She simply squelched any such thoughts. I learned that Stacy refused to date me when we first met because she thought I was too weird. No wonder she was keeping her distance when we went to Gay night at Great America on one of our first events together. It was all very illuminating.

In February of 1980 the Aquarius opened the movie *Cruising* with Al Pacino playing an undercover cop who infiltrates the gay leather scene looking for a serial killer. The gay community was urged to protest it saying it showed the gay community in a negative light and the men at Stanford's gay people's union (the GPU) sent the Aquarius a letter telling us we should not show it and why and if we did they would protest it. John was amused, but I was mad. They hadn't even seen the movie. How did they even know what it said about the gay community? I felt compelled to write a letter back telling him that we would show the movie because that's what we do and besides the movie might open the door to more gay movies. So they were welcome to protest, but many of us working at the theatre were gay or lesbian and we would appreciate it if they kept it civil. John and I agreed that the protest would just create more publicity and interest in the film so it was a win for us anyway.

In preparation for this movie opening John alerted the Palo Alto police department about the impending protest and invited them to a private screening we would provide during the day. Half a dozen rather tall officers came to the screening in full uniform and sat in the back row. Me and my friends occupied a row a few yards from them and I was strongly conscious of their feelings when the opening scenes showed two cops parked in their squad car at night while one of them was getting a blow job from a prostitute. The protests were about how the movie made gay people look bad, but no one said anything about how it made the police look bad.

The whole idea of a cop going undercover as a gay man was fascinating to me on many levels. The film didn't just skirt around this transformation it recreated the entire bar scene filled with men clearly doing things to each other (though all the explicit material had been cut). The sound track was so good some of us bought the album. The bar scenes and the men looked completely genuine and were in fact actual bar patrons of a bar called the Mineshaft, though the bar itself declined to be part of it. But the movie was less satisfying. The comments my friends and I were making turned to laughter at the lack of direction and clumsiness of the plot.

The movie left it ambiguous about how the Al Pacino character felt about homosexuality and how much he participated as a bar patron, but by the end of it I could feel that it had left an imprint on him that was somehow sexual. I didn't think that the film maligned the gay community. Sympathy was generated for the first gay man who was murdered and the killer had psychological problems, possibly of internalized homophobia, but I did not think that it implied that being gay made you a murderer or encouraged the murder of gay people.

The protestors kept a polite distance by standing across the street with their signs to boycott the movie. Cop cars drove by all night and John had a staff member inside the theater in case someone tried anything. I had silk screened a t-shirt with the words "Cruising. It's only a movie" using the same typestyle as the movie. A reporter asked me if I had made the t-shirt myself and why. I rambled on a bit about how I thought the movie was just a bit of Hollywood trash.

"It's no more about the gay community than *American Gigolo* is about male prostitutes," I said referring to the movie we were showing at the Bijou. But she rewrote it to say "It's as much about the gay community as *American Gigolo* is about male prostitutes." I knew nothing about male prostitutes, but yes *Cruising* actually had recreated a sector of the gay community. Just not the one they wanted seen.

I crossed the street to chat up the men who were protesting. The man who wrote the letter told me that the movie gave a negative presentation of the gay community. Well there are movies that have positive depictions I countered and gave the recent French movie *La Cage Aux Folles* as an example. That the movie actually showed a gay couple seemed positive to me even if it was played for laughs.

"That movie doesn't represent me either," he said. I didn't really get it about representation or what was being asked. I mean I was never going to see a depiction of a Eurasian British woman in an American movie let alone a lesbian one nor would I expect to. Hollywood was its own world. I loved the movies for allowing me to be someone other than myself.

To me representation in film was the realm of a documentary like *The Word Is Out* which interviewed actual gay men and women especially older ones with history to tell. Fiction was about stories of human interest and that often meant humans doing nefarious or taboo things in subcultures not often seen. Novelty was the stuff of movies. As for inspiring the killing of gay men I wasn't sure that was logical.

Movies usually showed women being brutally murdered. Did that inspire more murders of women?

Meanwhile, in the city there were 200 protestors making it a much bigger scene, but for once I was glad to be a bigger fish in a little pond.

It would take a few more years for me to appreciate that films could be made about gay people in the same way that they were made about straight people because their lives were historically interesting or they were interesting people. But until then all I asked was that lesbians weren't killed in the end, an effect I found devastating when I saw a lesbian couple who actually kissed in the movie *The Fox,* a 1967 film I saw as a retro film at The New Varsity. Based on the D. H. Lawrence novella the women were living together on a cabin in the woods. At the end a tree falls on the femme character killing her while her lover is left with the man who felled the tree. The message was clear—a lesbian romance had no future.

I continued to be intently interested in any hint of a romance between women in films. We showed one at the Bijou about track stars called *Personal Best.* It had a love scene ten minutes in, which was when a few people would walk out, conservative looking straight couples. My mother too thought that scene was porn. Any scene of women making love was considered porn apparently. Conveniently the male gaze of heterosexual films allowed me to observe women as they were being kissed. I was particularly fond of movies from the 1940s with their smart sassy women—Rosalind Russel in *His Girl Friday,* Katherine Hepburn in anything, ditto for Lauren Bacall. These movies showed me how women and men flirted in a way that was subtle and filled with innuendoes. And the women were often professionals, independent in some way. The movies of the '70s felt bereft of women heroines in comparison.

I found some film buffs among my friends at school. I met Rachel in my photography class at Foothill College. She was friends with Lois a single mom and Doug a gay man in the class. They were a little older than the norm of students so more interesting to me. Doug organized a group photo of all of us with a handful of his friends and by the time he shot two rolls of film we were used to hanging off each other. We also went with him to The Answer, a gay bar in town where we danced and I flirted with Rachel. At the end of the evening I kissed them both goodbye. Rachel gave no reaction and I was reminded of the scene in

The Big Sleep with Lauren Bacall who gives Bogie a kiss. "It's better when you help," went the line.

She was not much taller than me and plump in a pleasant way that filled out her narrow face and her big round eyes, her blond curls falling to her shoulders. She loved good literature and had a collection of hip music albums. Plus we shared similar reactions to the movies we had seen.

One evening she invited me to a gallery opening in downtown Palo Alto not far from the Bijou. It was just the sort of lively, but intimate party that characterized this suburban university town. We were duly welcomed by the owner whom Rachel had befriended when she first came to the area from New York. We stayed for the entire evening enjoying the interactions between Richard and the public and his tall blond sisters, his tall wife and nearly full grown son. We were family by the end of the evening so we joined them for dinner after the opening and then I gave Rachel a lift to her car on the back of my bike. We lingered by her VW bug inspecting the darkened storefront. I played with her hair assessing her receptiveness before I started kissing her. We leaned against the wall lit by the streetlamp.

"I don't know how to kiss really," she said, "I'm just making it up as I go along". She told me she had only been involved with one person before.

"Only one person in 25 years?" I said finding my tongue. I looked back on all the women (and men) whom I had kissed along my journey so far, feeling some shame for it.

"Yes a veritable innocent," she said endearing me with her self assessment in such literary language. Cars passed and some slowed. It was hard to hide that we were two women together. One car of rowdy lads backed up and one of them leaned out the window and asked us if we'd seen a man on a bicycle. Then stared at us for a bit. We pocketed our hands and kept a respectable distance when we saw a man walking down the other side of the street. He asked us if we liked Jack Nicholson and said we should see *The Shining*. It was on my list. He walked on and we resumed kissing lingering for two hours unable to ask the other to our home. That would be too forward so early in the game.

I saw sexual innuendos everywhere even in our projectors. I told Tim and Stacy on their visits to the booth late at night how the sound of the giant reel of film as it was rewinding on the projector sounded like it was masturbating. The sound getting more and more urgent with the weight of the film as it returned to the reel culminating in the slap slap slap of the end of the film against itself as it was released from the take up reel. Then the machine groaned as the brake was deployed. This made them laugh as it seemed to confirm my theory.

The crowning event of the year was the Pride parade and I wanted to ride my motorcycle with the Dykes on Bikes. I was now fully outfitted in a classic leather motorcycle jacket with its oversize brass zipper crafted by a German leather worker with a shop on Market street known simply as Tauber Leathers. Angel, who was with me at the time, said I looked cute in it. That was enough for me to buy it on the spot though I rarely spent money on clothes, let alone $240. I planned to wear this jacket everyday I rode the bike, so the price per wear would be minimal I reasoned. Later I spent another $200 to have pants made that would zip up the side seams like ski pants. The shiny black leather was so thick I would creak as I walked, but the suit shed rain and kept me warm. The tough as nails effect was enhanced by a pair of Gorilla brand work boots with satisfyingly bulbous steel toes and a stacked heal that gave me some height. The only thing that wasn't black was my full face white helmet. White for better visibility.

It wasn't hard to persuade Angel to ride with me in the parade. The more interesting question was who would be our passengers? Angel invited a woman she was dating at the time. Elly had gone on vacation and I had broken up with Glenda so she was out of the picture completely. I invited Rachel, though we were so new as a couple. Everyone had some vague plan for the parade so I decided to organize what I wanted to happen. I went to find Stacy so I could persuade her to pick up our two passengers at my house early enough to get us to the assembly point of the parade. We were riding our bikes on the freeway and didn't want to risk it with passengers. Stacy brought a friend too so we all had a buddy. The June weather was perfect and the morning air brisk enough to warrant our jackets.

"May the force be with you," I said holding up a fist as we pulled out of the driveway and headed for the freeway.

The Dykes on Bikes were a bonafide formally organized lesbian motorcycle club. The members headed the pack and allowed non-members to follow at the rear. There were at least 50 of us. The leaders walked the pre parade line-up and shouted out tips to us. One tip being to take out the fuse for our headlamps so we wouldn't run down the battery with all of the honking of our horns. And warnings not to let our wheels get caught in the rails of the tramline.

That year in an attempt to appease the public and show we were not perverts, the more salacious members of the gay community, the drag queens, the butch daddies, the naked man with the boa constrictor and the Dykes on Bikes were pushed back into the middle of the parade. Instead of being the lead group bursting forth to signal the start of the parade we were contained at a more sedate pace within it. So it was a long wait before we could finally roar out screaming and honking our horns to cheers and cameras, some press photographers getting between our two lines for a low angle shot.

We had to stop often to let the rest of the parade catch up. This allowed us to be more thoroughly admired and lots of lesbians watching from the curb stepped out to ask if they could have their pictures taken with us, especially Angel and her girlfriend in their complimentary lavender and pale blue pants. And with every start we were yelling and honking. We looked at the crowd as much as they did us and spotted our friends from the GPU. Leathermen smiled at me. Women smiled at me. I was grinning all day. Someone ran out to hug Rachel, a friend from Foothill there with her lover. It was a heady experience to be so out in the open in broad daylight. I felt like a hero in a ticker tape parade. I'd never been so publicly welcomed and so celebrated for being the one thing I was so conscious of being and took such pains to hide.

As we rode into the Civic Center a woman in a dress ran out and hugged me. It was Lani Ka'ahumanu from Oz, reminding me how she knew me with Panda. I was beginning to feel how far my community was stretching. We already knew this event in our fair city was the nexus of so much of the gay community.

At the end of our ride we passed several bikes that had died and were being pushed, and a cluster of women around a bike where the passenger had got her shirt caught in the spokes. Several women hacked it off with their buck knives. We weren't butch dykes for nothing. I was pleased with the success of our outing and we went off to find our friends at Lotta's fountain my designated meeting point where we were joyfully reunited with Tim and Doug, then returning to stand under the rainbow flags at the Civic Center to watch the rest of the parade come in.

"I'm glad you were with me today," I said to Rachel at the end of the day and squeezed her hand. She was surprised and squeezed back.

Chapter 20

The World of Men

I came out of class so mad I threw a hefty text book as far down the open air walkway as I could, startling a student yards away. Foothill College had a good number of classes that I could take to continue my interest in theater, but the perspective was much more job based than it had been at UC Santa Cruz. At first I liked it; I liked knowing that there were jobs in acting in TV advertising and what types were in demand, but then it soon became clear that I wasn't going to fit a type. I wasn't even going to fit my sex. But did it really matter as long as I was learning the craft?

The acting class took place in the theater where we pulled chairs into a circle on the stage. The teacher liked to do improv exercises, but he wouldn't say what he was going to ask us to do beforehand. He would just announce that we were about to do one and the same two guys would jump up game for whatever scenario he put forth. They had clearly been in his classes before. It didn't seem fair that they already knew how class was structured. I didn't get a chance to do an improve exercise, but at least we would all have a chance to perform a monologue since it was an assigned task.

I chose one I already knew, partly out of laziness because I already had it memorized and partly because I wanted to incorporate the suggestions my last acting teacher had given me when I was at Santa Cruz. It was also a nice thought provoking compact monologue about a universal subject— contemplating death. The play itself was a popular one for theater at the time—*Rosencrantz and Guildenstern Are Dead* and easy to perform because it really had only two characters, with Hamlet as a walk-on. I was familiar with it from when Caesar did the scene from it for his director's class with me and Cindy. So I already had a soft spot for Rosencrantz, one of the two escorts charged with delivering Hamlet, the Shakespearean character, across the ocean.

At Santa Cruz it was not unusual to use text from a play in a completely different context in order to create a new opportunity for theatrical storytelling. I had done it myself by using a monologue from *Waiting For Godot* in a modern dance piece. So I happily settled in to working on my monologue presentation.

When I came to class and sat on the floor of the stage the teacher asked me what play my monologue was from. When I told him his expression changed from receptive to slightly hostile. What character are you playing he asked? I told him.

"Why didn't you consult with me about this?" he questioned me. "I know in some avant gardé theater a women might play Hamlet, but this is a beginning acting class. We are to act the roles as they are written" I looked at him blankly. It never occurred to me that I should have to consult with him just for a class assignment. He went on. "And why would you want to play a man's role when there are so many great roles for women. Lady MacBeth or Hedda Gabler for instance?" I knew those characters. I had read them in high school and neither had appealed to me. They were both about women whose power was limited because they were women. They spent the whole play trying to work around the shackles of their sex. Not to mention that these characters were white and I couldn't pass for white either, but I knew he wasn't allowed to complain about that.

"I wanted to do a monologue that wasn't so personal," I attempted to explain. Personal to the fact of my sex I meant. It wasn't worth going into the limitations of being female, he clearly believed theater to be equally filled with great opportunities for women. I hadn't found this to be so. The only monologue I could find for a woman that wasn't about being behind the throne or behind a man who was a gatekeeper was about not wanting to birth a child just for the sake of producing an heir for her country. It was from an obscure play about Queen Christina. The queen that had made Greta Garbo the iconic lesbian heartthrob in the movie *Queen Christina* striding about in men's clothes and kissing her ladies maid. And it had that amazing final scene of her looking enigmatically at the horizon from the prow of a ship. I probably should have done that monologue, but I wasn't done with Rosencrantz.

"What's not personal about it? It's about death. You can't get more personal than that," he said. Yes but death was universal to both sexes not just to women. I hung my head. I was here to do a monologue not discuss sexual politics. He wasn't going to get it anyway. And I wasn't prepared to argue with his objection that I had used a monologue out of context of the play. My first encounter with monologues was from an entire book of them that we used in high school. We were invited to perform any of them whether we had read the play or not.

"Go ahead and do it then," he conceded and I began setting the scene of getting into bed and winding up an alarm clock. This had been the suggestion of my previous teacher who saw the monologue in an entirely different context, more in the realm of a Noel Coward play. I started into the first lines of the monologue feeling the existential humor of the line "dead in a box", but my teacher was not smiling. The class was tense after all he had said wondering how I was going to get through this. And then I forgot the rest of the lines. I stopped and just hung my head.

"Well I don't understand why Rosencrantz is getting into bed with Guildenstern, but I like the part where you're winding up the alarm clock," he said and then my turn was over. I got up and went back to my chair fuming until class was over. A classmate came up to me on my way out. A man a little older than me.

"I would have lost all my lines too, if he had dressed me down like that before I went on," he said. I nodded appreciating his sympathy. He also told me that the play was a personal favorite of this teacher who was right then directing the play for a performance. I could see that what happened to me wasn't personal to me, just to my sex. I still went out the door mad. At least I could throw something like my text book. The girl who was startled by it landing at her feet asked if I was aiming for her.

"No," I said," I was just mad at something from class." I picked up the book accessed the damage and went on with my day.

I did finish the class, going through the next exercise which required partnering up with others in a scene, but I lost my enthusiasm for theater tethered as it was to pre-written scripts. I turned to other venues. I was required to take a communication class, but I was too terrified to take public speaking, which likely would require debating one side of an issue. That felt like a man's domain too. I always saw both sides of an issue. So I took group communication which was fun because it allowed me the opportunity to talk to other students about interesting topics. But then the teacher, another man, divided us into groups that separated me from the other articulate students and put each of us in groups with painfully shy students who would hardly talk at all. I was annoyed and found other ways to interest myself by writing provocative statements on the board for discussion.

"A woman cannot truly know herself until she understands her sexuality," I wrote. And the teacher did duly respond with interest, but he didn't offer it as a topic.

"This is certainly true," he said, "but wouldn't it also be true for a man?" He countered and proceeded with his own class programming. I was not given a chance to disagree, nor did I have the words. All I knew was that women were not encouraged to explore their sexuality at all, but for men it was all about exploring their sexuality. The culture encouraged it often at the expense of women. I stopped writing messages on the board. He had silenced me, but I was on to him now. He wanted to connect with his students in an attempt to be relevant. I decided to change my appearance. The following week I dressed like a hippie in my bell bottom Levis that I had patched with all the scraps of fabric my mother and I had saved from our sewing projects. I wore my old wire rim John Lennon glasses to class over my contact lenses which meant my vision was out of wack, but it was worth it for the effect.

Angel and Stacy saw me from across the campus. "Isn't that Amanda," Stacy said ready to come over and say hi.

"No it can't be", Angel said, "she would never dress like a hippie."

My communications teacher seemed to like my outfit and started to address issues of social justice my way. The next week I wore the very feminine floral dress I had a dressmaker sew for me in Thailand. It was supposed to be a tailored shirt dress, but the silky fabric made it into something much more feminine than I intended. And it required wearing feminine shoes and not my usual boots. The teacher paid me no attention, but a male student who had been friendly with me suddenly withdrew as if I had been lying to him about who I was. If I was learning anything in this class it was that clothing was a powerful communicator.

The next week I wore my three piece suit. And the vintage wing tip shoes. The suit seemed ok to wear even at this more conservative campus. Menswear for women was enjoying a fashion trend. By now the teacher was onto me. He made a joke in class that I was going to be remembered long after the class. He didn't say what I would be remembered for. I was pointing out that a suit was a power statement for a man, so why was it just a fashion statement for a woman or was it? But he had acknowledged me and I gave it a rest for a bit and wore my own clothes and participated in class assignments as directed.

Then one week he took me aside and asked me why I wasn't at a four year college. I was obviously too smart for the junior college set. I didn't know what to say to that. What did the question even mean? That because I was smart I ought to be pursuing a proper degree at a university? But this school was the best I could afford while saving money by living at home. Or did it mean that the students at this school didn't deserve any better than what pablum he was offering? He wasn't going to offer any more to the smart students in class. And this was a required class so we just had to get everyone through it. I left it at that.

I had thought of being a teacher myself, but there was no way I was going to with the homophobia so focused on adults who might influence children. I wasn't going to wear a bag over my head at the gay liberation events as I had seen teachers do in Santa Cruz. I wanted my freedom.

I gave my communication class one last outfit before finals week. I wore my leather jacket, blue jeans and Gorilla boots with the t-shirt from the Deluxe bar. I completed my outfit with a heavy black belt and a biker wallet at the end of a chain. My keys were already on a chain so I tucked them into the belt and they jingled as I walked. I topped it off with my leather man hat with the shiny black visor. It was a policeman style hat that evoked a combination of authority and subversion of such authority. I braided my hair back and tucked it into the back of my jacket. I was now a recognizable stereotype. There was actually a man on campus who wore this outfit with a black leather vest, but without the hat. And the movie *Cruising* had been full of this look. If people didn't know how gay it was, they read it as motorcycle bad ass. As I walked down the hall people sitting in their classrooms looked up as I walked by because of the jingle of keys. No one in class spoke to me. I had reached maximum alienation of everyone. I enjoyed the effect, but it wasn't me.

What was me, I realized, was a student willing to fulfill my obligations to my parents and thus my status as a middle class person by finishing a four year degree. I'd been going to school for four years now with nothing to show for it. I had lost the desire to study theater at this school and had focused on art classes—watercolor. My teacher Bart De Palma was the brother of Brian De Palma the Hollywood movie director whose film *Dressed To Kill* had recently played at the Aquarius. Mr. De Palma once described how his brother had come to his art opening at a gallery and marveled at how supportive everyone was of his paintings. In Hollywood he said all his peers came to his openings ready to tear his film apart. This did not make Hollywood or filmmaking sound inviting. Achieving anything in my life was hard enough without battling a whole culture of people hoping for you to fail.

In order to acquire said degree I would have to choose a major palatable enough with a culture neutral enough not to alienate me any further. I didn't know that this was why I felt so at odds with my schooling. I didn't yet understand the concept of cultural alienation or marginalization. As far as I could see no one understood where I was coming from. At least not enough to help me align myself with a career path that would enlist me in the upwardly mobile middle class. As a student I just thought of myself as stubborn and lazy by nature, but the time had come to kick myself along or "buck up" as the British would say.

I went to the administration office and browsed the rack of pamphlets that described what AA degrees were available, picking all the ones I could see doing that wouldn't require either reading or writing. Reading and writing took up too much brain space and made me argumentative. It couldn't be math heavy either because I was too careless for math. That left me with three degrees more related to a trade than an intellectual profession. One stood out — Communication Arts. The same career that Paul from College V had pursued. That wasn't so bad I said as I discussed my choices with Tim. My art skills weren't of the fine art caliber, but neither had Paul's been.

When my father saw me with the drafting tools needed for the required drafting class he was very happy. You can get a job with drafting skills he told me. Drafters were a part of his engineering world. My mother too was pleased since commercial art related to her work in market research for advertising. She told me my choice was more useful than just doing an English degree. Parental approval. Check. I could now focus on what I needed to do to complete a four year degree. Had I picked journalism, Berkeley or San Francisco State would have been the schools to go to, but journalism no longer appealed to me. The writing was too formulaic and the topics routine. San Jose State offered graphic design classes and a Bachelor of Science degree in Graphic Design. It was ironic that I would be in the sciences after all. San Jose State was also the very school that my mother had long ago told me was beneath me. It was a come down from the U.C. system, but I was ok with that, because I could afford it.

Towards the final year of my degree I moved in with Tim and Stacy. It made sense. Tim and I had already lived together in a shared house in Santa Cruz. It was more affordable than renting an apartment solo while still allowing us the autonomy of adults. My father too wanted me to establish my independence away from home. He had married again, a woman who had been his secretary in Thailand. Ah Joi had contacted him while going to school in the states just after my mother left him. He courted her and then she immigrated to the U.S. with her two children. I enjoyed his new family and Ah Joi's cooking. (I learned later that Khun Ya had instructed her to both feed me and speak Thai to me.) I packed the meals into a Thai lunchbox to take with me to the theater.

I'm not sure what prompted my father to tell me I needed to find my own place; it may have been that he didn't want the children to know I was gay. When I was with Angel he told me that the kids thought she was a boy so I was not to disabuse them of that notion. My mother certainly didn't want to take me in either, though she had acquired her own house. She did not for a minute agree with the Thai family custom of keeping your children at home for life. She had her own love life to manage.

I worked full-time so I could manage rent. I left it to Tim and Stacy to find a place and went off to Thailand. They found a three bedroom house in the Barron Park neighborhood of Palo Alto. I didn't feel lonely anymore, living with my two best friends.

Then I was fired. The new manager didn't like that I was basically in charge of a crew of my own friends. He had his own ideas about who should work where and paired the two most immature guys to work at the Bijou. We had always made sure they worked with women so we could temper their shenanigans. I said nothing when he was upset when one of them rode his moped up and down the aisle after hours, leaving scorch marks on the carpet.

Meanwhile he made a new rule forbidding the acting manager from hanging out in the manager's office at the Aquarius, which was stupid because that was the only place where you could look out onto the lobby and make sure all was good to start the film. He was making the point that I was merely a projectionist so my place was to sit in the projection booth at all times which would have been extremely unpleasant. He clearly did not like a woman manager being in charge. So I ignored the rule and one night he came by the theater unannounced and saw me leaning out the office window talking to the crew. He was with his boyfriend a younger man who had worked with him at another theater. It was clear to me that he wanted to hire his boyfriend so I had to go. He made a show of storming up the stairs to the booth to tell me that I was in violation of the rule that the office was off limits. Then he told me I was fired and stormed off again.

It wasn't worth it to me to try and tell him how this interfered with the running of the theater not to mention needing a secure place to count the take at the end of the evening. I was sure he would find some other bogus reason to fire me. After I was gone he called me up mad at me for still having the keys to the theater as if I was a criminal and was going to use them to rob the theater. I said I'd come by the office with them. I was mad, but I refused to give him the satisfaction of seeing me react. Instead I made him a gift. In my silk screening class I created a poster with the words "Piss Off" painted graffiti style across a brick wall in bright pink and green. It was of course my final words to him, but I made up a story so I could give it to him with a smile in the very office I had been forbidden to use. I had the poster rolled up in a mailing tube when I went to drop off my keys. He smiled and was very courteous as I entered the office that was now his domain, but had once been mine.

"This is for you for the office door," I told him watching him as he unrolled the poster from its tube. "So it will be clear that no one is to enter it," I added. He smiled at the poster and accepted the sentiment of the gift as sincere though I'm sure the underlying message did not escape him. And he did indeed post it on the office door. It had my signature on it so the crew made up their own version of how I had been fired for giving him this poster.

I was soon hired at another theater. This one was not part of a chain, but was a little hole-in-the-wall owned by a woman with the German name Heise. She did not care that I had been fired and listened to my side of the story without doubting my integrity. I felt calm in her motherly presence and was suitably submissive despite having arrived in my usual full suit of black motorcycle leathers. Underneath I wore my preppie uniform of Oxford button down LL Bean shirts with jeans. The ceremonial peeling off of leather rasping with the sounds of zippers and the transformation to mild mannered student persona seemed to amuse her.

Non-union projectionists were hard to come by and we got along fine. I quickly learned how to operate the 8mm projectors which had been designed for inflight movies on airplanes. The Festival Cinema showed old movies from the 1940s, classics like *Casablanca, Notorious, The 39 Steps,* and once in a while, *Gone With The Wind*. Heise sold tickets; she enjoyed welcoming the public to her theater. As I worked the candy counter inevitably someone would tell me I sounded just like Katherine Hepburn. We had a third crew member—a young man enamored of the culture of the 40s. He sported a classic preppie style and was slightly intimidated by me. The theatre had a cat named Ciné. We were a little family as it were and I loved the classic films that gave the venue a time capsule atmosphere with the walls covered in vintage movie posters. Heise went home to her apartment after the last show got in and I would do my art homework. When the show got out I would pop over to the New Varsity Bar and Restaurant one street over where Tim was tending bar. The two theaters were close in the way of extended family, both being owned privately. Both ran retro or second run movies and had a printed schedule. Both were managed by women. I felt at home with this theater family.

The emergence of VCRs and home theaters were still a few years away from eclipsing our world. The Festival Cinema was sold and though the new owner kept us as staff he soon realized this would not be a money making endeavor and closed the theater for good. Just as I finished my degree in that Orwellian year of 1984. I said goodbye to my five year movie career and got a day job as a typesetter and paste-up artist. A job that still required hand skills with a knife, but would in time give way to the desk top computer. I stayed with it, learning those skills too.

The Aquarius and the magnificent retro Stanford Theater lovingly restored by David Packard (of Hewlett Packard) are the only theaters remaining today in the old neighborhood. My job as a projectionist was one of the last analog jobs to go. Movies don't come on reels of film anymore, but on disks and projectors are just another push button digital interface. But I can still hear the sound of those reels of film clicking their way over the sprockets of the projector head. I took home the cast iron film splicer as a memento.

Chapter 21

Honoring The Dead

My posse and I rode with the Dykes on Bikes for another two years which was as long as I owned a bike. At my mother's urging my father had offered to buy me a car, out of concern for my safety if I agreed to sell the bike. I was driving a longer distance to San Jose State for school so I accepted the offer. The second year we rode, given the success of my strategy, we adopted the same Pride parade plan, but now we returned as veterans and I had upgraded my ride to a Kawasaki 400 so I could hold my head up with this sizable steed. The leaders rode Harleys which was only fitting.

Rachel rode with me and Angel had Stacy as a passenger as they were now a couple. They did not tell me the details of their courtship, but I did see them chasing each other at a run at one of our GPU dances and figured it was a lesbian mating ritual. Angel had on a tuxedo jacket and shirt with bowtie and Stacy wore a band jacket. They looked sharp and were much photographed. I wore my leathers with a hot pink silk t-shirt. The Dykes on Bikes were returned to our rightful place at the front of the parade and it all went by far too quickly.

In the year of our final ride in 1983, the mood of the gay community had shifted considerably with the impact of AIDS. Stepping out at the head of the parade was a man who was HIV positive wearing black leather pants tucked into tall lineman boots and a black leather vest with a peaked leather cap. He stood proudly carrying a rainbow flag and I saw death walking into our community. He looked perfectly healthy, but we all knew that the disease was a death sentence. The motorcycle club leaders handed out black strips of cloth and asked us to tie them around our arms to honor the dead.

It was grim, but the parade was even more densely attended possibly due to more positive coverage. Even our local newspaper, The Palo Alto Times, did a piece on the history of the parade in advance of the event instead of after, when it would be reported in the San Francisco Chronicle as a salacious news event. The gay parade, I learned from the article, was the single biggest tourist attraction in San Francisco. I was tickled. Imagine being a bigger attraction than the Golden Gate Bridge. Of course the bridge wasn't a one day only attraction, but still. I was thrilled to see mention of the Dykes on Bikes as one of the main entries.

This year we were joined by a Los Angeles women's motorcycle club called Leather and Lace so our number was over 100 strong.

Lesbians were the least likely population to get AIDS. This irony put a dent in the theory that God had brought AIDS to smite the gays because homosexuality was an abomination, but no one seemed to give this any air time. Lesbians didn't count and I still identified more with the men. Seeing a large group of men in their leather regalia coming out of a leather bar one night was such a haunting sight it stayed with me evoking an other worldly culture. I wondered if I would even be allowed inside such a bar.

I imagined the back room where the floors were sticky and littered with empty popper bottles. That was the drug of choice—poppers. I had tried them once at UC Santa Cruz as I was prowling the third floor of A dorm looking for love. I stepped in the door where a Friday night party was going on and one of the guys handed me a vial and told me to snort the contents. I'd never seen such a vial, but I did what I was told just like Alice in Wonderland trying every god damn drug offered her. As I stood there waiting I didn't feel anything, then my heart began to beat faster and a minute later my head felt like it was going to explode. I thought I'd made a terrible mistake and was going to end up in the ER. And then the effect wore off just like that.

"What was that?" I asked seeing the smile on the man's face after watching me go through all that.

"Amyl nitrate. It's a heart drug, for heart patients," he said. "It's called a popper."

"Wow," I said, "what a roller coaster." I thanked him and left. It was a rush. Another drug to add to my drug experiences and I committed the name amyl nitrate to memory, but I had no interest in doing it again; it was too big too fast. But a few years later when I heard that gay men used it just before they were going to come, I could imagine what a bang of an experience that was. Then I wondered why gild the lily? Wasn't an orgasm good enough? Especially if you had such a big organ for its delivery. This was before I learned that women's orgasms were actually more intense, at least by some accounts. But poppers also relaxed the smooth muscles of the anus, thus its usefulness. Looking it up now, I see that death is a possible side affect among other things like stroke and decreased blood pressure to dangerous levels. And an animal study had shown temporary lowering of the immune system. So there we were. Gay men risking their lives for a short lived bang of an experience likely opening themselves up to proliferating whatever flesh deteriorating viruses lurked inside them.

The baths too, intrigued me for the promise of sex with strangers in cubicles. Though I preferred my men clothed in their leathers, moving sideways past each other to loud disco music. I followed the heated discussion about whether the bathhouses should be closed. Those on the side of keeping them open argued that this was one of the few places where gay men congregated which also made it a center of communication to inform the men about the AIDS epidemic. Such information amounted to flyers posted on the walls recommending the use of condoms. To do more would provoke rebellious behavior was the prevailing wisdom, not to mention be viewed as a criticism of the lifestyle of gay men cruising for anonymous sex in public places.

It was heretical to suggest that this lifestyle had anything to do with the onset of AIDS. How the party all night numbers game of sexual encounters might have an impact on how much a body could take. The number of STDs in the community reflected this lifestyle. While the treatment for these infections continued to lower one's immune system.

But this vision of anonymous sex in the backrooms of bars fed into my eroticizing of gay men and appealed to my impulse of conquest and non-monogamy, but of course I did not live this lifestyle nor was there such a thing as anonymous sex in public places for lesbians. It felt too dangerous. Men just couldn't leave two women alone. Not the gay men who called us "fish boats" when we walked down the Castro, but heterosexual men who viewed women as an open buffet of party aperitifs the moment we appeared in public. The world of women that I lived in was certainly not anything like the gay lifestyle.

Women were creatures who needed to be investigated emotionally before, as Sally Bowles put it in *Cabaret*, one could pounce. Though I was not even supposed to want to, which gave such a pursuit a delightful element of surprise. I did accept that maintaining a long term relationship was the mature thing to do, just like doing all your homework and finishing a degree. I pulled the usual all nighters to get my coursework in. I focused on my career and imagined the glamorous jobs I might get as a graphic artist.

But in time I began to feel suffocated. Rachel had anxieties about doing new things. She was nervous about driving her little VW all the way to San Francisco by herself, though she spoke of wanting to take art classes in the city. It was no good me suggesting she find a classmate to carpool with. She just refused to talk about it any further. We couldn't talk about clothes either because she refused to accept my assurances that she would look fine in clothes she felt she had to avoid. Nor did she want to exercise because she had asthma. Pretty soon there was not a whole lot she would allow me to talk about and I felt I was nothing more than a house cat answering to her nickname for me—Kitty. I braced myself to break it off with her and when I did we could not somehow remain friends and we saw each other not at all once it was over.

Of course I was never without a love interest, even if my attentions were not returned. I went back to work at the library one summer to help with the data entry of getting all the books into a digital catalog. I found new friends there, traveling to England the next summer with two of them. I didn't attend the parade as diligently, once I was no longer riding my motorcycle. It would feel like such a come down.

By the time I returned to the parade with Stacy for company four years later, the community had rebounded having sprouted all kinds of AIDS related support organizations from pets for shut-ins to meals delivered, to free clinics and counseling. Many organizations started by and staffed by lesbians. Project Open Hand for instance was created by a lesbian to provide and deliver meals to her gay friends. Straight allies stepped up to take care of the men they knew. There were so many AIDS support contingents it took an hour for them all to go by. Condoms and trial size tubes of lube were thrown from floats and the Sisters of Perpetual Indulgence gave away brochures on safe sex illustrated with bearded men dressed as nuns and an upbeat graphic style printed with purple ink. A rainbow flag carried by humans every five feet was so huge it spanned the width of the street. We threw coins in it; money that went to the food bank for AIDS patients. It made me proud to see us responding to help our own.

A few years later the AIDS quilt was being sewn in a storefront on Market street. Stacy and I went to see it exhibited at the Moscone Center. It was in the basement covering the entire footprint of the building. As I walked among the panels it felt like a war memorial only instead of battles commemorated there were clubs of country western line dancers, singers from the gay men's chorus, groups of friends, leather men. All a testament to the network of friends and lovers. And yet it was not about women. There was no Dykes On Bikes contingent or anything else I might have been involved with. It made me feel curiously detached from this war even as the gay men were dying in such numbers, the most beautiful first.

AIDS had brought death to our once vibrant community and created a culture of its own that permeated our movies and books and the stories people carried with them of gay men who died. The smell of death was in everything. It was a consciousness of death that had largely been missing in American culture.

My hairdresser and the cute Latin boy at work who dressed sharply and whose socks I would comment on when he delivered memos to my department both died. I was so mad when not one of his work friends at the memorial for him dared to mention he was gay; only that his family had abandoned him.

The sardonic pairing of sex and death marked the tone of the day filling us with images of emaciated men with lesions on their skin and a wit that got more biting as time went on. It was a cruel, unpredictable death. Though some lived quite a few decades before succumbing as our friend Doug did, isolating himself increasingly in cynicism.

I was glad that the community was forced to mature and realize that we would have to protect ourselves because the rest of society refused to look. It was a pandemic that wasn't shared, orphaning us as the straight world carried blithely on. And we did learn to secure our lives and our partnerships with legal documents though I thought gay marriage was taking it too far. Why would we want to take on such a patriarchal institution with so much baggage? There were more pressing concerns when we could still be fired for being gay?

As the AIDS epidemic went on those who survived stood out. I came across an article in a gay newspaper that explored what were the commonalities of those who seemed to live longer. It spoke to how to live in the face of death and offered a structure.

Number one was to come out so you were not spending so much energy supporting an elaborate fabrication of who you were while living a double life. I couldn't agree more.

Second was to monitor your health. Well duh. But yes I was paying more attention to living a healthy lifestyle and so too was the community.

Third was to tend to your community and put energy into helping others who were dying of this disease. This was a sentiment I could apply to other communities and later carried to other issues such as the planet. The idea being that it was best to live in solution rather than in despair at the possible outcome, or try to escape with distractions.

And finally work to change laws. Engage in the political process. I believed in being out and was motivated to talk about issues. I wasn't inclined to get further involved politically, but I understood this final principle to be about working to make the political system care about your people. I liked the whole package, geared as it was to coming out and I appreciated this wholistic approach to working the system. It was the first time I considered myself to be part of a whole system.

The gay community had come of age by embodying a message of liberation and agency. With AIDS came a larger sense of community and of the future. The struggle to survive, paired with the influence of feminism prompted the community to pause to reflect on what was family. Such reflection spurring a boom in lesbian and gay therapists. In the end the community seemed to long for integration with their straight counterparts embracing that most conservative of institutions—marriage. I was so put off by this turn of events I pulled away from gay politics altogether and towards the culture of women. Towards what could be imagined if women were to make the world.

Chapter 22

I Am The Most Beautiful

As I became immersed in the feminist thoughts permeating the air I started to wonder what it was about Thai women that gave them so much self assurance and power. Something I felt was missing in the women who were my peers. My American friends were intellectually vigorous, but seemed to cave when it came to self worth. It was a stark contrast to the self assurance of my Thai peers who were just more comfortable in their skin. It was not even what they talked about; it was more just an accepted fact that Thai woman had authority no matter what their place, but where did it come from?

Thai women, my mother complained, talked constantly about what was beautiful. She made them sound shallow in this fixation. But maybe there was more to it. A declaration of authority on these matters. I remembered spending a weekend at the beach with a group of young Thai women, my two cousins, Neung and Nor, and a friend of Nor's. In the morning after we had dressed I found the three of them assembled in front of the large mirror on the wall. I joined them to look at our reflection. We were dressed in our seaside holiday outfits, peasant blouses and capris. We smiled at our reflection. Then with the formality of a ritual someone spoke.

"I am the most beautiful of all," she said.

"I am the most beautiful of all," said the next without denying the statement of the first.

"I am the most beautiful of all," said her sister. Then it was my turn. I was puzzled. What was going on? I had never participated in such a reckoning. I, who had spent my adolescence in America, had learned to be modest. No girl ever declared her beauty in such a bald-faced way in the West, less she be labeled vain. Yet it was clear to me that I was the most beautiful of all.

Something in my childhood informed me of that—the Thai childhood spent at the center of my female dominated extended family. Still, doubt crept in to my mind. I was not pure Thai, being half white on my mother's English side. Perhaps I didn't quality for this impromptu beauty contest. I couldn't bring myself to speak, to declare my own beauty. So I just smiled with the others as we all looked in the mirror admiring our collective beauty. Then the moment passed.

I was never offered such an opportunity to declare my own beauty again, though others would do it for me as befitted protocol in the West.

"Its fun watching you cross the room," said a companion during intermission at a theater in San Francisco. I looked around at the corded lobby not getting her point.

"It's entertaining to watch all the men's head swivel to follow you. And you don't even notice them," she explained. "Oh that," I thought. I was dressed for the theater in high heeled boots and a long dressy coat open to show off my full sleeved renaissance style blouse over thrift store black velvet breeches. I loved dressing up. I did it for women and myself, not men. Men didn't understand fashion. And I had no use for the attentions of men.

I knew this friend considered herself a plain woman and had suffered for it in her youth, though she was tall and had the stature of a model; she could look quite regal in the right outfit. She too knew about the self-declared beauty of the Thai women, having spent time in the peace corps working in a hospital lab in a remote village in northern Thailand . We went to visit the village so she could reunite with the Thai friend she made.

As soon as we entered the hospital a crowd of Thai women came to greet her. They were so short in comparison that none reached even her shoulder in height. They took her arm, all wanting to touch her and when she sat down one sat in her lap. A latecomer came through the door. She was a plain woman with a pockmarked round face who took her place with the others. One of the women took up her introduction.

"And here is Suda. You can see she is as beautiful as before." And they all laughed heartily, Suda included. Later, my friend mentioned this interaction as one of the charms of the Thai women. This inclusion was clearly as important a lesson for my friend, as my memory of my youth looking into the mirror with my Thai cousins, self declaring their own beauty. For beauty, in Thailand, it seemed was not just a matter of chance. it was a birthright, a source of power not left to men to decide. This was a crucial point. For to be able to call a woman beautiful was a way to lay claim to her. I would later learn to do this myself when courting women. A woman who had not learned to declare her own beauty, I observed was adrift without an anchor or a pilot. Any tugboat could claim her and bring her in.

Thai women weren't only noted for their beauty world wide, they clearly believed they were the most beautiful. And perhaps this made it so. How empowering it was to have this sisterhood chiming in on its collective beauty. This inclusiveness creating a broad definition of what beauty was that allowed every women in the room to shine and reveal her own inner beauty. How weary I was of the stance women had to take in the States filling themselves with doubts about how they did or did not measure up to prescribed standards of beauty.

I was confused by the messages I had received in the West that beauty was in the eye of the beholder. Did this mean me? That I wasn't beautiful unless approved by the eye that beheld me? Why should I be judged by the standards of others? I could see for myself how my beauty compared. It was just a question of tastes and preference. Yet women in the U.S. never seemed to feel ok about themselves. I would try to tell my girlfriends how beautiful they were, but they wouldn't step in and own it. "I'm fat," said Rachel and indeed she was lovely in her plumpness, but I couldn't convince her it was a good thing. And she in turn would resent me for being thin and taking it for granted, not realizing the privilege I held. I did not remember this being an issue in Thailand. The main issue in Thailand was how light your skin was. The lighter the better, for skin tone was a measure of class. But among the village girls they held fast in solidarity that they were most assuredly beautiful.

Beauty we assure ourselves is only skin deep and it is shallow to give it so much attention. Yet we knew how important it was in making our way in the world. I see how it erodes our self esteem to see ourselves so judged by others. When a Thai woman declares her beauty it is the first step to declaring her full value and assessing for herself whether outside parameters have anything to do with it. She is then a realist. How much more powerful if we could divine not only our own beauty, but all of our own talents and skills.

I would eventually find such a tribe with these self declaring customs. They were a class of self starters; women entrepreneurs in business for themselves. Some had learned to believe in themselves. They had perhaps been mentored or attended workshops to bolster their belief for there were many guru cheerleaders eager to pump them up for a stiff fee. A whole industry of image consultants, marketing experts, social media consultants and writers. All this to help create a self made pedestal so that every day these enterprising women could throw themselves at the world as professionals capable of offering their self-proclaimed skill to others. And by this power they free themselves a little from the judgement of others; a key to embarking on a self directed life, I realized.

Chapter 23

Take Back The Night

Through the Gay People's Union I heard about the feminist march called Take Back The Night that would take place on the Stanford campus. I had not been afraid of being out at night. I had always gone out at night at UC Santa Cruz, which was, after all, the rape capital of the country. But I didn't know that women were at risk no matter where they were. My mother started to warn me not to go to gas stations at night if I was alone. It annoyed me that I would have to think about these things. She herself was usually accompanied by a man and though I did have Tim as company on many an outing, I was not going to build my social life around being with a man. It wasn't in my trajectory as a lesbian to frequent the watering holes of heterosexuals and arrange myself in attire to attract the attention of men which seemed to be where trouble starts. If I had to frequent such public space I planned to simply ignore men and avoid interacting with them. Later this ignoring was described by my partner as putting out a vibe that repelled men and she gave a kind of shiver which told me that I had successfully projected that I wouldn't give them the time of day.

The whole point of the Take Back The Night march was to raise awareness that women were limited in their freedom because of male violence. So I joined the march, a not very big one. We marched, we chanted "Take back the night" and listened to a speaker give statistics of violence against women. We felt safe in such numbers, but then we would be alone and vulnerable again. Stanford offered an escort service for women walking alone at night. The more I thought about this the madder I got. Why should I have to call an escort service. If men felt they could use their strength to force themselves on a woman, then women had the right to defend themselves, I told my mother. To kick them in the balls if it came to that. She didn't like this idea at all. She seemed to want to protect men from me and such thoughts. She prided herself in being able to hold her own in a man's world. This meant she negotiated her way in the society of men by joining in the banter of the battle of the sexes; a cultural exchange that offended my diplomatic upbringing. I was not out to take sides in a discussion of which was better the superior sex. I simply assessed the reality of a physical power difference and decided I had to take a fighter stance. I had already been given instruction in high school on the basics of self defense by two police officers who had come to our gym class to show us how to put our keys between our fingers or roll up a magazine to use as a weapon. How to avoid places where we might be trapped alone. We had a right to defend ourselves, they were telling us, this new generation of young women.

I felt safer once I got a motorcycle and encased myself in leather head to toe. In fact women started to cross the street when they saw me walking down the sidewalk. I clipped my keys to the end of a chain and swung it around like a weapon thinking to clock someone in the noggin. The chain bearing the weight of the keys immediately wrapped itself around my wrist and was useless. Often I ended up hitting myself with it. Dang it. I was just a fraud. I wasn't going to kung fu anyone with my flashy key chain trick.

The Take Back The Night event had introduced me to a personal kind of activism, one that invited me to participate. Through the Gay People's Union I found out about the speakers bureau that sent one lesbian and one gay man to high schools so students could ask us questions. This was worthwhile, seeing as I had not too long ago been a gay student who had never laid eyes on a live gay person. The students were so afraid to speak they passed their questions to the teacher on slips of paper. Totally forgettable innocuous questions. Did gay men wear speedo swim trunks instead of underwear for instance. We kept our answers short and diplomatic. Then a newspaper reporter wanted to interview a gay teacher for a story. This was after the defeat of a proposition that would have mandated the firing of all gay employees in public schools in California. The one out gay teacher (the drama teacher) at my alma mater was going to be interviewed but then thought better of it, so someone offered my name as having been a gay student at the school. When the article came out I was quoted as having said that because the gay teachers at the school were closeted, I didn't have any role models and my isolation was made more severe. I hadn't intended to cause any trouble to the school, but I heard plenty of the ripple effect of my statement. Parents were calling the school demanding to know who the closeted teachers were so they could request that their child be taken out of their classes. The dean (a lesbian classmate of mine) told these callers that such information would not be divulged and no student would be excused from any teachers' class. Then the closeted teachers got on my case when I showed up the next week to speak on a panel about being gay.

"You outed us," this teacher said cornering me outside the classroom.

"But I didn't give any names," I said perplexed.

"You outed us as an institution with gay teachers," she said. I didn't believe in outing people, but it had never occurred to me that I could out an institution. I explained that the drama teacher was going to do the interview and then didn't so it came to me. But that didn't really excuse what I had said.

"Do you stand by your having outed us as an institution," she asked. That's when I realized there were sides to these issues. That if I stood up for myself, someone else would be impacted. I stepped into an adversarial role.

"Yes" I said. She sighed and marched off. From the podium I acknowledged that the impact of my words had put the school in the public eye.

"There are gay people everywhere," I said, "lesbian nuns for instance," I added then sat down. I was on the panel speaking to the auditorium of girls and staff. It was as close to an apology I was going to give and not my most diplomatic moment, but nothing could take away from the triumph of telling my story at the high school where I had once had to be so careful about what I might say for fear I would be expelled.

The Palo Alto Weekly had a guest column spot for local voices. It was dominated by a particularly vociferous anti-gay, right wing Republican who once blamed the gay liberation movement for the death of a friend's son of AIDS. So in 1993 the paper was recruiting for more guest columnists especially women of color. I offered myself as a woman of some color who was an out lesbian willing to write in the vein of the "personal is political" a catchy phrase Gloria Steinem had coined. It fit my modus operandi perfectly.

"Why can't you write movie reviews or something?" my mother complained. "We have the same name. People are going to know you're my daughter." It did not look good for a marriage and family therapist to have such interesting family issues of her own. I don't think her clients cared that I was gay; it was she who didn't know how to handle what to say to having having the town lesbian be her daughter. That wasn't something I could help. I was on a roll with my first column *"Ten Good Reasons To Be A Lesbian."* The reasons included lots of cultural things like seeing all the lesbians at the Stanford women's basketball game. But the kicker was number ten: "You don't have to worry about men—getting them, keeping them, taking care of them. When the object of your love is a woman, you spend your time pursuing the concerns of women which are also your concerns". This was a concept suggested to me by a straight woman. And I meant it on a political level as well as a personal one, but I got plenty of letters from men who were outraged that I would consider living in a world where the concerns of men were not my concerns. "What about your father?" one asked. I had no idea what he meant, my father having so little concern for my concerns. I filed all the letters unanswered as a souvenir of my impact.

What got my mother was a line I wrote about motorcycles vibrating between our legs as we rode with the Dykes on Bikes. This line had even made it into Herb Caen's column in the San Francisco Chronicle the newspaper of the city that knows how. People had tried for years to get a mention in his column and I had made it in my first go of submitting something.

"Is it a matter of frightening the horses," I wrote to Mr. Caen "that a suburban weekly refuses to print the line motorcycles vibrating between my legs." He wrote me back that he liked my reference and printed something about how in the suburbs they still hadn't caught up with the times. The metaphor was too racy for my mother's British sensibilities as well as the Palo Alto weekly which had nixed that line and my entire report on the gay pride parade. My mother asked me to meet with a therapist who would mediate for us. A colleague she chose because she was a lesbian, not an out lesbian, but a lesbian nonetheless. I was amused and somewhat touched by this. My mother brought a copy of the offending column and presented it to her asking that she persuade me to stop with the off color jokes and gay causes because it was a liability to her as a therapist. The therapist took one look at the column and saw it for what it was in the eyes of the gay community—the writing of an emerging young lesbian finding her voice. There weren't too many out voices at the time especially in a suburban freebie newspaper. She tried to appease my mother by explaining that humor was going to be different for each generation. And as my mother pleaded her case further, the therapist finally told her it was too much to ask me as a writer to censor myself.

"She was biased," my mother said once we had left her office and we were on our way to dinner. I felt bad for my mother, but secretly pleased that I had been recognized by an elder lesbian for doing good work. My mother was never going to win this one I knew, but she was still my mother and I was grateful she was going to treat me to dinner.

The Palo Alto Weekly couldn't take the heat either as they were getting plenty of mail from readers requesting that the pervert be removed from the quest column section. And as it was a paper that arrived in their mailbox unsolicited and might be read by children, the Weekly complied sending me a letter to tell me my year long tenure on the paper was up. But *Ten Good Reasons To Be A Lesbian* caught the eye of an English professor at Stanford who wanted to include it in a Freshman English writing text book he was putting together. It made me proud when I got my copy of this thick book, *Encountering Cultures: Reading And Writing In A Changing World* by Richard Holeton. I saw my piece listed in the contents alongside Alice Walker, Maxine Hong Kingston, and a number of other writers I admired. When I called him up to thank him he sent me a check for $200. It was my first paid piece. But more important I felt I had succeeded in doing something different. I had taken what was considered a depraved social status and made it into a social advantage with some subversive humor thrown in. I was never gonna accept a victim status. I was after all a Thai woman who had the right to state that she was the most beautiful woman in the room and knew how to put a podium to good use.

Chapter 24

Take Back The Body

Tim was going to make me late to the movies again. I was pretty laid back when it came to hanging out with him, giving him all the time it took to answer his questions and wait as he tied his shoes just so and packed all the things he would need on whatever outing we were going on, but if there was one thing I was a stickler for it was getting to the movies on time. I was ok missing the trailers, which he felt gave away too much of the movie, but I wanted to be in my seat for the opening shot of the feature film. Every artistic decision the director put forth was made in that opening shot—the pacing, the location, how the characters were introduced and the tone of the movie.

But Tim was driving and so all I could do was warn him that I was not going to be happy if we were late. And we would still have to walk a block from where he parked. Things were always tense at this point, but I could still make up the time if I ran as fast as I could once parked. This made me so winded by the time I got to my seat that I was breathing hard and even coughing for the first few minutes of the film. I was clearly out of shape. I was a good athlete in school, but I hadn't done anything since in the way of regular exercise.

When I talked to Tim about it, he too wanted to be in better shape so he would be ready for the ski season. He suggested we jog together. That didn't exactly excite me, but I had recently read about an exercise course that was being implemented in various cities called the Parcourse. It was a built environment that reminded me of an obstacle course. You followed a trail and the course had stations for push-ups and sit-ups and various other exercises with posted instructions to tell you how many reps to do. And best of all it was free. No gym membership required.

And there was one on the Stanford campus that anyone could use. It was the nicest one too, as it looped past Lake Laguanita and followed pedestrian foot paths. My attendance at events at the Stanford Gay People's Union had given me a sense of belonging that invited me to use the campus as if I was a student. Parking was available after school hours. Tim would drive us there and we would start our warm-up exercises in the lobby of the gym when it was cold and do the course three days a week. Tim coached me to improve my reps on the pull-up bar. This made me feel purposeful. I imagined myself as one of the astronauts in *The Right Stuff.* I didn't even have to be a jock and join a softball team to keep in shape; I could just run this innocuous and scenic obstacle course. Soon I could run for my seat in the movies and land in the chair without breathing hard.

Lisa who was my girlfriend at the time, also joined me on the par course when Tim wasn't available. I had met her while working at the public library that summer entering books into the data base. I didn't even realize I was flirting with her when I would scoot myself into her way on my office chair on wheels as she walked through the work room. Lisa was intrigued by my Thai language skills, as she was a linguistic student. We hung out together and she wanted us to be inseparable best friends. When I told her nobody got that kind of attention from me unless they were my lover she gave in and allowed her attraction to me to manifest into love making while making it clear that she would eventually meet and marry a man.

It was Lisa who introduced me to martial arts. She was pursuing a degree in International Relations, so had become acquainted with the international house at Stanford. They had parties involving food and cultural events. She invited me to go with her on Asian night. The cultural event scheduled that night was a performance by a Chinese couple dressed in silk outfits doing a choreographed martial arts demonstration involving weapons, flying leaps and mock battles. I was enthralled by the fierceness of it and the visual excitement of watching them. If this art dance form was considered acceptable in the United States then I wanted to embody this skill as part of my own Asian persona.

Once I had a better paying job as a paste-up artist and no longer worked at night at the movie theater I started looking for a martial arts class. Karate schools were so numerous each town seemed to have one. I picked one where the teacher (a white man) emphasized the self defense aspect rather than the fighting sport of it. I immediately felt at home after the first class. The movements were so similar to Thai dancing poses I thought there must be a relationship between Thai dancing and martial arts, plus it brought back all those kung fu movies I had watched as a child in Bangkok. And of course in the U.S. there was the iconic TV series Kung Fu which I watched faithfully because he was biracial too, though he was played by David Carradine a white man. Most people forget that part, Grasshopper.

That show by itself may be why people expected an Asian face to pop out with pithy wisdoms. There were, in fact, very few Asian people in my karate school; they probably wished to avoid such a stereotype. All the wisdom spouting Buddhists I would later hear offering Eastern wisdoms were white Americans giving dharma talks. That my martial arts teachers were also white were another example of such cross cultural pollination and suited me. I soon felt the benefits of my new sport. The horse stance, the most basic of forms and the foundation of karate moves, had in a few months strengthened my upper thighs and fixed my bum knee, the one that had bothered me from a ski incident years ago. And the exercise improved my lung power further. This was indeed empowering.

The second move I made to take back my body was to tend to it anytime I was in pain.

Tim, whose lanky form had caused him back aches all his life, had a chiropractor. This was before this form of bodywork was common and many people thought it was quackery. But I trusted Tim's judgment and his engineering dad's perspective that he so imbued.

Peter, his chiropractor, was looking for candidates to help with a research project that was analyzing hair samples to find out what healthy people's chemical makeup might be. Tim had such a poor immune system he was always catching whatever bug came by and had it longer than anyone else, so he volunteered me, who never seemed to get sick at all. This I attributed to my genes and lots of exposure to third world germs. When I came to understand the human micro biome there was a lot of truth in the latter.

I was not, however, immune to doing stupid things with my body and one day I hurt my back while trying to dive into an upholstered chair head first at someone's house. The arms turned out to be harder than expected and as I summersaulted over it into the seat it shifted one of my vertebrae out of alignment. When Peter told me how manipulation of the bones worked and how muscles were affected when bones were out of alignment it made so much sense so I was relieved to go to him and have his help to fix my back.

There would be plenty of other fixes he would help me with over the years and one day I asked him if getting old automatically meant that you were in for a lot of aches and pains. He told me that it was more that older people were a collection of injuries that had not healed properly. I remembered my bum knee. The one that wouldn't heal until I had strengthened my upper thighs in karate so much it took the strain off the knee so it could heal. Getting old I realized was a study in navigating safe passages for the journey of the body as well as the mind and spirit. I vowed to properly heal every injury. I did not want to end up with a body full of old injuries.

I also learned to fall quite splendidly in karate which would turn out to be good training for the perils of old age. When my peers would sustain injuries in falls I realized that they had no recourse but to try to stop the fall as they flayed against gravity. When I felt myself falling I would go with it rolling into the fall when I felt the point of no return. I still ended up splayed out on the ground, but no serious harm done. I fell off my foot powered scooter once rather spectacularly one rainy day and had to have stitches in my chin, but no bones broken, and I was back working in a day. Karate was actually teaching me an aging skill. How useful and unexpected was that?

My mother was disappointed that I hadn't taken up tennis which she had loved all her life playing into her 80th year. My Dad played too and so did my grandmother. In Thailand it was very much a game of the upper class and was highly promoted at the Sports Club. But tennis, the competitiveness of it put me off. And that it required running after a ball. I was afraid of being hit by balls. It just wasn't my game; there didn't seem to be any point in it. Learning to defend myself was something I did find useful. And it was my mother after all who had been concerned about me being alone at night on my motorcycle getting gas at an all night gas station. As if a man or a car full of them would drive up suddenly and abduct me away for a gang banging or just rough me up for sport.

My karate training engaged my voice too. We were trained to yell the kia yell to add emphasis to our defense techniques and as a psychological assault on the perpetrator. Similar to learning to yell "no" in the anti-rape training women were taking at the time called Model Mugging. This discipline taught a more rudimentary self defense that involved a live target covered in protective padding.

Unexpectedly, the yell translated to other parts of my life when I was being attacked in verbal disagreements. Raised as I was to deflect disagreement by simply declining to respond, like a good Buddhist avoiding conflict, I was in no way equipped to respond to the fighting style of my American girlfriends. Lisa had the experience of five siblings all honing a negotiation style that involved bullying and verbal haranguing. She would badger me into agreeing with her and was then disappointed that I wouldn't answer her back. But shortly after I had taken up karate I suddenly found myself shouting back. It was just a nonsense syllable and it made us both laugh, but it surprised me that I could now connect my voice to a response in real time.

I had been the sort of person who would suffer what I felt to be an insult and then go home and think up ten clever things I could have said to put the person in their place. But I had spent so much of my life thus far suppressing my feelings, that I was disconnected from the moment of exchange. Now karate had installed in me a voice at the point of impact. This would prove to be the most immediately useful feature about my training. And now that I could verbally defend myself I wanted to have something to say. I would spend a great deal of my life going forward accumulating information to back up my responses.

Learning to defend myself engaged me in thinking through possible assault scenarios. It trained my mind to a broader awareness of my surroundings, anticipating spaces where people might hide. It disturbed my mother that I was training myself to harm another person—men to be exact. This factor upset a lot of people, but it empowered me. As I practiced through the given scenarios of the defense moves—someone choking me or pulling a knife on me—I practiced deflecting away from these assaults, then laying my hands on my perpetrator and throwing them to the ground stomping on their head and their groin. We did not practice killing them. Just incapacitating enough for us to run away. It was drilled into us that we were not to pick fights, just defend ourselves. And once in a while, our instructor would have us practice defusing a situation with words. Hold up both hands, step backwards, look them in the eye and say "I don't want to fight" as calmly as we could.

Learning to defend myself calmed me and gave me an outlet for my anger at a world where I was put in a position to be dominated or humiliated. Being hit accustomed me to the physical assault so I could distance myself, and my training would kick in, engaging the part of my brain that solved problems as I determined where to deflect the blow and how to strategically inflict one. Coming to class helped dissipate the anger I accumulated throughout the week at being misunderstood or not being heard at all. The fury of my anger was sometimes unexpected and startled others.

One afternoon I was trying to give feedback to a woman in my writing class who had just read a story about how her father forced the family to endure very long car rides as he indulged his enthusiasm for the new interstate highways. The all day car rides made her and her brother miserable trapped in the back seat. So visceral was her description I was reliving her plight.

As I struggled to intellectualize my response my teacher asked me "But how did it make you feel?"

"Feel?" I said as if this was a novel quantification to judge a work of art. But since she asked I let her have it.

"It made me feel like killing him," I said adamantly. My teacher drew back speechless and I felt every man in the room flinch, recoiling at my words. How could a father doing something so benign as going on a road trip prompt such homicidal thoughts? I could hear them thinking.

I wondered myself why such a scenario would make me so mad. More to the point, given how strong my feelings were, should I even be trusted to express them? I was clearly highly over reactive at the slightest suggestion of a woman (or child) being powerless.

A week or so later I ran into the woman who wrote the story. We stopped in the middle of University Avenue during the lunch rush. She was apologetic. "I was too young to do anything," she wanted me to know as if she owed me an answer. But she was just a child I thought; she wasn't to blame. I assured her I understood. It was a good story to evoke such a reaction. She had broken the silence of women, expressed the powerlessness of children in a male dominated nuclear family. A typical situation in American culture. Where I came from women kept the power in a household.

I had been 29 when I took up karate. In a year the workouts toned my body into a hardened instrument. When I turned 30 a sense of liberation came over me. Thirty was so firmly a demarcation of adulthood that I felt suddenly free from the expectations of my youth and the obligations of my family. I had gotten a college degree (though it took me eight years to pull it together, so unimpressed was I with the choices). I had a full time job that was not a night shift and was even related to my degree—I was a paste-up artist and typesetter at the Palo Alto Medical Clinic. Having achieved the bare minimum I figured I had convinced my family to give up on me.

I lived with Stacy and Dave a gay man I had met at work. We were renting a house from my high school librarian. We called ourselves Seale House after the name of the street. It so happened that Dave, Stacy and I all had birthdays a week apart. I suggested we could celebrate together in one giant party and invite our separate groups of friends.

I had designed a flag for our gay/bi/lesbian household at a party that Dave hosted to design flags for flag day. We all liked my turquoise, pink, and purple flag so I made it room size as a backdrop for our party.

Thirty, I figured, was where youth ended and so I must now be at the pinnacle of my physical self and I was going to show off my toned karate made body. Cirque de Soleil had just had its debut thus its modern styling served as my costume inspiration. I made a bonnet from the turquoise flag material with a hot pink headband. And I wore a turquoise spandex unitard that showed off every line of my body. I topped it off wth a hot pink sweatshirt and my bicolored elf shoes. I invited lots of people, both old friends and new from many arenas of my life; it was a terrific party.

I had by then learned another vital lesson of the mind and body. After a few years with Lisa I grew tired of being so controlled by her dictating to me how I should treat her. And when an old high school friend I had had a crush on wrote to me to tell me she wanted to explore her attraction to women as she was experiencing a desperate crush on a woman colleague, I flirted with her blatantly in our correspondence over discussions of Virginia Wolf and Vita Sackville West. Finally we agreed to meet in person. She paid me a couple of weekend visits during this time and stayed with me as a houseguest. I agreed to "help" her with this exploration of her sexuality. I kept our affair from Lisa and instructed my housemates to too. Lisa knew I was attracted to her, but I lied to her with explicit details about how nothing had happened between us.

I had no idea how keeping this secret would squelch my creativity and my voice. I thought I could have my cake and eat it too as it were. Why would it matter so much if I kept this lover a secret? It wasn't my rule that I had to be faithful to just one person. Especially a woman who didn't want people to know she had a woman lover and kept our relationship from her family and friends a secret out of homophobia. So I kept my secret lover from her, thinking it wouldn't make a difference. But it did. I felt the information wanting to come out in a visceral bodily way as if I might have to throw it up. I had to steel myself against its thrust just to eat my breakfast some mornings.

I couldn't trust myself to speak freely about anything or make the spontaneous jokes that would come to me. I was in fear that I was going to give myself away if I so much as opened my mouth. And when Lisa and I were together having a perfectly lovely time watching a sunset sitting on a hillside, for instance, I would want to tell her this secret. Which would of course turn that lovely moment into a crisis. So I didn't. I waited it out. Waited until she met someone else—the man she would marry. It didn't take long.

But I vowed to myself that I wouldn't do it again. I would fight to maintain my freedom to speak. The price of not being able to do so was just too high. I vowed I would live a life centered around being able to speak freely.

Chapter 25

Take Back The Goddess

While standing in line for the Porta Potty I took in the beautiful San Francisco June day. The year was 1981. There were fifteen maybe twenty Porta Potties lined up in a bank of them on one side of the Civic Center. I was so happy to be here at the rally following our triumphant ride down Market street on our motorcycles leading the march. My black leathers marked me as a participant of the contingent down to my steel toed boots.

I looked around at my peeps. Every one of them, like me, a gay person who likely faced every day living a double life. A life of secrecy or part secrecy. A data base in our heads of all of the people in our lives who knew or did not yet know our secret identity. It was important to remember who we had come out to so as not to inadvertently step on that landmine of shock and uncomfortable silence. To come out had to be planned with carefully chosen words to entrust an individual with this information, even if we were going to do it casually. But it hadn't reached the casual stage yet. We were still in the world upturning part when "coming out" guaranteed the recipient of our news would be in shock. Then they too would keep the news a secret. So each person had to be told. One by one.

My father confronted me first. Just after my mother left him and I had come home in the aftermath from college. He announced it without preamble after dinner one evening sitting in his usual vinyl swivel chair. A tumbler of red wine in hand.

"I know you're not normal," he said, "you like girls." A foot waggle accompanied this statement. I sat dumbstruck by his words, not so much in shock, but in surprise waiting for what would come next. "Your mother. She thinks it's my fault. So you have to tell her."

"Ok" I said tentatively. I heard his logical yet emotionally nonsensical mind going over things. The implication was that she had left because I was gay and it was his fault. So I had to make it right by owning up to it so she would know it was not his fault. He also blamed the women libbers putting ideas into her head. Yes that was closer to the truth. It helped that the feminist movement was supporting women in finding their own path of fulfillment in life, and not putting up with unsatisfactory limiting husbands.

I knew I had little to do with her leaving him, but I agreed to tell her anyway. When she came to visit me at college the next month she offered me the opportunity by asking about my social life. I told her that I told men I was bisexual.

"Well that must intrigue them," she said.

"Hmmm," I said. That was not quite the reaction I was looking for, but it would do for the time being.

I was not quite ready then to declare my full identity as a lesbian. To come out as a lesbian seemed to be more radical than coming out as a gay man. Lesbians were so invisible that it was not even a conceivable concept for some. Queen Victoria is said to have declared it didn't exist, but that is just a myth. The law she signed forbid child prostitution and sex with minors and an amendment was attached to address "gross indecency" between men, but lesbians were not mentioned for fear that this would actually encourage women to investigate their sexuality.

Gay men occupied a place in literature as witty men of the theater —Oscar Wilde for instance, the last man jailed for the offense. And ballet, of course. Gay men also proliferated in the professional domestic arts as interior decorators, hair dressers, florists and wedding planners. All stereotypes shored up by enough actual gay men to be credible. Professions that had relationships with the public—mostly women. They supported women and their heterosexual mainstream lives. In that sense they were integral members of society with places in it to call home.

But who knew any lesbians? To be a lesbian was to live in a world not centered on men, quietly undetected in "Boston marriages" with other 'spinster' women, some dispensed with being women altogether, dressing and living as men, joining the army, or becoming cowboys, equally undetected in history. Once women entered the work force, lesbians were often found in blue collar jobs as electricians and bus drivers, and the armed forces, and libraries too, for the studious set, but still not highly visible to mainstream life. Later lesbians emerged as high tech workers and backstage technicians and, as soon as possible lesbian therapists.

At the time of my coming out I knew of no lesbians in history or otherwise, but I did understand that lesbians were interesting in a subversive sense of being sexual outlaws, seen mostly as a sexual fetish, but subversive to society for rejecting the world of men. Even feminists didn't want us when Betty Friedan, the president of NOW (National Organization for Women), gave us the epithet The Lavender Menace because she feared that the appearance of lesbians would allow the public to dismiss the women's movement as man hating. This simply gave rise to lesbians organizing within the movement with a great deal of humor and theatrics under the name she had given them until lesbian concerns were finally allowed to be addressed.

To occupy a lesbian identity was to jump off the grid of society, that out of necessity, required innovation. In time I would see this mindset of innovation showing up in emerging movements with lesbians supporting and promoting electric cars, tiny houses, permaculture and other aspects of reinventing how we lived. As I was coming out I dipped in and out of the ideas of the times, of a lesbian nation overthrowing the patriarchy for instance. Lesbians were buying land, mostly in rural areas, to create women only communes. This radical lesbian separatist movement paralleled the rise of the creation of women only spaces, women's bookstores, women only cafes and the historic women's building in San Francisco. Santa Cruz had a women's bookstore where I stood one day reading the latest Rita Mae Brown novel. I was beside myself with glee that lesbian characters would actually appear in a book. But I did not have extra money to buy books. And her first book, *Rubyfruit Jungle* the loosely autobiographical, spunky tomboy, coming of age story, I did not find until after I left Santa Cruz.

My mother was hoping my lesbianism was just a phase encouraged by the outrageous atmosphere of College V with its slight leaning into kinky theatrics. When I did declare a lesbian identity I told her about lesbian separatists. These were the lesbians who went out of their way to protect their spaces from male energy—coffee shops and support groups et al. One all female household I visited proudly introduced that even their dog was female. It was a heady concept, but I only stuck with it for about two weeks. It was too contrived. Here dykes were trying to expunge male energy from their lives yet they wore men's clothes.

"Because men have the power in society," one told me. The logic of this was too much for me. I was a proud member of the Transvestite Revenge Squad. I preferred to subvert society by cross dressing at social functions or alternatively dressing like a drag queen. I had no illusions that actually dressing in men's clothes was going to get me power. Society didn't work that way. Such dogmatism annoyed me. The lesbian community in Santa Cruz was in part why I kept my hair long rather than align myself with the regulation dyke haircut and flannel shirt uniform. They didn't seem to want to date me anyway so why bother.

But College V had provided me with a community that was open to sexual and gender fluidity. It was the bisexual girls after all who took me to their beds.

But once I was back in the more conservative Bay Area, the college life at Stanford felt palpably different. It was so straight and culturally white that I would joke that at Stanford even the minorities were white. Meaning they were eager to excel in a mainstream achievement oriented manner that did not allow for any real cultural diversity. After Tim and I crashed a party to compete in the best undressed competition promised on the flyer I could see that there was not an iota of kink in its DNA and we weren't even cross dressing. I missed the gender bending culture-challenging atmosphere of College V. I avoided hanging out with Stanford students at all except at the Gay People's Union.

At least we had San Francisco the gay capital of the world with the largest gay and lesbian parade in the country. And on this day that was given to us to take over the streets and the civic center we could be completely out and yet anonymous in our numbers. I soaked it up standing in the sunshine in that Porta Potty line. No one here could possibly assume I was straight and that made me feel liberated.

When I took my turn in the Porta Potty I discovered that my period had just started. I was so startled by this reminder of my female body that I felt betrayed. Here in the midst of feeling high in my androgynous butch identity amidst my peeps I was being rudely reminded that I had not escaped the biological fact of my female body. And then I was equally startled at my own surprise at this. Gone was the woman network of my youth in Thailand reminding me of these female functions. I did not have that support anymore. I reached into the deep interior pockets of my motorcycle jacket for the minimalist O.B. tampon I favored. At least tampon technology would help me defy this femaleness for the rest of the day. And again I could push away this intimacy of my female reality.

I did not give much thought to this disassociation from my bodily functions until a few years later when I became lovers with a woman 14 years my senior, with the voluptuous body of a fertility goddess who was the mother of three sons.

I met Louise through my mother, who had by then become a behaviorist specializing in autism, which was why Louise had chatted her up at a party and invited her to come to her house in Woodside. She wanted someone who could help her with her severely developmentally impaired autistic son who was nine at the time.

I happened to drop by to see my mother just as she was going to Louise's house so she had called to ask if she could bring me along. Of course Louise said yes. Louise loved meeting people. So my mother drove us into the town of Woodside and up a private road to the top of a hill. It was dark and I had no idea where we were, but the view told me we were high above the valley floor elevated and removed from life on the peninsula. Louise came out of her yellow ranch house ablaze as it was with light and welcomed us in. She offered us ice tea as we seated ourselves in her open plan living room. The glass patio doors to the pool and beam ceilings so much like the house my parents and I had lived in only somehow grander. Perhaps it was the floor to ceiling bookcase full of expensive art books that did it. Or the bright yellow and blue stuffed parrot spreading her wings on a branch atop the bookcase.

Louise, ever the hostess, made us both feel at ease, but slightly expectant of what she might ask of us. She was a big woman, at least a head taller than us, with brown hair and the bluest eyes I had ever seen. I didn't expect to be more than a witness to her friendship with my mother, but she had taken one look at me and set about to find out who I was, asking me questions about my life, my writing, what the book I was writing was about and my karate practice. She was looking for my source of power, I would realize later, when she described me as a physical perfection much like a thoroughbred horse trotting by that made her say "I want that."

I was telling her how karate was based on the horse stance which had been taught to monks to keep them awake during meditations. The leg strength required made them fit enough to fight off bandits on the way back to the monastery after shopping for provisions. And soon I was standing in front of my mum and Louise demonstrating the horse stance with its squat position as if one were straddling a horse. Louise was so impressed by the confidence of my stance and my commitment to this practice that she went down to my karate school that week and signed up for class. She also signed up for a weekend writing workshop I told her I was attending at Hidden Villa, a community ranch in the next town.

Louise had already made sure I would return just in case it was me she wanted all along. She asked me that night to join her for an afternoon of horseback riding. I had in fact been envisioning a life with horses and had told her that evening how earlier that year I had gone to the coast and rented a stubborn old nag at a ranch. I could hardly get the horse to move more than a few feet from the barn, so I just patted it and talked to it affectionately.

"One day I will have a life with horses," I thought to myself. I forget now why I wanted such a life, but as they say, be wary of what you ask for. Louise took me for a three hour ride through the hills surrounding her house. I was so sore when I got off I could hardly stand upright as Louise watched me with a slightly bemused look at my crippled attempt to walk. Later when I asked her why she had ridden me so hard that first day, she said she had wanted to wipe that self satisfied smile off my face, and force me to admit that I had had enough. I did indeed say no when she asked if I was game to gallop up the final hill before us. As charming as Louise was, she had a dominant side and enjoyed being the boss.

Louise was well practiced in a stealth-like seduction that I didn't even realize was coming when one day we were sitting in a field and I was chewing on blades of grass. She picked a grass stalk too and poked at mine playfully, but so gently it was like a caress and I felt the air electrified in this intimate little love making act. I succumbed to her charms delighted to be so expertly courted. She asked as eagerly as an innocent young girl making friends if I would come to her house again. And then again until she asked me to stay the night.

I dressed for that night in my tight Sasson jeans and a red checked cowboy shirt with snap pearl buttons. A white cowboy hat topping it all off. The cowboy hat did not impress her, but the lemon scent of my shower gel signaling my preparing myself for her as a lover did. Soon my mother suspected something.

She called me up at work when she realized where her introduction to Louise had led me.

"You seem to be gravitating toward a mother figure," she said. "Are you sure this is good for your overall development?" I nearly laughed. How like a therapist. How like having a mother who is a therapist. I may have been rendered speechless. What I wanted to say was "So, who cares? Doesn't everyone need a mother figure?" I mean whose fault was it that I might need a mother figure?

It's true, Louise was taller than me and much stronger. She dressed like a mom too, but would also stride about in a tan jumpsuit worn alternatively with flip flops or a pair of battered riding boots. Her straight brown hair cut level with her chin framed her mischievous smile. All Louise had to say to me over the phone was "sweetheart" and my heart would come undone and drop through the floor.

Louise's mothering nature brought out another side of me, one that shed the tough hard ass dyke in black leathers. One night, not long into our relationship, when she asked me to fetch her glasses from the bathroom I jumped up naked from her bed, walked across the terra-cotta tile floor to the bathroom and returned triumphant with her glasses.

"You're really sweet you know that? I'm just seeing that now," she said when I handed them to her smiling. I felt redeemed to hear her assessment. The leather suit had just been a protective shell all along. This was who I felt I really was.

My mother gave up on her intervention and the next week came to the house for dinner with all who happened to be there. Louise's best friend Clea, a tall German woman she'd been lovers with at Stanford, and her teen daughter Allegra, who'd been a friend of the boys since childhood were there, as well as a young man who rented a room in the house. It felt so companionable watching my mother join in the ordinary conversation I knew it would all be ok and I set about to move into Louise's household. Sealehouse was down one anyway since Stacy had moved to Santa Cruz. And Dave was content to move out on his own.

Life with Louise was one social event after another, her days filled with riding and meetings with friends, for she did not work, not really. She had indulged a life of leisure, stopping just long enough to get a real estate license to bring in some cash to bolster the meager funds from child support and rent money from the studio adjoining the stables.

Having prioritized a life of illicit affairs with women while she was still married to a man, she was an unabashed hedonist comfortable with her body however much weight she put on. I asked her how many women there had been, but she had never kept track.

"You didn't make notches on your belt?" I asked as one who kept meticulous records of everything.

"It fell apart," she said alluding to the belt becoming more notches than belt. No one had been safe from her ardent pursuits, from the babysitter to the hairdresser, to the Egyptian diplomat to the UN. Nearly every woman she introduced me to in her large network of friends had at one time been her lover. I enjoyed Louise's lust for life as much as these others. She had no qualms about anything. In the bedroom nothing was taboo including menstrual blood. We just laid towels down if one of us was bleeding. I made a handprint of her blood on her stomach once and lay my body on top of it. When we came apart again the blood was gone.

I was eager to hear of her experience of giving birth and her status as a woman in the equation of motherhood and as the wife of a man in her role as homemaker. A man who was bent on pursuing his entrepreneurial dreams and had insisted they leave New York against her wishes.

Sometimes I challenged how she was raising her sons in this same patriarchal paradigm. The two older boys had been away at boarding school when we met. I was her first live-in female lover following her divorce. When they came back for the summer she made an appointment with a male therapist for the purpose of breaking the news to them. She wanted to give them space to react with the support of a man. They already knew she was a lesbian, but now they faced the prospect of having to live with their mother's lover.

"She's not even white," said the eldest, who was prone to expressing aloud the biases harbored by this East coast social registry family in all its WASP glory. The middle boy, who was the social one of the family requested that we were not to reveal our status in front of his friends with any displays of affection or references to our relationship. He also requested that Louise take down all the artwork with naked women in them. This included an impressive carved head from Mexico hanging over the fireplace. It was a mask representing the sin of lust, the face red with passion, the tongue actively pursuing a tiny naked woman caught in his beard. Louise duly replaced it with a wooden fish. But she put her foot down at taking down the delicate series of framed etchings each of a nude woman standing in a creek. They had hung in her grandmother's house she told the boys implying they had nothing to do with lesbians.

I was gratified when Clea's daughter came over to hang out with the boys and immediately asked what happened to the Mexican mask. She was herself an artist and a horse whisperer. She was the cool girl the boys respected completely.

"Why has it been replaced with this boring fish?" she asked no one in particular. Louise and I held back any explanation. It was satisfying enough to have a peer of the boys themselves take them down in her own way.

The boys carried on occupying the house with their usual boy habits. They peed in the bushes on the property and sometimes in public.

This privilege outraged me; there was something so arrogant about it. Louise explained that their father had done the same and thought nothing of it. But she was also the kind of woman who wore skirts when she traveled to undeveloped countries so she could squat down in the middle of a dirt road and pee fully covered.

On hot days they would walk through the house shirtless. I had no objection to this, but I saw my opportunity to make my point. We had no neighbors to speak of since the property sat on five acres of a brush covered hilltop. So one day I too took to walking through the house shirtless. No one could make any comment at all. Indeed what could they say? My body was in top form and my breasts revealed what perfection their mother was privy to. The boys ignored me in silence. By dinner time Louise had taken my point regarding male privilege and told us we were all to wear shirts to dinner. I was satisfied that I had left my feminist mark on their upbringing.

Surrounded as I was by so many Americans with their privileged ideas I felt my lack of kin intensely as it was clear that I would never be part of anyone's family, orphaned as I was by my mixed race and sexual orientation. But I could at least birth a human who would look more like me and was raised with my sensibilities and values. I binge read back issues of *Mothering* magazine, books about child raising, homeschooling and how societies were set up to help or hinder child raising. I had conversations with my imaginary child, telling it all about how the world worked. I questioned Louise about being a mother. She was proud as a woman of her social class to be able to produce sons, but knew full well how women were kept in their place. She told me how her husband's golf club back in New York had a separate entry for women for they were forbidden to enter by the front door. I was appalled at this archaic tradition. When the feminist movement emerged Louise saw a revolution was coming that would change all this. She told her mother that things had changed; it would be different for women of her generation.

"Nothing has changed," her mother said emphatically. In time, Louise would come to agree with her. The world would not budge to center women in a way that respected and elevated her role as the creator of life. Women would in the end still be stuck with the child rearing part of the equation while men were free to follow their passions. And indeed post-divorce her husband would not put in even a day to care for their disabled child. Louise was the one who would have to manage this boy's entire life as well as his day in day out care.

The feminist books I was reading to ward off the ingrained privilege of her teenage boys introduced me to ideas of how a female centric society could be constructed. Louise, with her degree in Political Science, was as eager as I was to talk about how the world could be remade if women prioritized society. *Ms Magazine* was filled with articles discussing whether women's biology determined our social standing or if our oppression was a construct to be struck down. Should we protect women because their biology made them vulnerable or should we simply demand to be equal to men?

During this time Louise, hoping for additional information to guide her decisions, consulted a psychic. The psychic gave her a back story for her disabled son who did not have language. No words would he speak at all; just a few gestures of sign language as he ran his strange bouncy run through the house signing the word "more." The psychic told Louise a tale of his past life as a novitiate priest who died while during an initiation ceremony that involved being locked in a sarcophagus. And he had come to this life with his mental capacities diminished in order to recover from this trauma.

Intrigued by this imaginative story I made an appointment with the psychic too. She told me that I had been a man with many wives who had been somewhat abusive in his treatment of them so I had now come to this life as a lesbian in order to experience the perspective of the sex I had once dominated. This news dealt a blow to my righteous feminist anger. How could I label men as the enemy if I had once been a man who had abused women? Yet it seemed karmically fitting that I should be so mad at men in this life, and mad at the very act of psychological domination of a woman trapped in a socially submissive position.

Reincarnation theology as entertaining as it was in its storytelling and sense of justice, kept me a believer. Channeled information was of course at the mercy of interpretation by those born with these intuitive skills. Intuitives were just as easily influenced by the culture and religion they were raised in as everyone else. So it was all to be taken with a grain of salt, forgotten if it wasn't useful, expansive if it was, but more often than not it spoke to me. Humans are made of stories, created from stories and guided and motivated by stories. Far better to have a good one than none at all. Far better to have an ideology that attached no particular gender to one's soul than to cast one sex as the lesser one to be dominated and controlled for all of eternity by the other as the Christians would have it, silencing women in the process.

The irony of my past life as a man softened my stance toward men as the sole arbiter of a patriarchal system. They were after all born into the sex that was forced to uphold a system in very narrowly defined ways just to be a man, a system I had now to navigate as a woman as a karmic comeuppance.

The only way out for a woman as far as I could see was not to have children at all, and simply boycott a world that refused to help raise its children. This would, in the end be my decision, for I could see that I did not have enough support among my friends to have any help at all in raising a child. Not in the US. None of my peers were interested in collaborating with me on this project. Louise too was lukewarm about it. In the end I felt that I was no match for the cultural influences of American materialism. Any child raised in the U.S. would render even an offspring of mine a product of advertising. So I gave up on motherhood. But what of womanhood?

One day Louise came back from Robert's, the town grocery store where there was a massive bulletin board covered in flyers offering trucks for sale, boarding for horses and just about everything the town had to offer this moneyed population. Louise said she had seen a flyer for a goddess circle promising to introduce women to the pagan arts over the course of a year. She thought we should take this year long class together and called to sign us up. I was intrigued and interested. The teacher wanted to meet us first, so we drove to her house on the coast where classes would be held.

"Oh yes I see," said Pamela as she came down the outdoor stairs to greet us. A tall women with a youthful energy though her hair was prematurely gray and would eventually turn a radiant white. She was different from feminists I had known, a teacher of women's spirituality, but not apart from men and not in defiance of men just more slippery in her negotiation of the world. She would tell us there were times when we would have to stay hidden and how to know when to be visible.

She did not say as she came down the stairs why she had wanted to meet us before admitting us to her class. Maybe because we were a couple and she was not sure how the dynamics of the group would be affected if two of us were together, but we seemed to pass muster. She recommended that we not partner with each other in class so we could develop our own paths in the course.

Every month we would come to her house to perform the rituals that marked the seasons of this earth based tradition. She talked a lot about initiation rights and how young girls who had begun their periods would be celebrated by the community of women and welcomed into it with ritual and how she had offered this celebration to her own daughter. She had written a book about the medicalization of birth in American Society. How male doctors had disempowered women in the process. How witches (the original midwives) had been persecuted and burned at the stake which was why we had to know when to stay hidden.

This emphasis on women as the sacred channel of creation did much to open my mind to appreciating how powerful women were in their connection to this biological mystery of creation. How powerful the fact that we bled every month and created the womb lining anew again and again. In this context it made sense to me that women would be worshiped in pagan times as the arbiter of fertility. That society would be organized around this fertility and the power of women to create life. My 7th grade teacher had been right—women had the power to give birth which men would never be able to appropriate. Our patriarchal society's failure to honor this innate power of women was simply an insult and a denial of the divine feminine. For even if we didn't have children this denial debased our standing in society in a way that I was just beginning to understand now in my '30s.

As I came to know the divine feminine I realized how lost I had been as a lesbian with no anchor to a female power or for that matter the earth beneath my feet. And having had no emotional connection to men and no desire to follow the usual path of women seeking a man and creating a family, I had until now held myself aloof from society and from my own life. I never really felt a part of it, a part of American society and social relationships.

And as an immigrant, I felt disconnected from the land I lived on as well. I mean, what did this American history and its native history have to do with me? Emotionally I saw myself hovering far above the earth not quite committed to occupying my body enough to express any emotions. I longed to belong to something and I missed having a family that centered me as an important person. In the context of this goddess circle I could see how far away I was, hanging out in the ether as if I didn't really have a purpose here on earth. I was just an impartial witness.

Pamela taught us about the Ohlone tribe who had occupied this land where we were seated, creating the tall cliffs with a big mound of mussel shells. And she would send us outside to create ritual in the sacred forest near her house and in the waves on the beach. We went on walks to look for messages that spoke to us in what caught our attention. In the rituals we performed on this land I began to feel a sense of support from the land itself. If the divine feminine could be accessed through the land, then the land that I stood on was a loving entity communicating with me and supporting me. These thoughts did more to pull me down into myself and speak to me of my purpose than any formal education. By the end of the year-long course I felt that I was indeed a priestess initiated into the divine feminine. And I even grew to appreciate that as a woman I would bleed every month as a sign of my power. And what a truly amazing thing that was, even for a lesbian. Maybe especially for a lesbian, for we loved women and lived a world centered around women.

Chapter 26

Cover Girls

In the two years we had in the paradise of Louise's hilltop home the Berlin Wall came down and we celebrated with Clea, who was a teenager in Berlin when it went up. Then the Loma Prieta earthquake happened with just Louise and her youngest son in the house. I made my way home from work through long lines of traffic. That night we had no power so I baked potatoes in the fireplace. The next day dramatic photos covered the front page of the abbreviated San Francisco chronicle that had been put to bed the night before in the dark. I couldn't bring myself to return to work, as if life was just going to continue on as usual so I stayed home, realizing that I didn't want anything to do with any of the people in my office during this high holy occasion of the earth shaking. Louise had that sense of awe I craved for the natural world that was less and less expressed down in the flats of Silicon Valley.

At the end of the two years Louise had to sell her home to fulfill her contract with her investors—the ex lover real estate agent who had offered to help her buy her half from her ex-husband. So we set about looking for a new home and packed our books and our two cats, hers and mine, and relocated to a more compact cape cod style house by the creek in Menlo Park. Her disabled son did not come with us, for he had been dispatched to a group home in Mount Shasta. The horses we boarded at Hidden Villa.

Being in town again a stone's throw from Palo Alto I felt more connected to the community life in downtown where I was able to pick up the Palo Alto Weekly every week at a sidewalk kiosk box downtown. One day I was annoyed at an article about a lesbian couple parenting children because they had chosen to remain closeted. I wrote the Weekly a letter accusing them of perpetuating the closet by not covering the gay community that was out. A writer contacted me and asked if I knew those who were out. I pointed them towards the Gay People's Union at Stanford where she duly went, but she really wanted a couple to showcase not an entire group so after talking it over with Louise I volunteered us.

A lovely woman photographer met us at Hidden Villa where we did a photo shoot of Louise and me riding the same horse (which we never did) and then photographed us sitting together in the field after, me with my arm cosily around Louise, who had her head up against my chest. Both of us looking at the camera willingly vulnerable to its inquiring eye. This was to be the cover shot. We would be all over town as the face of an out lesbian couple in the suburbs. Before my mother could see it, I called a friend of hers who had a gay daughter and asked her to call my mother and tell her what a good thing it was I had done for the cause. I also called a writing group friend who was a member of PFLAG (Parent's and Friends of Lesbians And Gays) and was on the speaker's bureau with me. She called my mother too. This helped and kept my mother from saying anything prohibitive to me, but when she came to get her copy at my workplace and we walked to lunch downtown she made sure to keep the paper folded over our photo. I realized what a continual challenge I was to my long suffering mother. But Louise and I celebrated our public appearance by showing up at the Weekly to ask for 50 copies of "our" issue.

"Oh look it's the cover girls," said the receptionist. We told them we wanted to send copies to all our friends. We loved that we were making lesbian history together.

Louise had also discovered poetry. At first she wanted to be a ham radio operator so she could make contact with the world, but once she started writing down verse, poetry was her chosen vehicle. And since she had a nose for society's highest echelon wherever she found herself she was best friends with JoAnn Loulan a well known lesbian speaker. JoAnn had significant star power, sported a lions mane of curly hair and could speak extemporaneously, wowing the crowd with jokes and insights. Her book on lesbian sex sold more copies than any lesbian book, people would whisper as she walked by at a lesbian event. She spoke her mind and was always trying out new ideas. She introduced Louise and then me to the lesbian Cliterati as one of the writer's wittily called them. These were lesbian therapists, a daughter of a Republican Bush cabinet member, a writer of juvi fiction who had been lovers with Louise, and her midwife girlfriend. Contact with this esteemed group gave us exposure to the makers of lesbian culture on the West Coast.

When Karla Jay, an early lesbian activist out of New York, sent out a query for submissions for her lesbian anthology project we both submitted pieces. Louise with a poem about being a mother of a disabled child while I offered two short pieces, a playful one about being a lesbian vampire seducing curious straight women and another about my experiences as the guest columnist at the Palo Alto Weekly. Our short works were interspersed with longer articles that became the book *Dyke Life: From Growing Up to Growing Old: A Celebration of The Lesbian Experience*. Karla, who had been a long time activist of the Stonewall era, had a knack for community organizing and she scheduled several fun group book readings.

As my writing tasks made me more of a public figure my thoughts became more focused on my identity and Louise felt neglected. We managed to make the house more lively by inviting a very butch Canadian lesbian to live with us; her short haircut shorter than I'd seen in some time. Laurie had recently been lovers with JoAnn. JoAnn's very femme persona with her mane of curly blond hair paired up with the Laurie in a classic butch femme coupling that JoAnn had decided to re-introduce one day from the podium. She came up with a butch femme rating scale that her audience could participate in. A volunteer was summoned to the stage and JoAnn would call out the numbers from one to ten with ten being the most butch. The audience would applaud when she called the number they thought most fit the volunteer on this butch/femme scale. Nobody quibbled with this ranking game; we all knew what she was talking about and enjoyed the process.

For decades the butch lesbian had been suppressed in favor of androgynous presentations promoted by feminists. The Butch Femme model was considered a throw back to the role playing of the 1950s and a regressive heterosexual format. Their relationship didn't last, but butch lesbians were liberated again in ever more dapper outfits, visible proof of this cross dressing desire of lesbians. And though I still would not cut my hair, that year I rented a tuxedo to attend the Bay Area Career Women's holiday party with Louise. Laurie, and the rest of JoAnn's entourage were all couples who seemed to fit the butch femme paradigm, but not too obviously. The career women of this club were largely closeted professionals, which was why their name did not contain the word lesbian.

Laurie was closer in age to me and brought with her a more urban hip energy to the household and she was definitely out. Her parents had been working class socialists who supported her coming out, which gave her a strong sense of herself that she used to advance the cause of lesbian visibility. She would, for instance, make my mother acknowledge her by talking to her about me as if I were family. My mother had to overcome how uncomfortable she was with such a butch presentation just to be polite and this delighted Laurie. Her anecdotes about working in a women's shelter and her current work with queer youth taught me a more political way of being in the world as a role model and advocate. At about this time I started a gay straight alliance at work with a co-worker who was also out—a lesbian nurse who goaded me into using the interoffice mail to deliver our flyer with interesting repercussions. HR contacted my boss, wanting to know if this flyer should be treated as official clinic policy. It wasn't; we were just being subversive.

It was at one of our mixer events that Louise met her next lover, then a med student doing her internship at Stanford; we incorporated her into a polyamory arrangement Under our open relationship agreement Louise and I agreed to keep each other appraised of our extra curricular activities. Louise had already had another lover within our relationship and I too had one other with a lovely artist friend from the photo department at work. The presence of these other women in our lives made us feel we lived in an abundance of love emblematic of our bonds as a community of women. Louise's lover at one time joining us in our bed, but that was just too much flying sweat for me and I told them to go ahead and meet on their own.

I was enamored of the potential of love to connect everyone in the community in a sort of lesbian style six degrees of separation. It was part of the lesbian zeitgeist to regard monogamy as a patriarchal concept. It also exemplified the tight bonds of women to care for each other through changes in relationship status from primary partner to best friend and confidant. This fluidity of roles was a common phenomena in the lesbian community so often small in the underground days of being closeted. Even at College V I saw a photo exhibit showing pictures of couples to highlight who had been lovers with whom over time in her lesbian circle. It was such a factor of lesbian life that we all laughed in recognition when the television series *The L Word* used the visually witty white board chart full of arrows connecting names in a wild circle of contact tracing that would symbolize the ecology of lesbian life. Still there would always be lesbian drama that women, wielding a portfolio of communication skills, could readily dish out to process their feelings of betrayal when things went south.

Louise and her new lover broke our rules of transparency. The lover didn't want me to know of their relationship in case I spilled the beans to her partner who was the same lesbian nurse I had collaborated with at work on the gay straight alliance. Her relationship with the nurse had been constructed following the conventional marriage model of exclusivity and coupling and included dual ownership of property. This sounded so stultifying to us that we wanted to liberate her from such a loveless and restrictive marriage.

Laurie moved out, having found herself another girlfriend and a place closer to the action in San Francisco, so we had the spare bedroom free just as the new lover started to come over for dinner. When Louise proposed that this new woman move in with us I didn't know they were lovers, but I could feel the erotic energy on an unconscious level and took it to mean that she was available to either of us. The incoming lover played along and allowed me to befriend her as a potential love interest even going out with me separately. In innocence and trust I walked into this duplicity as the three of us engaged in conversations of how we were creating an inclusive extended family that would enrich us all. After so many years in her dead end relationship, the new lover was so enthralled with having even a partial share of Louise that she was happy to consider this arrangement. She knew Louise still loved me as family and wasn't intending to leave me. She consoled herself that she had Louise in their private love trysts. I didn't even suspect their hidden affair. My blind spot was so huge I was the last to know in our community which was a lesson in itself. The nurse immediately suspected after discovering the telltale clue of finding a fox tail sticker in her partner's underwear after Louise and her partner had gone riding together.

As time went on the tension of their secrecy drove Louise to seek advice from a psychic who told her that if she kept this secret it would drive apart her relationship with me, and wrap her heart in increasing strands of darkness until she couldn't love either of us. This warning was enough for Louise to announce to her lover that she was going to tell me the truth that very night. The lover fearful of an emotional blow out wanted to flee, get in her car and drive to Nevada, but she didn't and we sat in the living room and heard Louise's revelation.

The truth struck me not as a betrayal so much, but as a solution to our two separate relationships with this woman whom I was now prepared to love. We already had something of a bond for she spoke Thai having lived as a Peace Corp volunteer in Northern Thailand. I was thankful that Louise had decided to come clean for we could then consummate our threesome which we proceeded to do that night in a celebratory mood in Louise's queen size bed.

I would be alright about the betrayal I thought, if I could just repair the false narrative with the details of the true one. Being as meticulous as

I was about recording events and conversation I set about to reconstruct the truth. Louise revealed to me all the assignations they had had—in a field on a horse back ride, at a motel, etc. This process we did not share with the lover for it made her uncomfortable exposing her guilt and her privacy; she wanted to put the past behind her as quickly as possible. When I was done reconstructing the sequence of events we were happy for a time and even went on vacation together to Thailand and that Northern village of her youth.

But one afternoon I came home from work to have lunch and heard them in the throes of passion in one of the bedrooms upstairs; the one we didn't all share. I paused for several minutes wondering if I should announce myself. Surely they had heard me come in. And I had a right to be part of their coupling didn't I? I climbed the stairs saying something like "hey there" in a suggestive voice to announce my presence. But this turned out to be the worse thing I could do, for I had caught them "in flagrante", as they say, busting them on their continued secrecy. Before my loud footsteps made it to the landing, the door to the bedroom was slammed shut with such force the meaning of it could not be more clear. Stay the fuck out. I beat a hasty retreat and sat in the living room until Louise came out and explained how vulnerable a moment I had interrupted.

This intrusion on my part would set fire to our Camelot. My discovery made it clear that they were carrying on a reality that didn't include me—a separate reality that had a narrative arc of its own in conflict with our vision of a lover's community. We continued to eat dinner together, but could no longer speak freely to each other. And I was for months consumed with regret at having walked in on them. I woke up regularly at 4 a.m. haunted by my regret. Every meeting between me and the lover was fraught with unresolved tension driving me into hyper vigilance for every shift in the mood of the household.

Ours was now so complicated a situation that the therapist we sought out to work through it all charged us extra. At the first session she pointed out that since the lover was now the primary sex partner it would make the most sense if she slept in Louise's bed. So I switched with her and moved into the spare bedroom. I would still be a member of the family, but not the primary partner. I accepted my demotion as the sacrifice I would make to regain harmony and secure my place in the household. Their eroticism they inadvertently shared with me through the wall between us and I greedily made use of it for my own pleasure.

Why I didn't move out then was a question I refused to consider. Had I not been imprinted by the polygamy of my Thai family? The fascinating yet common place reality of my grandfather's two wives sitting down to dinner together every night discussing the household schedule long after he had died. Having family was better than no family at all.

I grasped at the one thing left to me—the telling of our story. I would save myself with poetry. Poetry allowed for metaphor to stand in for factual detail, and would contain the new narrative I had to write of what had befallen our vision. Louise saw it as a sign that I was on my way to healing so encouraged and even helped me with some of the stanzas reporting to her lover that it was all good. I would soon be over my grief and arrive at acceptance.

Nine poems later I was satisfied I had my story safely contained. I typeset it at work using my desktop publishing skills to create a chapbook (a poet's booklet) with a cover that sported a Celtic design of three horses' heads nose to neck in a circle. I made some 50 copies on the office copy machine, borrowing the booklet stapler from the printshop to put them together. And I mailed them out to all of our friends. Some wrote me back their thoughts. The writing had repaired my mind, wrecked as it was by the shredded narrative of falsehoods. Sharing it had made me whole again.

When Louise admitted that it was humiliating for her to be so exposed I was surprised. She had always lived her life so shamelessly thumbing her nose at convention as she shared her charms liberally with all who attracted her eye. We loved her for it as if it were her profession, her artistic expression. But seen through my poems as a story of a vision of community attempted and lost, it became something else. It gave me a moment's pause that I had wielded such power as a writer.

"At least I didn't send one to your mother," I told her referencing how her ex husband had complained to her mother about all the women Louise had affairs with that somehow justified his affair ending the marriage. I still felt betrayed enough to think publishing my poems for public consumption was a fitting karmic retribution—my bid to have the last say.

The little chapbook with its unassuming title "Nine poems for three" sat on my friend Stacy's coffee table and attracted the attention of another writer who contacted me to ask if some of the poems could be included in an anthology she was editing on the topic of lesbian polyamory for the *Journal of Lesbian Studies*. Mine would be the one failed trio relationship. I gave her six from the original nine and wrote a new erotic one for the lesbian only audience. In this context the poems became a part of lesbian cultural history, a signpost of how lesbians had tried to remake the world by stepping off the couple centric grid of traditional coupling in the West. The very couple centric pairing that had torn me away from my extended Thai family and detonated the richness of family relationships I had known as a child in that world and which formed my entire community.

Later in a gay card shop on Market street I laughed out loud when I saw a vintage style card of a 50's family dinner with the fake caption that summed it all up. "One nuclear family can ruin your whole life". So despite my demotion to second wife status, I stuck it out and we moved on. The poems and the story they contained were never mentioned again.

We continued to live together as a family and planned a birthday party for Louise's 50th birthday to which all our friends came dressed in their finest. I knew that the lover, who was tall and a lot more butch than me both in personality and in bed, would make her debonair appearance in a tuxedo towering over me in both rank and stature. I stole the show by falling back on an outfit from my College V days, a classic little black dress; a vintage black brocade sheath with spaghetti straps and a bolero jacket. I accessorized it with a tiny hat with a veil. My patent leather pumps and sheer black stockings completing the outfit. Everyone who came in the door gushed over my transformation into the femme fatal persona they didn't know was in me or had long forgotten was me.

The house filled with women—all friends of mine or of Louise's. Our teacher, Pamela, came and led us in a ceremony to celebrate Louise's milestone birthday. She had us stand in a circle and each say something to commemorate our relationship with Louise.

"Thank-you for the adventure of our lives together," I said. Afterwards I asked Stacy if it sounded like I was speaking of our relationship as if it were over. "Yes" she said with such finality that I felt like I had publicly announced it.

The lover, who was never very imaginative about expressing herself let alone making public statements stuck to a simple "I love you."

With the support of my friends and some champagne I got through this turning point and could even celebrate this commemoration of our lives together. Then it was time for cake. We had had two cakes made. The lover and I each carrying one into the living room to Louise. We both knelt before her to show the message inscribed around the perimeter of the cakes. On one were the words "Having her cake" and on the other "And Eating It Too." In the middle were the numbers "5" and "0" plus the usual candles for her to blow out. Having organized all this we had managed to be a family after all.

Soon enough I found another girlfriend I could bring into the house freely and develop my own private love relationship with her. This alleviated the tension considerably though it did not improve my relationship with the lover who treated me like a least favorite sibling; we moved around the house cordially enough, but with little to say to each other.

It was not until I lost my job, that Louise, fearing that I would become permanently dependent on her, ended our relationship. Standing in the door of my tiny writing room in the library she asked me to find another place to live. I shed a single tear at this request turning my face away from her to swallow my pride and pain. Somehow living life one day at a time as we had done had gone on so long that I had been lulled into the sense that such an arrangement would continue indefinitely. But the writing had been on the wall for a long time now and I told Louise I would start looking right away. I didn't have much to pack just a bicycle, my clothes, ten boxes of books, a few photo albums, my journals and the manuscript of my book. I threw in a copy of the cover story of us in the Weekly as a souvenir, and swiftly moved out in one afternoon with the help of my new girlfriend while Louise and the lover were out riding.

PART III. OFF GRID LIVING

Chapter 27

The Low Tech Road

"But a tampon doesn't take up very much space in a landfill," said my housemate at the kitchen sink watching me mix up red dye for my art project. To demonstrate my departure from the tampon, I was making a tampon lei and was mixing up red dye in a bowl so I could show it was a "blood" saturated tampon lei. The lei took an entire box of O.B.s (which had no applicator and was thus my minimalist brand of choice). I dyed just the tips, leaving the tops and the strings clean so people would know this was art and not actual used tampons. My housemate was trying to get to the bottom of my rationale for wanting to use an alternative.

I had used a sea sponge for several years. Inserted into the vagina the sponge worked quite well. Squeezing out the little sponge in the sink did not gross me out. I was visually intrigued by all that blood, watching it wash away down the white porcelain bowl under the force of water from the bathroom faucet. I wanted to express this visceral-ness somehow. And so had embarked on an art project which my techie housemate was now observing as he tried to understand my motives. I appreciated his willingness to discuss the subject. He was a well intentioned young man and a software engineer at Motorola. He was the best paid of all of us in this communal living household in the mid '90s. Out of respect for his scientific mind and his appetite for innovation, I searched my mind for my underlying reason for wanting to cut my ties to the tampon industry, or should I say cut the string—that skinny wet reminder of my dependence on these all too necessary feminine hygiene products.

My mother had been a solid tampon woman, fully appreciating how it liberated women from the bulky pad. And I was just as eager to graduate to the tampon right away for they were so small they could be kept discreetly in a purse or backpack. No other option was considered though my mother had been required to discuss an alternative product at length for her job. In the '70s while working for an advertising firm she conducted focus groups to address the marketability of new products mostly, food products — pizzas and colas that would show up in our fridge. She did not, as far as I know, bring home a feminine hygiene product under study, so much did it disgust her. It was a rubber cup that would catch the menstrual blood which would then be disposed blood and all. The women in her focus groups all found this idea disgusting. I listened as she told this story for the entertainment of her women friends. She concluded that it was a product only a man would invent and her friends laughed in agreement. (Though decades later a woman would develop the Diva cup from silicon rubber that was marketed as a reusable cup.) I was too embarrassed as a 15 year old teen to join in the laughter my mother prompted. I agreed with the neatness and convenience of the tampon. The idea that other products were constantly being tried did keep my mind open that a better way might eventually be offered.

In an article in *Ms Magazine* I read about women of other times sitting on little tufts of moss in retreat together leaving their men and children to fend for themselves. This was an intriguing idea, especially the retreat part. The giving back to nature of one's own blood was also a nice touch that spoke of a very intimate relationship with the earth. It was also in *Ms Magazine* that I learned that a sea sponge could be pressed into service and used instead of a tampon. I immediately pursued this idea for they were easy to find and cheap. And being natural gave me a connection to nature reminiscent of a bit of moss. It freed me from a dependency on the modern world, reminding me once a month that I was forced to enter a store to buy a product I couldn't live without. Being free of such an industrialized product felt liberating.

Yes my roommate was right, saving space in a landfill was hardly justification for giving up such a product of modern convenience. In the mind of an engineer it would seem ridiculous. I could have talked about the embodied energy and resources that went into the making of the tampon, but we hadn't yet dialed energy use into the eco-equation and that too would seem insignificant. And as far as filling up the landfill it was construction debris that was the biggest culprit followed by packaging from the sale of consumer products not dirty diapers which came up so frequently in conversation. Women always seemed to be the first to blame themselves for something.

Standing in the kitchen of our rented house in Portola Valley I looked out the window into the garden which boasted a hot tub the housemates had pooled money together to buy. In the opposite corner was a compost pile where I had dug up worms for my first worm bin. The view from the deck of this rambling California ranch house, surrounded by pine trees made me feel like I was living in the woods.

"It's really more of a spiritual thing," I explained glancing up at him. I could see this didn't explain it at all so I took another tact.

"For instance, I think how if I were marooned on a desert island and were to go swimming I might get eaten by a shark just because there were no tampons available." Later I would learn that much more blood would have to flow to attract a shark, but the scenario would suffice. Men could identify with this need for independence—the self-sufficient cabin in the woods and all. My housemate gave a nod of partial understanding, got his glass of water and went back to his room at the other end of the house.

I hadn't lived in this house long. After my life with Louise ended I had returned to group housing as my only affordable option. The room I found to live in wasn't even a room. The sprawling California Ranch house had six small rooms, but mine was a makeshift room. It had been created to keep the rent low by allowing for one more person to occupy the house. An engineering student had put it together by making a wall the usual way from 2 x 4 studs covered with drywall. This structure was then moved into position and clamped to the exposed beams of the roof. Exposed beams were the style in these ranch houses. The makeshift wall provided privacy but wasn't pretty—the studs were exposed on the inside. When I came to live in it I was told by the men in the house that I was required to take the room apart and live elsewhere when the landlord came to visit because they hadn't had permission to build it. They would help me they said. I could see it would be a major production to coordinate this room disappearance, but I agreed to it because I had been searching for months and this was the only room in my price range in a shared housing that was willing to live with someone over thirty. Young people wanted to live with people their own age. In this house the occupants were closer to my age.

The sheet rock made the disappearing act cumbersome. So I took it upon myself to improve on this design drawing on my experiences from my summers at the children's theatre. Remembering how the sets were created with canvas flats I decided to replace the sheet rock with fabric I found on sale — a bolt of ironing board material. I was pleased with what a chic wall covering the silver covering would make, slightly futuristic like a 1950s sci-fi set. I sewed the widths of fabric together until it was big enough and carefully stretched the fabric across the 2 x 4's and stapling it to the wood. Then I painted sheets of masonite white and screwed them to the inside of the wall; this made the room look normal once you were inside it. For a door I hung panels of curtain fabric, one on each side of the 4" thick wall giving the illusion of a door flush to the wall. Once inside my cosy room, the huge plate glass window looking out at the hot tub in the side yard made it seem larger than the 9' wide by 12' long space. At the far end was a floor to ceiling bookcase which I used for storage. My homemade bed platform Tim had built at College V fit nicely against the opposite wall of the narrow room. Tim had given me the bed when he moved into an RV because he wanted to own something rather than rent, and drive to ski resorts when he became the downhill racer he dreamed of being. I heated my fabricated room with a plug-in space heater I kept under the bed so it was the bed that got hot first. The landlord came to visit only once and my modifications made it much easier to disappear the room into the basement. I stayed in a vacant room a roommate had just vacated.

The rent was so low at this Portola Valley house I did not feel any urgency to get another full time job. I could freelance; free myself from a full time job altogether and maintain my career as an artist.

I did not want to be a part of the tech industry. I wished to avoid anything to do with tech. I had an aversion to computers and programming. In my last years of high school my father, fearing obsolescence as an electrical engineer, built his own computer from Heathkit, the electronics kit maker that taught Steve Jobs how to think in terms of components. It took my dad a year to build this homely computer working a few hours every night after dinner. He was so proud of it he offered to build another one for my aunt to use for inventory at the venetian blind factory in Bangkok. My aunt would pay my airfare to deliver it and teach her staff how to use it. This I did, but when I sat down with the two women who were so eager to learn from their teenage teacher I couldn't get past the first blinking green prompt. My father had shown me how to log on, but sometimes it would work and sometimes not. If it didn't work he would take over and fix it, not explaining to me what the problem was. I knew there would be a chance I would fail given this experience, but I wanted to go to Thailand so said nothing. And sure enough what I was supposed to enter didn't work. I was so humiliated I started to have a meltdown banging on the keys, but the ladies talked me down gently assuring me it was alright. My father hadn't bothered to test my knowledge either. Despite his brilliance or maybe because of it, he had no clue how to be a teacher, how to explain things. But the computer was delivered at least and later my uncle, a civil engineer, got it going.

I was reintroduced to the green screen in college on a field trip to a printing company and though I wasn't required to learn to use this typesetting machine, what it was doing made sense to me. In lettering class we would work for hours painstakingly drawing and inking words such as one might see on a t-shirt. It was part of the allure of lettering to perfect such hand skills much like a Japanese calligrapher and requiring the same zen like calm, not that I wanted to spend the rest of my life doing such work. I wanted to be a graphic designer coming up with snappy ideas. I knew though that the entry level jobs would be in paste-up. Computer generated type dispensed on photo sensitive paper and affixed to the paste up board with a sticky wax spread on the back.

Paste-up artist was indeed my first job out of college. I used an Exacto knife to slice these sheets up and position the pieces. The inevitable corrections required cutting out the typo, removing it and mortising in the correction. Such knife skills were so important to our work that my then girlfriend Rachel, who also had a paste up job, made herself a costume fabricating the blade from stiff silver paper so she could go to the company Halloween party as an Exacto knife. The cylinder of the blade being big enough to fit on her head. Such was the level of creativity displayed by the armies of paste-up artists in the ranks, madly pressing deadlines to put newspapers to bed.

When I got a job as a typesetter at the Palo Alto Medical Foundation I accepted the training needed to sit at the desk size *Varytyper* machine and program what fonts and size I wanted the text to be. The green screen became my friend. I and anyone who fancied themselves a writer wanted to get their hands on a computer with a word processing program as soon as possible.

I had thought I wanted to create ads for Levis because they evoked so much of the American West. In one TV ad a woman dressed like a cowboy lounged across the front seat of a wagon evoking James Dean, as she called out "Travis" to an old house on the horizon. Very like the movie *Giant,* very sexy and butch. We never find out who is this Travis.

As part of my degree program we went to visit the Levi headquarters in Levi's plaza in San Francisco. There it became clear to me that their goal wasn't to preserve the history of the American West as they had done with their classic 501's. Their expansion into fashion became all about selling the Levis brand. And they worked way too hard at such a shallow task.

"If you're not completely exhausted at the end of every day," the art director told us, "you're not doing your job." Really? Why would anyone think that was a good model of how to live?

I loved creating stories, but TV ads didn't go far enough. When I found a letter my mother had kept from an acquaintance describing their stay in Thailand, the awe and wonder that were expressed showed me the appetite Westerners had for the exotic. I knew so much that this American traveler could only wonder at; it showed me how much I could reveal that might be puzzling to a visitor. While the weight of my cross cultural perspective demanded to be explained. I was tired of explaining myself. I decided to write a book. I figured I could whip this book out in a couple of months.

A month later I only had two chapters. I had too many questions about how to write such a book so I enrolled in a memoir writing class at Foothill. I got my first computer. My father helped me shop for it. He was pleased that I was writing down the family stories and was happy to encourage my writing with this new word processing tool.

Typesetting meanwhile underwent a sea change with the desktop computer. I learned Pagemaker and weathered the transition, glad to be rid of the photo chemicals required by the old machine now replaced by a laser printer. But no longer were my knife skills required and without the whip of the Exacto knife and the threat of having to mortise in corrections, I stopped caring and looked for other things that needed fixing.

I was tired of the phone being buried under piles of paper so I redesigned the desk the carpenter shop had built from 3/4" ply. I brought in my circular saw to cut it up myself because, as I told my boss, it would take me too long to explain what I wanted and then they would tell me it couldn't be done. All I had to do was slice a piece off the desk the width of the telephone, slice the corresponding side of the desk and invert that corner so the desk dropped down to hold the phone and the stapler and pen holder. Tim came by to help me carry the desk outside so I could do the deed without covering the office with sawdust. I was pleased with the result. Changing my built environment had improved my mood. At least now I could find the phone.

But my slacker attitude and my typos caught up with me, and I was fired for "incompetence." I was 36. Ten years I was at this job and only now had they figured out I was incompetent? It was clearly an excuse. This was when Louise decided to ask me to leave. My cat got run over while I was out looking for another place to live. In my grief for both a comfortable life and cat I thought to leave the Bay Area and move to Hawaii.

"When are you coming?" asked the friend calling me at work on that very phone I had designed the desk around. She owned a flower farm in Kuai where I could wield a different kind of knife, cutting flowers for her online flower shipping company, the first online business in the state of Hawaii. But I could't leave. I had already found a new girlfriend.

Catherine was introduced to me by the secretary down the hall from me. They knew each other from dance class. Gayle had told me about Catherine when she came out to her as bi and Gayle asked me if I thought bisexuality was actually possible. I patiently explained that I had known many bisexual people and thought sexual preference was more fluid than not. Gayle had told Catherine about me too.

One afternoon I spotted a woman waiting in the lobby sporting a black leather bomber jacket. As I looked her over wondering who was this attractive woman she answered my questioning gaze and told me she was a friend of Gayle's. She was just waiting for Gayle to finish work so they could go to coffee.

"Hmmm," I said, "you don't see many black leather jackets in these parts." Then I walked back to my office. Catherine later said I was speaking to her in gay code. A few minutes later Gayle came to my office and asked me if I would like to join them. On the walk to downtown we were flirting so briskly Gayle was completely lost in the gay references and movie lines.

"Come with me to the Casbah" I said as we approached our destination, stooping to the most obvious of pick-up lines. I was so buzzed with the electricity of meeting a woman my age who was so immersed in queer culture that she had chosen to identify herself as bisexual, I didn't care how cheesy it sounded.

I learned she had just finished a documentary film about the bisexual community (which interviewed leaders of the movement including Lani Ka'ahumanu). By the time her film *Queers Among Queers* played at Frameline the San Francisco gay film festival, we were dating. She was the girlfriend who entered my life just as I was suffering through the ending of my trio with Louise. Bring me a new girlfriend I had said to the universe from the depths of my pain; "someone beautiful and not too young." Catherine was indeed beautiful, with a head of blond hair falling in thick waves past her shoulders like a 1940s movie star. She was my same age and size. I was struck by the irony of her being just a month younger. Not too young I had said in my request. Did that mean I too was not too young now?

So, having been granted my wish, I had stayed in California. I collected unemployment and hired myself out as a bookkeeper, graphic artist, carpenter and professional organizer. It was my flower farm friend who had shown me an article about professional organizers that introduced me to this freelance line of work that would bring me back to a hands on work that used both my design skills and my hand skills. Catherine got me a part time job, one that would tide me over as I built up my organizing clientele. It was a job she had done as a videographer that required the use of video cameras in a studio like setting. To train for the job I had, at her suggestion, enrolled in a television broadcasting class at Foothill College. It was in fact for the TV class that I had decided to use my tampon lei as a prop.

A Stanford student in the class had invited me to appear as a guest on his TV show, to be broadcast over the student cable channel. My host aspired to be a late night TV show host and was devoting his expensive education to becoming a comedy writer. (Stanford didn't offer a TV production course which was why he had come to the Foothill class.) I recognized an opportunity to push forth my tampon free agenda and my host agreed to the skit. Catherine came to the set as my assistant.

A lei of course would naturally be worn with a grass skirt. Capitalizing on my not quite identifiable Pacific Rim beauty to appropriate nearly anyone's cultural heritage that I might be mistaken for, I borrowed whatever might serve my interest. This being 1995 we were not "woke" yet to calling out the concept of cultural appropriation. So I stripped to just bikini bottoms donning the grass skirt and the lei to cover my breasts. I had devised to portray myself, with tongue firmly in cheek, as a primitive semi-indigenous person who might after all have something to offer the modern world with my use of a sea sponge. My English accent would, I knew, add an additional layer of irony. An indigenous person of color who had been internationally educated was still unexpected in American culture, less so in British culture. I had seen this point played for laughs in a Michael Cain movie involving a tribal chief in deepest Africa.

It further amused me that my host, a closeted gay man, would have to pretend to appear as though he had a working knowledge of a woman on her period. Thus we managed to ad lib our way through the skit and had quite the rapport over the part about wanting to be rid of the wet string between our legs.

The show was sophomoric in the extreme and despite Catherine's warning advice, no one had bothered to do a sound check to discover the annoying buzz on the soundtrack from all the crossed cables on the floor, so it never aired. Still, I was satisfied that I had made the most of this particular adventure to undermine the corporate monopoly of our daily lives even if only the cast and crew and my new girlfriend witnessed it. I relished my anti tech use of a nature made sea sponge inside my person. It was so quietly subversive that it kept my spirits up just to be able to practice such an idiosyncratic habit so far from the sterile world of tech.

While everyone else was chasing the latest innovation of the day— the flip phone my housemate was working on at Motorola due out the following year, I was quietly taking a low tech road.

My relationship with Louise had lasted five years. Gone were the horses, the intrusion of teenage boys and the values of a high society debutante of the American upper class. My new life would return me to the movies Catherine and I both loved and to dance performances Catherine introduced me to. So much did we share of cultural history and gay culture as age mates that our calendars were filled with events. Soon she asked me to move in with her to a house with a garden and a cat which I would call home for two decades.

Chapter 28

Woman Grows Bigger Brain

My new videographer gig required that I sit behind a two way mirror to observe a support group of women with metastatic breast cancer. I would be using two remote controlled cameras that could be moved to capture whomever was speaking in the group. The recordings I made of these groups would then be analyzed as part of a study being run by the psych department at Stanford; ostensibly to prove that support groups extended the lives of metastatic breast cancer patients, but also to study and categorize their expressions.

Catherine had been the videographer for the group for two and a half years. She had been moved by the stories of these women whose diagnosis brought them up against impending death. Death had been an early visitor in her young life as six of her gay friends had died of AIDS. But she had to get a full time job post divorce so she could keep her house, and she wanted to hand over this task to someone she trusted so she nominated me. I too would in turn be touched by the messages imparted by these women. I would also find out more about myself. I soon realized that my attitude towards death was quite different from those who stepped into the observation room with me. Therapists, medical students and journalists would express pity and sadness about these women's fate, condemned as they were to an early death.

"You did know this is a metastatic breast cancer group?" I wanted to ask them. The diagnosis meant facing an early death. But it was the idea that they were faced with death at all that was prompting the reactions of these observers. Several of the women had died during the course of the study. But I wasn't taken by the tragedy of it. After all I didn't know these women. I was more exhilarated by the idea of what facing one's death might prompt these women to reveal or do in the face of death.

One woman whose death was indeed imminent made sure she looked her best and dressed up for each meeting. She earnestly kept up a good front as if it were her job. Her teenage daughter said it confused her how her mother looked so good. I also recorded the families support group so I could see she hadn't been prepared for her death and was mad about it. Another woman played on the tragedy of her own story and talked about how she didn't want to plant her tulip bulbs in the fall in case she wouldn't be there to see them come up. She said the same thing the next year until I just wanted to say plant the damn bulbs already.

Another much younger woman had a husband who was already picking out his next wife and wanted her opinion. This story so infuriated me I wanted to run him over with my car, but my attitudes towards death remained equanimous. I thought this might be rooted in my Buddhist upbringing and the sense of acceptance that all life was suffering. Not to suffer was therefore a subversive act. If you were not suffering then that was reason to celebrate. This was how people seemed to feel in Thailand. The word "sanuk" which roughly translates to fun implied a whole cultural quest for celebration and group enjoyment. In American society nobody wanted to talk about death. Though this didn't necessarily mean that they valued life more.

At a staff lunch I tried to express this acceptance of death being due to my Thai upbringing and a co-worker asked me if it was because the Thais placed less value on life. I was dumbstruck by this statement that Asian people didn't value life, so stereotypical was it. So old fashion a judgment of Asian people. How was it possible to think that a human of any race didn't value life. I looked around to see if others at the lunch table would come to my defense. No one did, not even the therapists. It was going to be up to me to defend myself.

"No," I said, "we just don't take so much responsibility for death." My words felt inadequate. I was trying to be diplomatic. Americans seemed to operate as if death was a failure of will, something that needed to be fixed with medical intervention or a motivational training towards a goal to live for. The therapists talked about how one of the women had given up and hadn't made it to her daughter's graduation, as though in dying she had failed. What about her suffering? I asked myself.

I spoke no more of my feelings around death. Nor did I trust myself to work with clients facing death, either their own or of a loved one. How could I explain that I did not possess any of the expected reactions towards death? That I couldn't get into the tragedy of it. That I was in fact excited by the prospect of death pulling away the veil of societal obligations and personal pretense.

One week a much loved woman of the women's group summoned the group to her bedside, as the end was near and she had been unable to make it to the group for some weeks. She wanted to say goodbye. I was invited along to film the group with a camera on a tripod. I could hardly contain my excitement at the privilege of being there. Luckily no one paid me any attention. One of the woman asked their dying comrade if she had any final insights to offer the group.

"I didn't do the work" she said and smiled at the irony of the lateness of this realization.

What did this mean I asked Catherine. She told me it meant she felt she hadn't done the work to prepare herself for death. To look at her feelings about death and know herself. The therapists talked about how one person or another was avoiding doing the work, the work of arriving at your death bed with no regrets. Or as the Tibetan Buddhists would say "remember dying" as a prompt to do what you needed to do with your life. The dying woman had done the work, Catherine added; she just set very high standards for herself. She was an accomplished woman, and she had been a leader in the group. A common refrain of the women was that they needed to take the time to know who they were and not just what was expected of them. To even know what they wanted to do with the time they had left.

Outside of the psych lab, the stories of overnight wealth in Silicon Valley from tech companies going public permeated the air. All anybody could talk about was what company was hot. Young people entering the work force expected to walk away with their first million when they cashed in their stock options. It was hard not to feel I was getting left behind and should at least try to get a job in a tech company. But I had tasted freedom from full-time work and I wanted to find out how far I could make it on my own.

A freelance writer I had met while working as a typesetter told me he had figured out what he had to make per week in order to pay his bills, the idea being to stay free by keeping your overhead low. I thought this was a good rule of thumb. To work just enough to get by. That way I could spend my time writing and pursuing my own interests. The counter culture had been buried by the rising tech gold rush, but the message the dying women imparted confirmed so profoundly the search for a meaningful existence over pursuing conventional expectations that I felt I was on the right path.

I decided to grow a bigger brain. Based on recent studies at the time proclaiming that adults could indeed continue to grow their brains I saw no reason why I could not improve on my own brain capacity at the age of 36.

"I figure I can grow a big enough brain to become a doctor," I told a therapist at the Psych lab on our way to a nearby eatery for an end of term staff lunch.

"By that time you'll realize you don't want to be a doctor," she said. I smiled. It was true I didn't really want to be a doctor of any sort. A PhD was just a marker in the achievement driven metrics of my schooling. I had wanted to catch up with my illustrious peers in high school who were forever outshining me with achievements so proudly announced in every alumni bulletin. I wouldn't have to pursue these conventional achievements. I would set up my own.

I wanted to continue to grow my brain for I did not feel I had enough answers to satisfy my own questions. How did the world work? Was world peace possible or would humans always be driven to go to war? What caused the collapse of civilizations? Why did Rome fall? No one had answered that one satisfactorily. These questions would fuel my reading for some time. But just the idea of intentionally growing a bigger brain amused me. The audacity of it. As though I were in a lab undergoing brain growth stimulation funded by generous grants to further research for the betterment of humankind.

I amused myself with the brain growth project entertaining the veracity of the idea. I wrote an article announcing the discovery for readers of my personal newsletter, one I had created as a Christmas letter to explain my break up with Louise. I made it look like a real newspaper and this was such fun I sent it out more frequently as news demanded. It had the same type font and layout as the Wall Street Journal. I copied it onto buff paper to reference aging newsprint. The color of aging newsprint (a sign of the poor quality of the paper) was what spawned the term yellow journalism. I called it the *Wang King News* as if it were the newspaper of a city in China to reflect my Asian heritage. My British readers caught the reference to the slang word wangking meaning masturbation. A masturbation of narrative to service my own self importance. "All the news to get you off," was my subtitle. I framed my news in the third person as though it was worthy of attention. Under the headline "Woman Grows Bigger Brain" I reported the discovery of said woman noticing that her brain was indeed growing. This phenomena realized during a class in electrical wiring. I quoted my friend Stacy saying "I hope she doesn't grow one of those unattractive alien heads."

I had indeed signed up for classes in household electrical wiring. Having moved into Catherine's house I was aware that the bathroom exhaust fan was rattling noisily, signaling that a break down was imminent. I felt overwhelmed by the extent of home maintenance required in a house where I was sharing expenses. Electricians were expensive. My father had always done the repairs in our house. Someone in this household ought to know how to do this I concluded. The next week a flyer came in the mail from the state's Regional Occupational Program announcing classes in construction technology including plumbing and electricity as well as carpentry to be given at Sequoia High School only two miles away. This offering excited me so much I arranged my client schedule to accommodate the late afternoon class. It was two hours a day, everyday for two semesters. A whole school year.

I was one of six women in this class of some thirty mostly Latino men. The men largely ignored the women, but Jim our teacher gave voice to the inclusion of woman as equal participants to be integrated into the teams he had us form. We were to appoint a secretary who was not to be a woman. This immediately endeared me to him. The quizzes would be taken as a team he said. When the men realized that the women had the correct answers to test questions (because we actually read the text book) we became sought after team members.

One day the women were sitting in the classroom working on a quiz. The guys were working on theirs at the big work tables out in the work room. One of the young Latino men came to us to ask how to add up fractions. He hadn't had it in school he explained. My heart went out to him. This did give me pause. Here I had believed that men had all the advantages in life, but some of these men weren't even much bigger than me. One not even as tall as I was. I started recalculating my assumptions, taking back years of arguing that sexism was the ultimate demarcation of societal privilege over class.

I was also struck by his humility in asking a woman for help coming from what I had been told was a macho culture. I had not in fact ever had a Latino man in my life and only one woman. Now I was mad that my fancy education had not insisted we learn Spanish, but had pushed French for its literary value. I had been taking French since I was in grade school in Thailand because it had been the international language only a few years before. But Spanish was all around us in California and yet no one had even once suggested it was a good idea to learn it. It had been offered at my high school, but was somehow considered of lesser status than French or German.

One of the other women kindly explained fractions to this man in a few minutes with the classic pie shape. He just needed to add and subtract measurements for the class. Later I would refer this young man to a client to do a painting job and the client paid him more than he was prepared to for he too recognized this man's eagerness to please and better himself.

The class provided us with tools and tool belts with big leather pouches for holding nails, a small pocket for the tape measure and a hammer loop. (When I saw how much sawdust landed on my jeans I switched to khaki pants.)

"No pouches, no paychecks," Jim said quoting a boss he had worked for. The pouches made us so much more efficient, allowing us to have all we needed once up on a ladder. It also gave us a unified look as we executed the tasks at hand. We were now builders. The energy in the class shot up as soon as we got on our feet. The guys nearly ran over each other in their excitement. We were actually going to build a house. Or rather a shed that would be sold to recoup the cost of materials, but it would be constructed just like a house with studs 16" on center and a roof with rafters we had to notch with "bird's mouth cuts" as they were called. Each of us learned to handle a circular saw and a hand saw. I was given top marks for hand sawing the most square cut in the class, owing to my trained eye from all the xacto knife work I'd done.

We worked outside in the school yard erecting two sheds, learning to pour cement for a foundation and how to make sure that foundation was square.

"It's just like mixing batter for a cake," I said to one of the women purposefully using a cooking metaphor as we watched Jim mixing cement in a wheel barrow.

"It's all connected," said my female compatriot offering me her wisdom of experience. She was an interior designer who wished to know more about construction so she could better direct the builders she hired.

"Entertainment centers are big right now," she told us, "everyone's getting them".

The walls of the shed went up and were bolted together so they could later be taken apart and transported on a truck bed. We sheathed a roof and constructed a door on simple gate hinges. With such a large crew it was all finished in a few weeks. One of the sheds we carried into the baseball field to be used as an equipment shed.

Then we came indoors to learn how to install plumbing, weld copper pipes and wire electrical outlets. This part really made me feel smart because you had to know something about electricity and if you didn't get it right you'd get a shock or spark a fire. The man next to me was doing just that having not listened to the most important instruction. Make sure the power is off.

Armed with my new knowledge and confidence I could now crawl up into the attic at home and figure out the wiring so I could replace the noisy bathroom fan that had started all this. I switched out a few light fixtures as well. The class went on to teach us how to tape drywall, lay roofing shingles and solder sheet metal together for what vent stacks came through the roof. I learned the origin of the phrase "irons in the fire" when I learned to weld.

In the lectures we learned about building codes and how systems worked. It fascinated me how a house was designed to connect to the town sewer system, water and electricity. When I saw how much lumber was consumed by the building industry I was prompted to read books on alternative construction methods and was drawn to natural building methods which were not so reliant on manufactured parts. I was very taken by straw bale building and could easily see how it was done, but I could not quite understand how a cob building was constructed. Cob was an old technique popular in England and usually with a thatched straw roof just like my childhood stories about *Milly Molly Mandy* living in the nice white house with the thatched roof with all her family members. Long after my construction class I drove all the way to Santa Barbara so I could learn this technique.

Cob building was very slow, I concluded, as you had to do so much manual work to force the cob mixture to adhere together in the making of a wall. But the materials were nearly free and renewable in the land itself. All that was needed was the mud at our feet, some straw and sand. We used bright blue polypropylene tarps to roll the ingredients together to mix it all together, but otherwise it was pretty low tech. The people who came to these workshops were makers, do-it-yourself shifters of culture who were not buying into consumer societies. To be able to build your own house from the materials at your feet was so empowering I would set out to join more builds around the world.

Jim had us take pictures of ourselves in action for our portfolio and taught us how to interview for a job. The whole point of the ROP program was to train people for what jobs were actually available. This included software training for office work and working in nurseries. (I had no idea selling plants were such a going concern. I'd never paid attention before.) Jim also wanted to talk to us about saving for retirement because he hadn't known to do this when he was young. (No one had taught me either so I was busy trashing my portfolio with internet stocks.) And he shared how he had designed his own house which he said was so small he could hear his son wet his bed in the next room. Was this a metaphor? I wondered.

During class I had teamed up with a pair of Brazilian brothers who were older and we worked so well together that I ended up hiring them to work with me once we finished the course. I gotten a job even before the course was over. The woman who hired me had been Catherine's supervisor. When she heard of my training she told Catherine she had a job for me as a site supervisor for a start-up called iScribe. The Dot com boom currently underway had made construction people scarce and office space scarcer. The job was to remodel a storefront that had sold auto parts into office space. The site gave me the opportunity to solve lots of interesting projects. The most challenging was to find fittings that would convert a sink into a shower without breaking into the wall. I installed a handheld shower where the spigot was. I also assembled a folding basketball hoop that none of the guys had been able to figure out.

"How did you do it?" My supervisor asked me impressed.

"I read the instructions," I told her. "Eleven pages of them". She laughed. How did guys learn things I wondered when they were so book adverse?

I asked one. He told me he would find someone who could do the task and ask them to show him. Hmmm. Well in that case I thought, there was plenty of room for me to figure out all kinds of ways to do things just by reading. But now I knew I could also ask. I liked to compare different techniques, mix things up a bit.

The Brazilian brothers and I continued to help with the remodel of three different buildings for iScribe as it competed to be the first to expand into this new market of online prescription apps. We drove into work in our old beat up cars to a parking lot full of brand new BMWs and an office of young people the company catered to with amenities and free snacks. The job market was so hot that students were stopping out of college to take these highly paid jobs. But as far as I could see all that these workers did was sit in cubicles with headsets on, to either sell the product or troubleshoot it. The telephone system and what music played while on hold was the most crucial component of the office. While software designers on the payroll sat in corner offices surfing the web waiting for the next round of expansion.

The remodel was in part designed to attract workers and be as cool a place to work as all the other start-ups coming in on the heels of Yahoo and Apple. We painted the walls to go with the company logo. The silver cabinet doors of the auto showroom were replaced with new doors laminated with the custom color of plum to match the logo. The doors were so finicky to adjust with those European hinges that I hired Tim to do the job. The basketball hoop had been fun, but I didn't have the patience to replace perfectly good cabinet doors with brand new ones. None of my team thought very highly of the gold rush fever of this boom. We did not aspire to buy BMWs.

No sooner had the finishing touches been installed to the final building (there were three by that time) than we got word that the company had fired two thirds of its staff. Their product was not going to make it. It was just an app for doctors to use to access medical records and write prescriptions. It was a free app paid for by the pharmaceutical companies in exchange for putting pop up ads of their product for whatever diagnosis the doctor was typing in. The very concept alerted me to how our capitalistic system was going to intersect with online technology. The best thing about the app was its name—iScribe. Our little start-up and its competitors would not survive as stand alone companies, but were bought up by large medical conglomerates, ones that ran hospitals and wanted a prescription app.

The boom bust economy model was no way to live I concluded. We slid into a recession so deep it changed the Bay Area business culture from one that catered to the good life for employees to one that would squeeze every last ounce of work from them as online technology and cell phones tethered them with electronic leashes. Workers logged on after dinner just to stay competitive.

My organizing colleagues and I saw a 25% drop in new clients. Home organizing was considered a luxury and people fired from their jobs now had time to organize themselves. With my construction skills I got jobs doing "handymanda" work a nickname a client gave me. So I installed organizing accessories to walls, banisters for the elderly and other little repairs.

Where I really excelled was in designing and installing closets mostly–flatpack ones, but also designed from scratch. Old hollow core doors I discovered made great shelves. I sliced them into planks and blocked the hollow part with scrap wood. The thick door edge looked great and they were flat and strong as shelves. They often didn't even need painting. And in using such reused materials I could then market myself as a Green builder. One job doing several closets for an eco minded client brought in $2000. My chronically disorganized clients who didn't consider organizing help to be a luxury also kept me going.

I had not been entirely immune to the gold rush fever, however, and had lost a shameful amount of money in the stock market—money from an inheritance from my frugal English grandpa just at the height of the boom. At least I wasn't in debt. This offered me some small comfort. I licked my wounds in shame beating myself up with regret in the wee hours of the morning. Ironically I had no particular goal for what to do with money, had I made the fortune I was envisioning. That was the irony of it. The financial system I discovered meant that the planet would be stripped of its resources just to pay off past debts regardless of need and turn it all into consumer goods. I grew less enamored of such a life and looked for ways to lessen my impact by living differently—smaller.

Others were beginning to question why we were consuming so much stuff. In 2006 a San Francisco group called The Compact launched a Yahoo group started by 10 friends who made a pact to buy nothing new for an entire year. They got a lot of press for their idea and were lambasted for being anti-capitalists intent on bringing down civilization. If that's all it would take, I was in.

Chapter 29
Thrift Is Not A Crime

There had been movements before The Compact that addressed the wasteful consumption habits of Americans, but they had all been under the guise of saving money which was an entirely different principle. The Great Depression was the compelling economic trauma that motivated this thrift. Thrift was still a value as I was growing up in America. I leaned into the thrifty values of my parents who taught me to save my money for something I really wanted; a pair of swim fins was my first saved-for purchase. The stories my mother told of having so little during the war also seeped into my heritage.

I had goals for what I would buy with my savings; a ski trip or summer camp, a unicycle. I learned to keep enough money in savings to cover emergency repairs of my wheels or replacement of prescription glasses. By the time we were in our twenties my friends had accumulated an average of $8,000 on their credit cards. This was three or four months income. Often it was due to emergencies or a pet needing medical care that started it. My parents were tough about money; they refused to spend money trying to save an animal. If it was going to cost more than $50 it was put down. My mother would simply tell me sadly that it couldn't be saved and I believed her.

When I saw that my love for theater and creative writing would designate me to the starving artist camp, I found advisors. Ernest Callenbach, the author of *Living Poor With Style,* had a subversive hippie ethic that convinced me the key to living your own life was not to become a wage slave, but to creatively find ways to make do. I was particularly sold on his treatise on panty hose being a symbol of corporate serfdom and his assurance that a woman would be unlikely to be strangled with a sandal strap. I was happy to dispense with pantyhose.

There was also the helpful suggestion that one could live on peanut butter and celery sticks. Peanut butter made adulthood seem manageable. Another book, *The Illustrated Hassle Free Make Your Own Clothes Book* from 1971 was also helpful. Such books were the legacy of the counter culture of the '60s. In the '90s Amy Daczycn, a graphic artist and a mother of a large brood living in the country, created *The Tightwad Gazette* a newsletter full of budget stretching tips. Her newsletter illustrated with lively graphics was such a success that she was featured in numerous magazines and eventually the compendium of tips were published in three volumes with the subtitle "Promoting Thrift As A Viable Alternative Lifestyle."

Alternative? Thrift was one of the core principles of Americans in the early days of self reliance and independence. But once the U.S. became the manufacturing arm of the world's consumer goods fueled by plentiful domestic oil production, the excesses of the '50s reflected what the American consumer culture had wrought with its gas guzzling big finned automobiles, shiny appliances and optimism.

After all, this industrious excess would soon put a man on the moon, a much touted achievement of American prowess. This was just about the time I arrived on these shores. It was also in 1968 that political unrest in response to the Vietnam War prompted another round of thrift, as the hippie movement spawned its DIY ethic to counter the exploitive capitalist consumer economy. But the whole point of being frugal, the counter culture implied, was so you wouldn't have to work so hard for The Man and thus preserve your time for meaningful pursuits rather than the acquisition of material things.

Soon after the counter culture emerged, Earth Day was founded in 1970 by a U.S. senator from Wisconsin who happened to see the oil spill off the coast of Sant Barbara. A public apprised of the impact of pollution by Rachel Carson's 1962 book *Silent Spring* was ready to jump on board. It was a rare coming together of the nation creating the Environmental Protection Act which in turn got us the Clean Air Act and the Endangered Species Act.

The Compact was rooted in these movements as well as the desire to spend less time shopping. It was a consumer driven solution to reduce our consumer footprint. Given that consumer sales were 25% of the economy no political figure would dare to suggest that we curb our consumption. That's why The Compact was called anti-capitalist and told they would bring down civilization. The founders of the Compact were not particularly political. They wanted to encourage their young families to spend their time together rather than shopping. What was political about their vow to buy nothing new for a year was that they had gone public with their group and it had captured the indignation of radio talk show hosts.

The Compact had only a few rules. You could buy underwear and socks, medical supplies, sundries and uniforms required by work or school, and items made by local craftspeople. Everything else you had to get second hand. The bulk of the conversations in the group were about home made cleaning and body care recipes, ways to re-purpose items, crafts, and a lively discussion about how to do without toilet paper. People, probably the same hippie era counterculture practitioners came out of the woodwork to share their old timer recipes and habits. One couple spoke of using his and hers bandannas instead of toilet paper and washing them after use. And no one even gave them any grief for such a revelation. This TP subject was so entertaining I wrote a summation for the group as a marker of how far people were willing to go to transform their consumer habits.

Advertising had not so subtly informed me of most of my habits. I hadn't thought to question advertising. My mother after all worked for a market research firm. Advertising was just a way to put the right product in front of the right customer, but thanks to Freud's nephew, Edward Bernays, advertising shifted to appeal to the emotions in a more propaganda style presentation. The human mind had to be managed Bernays counseled. Humans could not be trusted to behave rationally due to the unconscious urges of the Id which would prompt ordinary people to do irrational, possibly violent acts Bernays wrote. He set himself up as a consultant to help clients manipulate the human Id. He translated his uncle's books into several languages and came to the U.S. in the 1920s to interest Madison Avenue and the government in the application of this work. Under his influence, advertising became a medium that no longer catered to reason by touting the virtues of a product, but to emotions and the presumed desires of the Id. The stuff that dreams are made of as Bogart said in *The Maltese Falcon*.

Edward Bernays when hired to promote bananas by United Fruit in the 1950s also defended the company's interests in Central America where the newly elected president had suggested nationalizing the land owned by United Fruit. This was not as radical an act as it sounded. United Fruit which owned 3 million acres of land in the region had been given half a million acres by the earlier military government. In return United Fruit had developed the countries communication system, the docks and the railroad. And by recommendation of the military government, they had capped wages at 50 cents a day to keep labor prices low throughout the region. The new democratically elected president attempted to establish less exploitive labor laws while reigning in the power this American company had over the land. A company that had been granted a monopoly on the banana trade, thus excluding local people from cultivating bananas for a living.

Bernays framed this threat of the government taking over private property into a dread of communism, failing to mention, of course, that the land that had been given to the company originally. This new president was not a communist. He had merely recognized the labor party, but such nuances were ignored as Bernays framed the socialist platform as communist and fanned the flames of the campaign into an irrational fear that continues to this day.

My mother had a picture of a "communist" pasted into our family photo album. My father probably brought the photograph home from the office. Under the photo she had written the caption "a real live communist." My mother's caption had a whiff of irony about it. The picture showed a young man in peasant clothes staring blankly ahead. He was a prisoner of war captured along the border with Cambodia. He looked like a farmer from the fields. There was nothing to indicate he had the power to go up against such a powerful and super sized country as the U.S.. This just made me wonder at the gullibility of the American people. Why were they so afraid of such a simple man? Or of communism? Thailand had a military government, but we weren't being bombed by the U.S. We were an ally. So why couldn't communists be left to their ways?

In 1974 I visited communist Poland with my Aunty Lily, who owned a franchise of the Polish Ocean Lines. I was disappointed that no one wore uniforms as I had expected under an authoritarian government. One of our hosts, who spoke English, kindly answered my questions. I learned that not all industry was government owned. That would have been too much for the government to manage so they contracted with private companies for incidentals, buttons for instance.

Our hosts who were diplomats lived in very small apartments in the city of Warsaw. They slept on a pull-out couch in the living room so their daughters could have a room to themselves. The government had not yet built enough housing and strictly allocated what was available with long waiting lists for bigger suites. But no one was homeless. That was the whole point. In addition to these compact flats our new friends had privately owned vacation houses in the country and privately owned cars. Education was free, but you were only permitted to complete degrees for which there were jobs. This meant very few people could study theater or art (heavily controlled by the edicts of Socialist

Realism), but every graduate was guaranteed a job. Communism was grim in its restriction of individual freedom and enterprise, but viable as an operating system I concluded. More people had something to gain than not.

Edward Bernays went on to be listed as one of the 100 most influential Americans of the 20th century by *Life* magazine which gave him the moniker Father of Spin. In a democracy, spin was how the elite maintained control, after all, along with gerrymandering, vote suppression, and other tricks.) It was a close cousin to propaganda. We lived in a culture saturated with advertising, infomercials, and too much information telling us to be our unique selves, while making sure the parameters of convention were so narrow we never questioned how closely we were controlled. That's how much advertising had engulfed us. We were fish not seeing the water we swam in.

I could not detach myself completely from consumer goods, but I could fashion a lifestyle from repurposing things. Before The Compact I had learned the fine art of dumpster diving from a book published by an off brand publisher specializing in semi legal activities. Dumpster diving introduced me to the waste stream of America. It was a revelation to me that so much was being thrown away. Vacuum cleaners thrown out because the bag was full, many items thrown out because they were dirty. Plenty of broken things easily fixed. Stores were throwing out packages of food that were still good. In the U.S. people were so rich even poor people had stuff to throw away. I was sure you could live off this throwaway culture.

I still liked shopping as much as anyone especially for camping equipment, tools, and emergency supplies, but I liked the subversiveness of not shopping too. I once again sewed my own clothes restyling nice pieces I found at Goodwill which allowed me to show up at functions attended by my well heeled peers and still appear uniquely dressed in something not easily recognizable by a label. Despite my rebel ways I was still sensitive to how people assessed me by my clothes as all the angst of what to wear on free dress days in high school bore down on me. American culture was very much about how you looked and not so much about how you spoke as it was in England where there was such a thing as an upper class accent.

It was fashion that had invented "dynamic obsolescence" as a status marker and thus given birth to the throwaway culture, but fashion was also a tool of rebellion. The counter culture movement used colors and styles as a marker of anti-establishment activity including gay culture and punk. Fashion had played a part in the emancipation of women with the invention of bloomers for women's cycling attire. White dresses identified suffragettes marching for women's right to vote and today the pantsuit is worn proudly by American women in politics to honor this heritage.

How a woman presented herself also had its roots in the word glamour. A word that had once been associated with witchcraft. Glamour was used to enhance spells that required the subject to be enchanted by the appearance of the witch herself and thus be more readily amenable to the transformation she was intent on manifesting. When I learned this I wanted to incorporate fashion into my messaging too. What The Compact allowed me to do was veer off the habit of mindless shopping and approach it with my own purposeful intention. I could project a unique look that was timeless enough to avoid fashion obsolescence while still casting a certain atmosphere to enhance what interactions I had within a social setting. For everyday wear I still favored utilitarian work pants to project a sense of competence and a Han Solo vest for that butch flare.

Despite the reception and enthusiasm for The Compact, it wasn't a movement that really caught on. Not shopping was made into a style and and captured as movements are into the mainstream, compartmentalized into minimalism and simplicity. Framed as people trying to live a lifestyle unencumbered with things not as intentionally anti consumer— a stylish anti-style thing. Austerity was not my goal. But subverting the 25% of consumer spending and thus capitalism gave me a mission. I wanted to set an example not only of thrift, but of a focus on other concerns besides buying things. That we as a people should not accept that shopping was a reason to wage war. That it wasn't our "freedoms" that others supposedly hated us for, but our meddling in their sovereign countries. Freedom conflated with shopping became, during the Persian Gulf war, an American synonym for imperialism.

But most of all a low cost lifestyle freed up my time. I needed free time to spend writing to bolster up my own sanity, given all the psychological warfare and spin being waged on the populace. I also needed free time to invest in a handmade life less reliant on industrial capitalism.

Chapter 30
Peak Everything

Peak Oil was a conceptual turning point for me in how I would view the future. Peak Oil describes how it's not the running out of oil that will hurt us, it's the steady decline of oil that will send our growth oriented economy into a perpetual decline, causing world powers to become more imperialistic and war like, more destructive and planet killing as these behemoths fight over the remaining oil reserves.

Up until this revelation I believed, like everyone else in our optimistic society, that the march of progress was a fact of life. That the U.S. would continue to be the center of innovation. There was no reason to question technology and the good things that science would continue to discover to make our lives easier and healthier. At the time, the internet was still mostly for research, not socializing, but we had renewable energy, hybrid cars and compact fluorescent lights, plus the storage capacity of computers ,doubling rapidly, was cited as a mark that infinite progress would continue to amaze us.

Peak oil might have been a passing notion for me had I not been recruited into the Peak Oil movement. I was already connected in 2005 to the environmental groups coming out of Palo Alto. When a new course called Be The Change was offered Catherine and I enrolled in it together. The year long course trained us to become community activists by telling us the history of how the Bay Area preserved open space and the green belt through strategic zoning and teaching us how to approach local government to press for more such ordinances. We learned that smart environmental growth meant staying within city limits and encouraging in-fill development of empty lots. We were also warned about the folly of not allowing housing to be built along with the growth of our prized tech companies bringing in so many jobs. So it wasn't as if no one saw it coming —this housing shortage.

We discussed the psychology of early adoption vs conservative followers so we could encourage people to adopt these new innovations. The electric car was a tough sell then and hybrids were regarded with suspicion especially outside of the Bay Area.

Catherine had already bought a Prius. When we went to an environmental happening we would joke that it was a fifteen Prius event because of all the Priuses parked in the parking lot. She also put solar panels on the house and had a company we learned about come and seal up all the gaps in the house until it felt tight as a drum. I lobbied for us to buy a stove insert for the fireplace so we could not only burn wood more efficiently with little emission but whatever scraps we could find. The scene from *Dr. Zhivago* where he is burning their heirloom dining room chairs in the fireplace to keep warm had captured my imagination as a teenager. Plus I thought Julie Christie was hot. The idea that things could change in the blink of an eye especially politically and change your status from aristocrat to commoner resonated with my life coming from the high society of Bangkok to the low grade status of newly arrived immigrant.

It was through our Be The Change leadership training that I heard about a day long conference taking place at the Foundation for Global Community which had a large meeting room in a former auto showroom. I was intrigued and went alone. I soon saw familiar faces from other social justice events arriving. I sat down at a table of strangers. Richard Heinberg was the speaker. Throughout the day he asked us to discuss with those at our table our thoughts. At the end of the now grim day he asked what we would do with the information we had learned. I said I would write a report on the material and distribute it to my e-mail list which was all of 50 recipients. I gave a wry chuckle at this not very impressive number, but it was everyone I knew at the time from my close circle of friends to my network of colleagues in the professional organizing business.

What I learned from this peak oil conference was that there was no way we would enjoy the economic growth to which we'd grown accustomed going forward. I wanted to warn people that the economy was just going to be a series of boom bust cycles until we were forced by diminishing returns to reduce our consumption of fossil fuels. Given that oil money controlled so much of our government, it seemed unlikely that would happen.

At the days end one of my table companions, Bart Anderson, came up to me afterwards, accompanied by his wife Paula to ask me if I would send my essay to him. He wanted to publish it on the website The Energy Bulletin that he helped edit, which was a site that collected writings on anything peak oil and had been a suggestion of Richard Heinberg himself.

"Why would they want to hear from me?" I asked, "I'm no expert." He told me that as a woman I would offer a different voice amidst all the peak oil geeks who couldn't get past their obsession with numbers and projection models.

I wrote my piece and when it was published on the website my numbers went up on my own blog. It was rewarding to have more interest in my writing and I continued to write many more pieces related to my search for a sustainable lifestyle. Now that I was a reporter published on a website as forward thinking as the Energy Bulletin, I could justify spending a bit more money going to other conferences, workshops, and talks that I could then report on. In return Bart gave me books sent to the Energy Bulletin so I could read and review them.

I loved Dimitri Orlov's Russian perspective on the collapse of the USSR mostly because it compared the U.S. to its dreaded enemy and explained how the USSR likely fared better than the U.S. would, often because of its own flawed inefficiencies, stockpiling essential items rather than embracing just-in-time supply models, for example. Orlov also taught me about the boondoggle—time consuming tasks with dubious goals that actually served to postpone a collapse. I looked forward to this assumed collapse of the U.S. because of how enormously wasteful our consumer society had become. When I first learned that Christmas tree lights and decorations at commercial shopping malls and facilities were thrown out after Christmas along with the live tree because it cost too much to pay people to strip and store these decorations I was furious at such waste.

Another writer I favored was John Michael Greer of *The Archdruid Report* who was convinced that collapse would be a long slow decline rather than a sudden event. This gave his readers much more time to learn skills, localize our needs, and reduce our consumer footprint. He really was an archdruid, a spiritual leader in the pagan community. A spiritual basis would offer a much needed framing to remind us of what was important when achievement could not be marked by the acquisition of things. As the Slow Food movement, holistic medicine and a new generation of back to the land farmers emerged along with the crafting movement this was a style of collapse that could be called Slow Collapse. It appealed to me with its association with an ongoing practice rather than a sudden event.

The dire predictions of those more dramatic in their prognosis did not come to pass during the years that peak oil was actually determined to be happening so people went back to their complacent ways. Meanwhile the Energy Bulletin turned to focus on how we could teach ourselves to cope and transition towards a less fossil fuel intensive future and renamed itself Resilience.

Reskillling as it came to be called was a term coined by the Transition Town movement. This was a movement created by Rob Hopkins in England to organize a town towards localization and sustainability offering a model for other towns to pick up. Once I had apprised Catherine on the peak oil phenomena she too became interested and we attended our first Transition Town workshop in Berkeley together. Communication techniques were imparted on how to create community among ourselves in order to prioritize projects for our particular area.

Palo Alto created a chapter, but given that we lived in the high tech epicenter of the mantra of progress and perpetual growth we didn't get much farther than sharing extra garden produce and viewing movies on environmental issues.

I filled my book shelves with books I bought at the annual Bioneers conference in Marin where we listened to talks about how plants could clean water and replace our sewage system, biomimicry technology and indigenous practices that might have something to offer to a chemical agriculture world. I put my library together with a view towards the internet becoming compromised and the need to have practical advice on hand about plants, grey water use, building shelters and cooking food from scratch. I wrote essays on various homegrown topics for nearly a decade and was pleased to have inspired at least one other woman to write. In her book *Depletion and Abundance* Sharon Astyx spoke to readers from her home farm experience of how much there was to gain from a lifestyle of less consumption. She taught her homesteading skills at workshops on her farm.

I sold off family heirlooms. My father's vintage Leica camera brought in an astonishing $800 from a buyer in Taiwan when the dollar had dipped in value. My camera lenses I sold one by one and eventually the Nikon camera itself. Art students taking classes in film based photography bought these old cameras. Getting rid of valuable items when there was still a market for them made good sense to me as a professional organizer too though it felt like an emotional loss every time I gave up something I had loved. The Nikon had been so much a part of me just the thought of it in my hands, my mind poised to compose brought back memories of scenic overseas travel.

In turn I bought things that would teach me something, even if what it taught me was that it was not a viable solution. The hand crank washing machine for instance made washing clothes an intense chore even with a hand crank wringer. I'd have to be really desperate to make it a part of my regular life. The cheap 15 watt solar panel did power a 12 volt fan I used in my room and had potential so I saved the batteries from my electric scooter to use in case of a power outage. I used simple inverters to clip to these batteries so I could plug in a string of Christmas lights for emergency lighting. I wanted a hand crank sewing machine too, but more than that I wanted to learn to make shoes. A book from the library introduced me to this craft and I made a pair of sandal boots inspired by Roman gods. I signed up for a workshop in Portland where I sewed a pair of red and brown boots with yellow accents. So satisfying was this achievement that it felt like falling in love again. Somehow being able to make shoes was the epitome of self-sufficiency. Even Richard Heinberg had mentioned it in his book.

The Peak Oil movement thrived when the price of oil was high, but when fracking kicked in, prices went down and peak oil did not seem as compelling an issue. While the environment suffered even more from all the fracking, our attention was directed towards climate change. This movement was more political, not so much about re-skilling, but about pushing legislation and leaning on politicians. And still I prepped.

Preparing for the collapse of civilization as we knew it was largely relegated to preppers stockpiling essentials and guns in a way that struck me as selfish and nihilistic. What narrative were they listening to? What exactly was the zombie apocalypse they were expecting? Beware of what you prep for I thought. It may come true. I liked the Transition Town model of cultivating relationships in one's own community. I had seen Thailand weather the financial collapse of the Asian Tigers and it did not result in hoarding and armed fortresses. People simply returned to their family farms where rice was stored in huts on stilts big enough to rent out as an AirBNB.

Technology was robbing Americans of skills—map reading for instance and knowing where you were in your environment. Young people I was noticing no longer knew how to give directions. And when I sold my mother's car I learned that they didn't even want to learn to drive a car because they could just order up an Uber. I was appalled. That seemed very short sighted to me as a prepper. I was proud that I could drive a stick shift as well as a motorcycle. I came of age fixing and maintaining my ride, but fixing cars got more difficult with on board computers that didn't even have an oil light. I had to let that one go and find a mechanic I could trust.

There were others who were questioning new technology too. Bart collected the hardy old Dell laptops that he could repair and give away to those needing them; he bought them in bulk from Stanford's equipment department and taught me about Linux the open source operating system that appealed to my DIY people powered sensibilities. He gave me one of the Dell laptops so I could keep my old laser printer going since with every systems upgrade on my Mac I lost the use of some other piece of equipment. The tech that was supposed to save trees with the paperless office had become the menace of the environment, putting planned obsolescence on steroids.

Technology was somehow becoming more redundant, addictive and destructive of both society and the environment, not to mention people. I was referred to a client whose gaming habit had become so severe he still had not unpacked after moving six months prior, leaving the living room filled with boxes until his roommate threatened to evict him. Gaming? I asked. Yes that turned out to be a common addiction. The virtual world was even replacing sex as online dating led to online relationships that never meet in real life. I no longer worried about the population boom for I figured we had now reached peak people. The birthrate was already below replacement level in the U.S. and other countries were following suit as more women were able to earn their own income.

Meanwhile, addiction to porn created sexual dysfunctions along with escalating expectations for novelty and visual stimulation including making it a new normal for women to get their pubes waxed. Seriously? I had to ask some straight women friends for the lowdown on this. Having a relationship with a waxing salon was a dependence I hadn't even known to entertain. Being an old guard lesbian had its advantages. And as swimsuit bottoms got more high cut making it more difficult to keep those wily pubes tucked in I switched to a collection of snazzy board shorts.

I did keep my hair long because long hair heightened my Asian identity, where short hair diminished it. I preferred to be seen as Asian which also emphasized my beauty in a traditional way. One should have something to admire even if it wasn't exactly what one had in mind as an identity. No one would read a short haircut as butch on an Asian girl in this country so why try. Plus my girlfriends tended to have more to say about my haircut than me. After all, they were the ones looking at it. When my last hair stylist died of AIDS back in the late '80s it was my cue. Leave it long and another expense was gone. I cut my bangs myself and got a $15 cut and go for the rest.

When prepping became a reality TV show I was suddenly done with it. Did anyone really know how it would all end? Things might not be quite what it seemed now. The planet might be more alive than we thought with tricks up her sleeve. We might get input from the unseen, the unknown or just some other unexpected thing might come up. Preppers were so sure of what outcome they should be prepping for that it seemed a bit too prescribed.

All over the world people's lives had already collapsed, changed forever by war mostly initiated by foreign powers and by internal political changes that destabilized economies or having trading partners exiting as happened to Cuba when the Soviet Union collapsed. Yet life went on. It felt arrogant to be concerned with just preserving the American way of life. If there was going to be a collapse what then? Shouldn't we be creating another kind of life altogether? Why just stop at prepping? Society could simply evolve. Why not? And if not what would it take?

I was no longer interested in living in a prepper state of mind. I was more interested in keeping my wits about me to be able to see the emerging trends, the unintended consequences, and the cosmic joke of our collective mind arriving at an unexpected shore.

Chapter 31

Direct Revelation

"It doesn't matter what your religion is," Khun Ya told me, "as long as you have one." This was her instruction to me during my first return to the family homestead five years after my parents and I had immigrated to California. At fifteen I thought this was a very diplomatic approach to the topic, but I didn't quite know what to make of it. Both my parents were anti-religion, my mother having been force fed scripture by her devout Anglican father. In my grandpa's eyes I was pretty much a lost cause as I had never been baptized which made me a heathen. He didn't bother me with any sort of religious instruction save for taking me with them to church on Sundays. Church was a nice way to meet up with friends dressed up in their best clothes, I thought, while understanding not a thing I heard. It was mostly about how to be a good human I gathered.

My father rebelled against my grandmother's devotions to the Lord Buddha and on official forms where his religion was requested he would write "engineer." Between these attitudes of my two parents I had no formal religious training and was left to the animist beliefs that permeated all of Thai culture, which was considerable. There were spirits everywhere made visible by the spirit houses that were found at every Thai residence, spirit houses under special trees where spirits had been detected, altars of Buddha images in caves, altars by the sea with various sea gods. Due to the colored cloth wrapped around numerous trees just about anywhere you went theee were signs that spirits had made their presence felt. Interestingly my father still believed in spirits.

"You know the story your mother tells about the coffee table moving around?" he asked me once we were living in California. I nodded for my mother loved to tell Western friends about the seances my parents had had in our Bangkok living room with an American friend who could call in the odd spirit to play with them. One night she had asked a spirit to indicate its presence by moving the coffee table across the room. This it did so with unexpected speed while all the participants kept their fingers on the table's edge and ran after it to keep up. Then she asked it to return to where it was and again the table moved coming to rest in front of the couch once more, but then much to everyone's surprise the table spun 180° so the tiles which were painted with

Mexican musicians were faced the way it was before. It had corrected itself to comply with the directions given. This was what convinced all present that the spirit was real. None of them would have thought of that.

"They are real," my father continued, "Don't make trouble with them." I did not question him. I had lived all my life with the assumption that spirits or ghosts were all around us. The ghost story was a huge genre in Thai culture. Even my English grandpa had been a spiritualist taking my mother to a seance when she was a child. She told the story of the gathering in a community hall and how the man had said that a child in the back of the room (meaning her) had just been given a violin (which she had).

In my early '20s I fell in love with a Catholic girl who worked at the library where I had my first job as a page. She was older and had also attended a girl's school, one run by nuns. Sacred Heart Convent was the rival school to my school and I had been on their campus to compete in swim meets. This affiliation felt like a family connection. But though we shared a love of movies and literature so had plenty to talk about, the object of my crush was not interested in dating me. Nevertheless, I asked her my spiritual questions. Was there a god? If so there must be a spiritual reality. And if there is, what then was our purpose in life? To fend off my thirst for ways to contemplate what we could not know as we called it, she gave me Dante's *The Divine Comedy,* the Penguin edition translated by Dorothy Sayers. Such a lofty publisher of great books made me feel very scholarly as I caressed the three volumes, tapping them together on the counter of the ticket booth at the Festival Cinema the day she gave them to me. Dante was also suffering from unrequited love. He wrote his lengthy treatise inspired by Beatrice, a noble woman he loved from afar.

Beatrice summoned for him a spiritual friend to guide him through the underworld of hell. He dutifully recorded this exploration in his first book *Inferno.* I was hooked. There were lessons to be learned as to degrees of sin. I was amused to find that homosexuals shared the same level of hell as bankers for the sin of usury. These moral lessons interested me so I continued on with each level of hell more salacious than the last. I read steadily at my job at the theater.

Purgatory was refreshing as there was a chance to redeem oneself. By the time I finished *Paradisio* I was so high with the spiritual comaraderie I looked up from the final page at the movie posters on the walls and felt as though I was tripping on hallucinogenics. The ordinary seemed to vibrate a bit brighter. It had taken me nine months to get through all three books. I dreamed of learning Italian so I could read it in the original language, and of course, go to Italy.

I thought Catholicism was a very grand religion if one had to have one. I studied the famous religious art of Michelangelo and all the other painters from oversize art books from the library and was in awe when I went to see the Vatican exhibit at the Legion of Honor in San Francisco. Much gold was on display which seemed a bit materialistic and made me wonder what was the underlying agenda of the Church. In the end I realized that I couldn't become a Catholic. Not with the Pope laying down the law of the land for everything you were permitted to do or not. Having an authority figure in charge did not appeal to me. But I had made progress. I had allowed myself to believe in the divine. And I possibly possessed a guardian angel.

Like most Thais I already believed in reincarnation. That just seemed obvious and I was excited to have this confirmed for me in English by a series of books called *Messages From Michael* that bore some resemblance to my parents seances as they were also done over a Ouija board. The teachings of Michael were channeled by a woman with similar psychic talents. She delivered a complex hierarchal system of soul levels and archetypes. These teachings had lots to offer in the way of advice and fun anecdotes about famous people from history, along with practical advice on how to solve relationship problems. Other seeker friends of the '80s were taken by Carlos Castaneda, but he made me impatient with his unbelieving mind. I turned to the female centered narratives of intuitive exploration by Beverly Hills author Lynn Andrews skimming off Native American lore or ripping it off as some would rightly say. After awhile she wrote so many books of her convening with indigenous teachers all over the world that I stopped believing that any one person could have so many experiences. Wasn't one set of teachers enough?

In 1990, as the U.S. went to war in the Persian gulf with what looked to me to be the slimmest of pretenses, I became a skeptic. This act of imperialism so reminded me of the Vietnam War that I decided to pursue a study of imperialism in a concerted effort to understand if going to war was a common thread of the human condition. This took several years of intense reading beginning with Howard Zinn's *People's History of the United States* and finishing up with Naomi Klein's *Shock Doctrine.*

When I met Catherine she was just being introduced to Buddhist meditation by her psychiatrist. Buddhism and Western psychology fit together like hand and glove as long as you didn't press Americans too hard about reincarnation. Buddhist practice was very sensible and grounding. As it happened, my family in Thailand had also decided to take up meditation practice to alleviate the stress from all their business troubles. We happened to visit my home in Bangkok just at that time. It was my Aunty Ah Pahdt who gave us our first book on meditation called *Meditation in Plain Language.* She told me gravely that life wasn't really about material acquisition. She should know I thought, thinking of her love of jewels and her twenty foot long closet of custom tailored outfits. She took us to meet her Buddhist teacher at his forest monastery in Kanchanaburi, the town where she had a weekend house. It was an authentic Thai style wooden house where we could sleep on the floor without air conditioning just as the ancients had done. We went to a sound and light show to watch a reenactment of the bombing of the bridge over the river Kwai (much to the annoyance of Japan who wrote Thailand a letter every year requesting that this stop). Kanchanaburi was the location of that infamous bridge. At the monastery with its large open air pavilion my aunt's monk gave us instruction in English on how to meditate. It was quite a special introduction for Catherine as Buddhism was becoming her spiritual vehicle.

After a year of daily meditation it became clear that I was not as interested in Buddhist practice. I had looked into my mind and discovered that my entire internal dialogue consisted of arguments with Western psychology, the language of my mother's chosen profession. This revelation suddenly made me see how pointless my inner dialogue was and I gave up meditation except as a weekly social event at our nearby Insight Meditation Center.

Eventually Catherine told me that she hoped I would find some sort of spiritual path or we wouldn't have much to talk about. I'd heard enough dharma talks to realize that the lessons of Buddhism were already ingrained in me through the Thai language so I began to drift off and sometimes fell asleep which embarrassed Catherine. I was bored. Buddhism did not allow for flights of the imagination or stories. Stories were considered escapist. One was to stay with the breadth and concentrate on impermanence. Alright already. I was so imbued with impermanence I never made plans beyond next week. This was apparently a characteristic of children who were taken away from the country of their childhoods at a crucial developmental stage. Third world children a research therapist called them. They were the offspring of military people, diplomats and missionaries. I joined a local group, but we were so adverse to making plans we never actually met in person. Catherine, on the other hand, had plans for both of us reaching towards our retirement.

Finally Catherine gave me a book on shamanism by Alberto Viloldo, a medical doctor who had made contact with Peruvian shamans. I was completely in agreement with his description of the reptile brain and the many levels of brains up to the self actualized jaguar brain. Between the intuitive reptile brain and the visionary jaguar brain something about this system connected to me immediately and I decided to take a weekend workshop in Shamanism. That was the beauty of the Bay Area. Whatever you were into there was a weekend workshop for it.

The two day workshop was given by the Michael Harner Shamanic foundation out of Marin County. Much like the founders of American Buddhism he had traveled the world looking into shamanic techniques and distilled these methods to its essence in what he called core shamanism as described in his book *The Way of the Shaman.* Core shamanism involved a meditation technique some called lucid dreaming. This was a lot like a guided meditation except that you went on your own and made up the scenario and the story as you went. This was called journeying and was done to the beat of a drum at 220 beats per minute which induced theta brainwaves, the dream state.

"Spirits are real" I read at the top of the handout. Oh yes, yes, my soul cheered. Finally I was home. I could once again walk in the company of spirits. I left the workshop with my two spirit animals presented to me in ritual fashion by a classmate. There was only supposed to be one, but he said the other scampered in at the last minute. The first was a huge Bear. I felt supported by the strength and steadfastness of this guide, but he didn't talk much. It was the second one, Mongoose, who was the true guide. He was so talkative and intelligent. It was perfect that there were two, just as I had two nations of my birth family one of the West and one of the East. And with that I was off and running. I took more weekend workshops in various techniques from extracting malignant spirits to helping dead people's spirits make their way home to wherever it is spirits go. The workshops were fun and full of like minded spiritual adventurers.

In my journeys the spirits rewarded me with bits of psychic sight showing me things that my workshop partners confirmed were real.

"My guide is showing me that the exterior of your cabin is made of ash," I told a woman who wanted me to check that her out of state cabin had weathered the winter. She assured me that it was indeed built with ash paneling.

In the class on divination I told a young woman with a new boyfriend that I saw the two of them riding bicycles in a park and she said that was indeed one of their first dates. He was an older man and I told her his life was already so full of interests that she might feel neglected so to just let him have his space and she would learn a lot from him. This too seemed to resonate with her.

I didn't know where to go with this. I was already making a viable living helping people sort through their material possessions. It would be extremely iffy, I thought, to attempt to launch myself as an organizer of psychic clutter. I enjoyed the world of stuff and there was certainly plenty of it to keep me in business. I was adept at designing closets and storage space, organizing for efficiency and functionality and knowing where to donate items. It was very satisfying work that didn't leave too much of a psychic footprint from my client's emotional life. So I wasn't going to set up shop as a shamanic counselor.

I didn't really find it useful to ask my spirit guides questions of my own. I wasn't adept enough to interpret the answers plus the spirits liked it better if you were working on someone else's behalf. It was similar to interpreting dreams, but my dreams usually came with an emotional impact that gave me more clues. If I wanted answers, I preferred using a pendulum to answer yes or no questions. The pendulum was the most basic of intuitive tools as you only had two answers to discern. Yes or no. Other professional organizers who walked the spiritual path also used this tool and a colleague once taught us how to use one at one of our meetings.

What shamanism taught me was that the universe was filled with spirits which made me feel less alone. Not only that the spirit world was largely benign and eager to help. For one need only reach out and ask for help. I was beyond the concept of the guardian angel looking out for me now. I was in the realm of being a participant. But I had to be in a near desperate space to ask for such help. The emotional vibration of such feelings of being at a complete loss seemed to help.

Shamanic practitioners called their ability to access answers in a shamanic journey "direct revelation". Christians too understood this concept of being able to talk directly to God. And though I didn't work at getting a complete vision of the future or answers to specific questions I embraced the workings of the universe as a living entity that I could interact with. This do-it-yourself spiritual access to guidance suited me. But perhaps more important it gave me a degree of confidence to listen to my inner voice whether it was a direct revelation of god or not.

When Catherine and I broke up in 2014 after the first of the year I was in such grief that I wanted something that would take up lots of my time and give my inner life something to do. That same week my teacher Pamela, of the Goddess course with Louise, sent out an e-mail inviting people to join her in a study of the Tarot. I was familiar with the deck she used. She had designed it herself and written the companion book Tarot of the Spirit. Her mother, who was a painter, had painted the deck. It was beautiful and had both shamanic elements and a female emphasis as opposed to the usual male weighted one. All that was needed to bring in the feminine was to make one of the three male family cards female. And balance the rest of the deck between male and female energies too.

The Tarot appealed to me because it was easier to learn how to interpret the cards than to try and figure out the symbology my spirit animals were using to communicate with me. So I came to seek insights from the cards. If I was stumped by the symbology I could always refer to the book. The advice I found in the book would seem so right on that I felt like I had received psychological counseling. And the cards I drew were so often spot on, I felt that the deck was courting me to play with it even more.

Pamela's classes required frequent meditations, guided by her instructions addressing each card. The cards were based on the Tree of Life—the Kabbalah—a sophisticated system of addressing life's passages as one sought out one's purpose in life. I made the meditations into shamanic journeys so I could meet up with Bear and Mongoose and follow the instructions in their company. To use the shamanic journeying turned out to be super efficient, allowing me to access interpretations in my lucid dreaming just in a fifteen minute journey. Plus I loved being met by my guides as though at the airport upon my arrival home, hugging them each in turn.

During the COVID-19 lockdown Bear and Mongoose became my only source of hugs and touch. It was largely an act of the imagination as all shamanic journeys are, but the results were real. I could feel my heart open as I reached out to them and wrapped my arms around their furry bodies. Then I would sit and hold their hands relishing the warmth and touch of skin and fur.

I didn't exactly get religion as Khun Ya had counseled, but my off grid spirituality was rich in the same sort of moral guidance and spiritual backbone I had observed in her as the elder of the family praying every night to her impressive three tiered altar of Buddha images and amulets.

To be an agent of the goddess was a way to be awake to opportunity and allow serendipity to lead you to the work of the goddess. I was on a search for something, but I wasn't yet fully aware of doing so. It was a very monastic vision in the practical sense of focusing on everyday living. I was already leaning toward it with my work with clients and my own projects.

Chapter 32

Why Dogs Like Me

When I helped people organize their homes, what they had in their bathrooms boggled the mind, all those body products accumulated under the sink and in every last cabinet and drawer. While helping one client go through her bathroom we filled ten banker's boxes full of such products that were no longer in use. That was average for most of my women clients and now even the men are catching up.

We were mostly throwing out shampoos that stopped "working". Serious money was going down the drain and then it doesn't even work? It stops working halfway through the bottle? No wonder shampoo companies needed such aggressive ad campaigns. Many other clients too kept these half empty bottles hoping they would work if rotated back in between other brands.

Long before I became an organizer I had begun to reduce this reliance on body products, especially shampoo. It started with my adopting the zero garbage challenge, a popular concept in the late '80s. I started in the bathroom with shampoo as the prime culprit. I found a shampoo in a bar produced by some enterprising fellow, who made it himself and mailed the bars out to eco shoppers. It worked fine for me, though my friend's hair pouffed out like a lion's mane when she used it.

When I joined the Compact Group I learned from the forum that you could clean your hair with baking soda and an apple cider rinse, which was how people cleaned their hair several generations ago. This method soon underwent a renaissance and is called the No Poo method. I learned how shampoo would strip the oils from your hair which just caused the hair follicles to overreact by producing more oil, until people were washing their hair everyday just to escape this oily look.

When I tried the baking soda and vinegar method my hair literally squeaked. There was no residue at all; just a sense that I had finally rid my hair of product. I was sold. Even better I found that I no longer needed to wash my hair every other day as I had done with regular shampoo. I could go for a week or two and my hair looked great. A home ec book from the 50's confirmed that washing your hair once a week was all that was required in a pre advertising saturated world.

After a long time with the baking soda treatment it seemed a little harsh so I tried skipping it for a week and see if just massaging water through my hair would work. My hair wasn't quite as shiny but seemed to like this better. It acquired something of that wildly sexy grunge look men with long hair were trying to perfect, as opposed to the soft and silky billows of clouds that women with long hair are supposed to aspire to. This suited my butch persona. I began to think of my hair as its own creature that I would brush out like an animal companion.

If the apple cider vinegar and baking soda method was used widely in America in earlier days why did things change? I wondered. Part of this history lay in the pamphlets given to newly arrived immigrants to acquaint them with the American standards of living and hygiene habits. Soap and shampoo was thrust upon the arriving immigrants. People became so conscious of how they smelled that an entire generation of Americans were washing on a daily basis less they be mistaken for having just "got off the boat." Teeth were also of interest. When the army was recruiting they were shocked by the state of teeth in the ranks. To remedy this state of affairs they partnered with Colgate to educate the public and provide toothpaste.

I was aghast to learn that many commercial toothpastes had sugar in them. I adopted the baking soda and glycerin recipe a Compact member offered as an alternative, and that was another product I could dispense with along with the packaging. I confess though that after a few years of this I got tired of mixing up the recipe and started buying tooth powder in glass apothecary jars from a simpatico off grid couple who wrote the book *Good Life Lab: Radical Experiments in Hands-On Living,* describing their adventures building their own living structures in a dessert town. I wanted to support their inspiration. The jars could be reused for seed saving.

About the time the health craze took off, eco magazines urged us to look at the ingredients in our body products. There was a website aiming to expose the toxic formulas in these products by listing ingredients in them by brand. Any deemed poisonous were outed. Most of mine didn't pass, especially the moisturizers, which I was constantly researching. As a child I had eczema, a condition that worsened with stress. After a shower my skin would dry out so much I took to waxing it down with vaseline which would leave an oil slick when I sat in our black vinyl swivel chairs. As an adult seeking to relieve my condition, dermatologists prescribed expensive medical creams with cortisone that would stiffen the skin. I used it only as needed.

Later I learned to just apply baby oil right over my wet body and then towel off. But I would still apply lotions. I started experimenting with food product such as Crisco and that helped. But I felt like I was greasing myself up for roasting. I moved on to olive oil. At least it looked like the baby oil I had been using though Tim commented that I smelled like focaccia bread and got me an olive oil that had no scent. My eczema was gone. I knew I was on the right track when olive oil became a body product offered in tiny bottles by the most prestigious of body product manufacturers with a price to match.

Since I no longer needed to wash my hair so often I started to bathe less too. This had the benefit of leaving my skin more time to recover. It took me a lot longer to question the use of soap on my body. The onus of conventional wisdom about hygiene was so powerful that I was sure I would be making a major social gaff if I stopped actually washing with soap. A bathroom with a shower or bath was a required feature in all residential living spaces. That must mean it was a public health hazard not to bathe. Or did it? I researched further.

Before indoor plumbing even the best of society made do with a pitcher of water and a wash basin on a marble washstand. No one died. But they did seem to wear an awful lot of clothes. And someone once told me those empire dresses were tied so tightly at the breasts in order to keep insects from emerging. Hmmm. The Japanese had made long soaks in hot water an emblem of civilized culture. My own people in Thailand were fastidious bathers sometimes washing three times a day. Once on a long haul bus, I heard a Thai woman loudly proclaim in Thai that the smell of foreigners was assaulting her sensibilities something awful. I had to agree with her on that. In the tropical heat, foreign travelers sweated profusely and did smell quite strongly.

One of my friends mentioned that a wilderness survival expert told him that once you strip the natural oils from your body you are also stripping away a layer of insulation and will feel colder. This would make sense for emergency situations, but also got me thinking. Are we naturally protected where all skin issues were concerned?

In 2017 I read *10% Human* by Alanna Collen about the microbiome, one of the most exciting discoveries of the medical world. If beneficial microbes were maintaining the health of my gut perhaps the same was true of my skin. I also heard an old timer in a documentary about longevity talk about how sweat cleansed your skin. This was novel, since sweat was the biggest reason modern people showered.

Could it be that sweat was actually the natural cleanser of our bodies? Maybe we were supposed to taste slightly salty too.

There was little to be found on the topic, but I did find one family of four who had done away with soap and shampoos when showering and came through the better for it, even curing a skin condition. There was also a study that showed that indigenous people who had never used body products did not smell at all, but once they moved to urban areas and adopted the modern hygiene methods they stank quite a bit unless they were absolutely fastidious, washing daily in modern bathrooms likely full of expensive product. I was confident then that there was no point in soaping the body up on a daily basis if ever. I then learned from the book *Green Barbarian: Living Bravely On Your Home Planet* that dry brushing would exfoliate your skin and that's all you really needed to do, though I preferred to brush my skin in the shower with water as a lubricant.

During the COVID-19 lockdown I was living in the tiny house much more than I ever planned on doing. I had never bothered to try out bathing in the tiny. I had always showered at Catherine's. But now I was staying put half an hour away in my mountain home where I had just relocated the tiny. It was too cold in March and April and it just wasn't one of my priorities to heat up water in a kettle on the stove for a bath. Better that I make a mug of tea which would also heat me right up.

Social distancing was a good cover. I checked my scent frequently sniffing under my shirt and while I did detect underarm odor at first eventually I couldn't detect anything at all. Had I arrived at my natural indigenous state? Was showering actually a stimulant that was part of people's waking up ritual? Who invented the shower anyway? I was sure it was a sell job as much as the flush toilet had been. My reading on the history of bathing confirmed that the changes in bathing practices followed status shifts after the advent of indoor plumbing.

There was an example of status signaling in my own era. When refrigerators entered our lives people were so proud of owning one they wanted to advertise it as a status symbol, but unlike cars they couldn't just drive up in their refrigerator to show it off at church. What they needed was another just as highly visual a symbol. That's when Jello desserts became the status symbol to show that you had a refrigerator since only with refrigeration could you make these desserts. And make them they did in the most baroque architectural molds producing tiers of lurid colors. We laugh at these old displays because refrigeration is now taken for granted and home canning, kambucha, and yogurt have become our healthy eating status symbols.

I continued on my unbathing journey alone until finally an article in the *Atlantic* by James Hamblin came to my rescue declaring that we were showering too much. He was promoting his new book *Clean: The New Science of Skin*. He had researched the history of what was considered clean in a society, same as I had, and after doing his own no showering experiment had come to the same conclusion. After a few weeks he had reached, as he put it, a "detergent free steady state."

Body products companies were already trying to bottle beneficial bacteria as a product along with probiotic skin creams. The shampoo companies were also producing versions of baking soda, again at high prices. Some people just feel better if their habits are sanctioned by a company with all the necessary authority to make claims and explain the science behind it.

Not using soap at all remains a hard sell for those who venture close to me. I had a distinctive odor my closest friends told me, not a bad one, but a distinctive one. In the past this distinction was sought after by my lovers, but people were used to a manufactured scent now and nobody wanted to sport a distinctive smell of their own. A recent lover was not won over by my no soap showering, but her pets loved me. I had always been able to make friends easily with animals; now they came right over and claimed me as one of their own. Dogs especially loved me. In a bookstore where a small dog came to work with its owner, the pooch came right over to me looking to make friends. There's something satisfying about the approval of dogs as if you're doing something right for the entire animal kingdom. It made up for any offense I might be to humans. So I decided to stick with my new regime. I just keep quiet about it. And no insects have crawled above my neckline to warn of my feral status.

Chapter 33
Be Your Own Medicine

"You're grinding your teeth," my dentist told me, "I recommend getting a mouth guard. Would you like me to order you one?" I knew what a mouth guard was. My friend Stacy wore one and so did Catherine. At any sleepover house party it seemed as though everyone was popping in their night guard come bedtime. Interestingly, none of my male friends wore mouth guards.

"Er no thanks," I said.

I could hear my jaw clicking, but I didn't want to succumb to the recommendation of a mouth guard. It was bad enough that I wore contacts and hearing aids. I didn't want to keep expanding a life that relied so much on medical intervention and products. And why couldn't we control our own jaw grinding anyway? I wanted to explore my relationship with my jaw, give it a chance to atone.

So, every time I thought to check my jaw, I would let the tension there go until my jaw was slack. I found I had a psychological resistance to this slack jaw, as if I was displaying stupidity and might drool on myself while sleeping. Once I realized this I felt smarter for undoing the bad programming. I established a position with teeth slightly apart as my natural baseline and would practice it throughout the day and before I went to sleep. If I woke in the night and found my jaw clenched I would just remind it that this wasn't its job anymore and relaxed it back to the baseline position. Soon I found it came naturally and I wasn't clenching my jaw while sleeping. It had taken less effort than teaching myself to remember my canvas bags when I went into the grocery store.

Of course, like anyone, I had thoughts that drove me to distraction when I tried to go to sleep. Thoughts that would likely add to the clenched jaw problem. Luckily because of my long time journal writing habit I knew that if I wrote everything down I would know that my thoughts were safely contained and I wouldn't have to keep reminding myself of the insults I had endured during the day and what I should make of these events or whatever other problems were weighing on me. I kept my journal and a fountain pen by my bed. I wrote so much, I was always throwing pens away and then I'd have to look for one that worked so a fountain pen was my eco gift to myself when I decided to call myself a writer. A bottle of ink would last about a year. That made me feel secure. So if I couldn't sleep I would roll over open my notebook and let it rip. And just in the telling of my story or my list of worries my head would empty out and I would feel so drowsy sometimes I would fall asleep with my pen still in my hand.

It was far better than falling asleep in front of the TV as some did. Or more likely, with the use of sleeping pills. Sleeping pills were the gateway drug to anti-depressants one friend told me in my twenties. He was the first person I had ever heard describe the effect of anti-depressants. How you would go to think about something and your brain wasn't quite able to complete the thought. When he realized this he went off them cold turkey and the landing was so crushing he just sat in the corner all day. Clearly these drugs were powerful.

I remembered my mother taking sleeping pills when I was a teen. One night she had woken up looked at the clock and taken a pill then complained of how groggy she felt in the morning because she had misread the clock and taken the pill at four in the morning. I grew up thinking pills were scary stuff. After all, look how many women committed or attempted suicide by swallowing sleeping pills. One of my school friends had found her mother in such a state and called an ambulance, thus saving her life. Then she worried that her mother would be mad at her, but no, she was grateful.

I asked my mother once what caused birth defects and she told me the story of the thalidomide drug that when taken during pregnancy had caused tremendous birth defects in the fetus. The over the counter drug had been recommended for morning sickness, then removed from the market a few years later when these defects came to light. She mentioned it being in use when I was born, but she had not taken it. Well, thank god for that, I thought, but this cautionary tale stayed with me. Drugs were fallible and had in them the unintentional consequence of side effects. Some taking years to be fully understood.

No, I did not want to mess with pills. Some of my recreational drug-using generation embraced the idea that prescription medicines were a miracle and necessary for living. One friend kept a prescription for Xanax filled at all times. For the sake of this friendship I did not argue about such a dependence. Everyone is entitled to their own tools.

Another was a compendium of knowledge when it came to drugs. His specialty was the flu. He told me exactly what brands and what type of cold medicine to buy and what cough syrup. I had a fair number of sore throats in a year and whatever cold bug was floating around I'd catch. I became hyper observant about things that would irritate my throat and learned to head these invasions off at the pass arming myself with masks for woodworking and yard work and smog when I went to Bangkok. If I spent all night talking my throat would dry out, which might also cause a sore throat so if I would make some tea. There was even a throat tea full of licorice and other good stuff.

Licorice, I remembered, was sold by hill tribe herbalists in Northern Thailand. Thailand was already filled with memories of healing modalities. The village cures of my Auntie Sakorn with her tiger balm and throat medicines. She demonstrated this knowledge on me very viscerally in the summer of my fifteenth year. We were visiting the home of a relative. The walled compound was guarded by attack dogs. And when I forgot my purse in the car and ventured down the driveway to retrieve it two large dobermans came running from nowhere bearing down on me. Each managed to bite me in the leg before they were called off by their mistress. Auntie Sakorn beckoned me to her side and had me show her where I had been bit. I pulled up the wide leg of my bell bottom pants and exposed one of the bites. She took hold of my thigh and slapped my skin hard at the sight of the bite. Then she rubbed so vigorously into the muscle of this location that I near squealed out in pain.

"Is there another one?" she asked. I said no because I didn't want to suffer this treatment twice. But the next day the bite that wasn't treated was a deep blue bruise, but the bite that was treated was just a scratch. Hmmm I thought to myself. For a population of women who were proud of their beauty such a remedy would be valuable. I told Tim about it. He was disbelieving. "But you're pressing down on broken blood vessels," he protested. Well maybe that's the cure I reasoned.

Thailand still had Chinese herbalists and acupuncturists as well as their own home grown herbalists. So too were there Western trained doctors who stitched up my head when I had foolishly tried to walk on a wet stone bench only to slip and hit my head on it causing such a scene of blood, and relatives running all over the place to take me to the hospital. There were also dentists who put in my first fillings (without Novocain I might add which is likely why I'm such a hard ass today).

On my British side had been the National Health System for free dentistry and for my grandfather various operations. My grandmother was suspicious of hospitals and doctors, having had an elder sister die of pneumonia in a hospital when she was just a child. So my mother was not raised to run to the doctor for any little ailment and didn't worry much about every cold and flu I ever got. Neither of my parents seemed to get sick at all. I was lucky I had such good genes.

Western medicine was at its best for stitching you up and for surgeries to remove organs as when I had a hysterectomy because my womb was full of fibroids. When Catherine got cancer, however, I thought the treatment with chemo was barbaric.

I posted a statement to that fact to my Facebook page.

"I don't care how many statistics they throw at me," I wrote, "I am never going to go through chemotherapy treatment." There had to be a better way. I'd just as soon try anything else if I were in the same boat. Her treatment lasted nine months during which I accompanied her to just about every infusion session and folded a complex origami animal for each of those days. Enough to fill a large jar. So traumatic was this journey with Catherine I lost fifteen pounds of flesh I could not afford to lose because I didn't want to arouse her nausea with smells of food.

The year after Catherine's illness I recovered at one of my favorite activities to do in Thailand—I attended an adobe building workshop. As it turned out I had an American roommate whom I soon learned had had the very same breast cancer that Catherine had had only it was seven years earlier when there was no known cure for triple negative breast cancer. She was a microbiologist and was willing to try some of the alternative treatments she read about including giving herself coffee enemas, and completely changing her diet to such an extent that she became a chef specializing in this type of vegetarian diet. This story filled me with hope. It was not the only story I heard. Another woman I met that year had also had the same breast cancer and had chosen an alternative treatment protocol involving acupuncture and marijuana, which she grew herself. Both women had had surgery to remove the cancerous mass and both were obviously doing just fine with the treatment they had chosen.

The year of cancer I had my own little alternative exploration. My doctor told me that I had high blood sugar and diagnosed me with pre-diabetes. She told me to avoid eating so much white food i.e. rice, potatoes and pasta. A year went by during which I did nothing because I was taking care of Catherine so my numbers got a little worse. Now my doc was really getting on my case and telling me that the process of this disease would inevitably lead to pharmaceuticals. She had also warned me about my cholesterol. Clearly I knew nothing about nutrition. And she didn't know much either I sensed.

I started researching the whole cholesterol story until I could handily debunk what was the conventional advice at the time to eat a low fat diet. I also read a book on diabetes written by an engineer who then became a doctor just so he could publish what he had learned. I got myself a glucose meter as he had done and tested the result of everything I ate. The biggest culprit turned out to be whole wheat toast followed by oatmeal. Two food items that were supposed to be heart healthy. The engineer doctor explained how a low fat diet was useless. What we should eat was a low carb high fat diet. I dispensed with oatmeal and started frying up two eggs and bacon or sausages for breakfast with refried beans instead of toast; I had eaten a two egg breakfast for years before becoming "health conscious". The difference in my energy level upon returning to this breakfast was remarkable. I no longer felt a mid morning slump when I wanted a nap followed by being really hungry for lunch by 11:30 in the morning. I could now hold out all morning and eat a light lunch as late as 1 p.m.

I argued with my doctor that my cholesterol wasn't significant because there was good cholesterol and bad cholesterol. And really heart attacks were the least of my worries. I became a devoted paleo and declared I was a fatatarian interested in good oils like butter, lard and other saturated fats. I soon learned not to try to convince anyone else of what I had discovered. No one wants to hear health advise especially from a healthy person. The only thing we could all really agree on was to cut down on sugar.

While I was at the adobe building workshop, where I had met the friend who shared with me her cancer journey, I learned of a new health regime. Each morning we were offered a yoga class. I'd already been introduced to yoga at previous workshops so had added that to my routine ten years before it became so trendy. But this yoga class was different because this was the morning our yoga teacher announced that she had just drunk her own pee. I looked up at her curiously as the remembrance of the taste crossed her face with an expression that told me it was not altogether pleasant but doable.

Urine therapy, as this was called, is an Ayurveda practice that the adobe building guru of Thailand Jo Jandai had adopted and was teaching. Jo was a man after my own heart, willing to try new things just to see how it would fit into his life. He had been teaching about drinking your own pee as a remedy when you were sick and to recapture substances the body made for its own use. Well, if Jo was doing it there must be some merit to it I thought. My cancer journey friend told me how one dose broke the fever of her husband who had been ill. I would also learn that pee could be used to treat cuts and skin abrasions. Urea is, after all, an ingredient in plenty of high end body lotions. I tucked all this away in my alternative medicine chest.

Meanwhile, I happened to meet a Chinese medicine practitioner (a white American) who persuaded me to come in for treatment for my ADHD-like symptoms. Even after one session my brain felt sharp and clear. So I went in twice a week. My focus became so sharp that I started wearing myself out doing all the things I wanted to check off my to-do list. Meanwhile, my acupuncturist become my ad hoc shrink. He had a degree in psychology and he would bring to my attention what he was seeing with the diagnostic tool of Chinese Medicine. One look at the capillary veins in my eyeballs and he knew that I was agitated about something. While my pulse told him if I was in a pitched battle with some issue or some foe. He would ask me what I'd been thinking about, and tell me if I had the strength to fight whatever this battle might be or to lay off things for awhile.

If my feet were cold he would tell that my liver was being overworked from mulling over something and I needed to let it go or find a solution to release all that overthinking. His questions brought to my attention specifics of my life that I would otherwise ignore and only notice because I was waking up at four in the morning, obsessed with some problem that by the light of day was relatively minor. When neighbors let their dog poop in the sidewalk garden I had so painstakingly created, I was distraught about it trying to decide what to do. But mostly the battles I fought were on social media, or were a result of stage fright from posting something provocative. These sessions taught me a lot about what agitation I was causing myself.

Eventually my acupuncturist became too controlling and I suspected that he was doubling up on my sessions to make up for his dwindling client load. Every time I flew to Thailand there was hell to pay from the impact of the jet lag and whatever family drama I had to mitigate as property changed hands after the death of my father. Those weeks of recovery he had me in his office four times a week. Then he told me I couldn't go to Thailand if it was going to have such an impact.

This made me so mad that my blood pressure went way up and he warned me that I was heading for a stroke.

Now I was really worried. After all he had been right about so much. Was I really headed for a stroke? I drove straight over to Safeway after the session and tested my blood pressure in the machine next to the pharmacy. It was normal. Remembering my success with the glucose monitor I borrowed a blood pressure monitor from a client and monitored my blood pressure all week. I saw that the readings were perfectly normal until the morning of my acupuncture session. That's when I decided to fire him and find another acupuncturist.

I knew he would be loath to let me go and would try to negotiate. So I had to devise my exit plan, which took a good part of the evening to think up so unused to confrontational negotiations raised as I was as a non confrontational Thai by a polite Englishwoman. That evening I happened to see a movie about child abuse with a debriefing by Oprah. She talked about how difficult it was to walk away from an abuser because so often they did actually love you. This gave me insight into the care that my acupuncturist was delivering. He certainly cared about me and counted me as a friend. He had just overstepped his authority in a very paternal way.

The next morning when I went in to see him for what would be my final session, I told him we had a case of "white coat" syndrome here. This made him very nervous and he became super nice and solicitous of all I had to say which calmed me down a good bit. He spent half an hour talking to me, but I was not going to be talked out of my plan and proceeded with my script.

"Do I have free will?" I asked him as I lay on his table.

"Sure you do," he said as if I was asking his advice.

"So I'm free to come and go as I please?" I continued. He assured me I was as he pricked me with needles and let me rest. When the session was over I paid him and told him that I was going to exercise my free will. I wasn't coming back for the next two sessions. He tried to persuade me otherwise, but I was adamant. Then he said I owed him for the next session because I hadn't given 24 hour notice.

"I'll buy my way out then," I said, put down my money and I walked out. Twenty minutes later he was texting me offering to fit me in on Saturday. Now it was clear that my decision was the right one. I texted him that I wasn't going to come back at all. Two weeks later I had found another acupuncturist two blocks away. A lovely sympathetic woman who told me that acupuncture sessions were themselves tiring on the body and she wouldn't have someone come in more than once a week. That was a revelation in itself.

By then I realized that acupuncture may not have been the reason for my good health anyway. I had still caught a cold in the first year of treatment. Yet I had attributed it to the treatments because of my doc's confidence that it was the cure all for everything. I was just so wowed by the diagnostic tools being so right about my state of mind. It must have been something else that contributed to my well being. In fact I had taken up another health practice. One I never told my acupuncturist about. He never suspected despite his magical diagnostic tools.

Chapter 34

Pee Your Own Medicine

The health practice I had taken up was urine therapy. I'd been wanting to try it since I first learned of it at the mud hut build. A new lover encouraged me; she had practiced urine therapy at an ashram and cured herself of a hormonal imbalance. Prompted by such a testimonial and the transformative powers of love I jumped in. What did I have to lose? Urine was sterile and there were no adverse side affects. (Although I was later to learn that the body could react adversely as part of the detoxing process.)

Urine is a product of blood plasma, what the kidneys filtered out of the blood stream to keep its chemistry balanced. It was important to capture only the midstream of the pee stream to get a "clean catch". And what you got was a whole medicine chest of elements that the body didn't need that day, but could be used another day like leftovers from a good meal. This included hormones like melatonin or the excess of the vitamins you took and a myriad of other substances the body made. How interesting was that? Your body offered substances in this free pee stream that could cure you of whatever ailed you. Now that was self sufficiency.

I used a measuring cup because it had a handle. I filled the cup nearly full then set it on the counter. The taste was indeed unusual, but not revolting. At first I would wait until it cooled to drink it, but then I just went for it as warm as it had come out of my body like a hot drink. The taste changed depending on what I'd eaten. A little more acrid sometime, a little bit salty most of the time. Milder if I'd drunk a lot of water as I was now in the habit of doing first thing in the morning. Over time it got increasingly milder and at times it was so clear it tasted rather like coconut water, with hardly any odor at all.

It's hard to say what benefit this practice gave me at first since I wasn't suffering from anything, but I continued to do it just because it was so subversive. It was my little up yours to the pharmaceutical companies. After two years of this practice I realized that I had not had one cold during that entire time. My hair was full and healthy with hardly any gray and my teeth were no longer so sensitive to cold. I was also able to heal the deep cracks in the heels of my feet in about a week by soaking them in urine every day for ten minutes or so, an advantage of living alone. The same with the painful cracks that appeared every winter in my fingertips. But not being sick at all was a huge benefit. I also seemed to recover quite quickly from joint injuries I had sustained with all the physical work I was doing.

It wasn't a practice I shared with too many people in my life. They would be too disgusted. Catherine and her brother were disgusted enough when I told about how I healed the cracks in my heels. But occasionally I would mention it to an alternative health person. Most had heard about it and could assure me that this Ayurveda practice was indeed viable. A number of people did seem to know that jelly fish stings could be alleviated by peeing on afflicted areas. And on a slow news day Madonna had told of how she cured athletes foot by peeing on her feet.

As I sat down to write this chapter I thought I should actually read some of the literature so I could be more conversant about my adopted regime. I got one of the few books in English on urine therapy *The Golden Fountain* by a Dutchman— Coen Van Der Kroon— and was quite astonished by the seven pages of ailments listed that could be addressed with urine therapy. The chapter of testimonials from doctors and patients were filled with stories of rejuvenation, remission and recovery from cancer, AIDS, allergies, mononucleosis, chronic fatigue, and an assortment of other ailments.

The list of substances in urine was of such interest to pharmaceutical companies that companies collected urine and filtered out specific ones for use in the manufacturing of drugs. In Shanghai the city government collects urine from specifically designed public toilets and then sells this resource to this $500 million market which included insulin and growth hormones. One specialized in urikonase, an enzyme that dissolves blood clots. Stem cells too were found in urine.

Urine was what we were swimming in at the start the Dutchman explained, inside our mother's womb filled with amniotic fluid. During this 9 months of our gestation we ingested our urine and expelled it repeatedly. In fact our lungs needed to be filled with the fluid to complete development. Any surgeries done to babies in the womb leaves no scars. This vision of our floating utopia of origin gave me a warm comforting feeling all over to think that we could still access this fluid for rejuvenation later in life. The very fact that our body could excrete this fluid outside of our body for our own use in healing was considered part of the design, the Divine plan. One guru even suggesting that the Holy Grail was simply a cup used by a urine drinking practitioner.

"Drink from thy own cistern," was the advice in the Bible which urine practitioners interpreted as meaning drinking your own waters—the waters of life.

In India, shivambu, the word for urine, literally means the waters of Shiva and urine is considered one of the gifts of the body. A 5,000 year old document discovered in India speaks to this urine therapy with 107 verses describing the techniques and benefits of this practice within the larger disciplines of yoga and meditation. So once upon a time this feedback loop had been centered as a healing modality of the body. The practice still popular in India, where a former prime minister famously boasted of his devotion to the regime. His good health up to his death at 100 years old stood as a testament. Yet the techniques of urine therapy did not seem to travel well. Walter Cronkite himself had said no thank you in an interview with the prime minister.

This miracle of design described the kind of world I wanted to live in. Not the pill driven deterioration thought to accompany aging. Why shouldn't I believe in this divine design? And even more amazing, urine when drunk, stimulates receptors in the throat which then triggers the body into producing needed substances to repair and rebalance itself, including antidotes for snake bites or bee stings within 20 seconds of contact. Our body can thus self vaccinate using the toxins contained in the urine. It is a feedback system of intelligence that maintains the health of the organism. Goats and other mammals had been observed drinking their own pee.

If we chose to accept that the body is a self healing organism, much like starfish and octopus rejuvenating a limb, I was sure we would have a deeper appreciation for what our bodies were capable of and perhaps love our bodies more. The very idea filled me with utopian visions of a world of self healing organisms, all working in concert with the micro biome in the gut and the beneficial bacteria in the soil. We could heal ourselves and our planet too. Why weren't we more interested in this? We were not as a population that interested in health due unless we could find a performance booster to enhance our competitive goals.

Western philosophers such as Descartes, my college nemesis had declared the mind separate from the body, as if the human soul was reluctantly imprisoned in an imperfect body of savage and feral origins. Christian culture taught disgust with our bodily functions, especially women's bodies, whose functions brought women closer to beasts used in breeding. Westerners, I had long observed, operated from a place of self hatred of the flesh made even more salient by an economic system that could not afford for a minute to leave us to our own devices. The advertising for body products, I've already mentioned, have hammered home the notion that our bodies are nasty oozing smelly organisms covered in sweaty germs. We are thus blinded to our own body's ecstatic existence in the present moment in conjunction with the present environment.

"Drink from the fountain of youth the waters of Life," the Bible had said. Throughout Europe there are fountains featuring a little boy peeing into the water. My father had such a photo in his collection. One practitioner of UT speculated that these were the Fountains of Youth of the Biblical reference. And these fountains indicated that the town had developed a water distillation system—distilled water having the same effect as drinking urine, (minus the portfolio of biochemical goodies). Urine is similar to distilled water in that it has no electric charge. Drinking distilled water, I learned, was encouraged by practitioners as a detox.

With this Devine Design in mind I envisioned a spiritual movement based in nature rather than an economical one designed to exploit nature for profit and development. One day, at the suggestion of my urine therapy group on Facebook, I swished some aging urine through my teeth as is done in the practice of oil pulling. The aged urine had changed taste, becoming more tart and less acrid; it was a bit bubbly from fermenting. I could envision it becoming a liquor. The next day bits of plaque came off when I flossed. I found I could clean off all the plaque that before had stubbornly resisted flossing and all kinds of scraping that I had tried. I was sold. If this actually continued to work I wouldn't need to have a teeth cleaning every 6 months.

If I had a slightly stuffy nose I took out my neti pot and inserted fresh urine into both nasal passages. It cleared out the mucus right away without the bother of heating water and mixing in a salt solution. I did smell pee for a few hours with that first attempt, but I didn't notice it so much in later attempts.

I started to think about other ailments I could try to cure. Some had claimed they had restored 20/20 vision with urine therapy. I added the drops to my eyes in my morning regime. That felt fine, but it was too much trouble using a syringe so I took to bathing my eyes in urine filling a pair of swimming goggles with fresh morning pee. I put the goggles on and let my eyes fill with the fluid as I blinked 100 times as recommended. I'm not sure my eyesight was improved, but it might be keeping my close vision from getting worse.

As the fluid dripped from my eyes I used my palms to wipe it all over my face. Who knew maybe it would keep wrinkles at bay as one elder claimed. I washed my hair with aged urine and left it in, but it stunk so bad I ran to the shower to wash it out. But it did make my hair soft and easy to brush. I then decided to address my very dry skin using urine as a moisturizer.

I sat on a step stool by my shower pan and dipped my hand in a bowl of warm morning urine, shook off the drops and rubbed the pee onto the skin of my arms and legs until the moisture was absorbed. This proved more promising, as the pee slipped along the skin like a light soap and the odor changed to a sweeter one as the urine reacted with the chemicals of my skin. I continued and in a few days my skin retained more moisture than it ever had. Where I used to shed copious amounts of dry skin every day, my skin now had no dry spots at all. This made it worth incorporating as a daily practice.

The Irish used to bath their babies in urine to keep their skin soft. The practice went out of use and no one spoke of it, as I'm sure it made them sound backward. Women of Africa and those who had been enslaved in the States were also said to use urine bathing as a beauty agent.

I was loath to return to showering, which had always dried out my skin, not to mention using gallons of hot water. I also had to elaborately hydrate my skin with olive oil and other lotions. Now I didn't need to use any lotion at all. Why go back when I had discovered the cure to my lifelong skin problems?

My journey to off grid living had certainly not been stopped by convention. I was now a full fledged urine bather so I might as well own it. I did not wash my hair with urine again, but I would drip warm fresh urine onto my scalp working it into the skin. I styled it while it was wet and carefully brushed it out to the ends. It worked fine and didn't smell at all. I smelled like myself. A friend who hugged me attested to this.

The Romans washed their clothes with aging urine, so of course I had to try that too. Aged urine developed ammonia, which wasn't bad for lifting that ring around the collar. I still needed to scrub the ring a little with Dr. Bronner's. Two cups of urine and a capful of Dr. Bronner's worked best of all as a presoak making it much easier to release the grime from my clothes. It also worked fine for cleaning window glass and chrome surfaces just as ammonia would. Rubbed down with a sheet of crumpled newspaper.

I was further intrigued when someone said that the body was a distillation machine and suggested that if you were lost at sea and had the foresight to bring an enema syringe you could put seawater up your butt, hold it in the body to absorb as much of it as you could and when the fluid worked its way through your system it would make you pee which you could then drink. I ordered myself a syringe to try it out. It was indeed easy enough to do and should work as claimed, though it was a little bulky to pack.

One of my favorite Hitchcock films was *Lifeboat,* so being lost at sea had long been in my lexicon of survival scenarios. In the movie the captain saved himself by drinking his own sweat and he shows the glass inside his shirt. I had always wondered how a glass could save enough sweat. It would have been more believable if he drank his own pee as sailors have been known to do. But who was going to sell that idea to the filmmakers?

I'm sure I could even brush my teeth with urine, but I liked the tooth powder I already had. Instead I took my fermented urine and boiled it until it vaporized then inhaled the vapors hoping it would increase my lung capacity. This remedy was recommended for asthma and sore throats. It cleared my sinuses and had a sharp sensation like snorting cocaine. It didn't make me high, but I did feel I was increasing my lung capacity. This may have been just as a result of the deep breathing, but I liked doing it anyway. How better to occupy myself in the year of the lockdown than to snort urine vapors up into my lungs?

I will hasten to add that I did get the vaccine for COVID-19 when it came available. I did have my questions about vaccines in general and this one in particular. I avoided annual flu shots and preferred to boost my immune system. But I was also a willing participant in a collective society during times of crisis. I knew all my friends and family would worry if I did not comply. As for the rest of the medical industrial complex as much as I liked the idea of the Divine Plan I was not willing to decline all of modern medicine including antibiotics, surgeries, blood tests and other useful tools.

But despite my enthusiasm for urine therapy I could not get any friends to take it up. Not even those who had experienced its efficacy to break a fever. They didn't like it enough to make it a daily practice. One could say it was an acquired taste. People were more open to it being a cure for skin ailments and spider bites. For skin issues I could at least offer my own personal testimony. I loved reading testimonials. Stories of complaints unexpectedly cured, hair growing back, swollen stings receding and encephalitic reactions fended off. These were wondrous, uplifting stories of personal experiences. I read them as part science fiction of mortal threats to human frailty averted, part fairy tale of miraculous recoveries or just stories of enhancing our experience in a human body.

I was tickled by this gift of being able to pee your own medicine. Compared to my peers I was already in frightfully good shape as Catherine put it. And my mane of hair now had reddish highlights in the sun. Had I indeed found the fountain of youth? Time would tell. Time would tell.

Chapter 35

House of Mud

In the heat of the day, I stood on an oil drum looking out into the rice paddies and the hills beyond. All thoughts of the future pushed to the edge of my mind leaving me with a vague feeling of existential angst. My building partner for the hour, a Thai woman named Eh, looked up at me and asked cheerfully in English "What do you need?

"I'm looking for the meaning of life," I told her.

"Oh that you can find everywhere," she said with a smile as if it were in the very air we breathed.

I would soon learn that Eh and I had more in common than I had thought possible—a sense that the solution lay in localized self-sufficiency, and a desire to teach others, not to mention tarot cards and a New Age spirituality. The world having gotten smaller, she had just as much access to the same books and ideas as I did. I would continue to be surprised at what many of us had in common—a desire to experience a handmade life, an eco ethic of anti-materialism, a willingness to work together and get along with peoples of all nations. Each day this crew of some 30 women put our hands in mud for the task of erecting walls of a house. We ate together and shared living space as we devoted our efforts to this project over the 10 days.

I heard of the workshop through Pun Pun Farms, a sustainable outfit I saw listed on an earthen building network in 2008. I had become smitten with natural building and was thrilled to find a way to discover an aspect of my home country of Thailand that suited my own values rather than the highly acquisitive materialism of my Bangkok life. Thus I had embarked on a road trip given by Pun Pun to tour the north eastern provinces. We rode in the back of a truck farmer style, sleeping in rustic home built huts and using squat toilets exclusively. We visited organic farms that practiced sustainable methods and the new earthen buildings known as Baan Din (House of Earth).

The leaders of the tour were Jo Jandai, the founder of the adobe building movement in Thailand, and his American wife Peggy plus their son Tan who was maybe five at the time. The final destination was Pun Pun itself, an eco farm in the hills where Jo and Peggy had created an educational center to teach the skills of sustainable living to an international body of students. Jo had been the son of a farmer who had gone to Bangkok, following the usual path of young people hoping to better their life. But he was unique in that he recognized that there was not a better life to be had there when so much of your life was devoted to working long hours to afford a life that offered little in emotional and spiritual satisfaction. So after seven years in the city he returned to his family homestead.

Jo brought adobe building techniques to Thailand after a visit to the states where he saw the pueblos of Arizona. Walking inside these adobe buildings he realized that they were so much cooler inside and wondered if the same technique would work in the heat of Northern Thailand. So he aimed to try it out making bricks from the very earth beneath his feet on his farm. He succeeded in making several such buildings, but his pursuit of a hand made life from the land was a hard sell in an upwardly mobile society. No Thai girl would marry him. Then he met Peggy. This cross pollination of an interracial couple fit right in with my own world view and I followed their story with interest.

It was 2013 when I came to Thailand again to this women's building workshop. Peggy had joined forces with another American woman. Ginger headed the International Women's Partnership for Peace and Justice based in Thailand. The two had found Jeap, a Thai woman, who ran a non-profit that served to support ethnic minority students. It was for these students that we were building a house. The ethnic minority were what I used to know as hill tribe people. Still marginalized by not being granted full Thai citizenship, they were also teased by fellow students for their accents and tribal background. They left their homes to attend school so they lacked a supportive family and Jeap had taken them in. And thus the need for a house, which we would build. The building was already underway when our international crew of women arrived at the site.

The cement foundation had already been poured and the bricks made. We began our first day by passing bricks from hand to hand in a long line of women. With many hands to share the work the walls went up quickly. By the second day in fact. On the third day we installed the doors wedging them in with a mixture of mud and straw. Once the windows were installed we could plaster the walls inside and out then apply an earthen paint.

The temperature got hotter as the week progressed and one day I came to a dead halt halfway down the path to the stream. The 100° heat had leached out every last thought I had and left me with a feeling of blankness. What exactly was I doing with my life I had been wondering? What could I be doing with my life going forward? But nothing came to me.

Back home the recession had given my organizing business such a pummeling that 2013 was my worst year yet even with the emerging recovery. And my relationship with Catherine had essentially been stamped expired. Some of my long time friends were planning on leaving the Bay Area given that the high cost of living had squeezed out all but the moneyed elite of Silicon Valley. In this atmosphere my life had somehow run out of meaning and my skills were nothing more than a portfolio of antiquated analog hobbies—dressmaking, carpentry, bicycle repair, gardening, storytelling in various mediums and shoemaking. Skills geared towards an obsession with a post-industrialized society that never came. I simply wished to feel useful until I figured out how to weather old age and die without lingering, starvation being my choice.

It may have been that tour with Pun Pun that I'd taken in 2008 that had irrevocably pushed my life away from the aspirations I shared with Catherine for a comfortable house in the suburbs, one that was within range of San Francisco for our cultural interests going to dance performances and film festivals. After I got back from that tour with Pun Pun, Catherine was planning to remodel the bathroom. She asked me to look at some tile choices.

"This one looks more natural don't you think?" she said pointing to an earth tone tile. But the word natural in the realm of a building material had taken on a whole new meaning for me.

"What's natural about it," I wanted to ask her. "It's a commercially manufactured material attempting to look natural." But I knew such a comment would just sound obnoxious and wouldn't be constructive. So I picked a tile and we carried on. The bathroom got a fashionable remodel with a pebbled floor in the shower which appeased my desire for natural materials, but my path continued to be driven by different interests and values especially the desire to go small and reduce my carbon footprint.

On the second day of wall building, I was partnered with Khin a woman from Myanmar.

"Get on the drum," she said to me in minimal English. I looked at her to see if this was an order. "I am fat," she said by way of explanation which indeed she was. So I climbed up onto the barrel as she told me to do and she proceeded to hand me bricks.

As I stood watching a young woman gamely place bricks I felt compelled to coach her on her technique, something I rarely did outside of client work. And as we worked together we got to know each other. There were no shirkers. Everyone showed up and did their part, some with more talent than others, but nothing was so difficult that we couldn't do every part of it.

As I plastered the walls alongside my roommate, Susanna, I eased my angst by telling her about what was going on in my life. Susanna was dressed in a tunic over pantaloons as befitted her Malaysian home country and sported a natty wide brim hat. She spoke a British English and was bisexual, so was highly conversant in relationships with women. She urged me to get out on my own. But I knew I wasn't ready to leave Catherine yet. She was still my best friend; we just didn't have the same future in mind. I was headed in a different direction, but wasn't quite sure what. I was testing an alternative reality by coming to this workshop.

The house was being finished amazingly fast even though it felt like I was working very slowly. At the end of every day we would take pictures of what was accomplished usually with a pair of women in the foreground doing a yoga pose. There was something very feminine about this choice of presentation. And no one had to care how they looked. At the end of the day we washed ourselves, and the buckets, in the stream using handfuls of straw as a scrubber and then went for a swim in the pond. Back at the lodge I washed my clothes at the outdoor sink and dried them on the line.

In the evening we would gather in the dining area under the main house where the wifi signal was, and log onto Facebook. Facebook had become so ubiquitous that we were all thoroughly addicted, eager to post our updates for the day. It was the only thing about our little community that I questioned. Here we would work together all day, but at night we still wanted to trade comments with people back home. I missed the distance I could get by leaving home. I missed the long discussions I remembered from evenings at previous workshops and the visibility of books everyone was reading. Talking and reading together created a group understanding of emerging new perspectives. That was our reality in 2008. Five years later all that changed with social media.

By the middle of the workshop we had begun to friend each other on Facebook. And with all the tagging and posting pictures of each other, I no longer felt a need to report anything since my friends at home could see me happily posing with all my new mud covered sisters. I could wait to report my experience and give it the perspective of time. This skill was still left largely undeveloped by so much breaking news reporting. Only Susanna with her feminist training and writer's mind could beat me to these bigger perspectives which she now applied to the news of the missing Malaysian airplane, duly analyzing all the speculations and conspiracy theories in terms of our own hopes.

Some of the women even checked their phones at the building site. One of my Facebook contacts back home watching her Facebook stream came to realize that a childhood friend from Chattanooga was in fact attending the same workshop as I was. I was duly approached by Lisa from Chattanooga to confirm our mutual acquaintance. She photographed me and posted the picture to show our friend. This coincidence somehow leaving me unimpressed; so often did this happen these days. Yet it was an extraordinary coincidence that we should have come so far into the hinterlands to find we had a friend in common back in the States.

Facebook was now somehow an ersatz reality next to our daily immersion in mud. Mud that I spread over my skin instead of sunblock. "Clean dirt" I told Lisa who did not like getting her feet dirty though it couldn't be helped. We both tied our long hair back under our straw hats. She liked making things with her hands and was adept with a sewing machine, but had never done any building. And because she lived in Bangkok (with her Canadian husband) not far from my family compound we kept in touch and came to be friends. She would be the first of my mud hut sisters network in Bangkok.

In the last two days of the workshop we adorned our building with feminine touches. Jeap pressed ceramic medallions into the walls— round tiles painted with floral motifs. In the front bedroom two young women created vines of cob plaster climbing the walls. And on the curved walls of the exterior Tanya, my third roommate, a self described brutal Russian artist, fashioned a full size tree out of rocks and colored tile that she labored over to the end, even when we had all our bags packed.

In the wrap up at our last meeting it was obvious that people had been profoundly moved by the experience. We were awed that we had managed to complete a viable house in so short a time—a house for people we had actually met who would then live in it.

One woman said she was surprised to discover her own strength and ability though she had never done such work. The mother of a mother daughter pair commented that she was now confident that her daughter could look after herself in the world. Tanya said that she was not normally impressed by non-professional architectural work, but in this case she was. Susanna spoke of how so many of us likely came to this workshop with unresolved problems and issues, but in this community experience together, we would likely go home and find some shift had happened. This prompted me to say that I had already benefited and been filled with hope for Thailand after seeing how so many from disparate classes and levels of experience and education had been able to work together in harmony. Another young woman was so overcome by emotion she could only offer a single syllable before giving up. Khin from Myanmar I would now follow on Facebook as she organized her own building workshop. I had made many friends by doing little dances during the breaks and yearning in Thai for barbecued chicken.

Mud hut building agreed with me. The weight of the bricks and the stickiness of the mud had worked its way into my tactile memory so firmly that I would think of the house as a part of me and I of it when I saw pictures of the roof being put on after we had left. The profound satisfaction of having done something real lingered with me.

Chapter 36

Tiny House of My Dreams

When Catherine and I broke up we lived together for a couple of years until it grew too cumbersome to manage when we began to date other people. I dreamed of living in a tiny house on wheels. I went to the Dream Inn in Santa Cruz where I could rest my eyes on the smooth ocean as I took notes at a weekend workshop given by a young woman named Ella who had built her own tiny house. She lived in it with her harp, her boyfriend and a large dog. She was still in music school in Scotland when she discovered tiny houses, and knew right then that that would be how she would live on the earnings of a musician. She raised money for it playing her harp on the streets; busking, I learned, was the term.

As part of our divorce package Catherine offered to fund my acquisition of a tiny house of my own so long as it was not more than $24,000. As soon as she agreed to this I went on Craig's list and there found the house of my dreams. How serendipitous was that I thought. It was a little outside of my budget at $32,500, but it was the right size.

I knew that I would not have much room to park my tiny house anywhere I could imagine in the Bay Area. It was 2016 and the housing crisis would only get worse as residents dug in their heels against any new housing developments, especially apartment buildings. Nor would any town consider legalizing the use of tiny houses on wheels as a living solution as had been done in Sacramento and Fresno. So I would have to live in it illegally and by the grace of the neighbors. For it was a complaint driven ordinance, this business of living in trailers and RVs.

In the workshop Ella had likened the legality situation to gay marriage whereby the fact of it being illegal to marry your same sex partner did not prevent people from doing so. I thought this was a charming analogy. And having lived in gay marriage sin, illegally for so long, I figured this would be yet another bleeding edge of my semi legal, lesbian pioneering life. And like the gay community, those who had built tiny houses to live in were determined to find a way to legalize their way of life. It was basically the same demographic. Both communities were largely white, educated, articulate and privileged. Tiny house people wouldn't take no for an answer, but would find their way through the zoning system and building codes looking for leverage town by town. I was never actually for marriage gay or otherwise. I felt it would load more conventional expectations on what was already a conventional suburban life and I felt diminished by the idea. The whole point of being gay was not having to get married. (This is not to say that marriage equality wasn't a good thing. It was a needed legal protection, especially for women to retain custody of their children, and for the partners who were not the birth mother of their children.)

Ella offered an open invitation to everyone in the class to visit her tiny house. I went to see it with Pamela who lived nearby. It was the first tiny house I had actually been inside. And though it was small as a living space, it didn't feel small because everything was to scale and the high ceiling of the loft gave a spacious feeling of headroom. Ella said she could go smaller because even at this size there was still too many places where clutter could accumulate. Humans really didn't need that much living space, especially with the whole ocean to bathe in and several acres of land to roam as she had, not to mention our benign California climate.

The first tiny house on wheels was created by Jay Shafer, an architect who wanted to design the smallest possible house that would provide all he needed and still be a house. In this exploration he evoked the spiritual ideals of Henry David Thoreau, who in 1885 wrote his iconic book *Walden Pond* about getting away from it all. But in the context of Silicon Valley it also carried something of the miniaturization of electronics and computers that was helping us live smaller. There was one barrier to his exploration. Such a tiny house was technically illegal because zoning laws required houses to be of a certain size, varying from town to town. In Los Angeles it was 800 square feet. In the expensive town of Hillsborough just up the freeway from us it was 1600 square feet — the size of Catherine's house where we had at one time comfortably housed four adults, two dogs and a cat. Zoning for size was how towns kept poor people out.

When Jay Shafer thought to build his tiny house on a trailer it was no longer considered a house. In legal terms it was now a vehicle and thus could escape this minimal square footage requirement of a house on land. Thus the tiny house on wheels was born. And like other innovators he got the press interested in it, touting the virtues of living simply with pictures of the house with its classic gable roof and railed front porch. It was so adorable and picturesque it immediately became the cover story for the Sunday magazine section of local newspapers bringing it to my attention in 1999. The porch of the tiny house as a design feature struck me as a bit over the top American gothic, but the gable roof made it seem like a home to me. It was 8ft wide and 14ft long.

I was already smitten by the idea of tiny shacks for human use, not because of *Walden Pond* though the book was required reading in high school. Thoreau's treatise was largely a critique of contemporary society and not so much a how-to book. At the library I found two key books about building your own house. The first was called *Shelter* in which I was assured that building your own home was a human right. In this book I read about a man who renovated his own two bedroom house on the cheap while he was living in it, wrapping his sleeping bag in plastic sheeting at night to fend off the cold of an Oregon winter. This story made housing accessible to me in a contemporary suburban context. Another book Lester Walker's *Tiny Houses: Or How To Get Away From It All* encapsulated for me actual tiny houses complete with floor plans and photographs. One was Bernard Shaw's writing cabin which was built on a turn table so it could be moved with the sun. Yes I definitely needed a writing cabin.

As a family, we acquired a sailboat in my early teens. It was moored at the nearby Pete's Harbor where I was introduced to the idea that people could actually live on boats as they were doing there. Our boat was just big enough to have a cabin with a galley and a head that pumped your excrement right into the waters below, though we never once used it as day sailors. The idea that you could cross the ocean while living in such a boat just made such living in tight quarters all the more viable. A young man had just sailed solo around the world in a boat not much bigger than ours. I was equally enthralled by the books of Thor Heyerdahl describing his ocean voyage in a hand built raft in his book *Kon-Tiki* followed by *The Ra Expedition*. Seeded by the adventures of these adult lives I saw options for myself that would not require me to aspire to the goals of housing expected by a suburban nuclear family. A tiny house on wheels spoke to me of the maverick explorer lifestyle that it could offer.

After I took my tiny house class I returned to my mother's garage to remodel it into a tiny house with a loft bed just so I could practice building even though my mother didn't want me living on her property, nor did I want to live with her. The garage was so old it still had remnants of the old knob and tube wiring and no electricity had been available inside the garage since my mother bought the property, long ago while I was still in college. I was confident I could wire it myself. When she saw me up on a ladder wearing my tool belt running wire through the walls she made the memorable statement, "Well I never thought my daughter would want to be a plumber."

I did not correct her that I was doing the work of an electrician and that this would mean she would now have lighting in her garage. I just smiled at this blatant class assessment and what it meant to her that I had double backed on her college aspirations to rise above her working class roots. Her grandfather having been a horse shoer, and her father proud that he did not work with his hands, but was an accountant. Did she even know how much a plumber charged let alone an electrician?

I had learned all this from my construction technology class and was itching to use my newly acquired skills. In order to put into practice what I had learned in the class, I decided to cut out some windows to let more light in. I cut the wood out from between the studs and cut a window sill for it. The second window I cut to match an existing window in the same wall. This window I actually had to frame and make a window sill. I covered the openings with plexiglass waiting for the day I could build a real window sash

My mother didn't care what I proposed to do with the garage as I had so brilliantly fixed the hard to open shed doors several years before, by making them into sliding doors. This raised the curb appeal of the structure considerably and inspired her to paint the whole front of the garage brown with black trim, keeping the wooden door pulls I had made. Picking out colors and painting was more her thing. The building itself was built over the rock cliff of her property on stilts, so she didn't park her car in it, but just filled it with whatever junk she was discarding from her house. At least it had survived the 1989 earthquake

Later I insulated the walls with a broken hot tub cover from Catherine's that I cut up with a bread knife. After I had used up the hot tub cover I filled the cavities with discarded pillows. After several years of this I could finally cover the walls with wafer board ply made of thin shavings of wood which made an interesting visual surface. A client gave me a hammock so I cut a secret compartment in one of the walls to store it in where there was also a hook to hang it from with a corresponding hook on the opposite wall. But I was most proud of the sleeping loft, complete with built-in cabinet and shelves.

During this loft building phase I was running my table saw when I glanced out the window and saw a man on a bicycle admiring the view.

I took a break and went out to talk to him. He told me he was a carpenter himself and had stopped because he heard the sound of a saw. His name was Tim, a name I trusted I told him as it was the name of my long time friend from college. But he couldn't have been more different from my first Tim, being much shorter and not given to exacting conversation intent on nailing down the precise definitions of words. This Tim was of working class roots with a friendly hang loose style to match. He also noticed natural beauty as an artist would with few words just feasting his eyes on the natural landscape as he was doing outside my mother's garage admiring the view of the hills.

I liked him and took his number in case someone asked me for a referral to a handyman. Then I hired him myself on my mother's behalf when I realized the garage roof leaked and was going to ruin all the work I put into insulating the walls. Working with him on this repair was enough to allow me to get to know him. The repair didn't last more than a year or two and after another wet winter I had him back to frame a whole new roof. This was a huge improvement and made the garage look like a small house rather than two adjoining sheds built at different times. The two roofs adjoining being so problematic.

Having done so much work on this garage remodel I knew I could build a tiny house on wheels from scratch, but now I didn't want to. There was nothing special about erecting walls and running electricity. The fun was in the design of the living space. Thus this tiny house on craigslist was at the perfect stage to allow me to customize the interior to my needs.

As I drooled over the charming cedar shingled tiny house on wheels that I couldn't afford, I just had to write the builders a fan letter in answer to their story about the house. The weekend builders of this structure had designed and created it for their own use, to park on a property where they could take turns taking their family to spend the weekend. One was a roofing contractor thus the use of cedar shingles to cover the house. It had been finished inside to the point of having all the electrical work done and the walls covered in old reclaimed fence boards. The loft had a sturdy ladder built from reclaimed beams that came out of a barn. They had fitted it with quality double paned windows and it was fully insulated. After I hit send on my fan letter I received a phone call 15 minutes later from the seller offering it to me for $26,000. This was such a generous discount that I agreed to go and look at it the next weekend.

I asked my new friend Tim to come with me and he asked all the pertinent questions while I took in the reality of this rig. It was everything I had hoped for. The height of it gave me pause. It was taller than any normal shed and would be a lot harder to hide in a backyard. But it was exactly this height that made the inside of it feel livable, giving a mini cathedral ceiling affect with the 13ft height overhead as soon as you walked in the door.

As I fell in love with it John the seller raised the price another $2,000. Tim took me aside and told me he could build such a rig for $10,000. That was actually the price that Jay Shafer's tiny house company was selling their half built rigs for. I realized I should not have let John know quite so much about me by showing him pictures of the adobe house I built in Thailand at a workshop with my mud hut sisters. Clearly anyone who could fly to Thailand to build a house for somebody else could afford another $2,000.

What difference did it make to me, I thought. These guys didn't even own a house of their own and lived in rental housing here in this rural town of Gilroy. John made his living catch as catch can selling used goods at flea markets. The two had put a lot of work into this project and wouldn't even be able to use it themselves. I had the money to cover the difference. I grimaced at the extra $2000, but said yes and put down $100 in deposit. John already had a receipt printed out stipulating that the deposit was received and that I would have 10 days to pay for it in full. Ten days to figure out my situation or lose my deposit.

I had not yet asked my mother if I could park it at her house, but when I had shown her the picture of the tiny house she had encouraged me to buy it since it was so little money. In retrospect she likely didn't realize that it was a house on wheels because she thought I would be moving to Gilroy. I broached the topic to both her and her boyfriend at dinner the next night. Then I showed them where on her property I was thinking of parking it and thought it was a done deal, but no. When I wrote thanking them for agreeing to host me, my mother phoned me sounding furious with me and told me how impertinent it was of me to have sprung this on them without preamble let alone assumed they had agreed to it. Besides, the neighbors would not for a minute allow such a permanent fixture to be parked right next to the road.

I had in fact spent a sleepless night wondering the same thing. I had been so eager to land a spot that I had not allowed myself to see that it was not even close to an ideal spot, so unprotected as it was from the street and being just a spit of land that then dropped off into a steep slope running down to the creek. I accepted the possibility that I would have to give up this dream of a tiny house for want of a suitable place to park it.

If I had any social media skills at all this would be the time to put them to use, I reasoned. I posted an ad on Craigslist and Nextdoor seeking a place to park the tiny house. But I didn't just describe what I needed I offered myself as a helper with a list of all the practical skills I had developed from carpentry to sewing and shoemaking. My community on Facebook supported me by posting this ad to their page. I received several offers, but all too far away from my home territory. I kept at it. I posted pictures of places that might host a tiny house to remind my contacts of my quest. When I posted a picture of a rundown trailer park in an industrial area of Redwood City I figured I had hit bottom.

That weekend I went to a house party of lesbian friends where I showed pictures of the tiny house I was considering buying and my dilemma of not being able to park it anywhere. Stacy and her partner Peggy told me not to buy it; it would just become an albatross around my neck. But another woman took one look at my pictures and said "Why wouldn't you buy it? It's adorable." She could totally see the potential it had. She herself owned a piece of property zoned for agricultural use where she had a shack she could sleep in. The cost to store a tiny house in a storage yard would be the same as the cost of renting storage for all my stuff. And my stuff could just as well be stored inside the tiny house. It seemed like a viable option at the time and it gave me the mental space to fully commit to owning the tiny house. I had to fully want something before a way would appear. Such was the way the universe worked.

The next day I received an e-mail from someone I knew from my Buddhist group. Marianna and I had tried at one time to start a Green Sangha together, a Buddhist environmental group and we had done a solar oven demonstration for a day in the park. We were connected on Facebook. She had been watching my search and had a place to offer at the bottom of her backyard where, in the past, an RV had been parked by the previous owner. I jumped at it.

As soon as I got home I went over to measure the space at dusk giving me just enough daylight to see my tape measure. Yes it would fit with four feet on either side between a fence and a row of bottle brush bushes. I had my spot and just in the nick of time. I was overjoyed.

Chapter 37

Tiny House Build

There was still one more hurdle before I could have John and his crew tow the tiny house to the Bay Area. I needed a place where I could built the interior and fit it with a kitchen and bathroom. Ideally, a flat paved spot with lots of room where I could work freely for a month at least that it would take me to outfit my rig. If only my father were still alive he would help me I thought; his house was the perfect location with a large garage full of tools and a driveway tucked away from the street down a cul-de-sac. It was all still there, I would just have to ask my stepmother Ott, a woman I had been estranged from apart from a few formalities of civility since my father died ten years ago. It was all I could do not to be mad at her and my father for completely leaving me out of his will as far as his property in the U.S. was concerned.

I decided to overcome my estrangement and just ask her. She wasn't in town, but offered to speak to me over the phone. She asked me what was up in a congenial way. I put on my most humble respectful voice. When I explained to her my request she was amenable to it as long as she could still drive her car into the garage. Yes she could; the driveway was just wide enough. So she said yes, as if she had been waiting for me to ask for something—anything. I was so grateful I couldn't be mad at her anymore, and offered to do a number of clean up projects for her while I was on the property. Much of this turned out to be the chore of going through my father's things, which had been boxed and put into the storage shed behind the garage. I felt reunited with my father, talking to him in my mind as I went through his files, college textbooks, and work memorabilia. As a professional organizer I was cut out for this work. It had just needed me to show up to do it.

The day the tiny house was to arrive I was ecstatic waiting out on the street to direct John into the driveway. They were delayed as they negotiated their way into the Bay Area from Gilroy. But finally the white truck appeared and the peak of the shingled house behind it followed by his partner Phil's truck. The site of a house moving down the street was so eye catching that several neighbors came out to see it shouting out compliments in admiration. Thanks to all the shows on cable TV, people loved the idea of a tiny house and were fascinated by the miniaturization of living in one as though it were a spectator sport. It felt so good to have it so welcomed after my frantic search for a place. Once parked and leveled John and I stepped inside so I could hand over my $28,000 in cash. I was now the proud owner of the most beautiful and satisfying thing I had ever owned. The crew, which included both their wives, and the family dog, said their goodbyes and left me to it.

The first thing I did was call up Tim to come and help me paint wood preservative over those beautiful cedar shingles. I didn't want them fading to that grey weathered look that John and Phil were going for. We hand brushed it on. The house was so small it didn't really take that long and it turned the wood color to a satisfyingly rich tone. I would have to reapply preservative every two years or so, but it was worth it.

Since I had so much experience with designing closets for clients I started with the closet. I glued scrap 1/8" plywood into twin sets of shelves. I cut pieces of hollow core doors to hold up a rod between them. It took up the entire width of the back wall of the loft and was larger than most tiny house closets though it meant I would forever after put on my pants lying down.

I had drawn a floor plan with a ruler on a pad of graph paper. I couldn't be bothered to learn Sketch Up. But I really had no idea how I would execute the plan. I just made it up as I went along looking for things to repurpose. When Ott asked me to help her get rid of an old desk I took note of its potential. It was solid wood with a dark wood veneer bordered with a light maple molding around the entire desk top. The ample drawers pulled out on wooden glides and would offer lots of storage space. I told Ott I could put it in the tiny house.

"No way it's too big," she said. Watch me I thought and seized on the challenge. I had always wanted a wooden kitchen counter and that night I researched what product could best be used to seal it. I made a drawing of the cabinet space I needed custom fit to my largest pot and the mason jars I wanted to place on shelves. Using the hollow core doors I found in my dad's wood pile plus the stash I had saved, I built boxes for the cabinets and for shelves. Nice sturdy lightweight boxes with thick edges. I designed a pull out cart on wheels that would fit into the remaining space between the two cabinets. This cart I designed for my cutting board beneath which I could stash a trash can. Each additional thing I decided to build pushed my completion date out further than one month, but no one was pressuring me and every additional space saving trick would turn out to be useful.

When Tim saw how I had arranged all the cabinets he pointed out that I still had space where the drawers ended that could be made into a secret compartment so I proceeded to put in three more shelves 8" deep and this become my food pantry accessible only if I pulled out my sliding cart. This kept things out of view cutting down on visual clutter. I decided to make cabinet doors for the cabinets to further cut down the visual clutter which meant learning how to cut mortises for hinges.

Ella had advised not to build every day because you would burn out so I kept seeing clients and put in three days a week building while I spent my evenings drawing and researching ideas.

I devoted a lot of thought as to what I would do for a bathroom and shower. Ella had mentioned that using a shower in the tiny house was problematic because of all the hot steam fogging up the windows and creating a moisture problem which was why she bathed in the ocean. Bearing this in mind I decided that showers were not right for a tiny house as small as Ella's or mine. What then did a bathroom really need? I stripped out the conventional requirements until I realized that all that was really needed was a drain to let water out and a floor that wouldn't be damaged by water. Water coming in was easy enough to do, but water going out was a specially engineered objective. That was the only thing that was really special about a bathroom.

I ordered a shower pan specially made for RVs, which was the only kind that gave a choice of where on the pan the drain would be located so it wouldn't interfere with the iron beams of the trailer below. The fiberglass pan also had a high wall to keep water from sloshing out which basically made it into its own tiny room—a wet bath.

Once I had decided on the shower pan all I really needed was a good sink that would serve as a bucket bath. A bucket bath was what in Asia was standard equipment for bathing. Standing in your tiled room with the drain in the floor you had a bowl for scooping water out of a large jar (or bucket if that's all you had) to sluice down your body. It was a delicious way to bathe and what I had enjoyed throughout my childhood in Thailand.

There are no such bathrooms being built in the homes of my peers in Bangkok anymore. They all wanted showers and some had installed spa bathtubs so huge that it wasn't worth waiting for the time it took to fill them. I continued my research. Pinterest was so stimulating it kept me up at night thinking of how to implement ideas I found there. I dubbed Pinterest the crack cocaine of builders and would not allow myself to look at it after sundown for fear of insomnia.

When the shower pan was delivered I asked Tim to drill a hole in the floor for the drain. I couldn't bring myself to drill into my brand new oak floor. Tim loved the shower pan, but when he saw that I was proposing to make a shower surround out of corrugated roofing tin it gave him pause.

"So you couldn't just get a fiberglass shower to go with the pan," he said.

"No that would just be too suburban," I pointed out. The corrugated tin was my tribute to the favorite roofing material of the pre-industrialized Thailand of my youth.

"I knew I missed you," he said in response to my design choice. I was paying him by the hour after all. All of my projects would have some off-beat aberration that took much longer and had requirements no one else would think to do. Tim did me proud as he carefully attached wooden scaffolding to gently curve the corrugated panel around the corner of my wet bath. As a finishing touch he trimmed the panel with a wood shelf at the top that would just hold the fan I would use to vent steam out of the bathroom window. John and Phil had done well designing the placement of windows to accommodate a bathroom in this very corner.

I toyed with the idea of using a large ceramic pot as my water container, much like the water jars found in the bathrooms of my childhood. They were cement jars as tall as a child and filled with an ordinary garden faucet. But I scratched that idea because of the weight of both the jar and the water on my plastic shower pan. A plastic bucket would serve; I'd just hang it by a hook on the wall under a faucet. I searched for my bucket in a horse supplies catalog remembering from my time living with Louise and her two horses that those buckets for watering horses had to be resistant to both bites and kicks. I browsed the entire catalog and found an interesting ribbed black grain feeder with a shelf at the top to keep grain from falling out. It bolted to the wall and was plenty deep enough to fit my biggest pot inside. This horse feeder would make a great kitchen sink. And being made of plastic it was light weight. It fit perfectly centered into the far wall of the corrugated shower surround. To finish this "bitchen", as a fellow tiny house builder called it, Tim drilled a hole through the wall to receive a pipe to which I installed an ordinary garden hose tap as my kitchen faucet. I now had my bathroom.

Having reinvented the shower I would also reinvent the bed. Catherine and I once went to a bed showroom to buy a new bed. It was like buying a car if not more so, being all about the illusion of comfort and technology. As Westerners, we are sold on both, but the more comfortable we tried to get the bed to be, the less we seemed to be able to get comfortable.

I came from a culture of hard beds. A bit too hard, I would say even for the tropics where a hard bed keeps you cooler. But with every visit I would get used to it and when I returned home my soft mattress topper left me feeling all crumpled up. I pulled it off. I had slept on my 4" foam pad perfectly happily for decades. I figured I could reduce this to a 3" foam bed if I softened up the floor a bit with ensolite floor tiles people used in gyms and kids playrooms. I searched craigslist for a used 3" memory foam mattress topper. There were lots being sold, likely because people had discovered that softer is not better when it comes to beds. I happily adapted to my minimalist mattress as soon as I moved in.

I also threw out having a fridge. I just didn't have room for anything near a full size one and those little dorm fridges didn't have enough freezer space. The fridge was also severely compromised in efficiency by having a door that opened vertically, letting all the cold air fall out. I had it in mind to make a fridge from a chest freezer which others had done with a device to raise the temperature up from freezing. This created a fridge efficient enough to run on solar power. I had already bought a freezer just to try out this project long before I even had it in mind to live in a tiny house. So I decided to leave it as a freezer and just keep it outside in the yard. I preferred to keep lots of frozen food on hand, not to mention a quart of ice cream. I could easily make ice to put in a cooler I reasoned, and bought an expedition cooler with extra thick walls.

When all the kitchen and bathroom elements were finished Sheilagh, my Canadian girlfriend, came down from Vancouver to help me break it in. She liked the tiny house and said it reminded her of her tree planting job when she lived in very spare circumstances in the forest, even to the folding camping chairs I had set up for us. I hadn't thought about seating apart from having a straight back chair at my desk. The camp chairs didn't look right. Despite all my anti-consumerist sentiments I suddenly wanted my house to visually express a real home in terms of a house beautiful vernacular. And the camp chairs just made it look like a fishing shack.

After some thought I realized that I needed that most suburban of Western symbols of comfort—a couch. It didn't have to be a full on couch with overstuffed arms and a back full of cushions, but it did need to have some form of upholstered cushioning. I built a box with wheels to slide over my cooler and another matching one to serve as extra storage. Then I took some of the memory foam I had cut off when I reduced the queen size mattress to fit, and cut it up until I had two cushions for which I made covers. I chose carefully from blue green upholstery fabric to go with my now painted blue green kitchen cabinets. I sewed up the cushion covers with proper box ends. Much better. This little bit of concession to interior design was the house beautiful touch I was looking for.

But it was not until I finished installing all the bookshelves that the interior really said 'house". For to have shelves meant you had things to put on shelves. So perhaps ownership of things was what made a modern home even when striving for simplicity. It was my books that made it my home, just as Ella's harp made her tiny house uniquely hers.

I was now ready to move in, some months ahead of the Australian woman I had sat next to at Ella's workshop, who was building her home from scratch. I had been admiring her efforts as a Facebook friend.

A necessary hurdle of tiny house living for most people is downsizing and I certainly had my share of that to do. I cheated and put what dress up clothes I still wanted in a storage box that I pushed under the house along with another storage box for shoes and boots and one for bags and travel items. The books were harder to cull so I installed a bookcase in Ott's garage as a staging area to store books I wasn't quite ready to let go of yet. Culling photos turned out to be easy because I had made all the albums I wanted and what I hadn't used was so well organized I could just throw out entire decades of my life in an hour. That was satisfying to see where my hyper organizing paid off. I would sell most of the monetary valuables on e-bay while plotting to further outfit my mother's garage as an offsite storage area and workroom. My tiny house life would likely never be fully free of such off site storage because I was a crafter, a maker of things, a homesteader. Not a purist minimalist.

The tiny house was now ready to haul the two miles to the concrete pad in Marianna's yard behind her screen of bottle brush. I rented a truck and Tim hooked up the trailer and drove it over. It was time to move in. I moved my chest of drawers in with all the contents basically undisturbed along with my signature red desk. With my clothes put away and my dishes on the open shelves and my new toaster oven on the counter I was technically ready for actually living in my tiny house. But I was emotionally overwhelmed by it, by all the chores the house required. Chores that I had in fact chosen as part of the off-grid systems I had devised. And it was cold. Colder than I had expected to be.

"What have I done to myself?" I wondered

Chapter 38

What Had I Done To Myself?

The build had gone so well that I had not had a moment's doubt that what I had designed might not be conducive to everyday habitation. After all, the intention of my design was to have me living with an intimate relationship with my use of resources, particularly water, and the minimal use of refrigeration to cut down on food waste. The first few weeks of the reality of it were both magical and distressing.

The first night I spent at my tiny house in the backyard of my Buddhist sangha friend, I noticed a cat sitting on the garden path lit by the security light as though by moonlight. She sat looking at me in my tiny fairy tale size cottage. What a magical sight I thought, a welcoming omen. I opened the door to say hello, but the noise of the door scared her away. Indeed it was so quiet in that garden that I climbed into my loft bed under the eaves and fell into a deep sleep I hadn't enjoyed in some time.

In the morning standing by my dresser I was startled by the morning light streaming in. With the two windows on each side of the house being only six feet apart the contents of my house were sharply lit with daylight. I could see every dust speck. I immediately got out a cloth and started polishing all the chrome—on my Berkey water filter, my electric kettle and my vintage insulated carafe. Once everything was free of fingerprints and water droplets it sparkled as though in a showcase. I was reminded of the work of Joseph Cornell providing a tiny view into a tiny surreal world in his arrangements of objects in shadow boxes.

Thus the tiny house magnified the experience of living. The confined space, the strangeness of my kitchen layout, plus the added dimension of being so tightly connected to other activities further down the pipeline. Emptying a waste water tank, pee tank and poop bucket for instance. All of this created an intense feedback loop to every mundane activity having to do with cooking, eating, washing up and putting things away. It forced me into a state of hyper mindfulness.

And this was exactly what I had wanted. To be intimately involved in the entire cycle of my water, energy use and waste stream in order to see how much I or anyone could mitigate our impact on the planet. I just didn't know yet what such a lifestyle would require of me and this unknown made me feel a little uneasy once I moved in. Add to that the stress of being in a new place, working out new routes to all my clients and figuring out what to feed myself now that I was single. This was why moving was stressful, I reminded myself. My body reacted by being hungry all the time and I wished my outdoor freezer was full of frozen dinners.

I had been congratulating myself for having finessed my move into the tiny house by moving two or three boxes at a time while carrying on with my full schedule of clients. It did take longer, but I convinced myself it would be less painful that way, like pulling the bandaid off a little bit at a time. I was trying to squeeze as much of my old life as I could into the tiny house. Moving in a little at a time gave me time to find places for everything. I installed a lot of hooks for hats and bags. I fit onto the remaining wall space all the way up to the peak of the roof, all the artwork that reflected my identity. I hung, at the top, my Thai grandmother's high school diploma from St. Joseph's convent in Bangkok that she had so prominently displayed in her dining room. Below that the abstract collage I had done at art school of colored squares randomly arranged on a white background inside a checkerboard border. It was a design that I would later incorporate into my business card as a professional organizer. And I still had room to fit in my collection of drums—Celtic style hand drums and a Thai country style long drum. Making the house functional was a little trickier.

I had done numerous moves unpacking clients with crews of organizers. But those houses were so much alike, there was hardly any difference between one kitchen and another. The challenge of my tiny house was that it was unlike anywhere I or anyone I knew had ever lived before. Nothing could be taken for granted to function normally from the fridge to the sink to the toilet. I had purposefully deconstructed and reorganized basic systems and I had no experience using such systems on a daily basis.

Would the cooler keep my food cold enough? What would it be like to boil water for all my washing up? Would I be able to cook breakfast successfully given my regime of fried eggs, sausages and refried beans? How long would my butane cartridge hold out in my stove? Where could I buy more? What would I use for heat?

Winter is a hard time to move into a tiny house. The days are so short there is little time to tend to things outdoors. I came home to a dark house with an unlit entrance gate to open. Then it rained and rain seeped into my outdoor freezer. I had the wrong footwear for the muddy garden

I was to tend. The mud tracked into my house. My bicycle no longer had a garage to park in so I had covered it, but my karate uniform which was strapped to the carrier in a sports bag felt slightly damp when I put it on at class.

I did order a propane heater and when I saw a space heater at a garage sale I picked it up. But the house would not stay warm on its own. What was wrong with it? It had felt so insulated during the hot summer months, staying so cool inside.

A few days later, while wiping the floor I felt a draft and tracked it down to a half inch gap under the door. No wonder the house stayed cool. It was pulling cold air across it constantly. It took two trips to the hardware store to find the right weatherstripping. Then I didn't have any nails on hand to install the rubber flange, for I no longer had a garage. All my hardware was now at my stepmother's house two miles away. In the summer these were easy problems to solve, but the winter gave everything an edge of desperation.

My car was so full of stuff thrown in it for lack of storage I put my lunch in one day and I couldn't find it come lunch time. These scenarios were both ridiculous and maddening for an organizer.

I spent my evenings urgently researching. What was the proper temperature for food safety? I bought a freezer thermometer which compounded my fears because the temperature in the cooler was in the red zone hovering near 50°. I did not fancy food poisoning on top of everything else. I researched every item I kept in the cooler from the eggs to the mayonnaise. Mayonnaise I was relieved to learn could be kept at room temperature because it was so acidic. And eggs in Europe were kept at room temperature because chickens there were vaccinated for salmonella, unlike those in the states. Hmmm.

Cooking breakfast was at least doable. I loved my stove in a drawer. And I installed a hook to hang my iron skillet right next to it, and another hook to hang the pot scrubber I used to clean it. It was the washing up I had to reinvent. What kind of dish drainer could I fit and where? I prowled the aisles of Target and Bed Bath & Beyond looking for solutions to new problems I seemed to face daily. Why hadn't I thought of pot holders for instance or a doormat?

When the temperature dropped I braved firing up the propane heater, Mr. Heater (Little Buddy model). Little Buddy heated things up quickly and the 4" disk of burning wires felt like an open fire. I cracked a window so I wouldn't run out of oxygen until I realized that enough fresh air was entering through the drain in the shower pan. I also put together one of those flower pot heaters so widely demonstrated on youtube. Once I got all the right size flower pots bolted together and some votive candle holders to hold the four tea lights safely it worked beautifully offering a warm presence by my feet that didn't overheat like the propane heater. I used my electric space heater in the morning up in the loft. I also had a hot water bottle (courtesy of my Canadian girlfriend) to warm up the bed at night. A sleeping bag I had needed to store became my winter quilt.

Clients gave me all sorts of useful items they didn't need anymore. Thus I was supplied with pyrex dishes sized for a toaster oven from their bachelor days, silverware, pots, pot holders, tiny utensils from a VW van equipped to live in, plus containers to put it all in, and a weather thermometer. Very handy so I could watch how cold it was getting—48° this morning.

Some things I thought I'd do a certain way had to be completely revised. My vision of dish washing Thai farmer style required room to spread out three dish pans of water—two soapy and one clean plus room to spread dishes out to dry; all this usually done outside. I knew I wouldn't be able to replicate the three dishpans; I had two dish pans that fit perfectly into my sink with their rims resting on the edges of the sink. I thought I would just switch them out, but moving full dish pans of dirty water got old pretty quickly. And dishes seemed to get greasier in the process.

It brought to mind my first *Cat In The Hat* book. The one about the pink stain the cat in the hat was "helping" to clean up, but the pink stuff just moved from one thing to another until it got all over the house then shot outside and covered the entire landscape. That's what greasy dishwater reminded me of. Plus the waste water tank filling up prompted me to rethink even filling a dishpan.

I took a closer look at the drain in my shower pan, put a large mouthed funnel into it and poured the greasy water from washing a pan directly into it (to the waste water tank below). I scraped my dishes clean into my compost bucket. Then soaped each dish without laying it down anywhere. From my insulated carafe I poured clean hot water over the dish to rinse it into my dishpan, then put the dish in my dish drainer. Now I had soapy mostly clean water in the dish pan where I could throw in my silver ware to wash. This was in reverse order to how my English grandmother had taught me to wash dishes when I was 8, but it worked.

I found a minimalist dish drain at Bed Bath & Beyond that came strapped to a drying mat and laid it on top of my toaster oven.

That was another thing about my kitchen. It came in layers. To open my cooler I had to bend over, hold that position and pull away the couch bench that covered the cooler, then roll the couch bench back over it or I wouldn't have room to move.

I learned to remember all the items I would need from the cooler for each meal though I'm still forgetting at least one thing. For the evening meal the dishes had to be put away or I wouldn't be able to use my toaster oven. Was there anywhere to put things down that wouldn't be used so soon?

I discovered where. On my sewing table under the loft ladder, and on one bench, plus my chair in a pinch.

The floor being cold I put down a rug, but had to shunt it out of the way to get to the cooler, then put it back again. I did this with my feet. It got to be a little dance. Shunt to the right. Pull the bench off the cooler, then shunt to the left after I pushed the bench back. To use the sink I had to step into the shower pan which was often wet I realized so I took to standing on the walls of the shower pan and leaning awkwardly towards the sink. This bad posture would hurt later. What had I done to myself? I wondered.

I told myself I was living on a boat. It sounded more romantic. The yacht harbor where my family's sailboat was berthed in the '70s had a handful of people living on their boats. Yes the narrowness of my tiny house did resemble a boat more than a house. Those live aboard boats were the last bit of affordable housing one could own in the Bay Area, but they too had to go when the harbor was made over into condos and office parks. Though there was still a place for weekend sailors to park.

Other tiny house dwellers strived for normalcy with kitchens equipped with sinks and refrigerators. Even washers and dryers. But those tiny houses were at least twice as big as mine and a little wider. I wanted to be low profile. This necessity cut into any normalcy. I felt like I was on an expedition climbing a mountain from a base camp. I'd read lots of those books as a kid too along with the sailing books.

These tight quarters forced me to put things away all the time. The discipline of the tiny house was severe that way. And their were chores that could not be put off. Both the waste water tank and pee tank only took a week to fill, I would soon discover. That first week filled me with trepidation. But what really drove me to distraction was the unfinished curtains. I pinned a piece of fabric to the wall and that took care of the street light that kept waking me up and the neighbors looking in as they got in their cars in their driveway five feet from my house. I just couldn't open the curtains to let any light in because I didn't have a curtain rod to slide the curtain panel on. And I couldn't face going to any store on Thanksgiving weekend with all the doorbuster crowds. I longed for some sense of normalcy. I needed a break from all this hyper mindfulness living.

I texted Catherine to ask if I could come over because my house was exhausting me. She was happy to have me as she was missing me. She fed me turkey dinner leftovers and I built a roaring fire. What a luxury of heat. We put our feet up and watched a movie. I did not have a TV installed in my tiny house. I suspected I wouldn't have time to watch it. (I had installed a hammock hoping I'd actually have time to lie around in it. It proved to be a good place to read.) I stayed two days at Catherine's in my old room. Then having restored some sense of normalcy I began to miss my things and decided to go home and face the music. I would boldly empty the waste water tank.

I had bought an 11 gallon waste tank because I knew how heavy a 5 gallon bucket was and even with wheels this tank would likely be difficult to maneuver. It was my aim to empty my pee tank into it to dilute the pee so as not to burn any plants I was feeding with the nitrogen in the urine. I would then trundle the 11 gallons around to the trees and bushes that surrounded my house to water them via the handy outlet on the tank where a hose could be installed. Too bad the garden was already so well watered with all the rain. At least the plants would be fertilized.

The tank was heavy, but relatively easy to drag around even over the tall clumps of grass. A week was a short leash, but at least in the dry months a weekly watering of the garden would be welcome. I just kept reminding myself that urine was sterile as I handled these tanks.

The poop bucket gave me a month before I had to haul it out to empty into my rotating composting bin, an easier task. I also added the dog poop of the resident German Shepherd as it was part of my trade to pick it up thus closing the loop for both of us.

Gradually I adapted to the regime of the tiny house and it to me. I went to the Marine store and bought myself a deck tile to put in the shower pan. This kept my feet dry and the ergonomics of being able to stand at the sink was a huge improvement. I also made a dumbwaiter for the loft with a simple pulley attached to the ceiling so I could get my laundry crate down. I did laundry and washed my hair at Catherine's and we got in some episodes of *The Crown* with all its sumptuous living.

I invited some colleagues over to see my tiny house.

"What do you miss most ?" one asked.

"Space," I said. A place to put down random things. Otherwise I had pretty much everything I needed. I could also multi task like nobody's business. Check e-mail while frying eggs, put my contacts in without having to walk to another room. I would probably never burn a meal again because there was no other room to be gone in. And after a couple of weeks of the hyper mindfulness my concentration and my memory seemed to improve.

And there was still room for the unexpected.

Jane, the helpful client of the VW bus utensils, off loaded a vintage model of an animal cell that had been at NASA (in the department that studied mutations due to radiation). The cell model needed a home so when she retired from her job as a research technician she took it with her. I admired it every time I saw it in the condo she shared with her wife. One day she decided it could go. It was made of clear fiberglass upon which were attached all the parts of the cell painted in blues and green. It was so cool I told her I wish I had a bigger house to keep it in.

The more I looked at it the more I wanted it so I took it home to admire. I set it on the couch bench where the blue green base blended in perfectly with the blue green of my couch. As I dusted all the cell parts remembering my high school biology I realized the base was hollow all the way into the cell body. Perhaps I could get a light into it I thought. No bulb would fit so I retrieved a string of Christmas lights from storage, stuffed the lights into the body of the cell, plugged it in and there I had a giant Christmas ornament. What a beauty.

At nightfall my lit up cell was so beautiful and full of little lights it was all the holiday decoration I needed. It would be my pagan tiny house Christmas tree I decided.

How appropriate I thought. For some years now when asked what was my religion, I would put down that I believed in the divinity of cell division for that was as distilled as I could sum up my awe at life forcing itself into being with every seed and unfurling leaf. No matter what the conditions or circumstance, these intrepid cells of living beings of all forms still insisted on being born and carrying on. And so would I. And so would we all whatever might befall us I wrote optimistically in my Christmas post that year of 2016.

Chapter 38

The Art of Poop

Before the tiny house was even a figment of my imagination I built a composting toilet. It could be said that the tiny house was merely a vehicle for my life's goal to live a life processing my own poop. A dream that began to coalesce during the pivotal construction technology class I had taken some 20 years before. It was in the plumbing section of the class that I became convinced that the flush toilet designed as it was to connect to a centralized sewage system was a seriously bad idea. Not only did it use copious amounts of water and toxic chemicals to process our wastes, but given a good rain the poop would overflow the tanks and float out into the Bay.

As my construction technology teacher described this process he drew the tanks on the chalkboard to show the traveling poop. He did not mention how this problem could be fixed with additional tanks say. Nor did he give an opinion on our centralized water system, but somewhere between the lines I sensed a dissatisfaction with the process. So this first world system with all its claims of modern sanitation couldn't even keep poop out of the ocean? I thought to myself. This was a complaint that was so often leveled at Thailand when mention of all the picturesque houses on stilts along the river came up. Not to mention those fancy upscale hotels at the beach that were still dumping their sewage in the sea. I felt vindicated and indignant at the same time.

My fascination with poop might go back even further to a story I read in childhood. A story about the rich and poor. I knew I was a rich kid because of the amount of services and material wealth showered upon me from the moment of my arrival in Thailand while the poor kids were so poor they had barely enough clothes to wear everyday and one pair of flip flops and a school uniform with school shoes if they were lucky. The children of our staff at my house were lucky that way. My grandmother paid their school fees and bought their uniforms. They had very few toys if any and slept in one room with all their family. Growing up alongside this disparity in lifestyles was a daily reminder to me of this divide.

The story that I took so much to heart was about a rich kid who was put in a roomful of toys. When the adults came back he was crying because he couldn't decide what toy to play with. These adults (who in retrospect sound a lot like psych researchers) then put a poor kid in a room full of horse manure. When they came back that child was running excitedly around the room throwing horse poop in the air shouting "with all this manure there must be a pony". I loved the idea of this crazy kid seeing something good in horse poop. I also understood why the rich kid would be crying because he was alone with no kids to play with. I didn't want to be him.

I had often abandoned my room full of imported toys to join the poor kids making marbles out of dirt—the clay they found in the soil in the garden. It was clean dirt this soil and made a fine modeling clay nobody had to buy. And when the gardener cut down the palms of a banana plant it was a good day indeed. For he made us each a horse. First he cut a little notch ten inches or so from the end of the stem, poked a hole in the "nose" near the end and with a strand of bark string poked through this "nose" he made a bridle of the string looped around the "neck". That was one of the funnest afternoons as we chased each other around on our horses, the fine feathery tales sweeping the ground behind us. It was a reminder of the abundance of making do with what materials you had on hand.

The idea of making things from natural materials was apparent throughout Thai culture in the woven baskets made from coconut palm fronds. The the hard stems of the coconut palm fronds were good for making sticks for dried flower buds to be threaded onto to make a stalk of buds such as my grandmother would dye a bright color. Ordinary egg shells were elevated to a surface decoration on lacquerware. A ball made from wicker was used in a popular game similar to soccer but played in the air. The ball kept in the air with the feet and sometimes the head. I never played it, but it was fun to watch.

Making things from available materials did not stop with just natural materials, but also incorporated discarded manufactured materials especially automobile tires that could be made into garbage cans and planters. Square oil drum cans cut on the diagonal could be nailed to a stick to make into a dustpan. This constant recycling and reuse became part of my personal vernacular. Poop, however, was flushed down into a septic tank by the time I arrived, unless you count the pit toilets dug on farms and construction sites.

I first heard about composting toilets through my readings on eco solutions. I was entranced by this idea of recycling poop into soil much as had been done in China with "night soil" collection, a major contribution to sustaining fertility of the land.

On tiny house TV shows the camera quickly pans past the composting toilet eager to show how the miniature bathroom is indeed a proper room with a shower and sink (and sometimes even a tiny bathtub). If tiny house people did talk about how a composting toilet actually works we'd all be thrown out of town. Better that the public think these toilets are some kind of high tech poop processor turning turds into good smelling compost right inside the toilet.

This is not entirely the case. Take the Nature's Head, the most popular commercially available composting toilet on these shows; when the unit is full you must pick the whole toilet up and take it outside to empty the poop chamber into your poop dedicated composting pile. Some cheat and just line the bin with a plastic bag which they then dump in the garbage like so much dog poop. I do not need to tell you that this defeats the whole purpose of being an off grid eco loving poop composter. The Nature's Head was originally designed for use on board boats as an alternative to the kind that just pumped your deposit into the water below (as my family's sailboat did in the '70s). Thus the nautical term "head" in the name.

Composting toilets being quite pricey, I was relieved to find that all you really needed to make one was a five gallon bucket plus sawdust and straw. Sawdust to cover the poop and straw to pack around the poop once it is taken outside and emptied into the poop dedicated compost bin. The five gallon bucket system is the simplest toilet design possible. To make it more amenable it's nice to have a box to keep the bucket in to which can be attached a toilet seat. Nothing says toilet like a commercially made toilet seat. I learned all I needed to know about the bucket system from Joseph Jenkins, the granddaddy of American humanure composting movement (so to speak). His book *The Humanure Handbook* self published in 1994 became the poop movement standard. By the time I showed up it was in its 2nd edition and quite entertaining as he had collected plenty of lore and cultural information on how humans have dealt with this daily chore as well as the experiences of those who had put his advice to use. I was touched by a letter from nuns explaining how composting their own poop was an ultimate act of humility. Today you can read the book online for free or download a brief instructions only guide to get you started.

Another book called *Liquid Gold: The Lore and Logic of Using Urine to Grow Plants* by Carol Steinfeld refined my understanding of my options. From Carol's book I learned that separating the pee from the poop helps a lot to keep down the smell. In fact the Nature's Head has a urine diverting chamber to channel urine into a separate container that sits at the front of the unit. The plastic is translucent so you can see the pee level, but you have to keep an eye on it to make sure it doesn't overflow onto the floor. Or worse yet, get into the poop chamber making a doughy mess that sticks to the sides. Carol's book showed examples of DIY urine diverting toilets so I was confident that I could build my own.

It was not an idle experiment. I had a use in mind for such a toilet. I was going to do some urban camping at a piece of rental property Catherine and I bought as an investment (a brief one given all the pitfalls of owning low income rental housing). The property had a little utility yard with a shed where I could put the toilet. This land was a day's drive from home so camping in this little yard would save on hotel fees while I was doing maintenance on the two rental houses.

After much study of what components I might use in my design I made my toilet for about $20 and with a few upgrades it became my tiny house toilet. It works even better than the commercial ones that cost $1,000 or more. Unlike the Nature's Head mine has a catch basin for pee overflow because the pee tank is actually an oil change tank and has a depression to catch the oil going in, but also works to catch any pee rising out of the tank. I use a funnel attached to the top of the toilet box and a length of flexible hose to send the pee into the tank through the hole where the oil would slide in. A ping pong ball sits inside the funnel to block any smells so I did not need to vent the toilet to the outside as most commercial toilets do.

To create the top for my toilet I repurposed a wooden wine box. This seems to amuse people when they recognize the wine box. I sawed a hole in the upturned box and cut two short planks from an old pine shelf to prop the box up on these two "legs" to raise it to the right height. I slipped this box seat over a cardboard bankers box in which I hid the funnel and oil drain tank. From Ikea I found a stylish light weight black plastic toilet seat to cover the hole in the box. Inside the toilet I placed a small bucket on top of the oil change tank to catch the poop. It all fit together beautifully.

The toilet worked just fine for my urban camping experience though I just used it for pee and made visits to a flush toilet in one of the houses for poop. When I was building the tiny house I took out my homemade composting toilet and upgraded it slightly. The bankers box was just two temporary looking so I got another wine box to hold the pee tank and slipped the two plank legs into this second upturned box. Now it looked like a complete unit. I added handles to the sides so I could pull off the top box easily to empty the tank and bucket.

When my girlfriend from Canada came to help me break in the tiny house we both made a deposit in the poop bucket of my DIY toilet. I was satisfied that it worked, but I was not satisfied that I would see that poop and toilet paper every time I lifted the lid of the toilet seat. I went back to the drawing board on this detail and thought back to a publication I had read called *Dwelling Portably* a collection of tips for low profile living in a vehicle and sometimes in DIY ad hoc housing. The contributors of these randomly listed practical tips were often artists living simply and cheaply using found objects adapted to suit a new purpose. I would read a page at bedtime and knowing there were people who got by in this semi-homeless manner put my mind at ease and ready for sleep.

I had not realized how much anxiety was evoked for me by the threat of homelessness. In particular, the need to find ways to poop. One woman had written in a description of how she would use a sheet of newspaper on the floor of her van. She squatted over it, made her poop deposit then folded up the newspaper into a discrete packet for later disposal. It really could be that simple. As I mused over this I found a frisbee in my father's workshop that was probably given to him. I picked it up. In the quest for a solution every object becomes a possible solution. The potential of this frisbee amused me no end. It was plastic so was watertight and its convex shape was perfect for holding anything moist from running onto the floor. Nor did such a repurposing offend me as say an aluminum pie plate might do with its association with food. I would try it out.

I got a nice bucket with a lid when a client gave away a commode chair used by invalids. When I moved into the tiny house I stashed this lidded bucket in the shower pan. To use my system I tore a newspaper into quarters and lay a piece onto the frisbee which I lay on the floor. Then I would squat over it, make my deposit and cover it with sawdust from a wooden box I got from another client. The box had once held recipes in side by side compartments. I removed the compartment divider and it fit a scoop and a pile of sawdust perfectly.

Picking the newspaper up by the corners I would carefully lay it in the commode bucket and fit the lid back on. I felt much happier not to have poop open to the air of my living space. Nor did it require ventilation because there was no smell. And when it was full I could easily pick it up by the handle and empty it.

As for the dedicated compost pile I did not go the classic Joseph Jenkins route because I did not have the room to set up two dedicated composting bins to empty the poop into. (One to collect fresh deposits and one to season a bin once filled.)

I learned from some urban homesteaders that you could use a 50 gallon plastic barrel in which to store the poop, again packed in straw while it decomposed into soil. The 50 gallon drum has holes for air flow (and little screens on the hole to keep flies out). I did a version of this for my first year, employing a rotating compost bin I got free from Freecyle. I was disappointed that the rotation of the bin did not process the poop into compost like the crank on the composting toilet. It just slammed each saw dust covered deposit together into solid balls that one might use for cob building had I been interested in such an experiment. (A cob building is made of mud, sand and straw made into brick size balls or "cob". The cobs are pressed together to form a wall.) All those picturesque straw thatched white buildings all over the English countryside are made from cob. Quite a few are pubs now. But they were not, I'm sure, made from poop and straw. But who knows. Cow dung maybe.

My composting operation got an upgrade when I had a fortuitous love affair with a woman in Hawaii who had worked at a municipal composting plant. She was shocked that I was using a rotating compost bin for my humanure processing.

"Everyone knows those are the worse composting bins around," she said. She demanded that I immediately rid myself of this composter preferably wrapped in hazardous waste tape to warn the garbage men of dangerous bacterial content. Amused that we were having this conversation in bed first thing in the morning I promised her that I would put on my hazmat suit to do the deed. She then jumped up from the bed to stand at her standing desk tapping on her computer searching for supplies for a composting method using a fermentation process called Bokashi. She showed me a website that sold everything I would need to process my poop with this Japanese fermentation method. The particular kit they had was a pet waste disposal method which came with videos to show how it was done. I was immediately attracted to the black buckets with contrasting orange screw top lids. It was the screw top lids that particularly spoke to me. The kit came with a gallon of liquid EM—effective microorganisms—and several bags of bran that had been soaked in the liquid and dried. All for a hundred dollars. I did not even bother to see if I could repurpose some bucket I had lying around. It was so perfect as it was especially the smaller 3 gallon bucket. I ordered the kit right away and it arrived by the time I got home. The love affair didn't last, but this kit would be a game changer for my poop processing.

The instructions were on the box it came in. You just filled the three gallon bucket with two gallons of water added a cup of the liquid EM and a tablespoon of the bran. When the poop went in you added another tablespoon of bran and gave it a spritz with a dilution of the EM from a spray bottle (which also came with the kit). The bucket was then sealed between deposits. Once full the bucket was set aside for two to three weeks and the second bucket was put into use. Then when three weeks passed you dug a hole in your garden and poured the liquidated fermented poo into the hole. This I must say was so disgusting and oozy that I quickly shoveled the dirt back over it. Strangely enough dogs were extremely attracted to this brew. It must have smelled heavenly to them.

Digging the hole big enough was the hardest part, but luckily since most of it was water it seeped into the soil fairly quickly. I dug holes all over the garden bed, eleven holes in all over the course of a year. So it was just a once a month chore.

The instructions were to wait a week before planting into the hole. The high acidity of the fermented brew acted as a natural weed killer and for a while nothing would grow in that spot. After a week the soil would neutralize enough to plant a seedling or gallon size plant. I planted whatever I wanted. There was no trace of poop by that time and I was adventurous in planting food crops into the Bokashi infused soil. All humanure instructions advise using the processed poop with ornamental plants or fruit trees only, but I knew this was just a cultural bias unless the person had a contagious disease, but it was my poop alone so I wasn't deterred by this convention. I planted herbs, tomatoes, collard greens and even Jerusalem artichoke which was already rooted in the soil. We ate well and no one got sick. Also I, as the poop producer, wasn't ever sick which was why I figured it was safe.

The change over to the bucket with its screw top offered an opportunity to dispense with the frisbee and the newspaper cover as well as the sawdust. I was attached to the idea of a squat toilet because of its yogic health benefits. After much thought I took my step stool and placed it next to the open bucket, squatted on the stool holding onto the front of it with one hand while my butt hung over the side of the bucket and the deed was done. As instructed I sprinkled bokashi bran on the deposit, spritzed it with the EM solution then screwed the lid back on and tucked the bucket inside my shower stall just as I had with the commode bucket.

As for the urine in my pee toilet, when the tank was filled I poured the pee out into a bucket then diluted the urine with water at least three to one. I soon learned how much water to cut it with to avoid a telltale smell of pee as I poured it around fruit trees in my landlady's yard. Five times would do it. In a drought state like California water that didn't go into the ground seemed a criminal waste. Saving water to put back into the ground was the second most compelling reason that I wanted to live in a tiny house. In a conventional house water cannot be easily rerouted from the bathtub or shower, but in a tiny house every drop of water could. This was the beauty of it.

I still hooked up to the municipal water system to provide myself with clean running water, but I would later augment this with my rain catchment system that would provide enough water to keep a garden going. My landlord used her abandoned hot tub as a rain water catchment system too. That just left the dishwater or grey water as it is called. This I easily poured into a five gallon bucket outside straight from my dishpan. I was now my own sewer system. I had freed myself from a centralized system few gave much thought to, but were inevitably tied to.

The act of composting my own poop also changed how I felt about myself now that I had added value as a human. Not only was I using less water with this composting toilet, but I was also producing a product that was a fertilizer. My own body was generating a food to feed plants. No part of myself could now be called waste. I was an integral part of nature's cycle. There was something holy about that.

Chapter 40
How To Die At Home

At the outset of my freelance life after being fired from my day job as a typesetter, it took me three years to become a competent business woman, one who could sell services to strangers and convince them that I could indeed help them get organized and do it in a professional, nonjudgmental manner. I had plenty of help from my colleagues, long time professional organizers, who persuaded me to leave my rebellious bohemian ways at home and present a business like persona.They gave workshops at conferences about how to deliver an elevator speech with conviction, set your fees and your boundaries, and other policies in order to be taken seriously. They were mostly women and I loved their energy and solution oriented optimism. I dedicated time to helping to run our business networking chapter, sought out programs to keep things lively and informative and edited the chapter newsletter.

We had specialities. Mine was for difficult people—head cases, all the usual diagnosis likely to manifest a chaotic life. Other organizers referred me to those for whom they didn't have the patience—clients who got in their own way and were repeat customers. Repeat customers were money in the bank to me and allowed me to develop long term relationships with my clients. People are disorganized in very similar ways given the similarity of our daily lives, but their reasons for being disorganized was as varied as any life story. That's what kept me interested.

Later in my career, I got a message from an out of state friend asking me if I would help a friend of the family with some work she needed doing on her home. Repairs included a broken chimney that made the fireplace too dangerous to use and a leak under the sink. Sylvia, the client prospect, was a 94 year old woman who lived alone in a one bedroom cottage not far from my childhood home. I said I would give her a call.

She was at at a care home recuperating from a broken hip following a fall. On the phone she told me that all she needed doing was to have her leaking toilet replaced because, being immobile, she would not be able to go outside to turn on the water at the main every time she needed to use the toilet. When I asked if she could give me a key so I could have a look she said the door wasn't locked. That was my first clue that this job would be unusual.

Her house was tucked away down a long driveway that opened up into a flag lot surrounded by three neighbors. The yard was overgrown with knee high grass and a rambling vine covered the front porch with a thicket of dense old wood. A the end of the driveway, away from the house, was a garage that looked ready to collapse, one wall leaning precariously. I stood on the porch of her house and pushed open the door. It opened into one room. Two steps into the room I could see a large pile of bags covering most of the floor. Piles of books and stationery supplies occupied the coffee table and bags, baskets and boxes of papers and other items covered the couch. To the right was a stairway going up to an attic bedroom. The landing and the bedroom equally strewn with boxes of stuff. To the left a kitchen where every surface of the counter was covered with pie pans and plastic bags.

I walked around the pile in the middle of the floor to the bathroom which was equally dilapidated minus the clutter. The shower stall floor was rusted corner to corner and a foot up the walls with peeling green paint the rest of the way.

I sighed and felt a foreboding that I would somehow be compelled to do far more than I was being asked to do out of my own desire to set things right, especially as this was a referral from a friend. I put in a call to another organizer, offering her the job knowing that she could better defend herself and would have Sylvia sign a contract specifying work promised. (I had never asked anyone to sign a contract in all my years of organizing.) A week went by and Sylvia left me a message.

"I need your help," she said. She hadn't heard from the other organizer and would give me an advance to begin work on her house. Well now, that was different. No one had offered me an advance before and she was asking for my help herself rather than through a third party so I was assured that she was motivated.

I went to see her to pick up the check. She was a short, stout woman of few words but she wanted to show me pictures of herself on top of a mountain ridge with a group of people, including the friend we shared in common as they rested atop a peak. I was intrigued by this outdoorsy woman living her minimalist life in a house that was not much more than a cabin. Her most valuable possession she told me was her ice ax for she was an avid mountain climber. She wanted it to go to her best friend. I had seen it resting against the wall of her bedroom under the window.

I told Tim about the job as he happened to be working for me on my mother's place. He was intrigued and wanted to see the house. The clutter didn't bother him and after looking at the bathroom he thought we could whip it all into shape in no time. This gave me moral support and we both went to see Sylvia and he told her he could remodel her whole bathroom and enlarge it too by pushing into a nearby closet. She didn't want that she said and in private told me not to let him run away with the project. She also told me she had some carpet tiles we might put to use. I got that she just wanted to do the minimum, because she likely wouldn't have much longer to make it worth the expense. It was the same sentiment my frugal English grandpa had voiced when we suggested he get new mugs to replace his chipped ones.

"I wouldn't get the full use of them," he said so why spend the money was his reasoning. I was still worried about the clutter but she had told me she didn't want to bother with clearing it.

The first day on the job we met the neighbor who was very friendly and said she had been eager to get in touch with Sylvia to tell her she was going to tear out the line of trees between their properties and put up a fence. She chatted with me about my professional organizer services. Then she asked me what it was like inside Sylvia's house. I wanted someone, anyone to appreciate what I was up against.

"It's the worse I've ever seen," I said and she nodded with a bit of a smug smile. But it wasn't the worse house I had ever seen. I'd worked on a house three times this size with clutter so deep it was hard to approach the kitchen sink and a rat had jumped out when we started clearing things away. I had also worked in two homes that were so impacted that they were being used as fodder for a cable TV show about hoarders. All these jobs had taken a crew of 5 or more at least three days.

Later, I regretted my breach of confidence and began to feel protective about Sylvia. The neighbor might be waiting to buy Sylvia's land, Tim suggested and thus was waiting for her to be hauled off to a nursing home. This we knew Sylvia would hate. I had had another job with an elderly woman and knew that if Sylvia's social worker had so much as a glimpse of this clutter she wouldn't be able to allow Sylvia to return to it because it would be deemed a tripping hazard especially as she was returning with a walker.

Sylvia did indeed have a social worker, and once I explained this potential scenario to her, she said that I could box it all up and she would sort through it later. This at least gave me something to go on and I asked permission to take away all the recycling and trash. Then I waded into the pile armed with boxes. Wearing dust masks and gloves I tossed trash and filed the recycling bin time after time. I organized and boxed associated items together while Tim went to buy a toilet and took out the old one. I drove the old one to the nearby cement recycling center to be bashed into rubble.

As I worked through the pile I came upon a brand new stereo set still in its styrofoam packaging with a turntable and cassette deck player plus speakers. Sylvia had no memory of it and told me I could take it. It may have been a gift. (I sold it later on e-bay getting just enough to cover the cost of shipping, but not my time. I just couldn't bear to send it to landfill. Goodwill no longer took electronics.)

By day three I had the pile half cleared revealing a carpet so dirty with age it wasn't a color at all, just a strange gray littered with little bits of paper. We pulled up the carpet to reveal a cement floor painted porch red with a large crack running across it. A crack that was probably from the house settling much like the crack in the chimney. The crack in the chimney was why Sylvia didn't have any hot water. Which I only thought to ask about when she asked me to install a solar hot water heater.

And why did she want a solar hot water heater I asked trying to determine why she would go to the expense of installing such an expensive thing. Was she an environmentalist? She told me she had turned off the gas because the insurance company refused to insure the house until the chimney was fixed. So she had turned off the gas presumably in order not to have to worry about the house catching fire. This meant she lived in an unheated house. So did I, much of the time, and I didn't have any hot water either. I just boiled what I needed. Nor did I have house insurance. I was beginning to see my own fate in Sylvia's story.

She must have shut off the gas some time ago judging from the aging of the house. I asked her how she bathed. She told me she would wait until the sun warmed the water she kept in the three plastic trash cans she had in the front yard then bring some warm water inside in a bucket. How very like camping I noted. I rigged up a black garden hose to a garden sprayer which I attached to the end of the porch railing. This did indeed provide hot water, but would only work on a sunny day. A manufactured solar heater would cost quite a lot I told Sylvia so we dropped it.

Meanwhile Tim had found a very large oriental carpet at a garage sale for just $150 because there was a stain at one end. By day eight I had packed up everything in the room in boxes on one side of the room. That left the floor clear so we could lay the carpet. It rolled out from the far wall to about six feet from the near wall. So Tim went out and got linoleum tiles to run down the length of the room to make up the difference. It looked like a hallway from the door to the bathroom. Perfect. There was still a gap of a couple feet short of the fireplace which we finished off with Sylvia's red indoor outdoor carpet tiles that picked up the red in the carpet.

As we worked, Sylvia was undergoing physical therapy to learn to use a walker. She thought of more jobs for Tim to do. She needed a step with a railing so she could get up to her porch with her walker, and the pole to the mailbox needed to be cut down so she could reach into it. She was already short but now she was shorter and couldn't reach as high. She also permitted me to get her a new lockset so the door could actually be locked. Now we were talking. Tim started to paint over the rust in the shower with white epoxy paint and ended up painting the whole bathroom. It was easier than just covering the spots where the peeling paint had left holes. He installed the new toilet. It looked good, great in fact, save for the back of the door where we had run out of paint.

As she wouldn't be able to manage the stairs she had me bring her dresser down from her bedroom. She would use the pull out bed. It was in the grimy old sofa, the top of which was frayed. This shabby sofa disturbed Tim so much I offered to cover it with a blanket. The mattress inside looked brand new. We placed it so it would cover the stain in the carpet. I cleaned off the very dusty bookshelf and boxed up the very old books that had been in it, buried by several generations of new books. I set up the bookshelf as her home office filling it with her stationary and office supplies in all the many plastic boxes she had. Then I hauled up all the cardboard boxes I had packed up to the second floor leaving three in the far corner that were filled with paperwork. She asked me to set up an old fold-up patio chair to use with her card table and I set it next to the bookshelf.

Things were looking good; a bit like an English pub with the pale green walls. She wouldn't let us paint the walls, but I had found a framed landscape painting she didn't know she had and hung it over the fireplace. Using Coca Cola I scrubbed the soot off of the fireplace bricks. It actually worked. I used another painting to cover the fireplace itself.

Tim found a TV monitor among her things and hooked it up to a TV antenna that was still in its original package. He actually got it to tune in a couple of channels. Meanwhile, I pruned away the dead wood of the vine covering the patio and carted away all the vintage things stored on the porch approving each item with Sylvia over the phone.

All that was left was the kitchen. For that job I needed back-up. I asked my friend Stacy if she would come and help me with this scary job; I'd pay her of course. She had known Sylvia socially through our mutual friend and met her at their parties. We donned our protective gear and waded into the pantry bagging up anything that had expired or was obsolete. The cupboards were full of empty jars with their lids. All the food was inside a number of coolers sitting on the floor of the pantry. With all the rat poop in the kitchen I figured the rats ate anything stored in the cabinets, but couldn't get inside the coolers. No rats jumped out at us fortunately.

When I asked Sylvia about the leak under the sink she said a man who was trying to do her a favor had attempted to fix it some years ago and it had never been the same since. I took a wrench to the pipes in question and could see that the threads were stripped, which was the cause of the leak. No plumber is going to take this on I told Stacy. They would want to re-plumb the entire house. So we let it be, leaving a dishpan to catch the drips. No one would red tag a house just because it had a leak.

Working with Stacy gave me the opportunity to speculate with her on Sylvia's future. Stacy worked as an aid and caretaker to the elderly. She had also managed her father's time at an elder care facility. She was of the opinion that you get very little for what you pay those places. And you lose your autonomy. We agreed that despite the condition of this house Sylvia would be better off living in her own home under her own terms than going to a care home. She was waiting to escape the one she was in as it was. It made me realize that the real purpose of our mission was to allow Sylvia to die in her own home. Something people seemed to find alarming. Or perhaps it was the horror of being found dead—a corpse in a house for who knows how long.

The alternative—dying in a hospital was full of nightmares I knew, having weathered many ordeals to the hospital with my father who finally died of pneumonia after a long bout with throat cancer. I could see the helplessness in his eyes as he was subjected to all sorts of indignities and was woken up at all hours of the night to have his blood pressure taken to make sure he was still alive. He would have preferred to die at home, I'm sure, lying comfortably in his Lazyboy recliner. But his wife had a horror of waking up to a corpse, having already been there done that with her first husband.

Some fear dying alone especially Thai people, though why that made a difference I didn't know. Maybe it was the idea of realizing you were dying and having no one to see you off. But Sylvia lived alone and didn't much like people, Tim would learn later when he tried to hang out with her. Sylvia, who knew she wouldn't live long enough to fully enjoy a new paint job, clearly had no plans to do other than die at home. And to that end we would help her.

With the kitchen cleared out Tim lay a sheet of vinyl flooring through the pantry and kitchen, carefully cutting it around the doorframe. Then he built a very sturdy set of stairs to the front porch with banisters on both sides. That left one remaining job. I thought about it for a day or so as to how to shorten the mailbox in the simplest possible way. Once the pole was cut there was no way I could connect it to the base of the mailbox because I didn't have the tools to make a new thread at the cut end to screw it into the pole socket attached to the bottom of the mailbox. And I didn't want Tim to spend time digging out the pole that was set into asphalt. This would have to be a Sylvia style fix—to make do. I had Tim cut through the metal pole a foot below the mailbox. Then had him bind this section of pole to the bottom section overlapping the difference so it was the right height. He used two adjustable pipe clamps to hold the two sections of pole together. Then added red duct tape in sections for additional support. This gave it an op art look, and was in keeping with the reflector on a stick that had been taped to the bottom of the pole with black electric tape. I was very pleased with our arty solution. It looked on purpose.

I was now confident that no social worker, Fire Marshall or anyone else would be able to keep Sylvia from living in her own home. We had made her a nice studio bed sit and no one need concern themselves with what was upstairs. I went to pick her up. She first wanted to go to the post office so she could get her ballot and vote. This woman had her priorities. On the way, she told me, her knee ached just as it had when she went to the Galapagos Islands the year before. I was impressed. She had been there several times in fact.

When I got her home Tim was there to meet her. She made it up his two steps just fine. And he opened the door for her. She stood at the threshold looking into the house taking it all in.

"Who lives here?" she shouted into the house to acknowledge how different it was now. Then she walked herself in and settled into her lawn chair, asking me to bring her a beer from the fridge. When she handed me the check for the balance due, she told me it was worth every penny and said I could pick out a jigsaw puzzle from her collection. She knew I liked jigsaw puzzles. She wasn't really interested in doing puzzles anymore, even though I suggested I come over and work on one with her.

Tim was able to stay in touch with her. He had bought himself an RV so huge he had no where to park it.

"What were you thinking?" I asked him. When it came to vehicles he couldn't resist a bargain and he had a homeless friend who could live in it, he said, but then the friend disappeared. Probably arrested Tim said. The RV was some 30 feet long. He asked me if I thought Sylvia would object to him parking it in her yard. I told him to ask her. She said it was fine with her. As soon as he had moved the RV onto the lot I got a call from the neighbor who demanded to know if Tim was Sylvia's caretaker now and if he was living in the RV. I assured her that he had somewhere else to live, but if she wanted to harass an old lady because she didn't like that she had an RV parked on her land it was none of her business I told her.

"I have every right to be concerned about my 94 year old neighbor," she said and hung up.

Shortly after that Sylvia received a visit from the Fire Marshall, then from Adult Protection Services. The Fire Marshall just gave her a smoke detector and said she was fine. The Adult Protection Services said much the same thing, and her social worker, who had brought her things over the first day she returned, thought all was well too. Good, we had done it. We had gotten Sylvia what she wanted. To be left alone in her own home watching Double Jeopardy on her own TV. And for the first time in years she allowed people to visit her in her house, including the friend who had asked me to take the job. He wrote me to tell me how much shame she suffered from not being able to keep up her house and how happy he and his wife had been to see it so transformed. I was more than satisfied to have accomplished the job beyond my expectations and made so many people happy. Being a professional organizer had its rewards.

A few months later Tim called me up, leaving me urgent messages to call him. He had gone to check on his RV and knocked on Sylvia's door, but there was no answer even though he could hear the TV was on. Three newspapers were lying on the mat. Fearing the worse he had gone to the neighbor and asked the husband to check on Sylvia. He found her dead lying on her bed. The cause of death appeared to be a heart attack and not starvation as I feared. Tim assured me she had been able to drive and get around just fine. He was the last one to talk to her. She had told him she had saved an article about RVs for him that she would leave on the porch. It wasn't there. Had she died trying to bring it out to him? he wondered.

A member of the out-of-state family flew in to take care of settling her affairs. She had left the house to Habitat for Humanity. The organization would likely put it up for sale and not, as Sylvia hoped, create a home there for a low income family to move into it. I did not check to see if the annoying neighbor had bought it. That wasn't really the point anymore. We had fended off the neighbor for as long as needed, so Sylvia could pass from this world just as she had wanted.

Chapter 41

The Lazy Way

The year I spent fitting out the tiny house I did not return to Thailand as usual to attend the annual ten day women's building workshop, as I tried to do every year as an investment into what I called my mud hut sisters network. Anyone who would come all the way to a remote rural area of Northern Thailand to build a house from mud was my kind of person. But I was too burned out on building to spend my vacation building.

Instead, I went to Peru to see the work of pre Columbian civilization. I joined a tour with Freddy Silva, who was an expert in portals of antiquity, with whom I had toured prehistoric sites in England shortly after I had embraced shamanism. I had exuberantly danced my spirit animals at Stonehenge. Freddy taught us that ancient technologies had designed these sites as portals for humans to transcend the material world and get in touch with the divine. The mysteries of the pre Columbian antiquities was an enduring attraction in this way. But it was the perfection of those precisely fitted stone blocks that really impressed me. Surely this was a superior civilization. Perhaps an otherworldly one. No one in our current society could even figure out how it had been done. It just reminded me not to take anything for granted. Not even prophets of doom.

The next year I returned to the mud pits to help build another adobe home just a few kilometers from Pun Pun, the eco center where ten years earlier I had had my sensibilities tweaked by the vision of a sustainable hand built life. So much had I seen there that had influenced my journey. The composting toilets, the different natural building styles, the compact floor plans, garden plans, water filtration system and local appropriate technology and reuse had all played a part in my tiny house design.

Arriving once again by overnight train from Bangkok to Chieng Mai, the favorite city of digital nomads, I loaded myself into one of two pick-up truck taxis. Several other women from Thailand plus Clasina from South Africa introduced ourselves as we chatted on the hour and a half ride to Mae Taeng, the province where Pun Pun was located. Upon arriving, a quick look around showed me that almost none of the original mud and thatched roofed buildings were left. They had all been eaten by termites and replaced. Much had been learned in the process and the new buildings had a more permanent and finished look.

It was unusually cold out. So cold that we were all bundled up in coats and hats in what was supposed to be my tropical homeland, and there had also been unseasonal storms. Climate change was afoot. At the end of our walking tour of the farm, we were persuaded to doff our coats and shoes and start squishing our bare feet in a nearby mud pit. When everyone was in I put my arms around the shoulders of women on either side of me and started chanting monosyllables in a spontaneous expression of group bonding.

Nobody joined in though it made Ailsa, the 10 year old girl resident of Pun Pun, look up at me curiously. We had met before. She was a mirror for me, sharing a similar skin tone, dark hair, and Asian features. We had worked together two years ago when she joined us for her first build, gamely lugging bricks and climbing scaffolding for the entire ten days. Her Scottish mother, Lisa, was one of our instructors. Her father was from Burma.

The continuity of seeing her tugged at me. I was ten years old when I left Thailand and so much that I called home, but couldn't put into words. My memories were somehow embodied in the mud. Mud that in my childhood the children of my household had taught me to roll into marbles with which to play games, squatting on our heels on the hard packed dirt.

The longer I was away from my childhood home the more I wanted to embody within myself the Thailand I had grown up with, so that I could impart some of this sensibility to others. How I chose to walk, for instance, embodying the leisurely pace I grew up with. No one walks fast in the tropics. They don't want to arrive at their destination soaked in sweat. It is not so much a leisurely walk as a purposeful stroll. A child can keep up with this pace. When I came to the States I didn't think about walking fast. I just walked until I got there. I got up. I made my own breakfast and packed my lunch. Then I walked to school. There was no hurry in this entire equation. It did make me wonder now how hurry gets into the picture.

I tried to impart the sense that I had all the time in the world. As I got into the working world I embodied this trait as a refusal to hurry. Sometimes I would stubbornly procrastinate to keep the expectations from stacking up. In my mind I was a slacker, an identity subculture trendy in the '90s; I was simultaneously attracted to its defiant rebelliousness and repelled by its despair and lack of enthusiasm for life. My boss noted in a performance review that I was "lazy" except when I was doing something that was my idea. I was perfectly ok with this. Secretly pleased, in fact, that he had seen that I was self-motivated when self-directed.

Lazy is possibly the lowest insult in our production oriented society. Our stories of success so often contain the words "hard work" as in "with talent and hard work she built a successful business empire". This implies that talent is not enough, but must be coupled with drive and motivation in order to fully realize your potential.

"Not living up to her potential," was a comment my teachers frequently dispensed in their assessments of my academic performance. I did not get it. Potential for what? I worked hard. I completed assignments. I just wasn't interested in working extra hard. I did what was required. The word potential haunted me long after high school, as if it was my fault that I wasn't interested in the school's agenda, which was that smart kids with good grades got into prestigious universities which supposedly led to good jobs and a good life. I wasn't impressed by such a boring linear path. Where was the adventure in it? The collaboration with the unexpected. I clung to this innate right to be lazy and knew it had something to do with Thailand.

At this year's mud hut building workshop I met a woman who was the daughter of a tribal leader of a Karen village in Northern Thailand. Her brother sold organic coffee under the English title Lazy Man Coffee. Lazy ,she tried to explain to us, meant that it was organic since it did not require all the inputs of chemical farming. The English speakers hearing the word 'lazy' then attempted to explain to her that in English the word had a more negative connotation. I was intrigued by the context she had given us that lazy meant a collaboration with nature and thus was organic. Somewhere in that context was my answer.

In the west we have equated laziness with sloth, one of the seven sins. I looked up sloth and found that the sin of Sloth was not defined as laziness, but as an indifference to God. A lack of enthusiasm for the gift of life and what God wanted you to be. Somehow what God wanted you to BE had become what other people wanted you to DO. So it was handy to associate laziness with sin as a whip to drive workers. To claim laziness as a virtue must then be a subversive act in the context of the work world. This I could get behind.

I had seen signs of others who felt that work was something to be avoided. Or more to the point, needless work. I read *Cheaper By The Dozen* in junior high. In it I learned that the efficiency expert Frank Gilbreth would always ask to meet with the laziest man whenever a factory asked for his advice. For such a man he knew had likely devised labor saving ways. So being lazy was seen as an asset because it made you more productive. Other than that there was no call for laziness. There really wasn't an acceptable slow laid back space in American culture. Unless you were dying. Then again I'm not sure dying was acceptable either. Dying was a condition Americans seem to feel they could outwit with more effort.

Jo Jandai, who was the founder of Pun Pun, offered his own journey regarding work. After his seven years in Bangkok, when he realized that he was just making room and board, he had come home to the family farm where he only had to work two months a year to bring in the rice harvest and the rest of the time was his own. Westerners call this way of life subsistence farming and refer to this population as the poorest on earth. Meanwhile living in Silicon Valley the epicenter of wealth and technology I didn't exactly make room and board, given the housing shortage, and I had no farm to go back to. Who was the poor one in such a paradigm? I asked myself.

Jo didn't even believe in a university education. What good was an education to a farmer when he was not taught how to be sustainable. To Jo an education was just more consumerism. Because he embodied this life of leisure and was Thai, I felt that my being Thai also gave me an innate expectation for a life of ease. But I did believe in the pursuit of knowledge. Books could still be had for free from the library so no university was needed. Libraries were definitely a perk of living in Silicon Valley.

I had questions to answer. What was the cause of war? I wanted to know. How could imperialism be stopped? Why were Americans afraid of socialism? What were the non-technological solutions to climate change? What was a sustainable society? I wrote down what I learned from these books and posted book reviews. I pieced together a big picture and wrote essays as I went along. I looked for clues in popular culture and movies. With all this reading and writing I could no longer really call myself a slacker. Jo too had published three books and spent a great deal of time traveling away from home giving countless talks. And still in the back of my mind I believed in an ethic of laziness. Or rather a natural order of humans having to do much less work than anyone thought possible or necessary.

Civilization, we are told, came about as a result of agriculture creating stores of food, so that we might be secure in winter with no need to migrate in search of food. And, having stockpiled food and created leisure, we could then allow members of society to devote themselves to higher pursuits such as art, learning and preaching. This story may have been more about enslaving people to the land. Yet Asia, Africa and the Americas were all about food forests. Food forests were areas of cultivated perennial plants and trees that created a perpetual food producing environment. It did not require tilling the soil to grow annual, labor intensive crops. This "primitive" means of feeding ourselves right outside our door was not even recognized as farming by Europeans.

What's more, conventional farming could benefit from such primitive methods. In the '70s a Japanese microbiologist turned farmer named Masanobu Fukuoka developed a method of growing rice with less labor than any other farmer—a lot less labor. He did it by observing, then working with nature, delegating fertilizing jobs to animals and irrigation chores to natural forces. He called his method the do-nothing method. He believed that a Sunday farmer could feed his family just by maintaining certain chores. His book *One Straw Revolution* has become the manifesto of permaculture farming. After decades of being ignored he is finally being sought after for tips to returning to organic farming post-chemical collapse.

The do-nothing ethic was looking smarter all the time. For there is this: modern agriculture with all of its chemical inputs and fossil fuel transport miles and bare fields oxidizing carbon into the atmosphere, is the third biggest contributor to climate change. (The first being transportation followed by energy used for heating and power.) Not to mention that it was unsustainable for we now have only 60 years of topsoil left.

Food forests maintain the rain cycle, keeping fresh water where we need it instead of letting it flow into the ocean where it contributes to sea level rise. Food forests also act as a carbon sink sucking back into the ground all the excess carbon we might continue to release from the other sectors. While the vegetation dropped on the ground of this no-till method would replenish the soil.

So the lazy way was after all the sustainable way. It makes sense. The lazy way would reduce consumption and when people do no more work than necessary, it would subvert industry and capitalism and was good for the planet. That was what I was after. Life in rural Thailand embodied both my memories of a slower time and my vision of a Slow Future.

The house we were set to build this year was a few kilometers down the road from Pun Pun, at a site that would be the next phase of the Pun Pun educational center. Peggy's brother had already built the first adobe structure, which could be seen from the road, waiting a final coat of plaster and earth based paint. The house we were building was behind it deeper into the compound. It would be Peggy and Jo's house, a retreat away from the bustle of the Pun Pun farm.

We could see it as we approached. The concrete foundation perched on the edge of a large pond. There were pilings in the water where a pier would be built. It would be two stories high and had a compact footprint with a covered outdoor barbecue area. There were also iron beams instead of wood ones since wood now cost the same as iron. One of the reclaimed doors had a window put into it, an unusual feature in Thailand. The house itself had a modern look to it, a sort of Dwell magazine home for the earthen building set.

A few days into the build, just as we were coming to the top of the walls, we finished up early so we could drive to the Cat Lady's house. This was a woman who lived in an adobe house a team had helped her build in a little village between two rice fields. We sat on the lawn in her vegetable garden as she told us how everyone thought she was crazy to leave Bangkok and come out here to live.

"If I hadn't left Bangkok I would have died," she said dramatically. I could understand where she was coming from.

She had bought herself a little plot of land just off the road in this village. The house was outfitted with a large outdoor cat cage of cyclone fencing connected to the house with a cat run alongside the top of the wall that let the two cats in through the bathroom window. Next to the house a large outdoor kitchen with wood slat walls sat next to the house and behind it the garage. At the bottom of the garden was a guest house; those relatives who had thought she was crazy now liked to visit, but she didn't want them in the house stepping on the cats' tails.

As she told her story she mentioned that city people under 50 years of age were the most afraid of the country. This detail stuck in my mind for it put words to my own despair that the younger generations of my Bangkok family no longer valued the natural environment or even connected with it, so enclosed were they in cars and air-conditioning, indoor sports courts, manicured fields and chlorinated swimming pools.

I asked the Cat Lady how she got the idea to come to the country. She said it was through her government job that she was sent out to the country and she could see for herself that the people enjoyed a better quality of life. Her story was both inspiring and odd so focused was it on the cats who were famous and had a following on Facebook. It was a rich lady's story I sensed, since she likely had investments that had allowed her to buy the farm. Then she had to abandon it while she took care of her aging mother. Upon her return she had to clear a path into it with a machete. She did grow food, but just for herself and any visitors.

"They should have told us how the guest house could be an income," said Clasina who would later become a pivotal figure in my story. We were riding home in the back of one of the pick-ups together. I too had ideas on how to improve her homestead. She had talked of wanting to increase the fertility of her soil yet she was flushing away a perfectly good source of nutrients that could have been had with a composting toilet.

"She's just a crazy cat lady," I said, "she didn't need an income." And like most urbanites the world over she likely had never considered digging her composted poop into the garden that would then grow food. Even Jo said people just couldn't seem to get their minds around it and Pun Pun put their composted poop at the base of fruit trees and never in the vegetable beds.

The cat lady's observation of Bangkok people haunted me. I was left asking myself why were city people afraid of the country? I knew it had to do with the rapid growth of Bangkok since the '80s. It was true that we who were over 50 grew up in a Bangkok that still had a relationship with nature, living in houses that were not air conditioned and we had large gardens to play in. TV was only broadcast in the evenings and of course there were no smart phones and game boys.

Now city people flocked to the indoor shopping malls and spent their leisure time inside these hyper stimulating artificial environments to get away from the heat and polluted air. The air was filtered and cooled inside and with food courts, movie theaters and assorted entertainment the malls contained everything they could want. They uploaded selfies to Instagram accounts in such numbers that in 2017 the photo site reported that the Siam Paragon mall was the location of the most uploads in the world. Quite a testament to this indoor lifestyle and its status as a showroom. I could see the allure of these entertaining malls, but going into one made me feel like I was in an aquarium with limited air in my tank, so much did I want to get away from the gaudy consumerist displays of status items.

The two children who lived in the house my aunt had built rarely went outside even when their cousins came over to play; they preferred playing games on the large screen TV. How could I relate to children who did not play outside? An entire generation lost to artificial indoor environments.

When I talked to Peggy about it she confirmed that when Bangkok children came to Pun Pun they were afraid of everything. They fell a lot on the unpaved ground; they were so unused to walking on natural terrain. And I could see she didn't like to say it, but they were also already trained to feel the entitlement of their class and so refused to do things they thought beneath them like washing their own dishes. This annoyed me even more so much did it resonate with my observations; so much did it offend my class consciousness.

For the ten days I took refuge in life at Pun Pun. There were many working volunteers to talk to who came from all over the world with a desire to learn to heal the earth even if it meant sacrificing our own wants. We took our shoes off Thai style as we entered the guest houses and the dining hall. The tables we ate at were low to the ground so we could sit on floor cushions thus avoiding the need for chairs. This spared us the noise of them scraping on the floor. There were a couple of picnic tables with benches at one end for those not able to sit on the floor. Europeans of a certain age for example. This furniture-free life agreed with me as I had in my childhood often sat on the polished wood floors of Thai homes including the one my parents furnished.

My study of biomechanics and how the body needs a variety of movement had long shown me that you pay a price for the use of furniture with the diminishment of range of motion which led to diminishment of function of the joints. The Asian squat long seen as somehow primitive and feral had been exonerated by biomechanists as vital for proper elimination, the creative marketing of the Squatty Potty having driven this point home with humorous ads on Facebook.

There were no comfy chairs in this low furniture life. The beds were hard too, being nothing more than a 3 inch chip foam block. (Chip foam is what we put under carpets in the States.) This hardness was better for the body I had learned, for while sleeping the body moves in such a way as to adjust itself, realigning bones back to their optimum position. Those who found them too hard could request another mattress to double the thickness of their beds.

When in the dark I walked to the bath house I remembered how I had trained my feet to see. After reading Katy Bowman's book on foot health I had laid a path of loose river rocks outside my tiny house so I could force the bones in my feet to be pushed around as she recommended. The path also allowed me to walk to my freezer in stocking feet. Six months of this had given my feet new found skills, evaluating unstable ground. This gave me the sensation of "seeing" that had seemed so mysterious to me as I walked to the communal bathhouse along the darkened paths at night.

On the last day I said goodbye to Ailsa, not knowing when I'd make it back again or if I was up to another build, so tired had I felt. The adobe building movement to teach sustainable living techniques to all who were interested had matured since Pun Pun established itself. Now there were some 80 such groups and outfits teaching permaculture farming and natural building methods in Thailand alone. The participants too, reflected this change.

Unlike those who attended in previous years, looking for something different to do on their holiday, these woman struck me as serious about actually building a house for themselves. Yi Lin, my roommate from Taiwan, had moved to an island resort she had loved as a child and had run tours both on bicycles and by kayak. She was now looking for ways to help the locals make a living that would preserve their way of life. Two Thai cousins already had a garden and were interested in using permaculture cultivation to develop it. Syri, a Japanese woman who had trained as a chef, had her grandparents farm to return to. A young Thai woman grew micro greens on her balcony in Bangkok and sold them at a farmer's market, awaiting the day she could move to the country. And then there was Clasina actively looking for land to make her food forest home. And I too had moved further along my sustainable journey in my own lazy way.

Chapter 42

A Farm In Mae Taeng

When I got back to Bangkok my girl cousin was eager to meet with me to make me an offer for my share of a piece of land the family owned where we had had a factory to assemble Venetian blinds. She wanted to buy the land from the other three heirs so she could get investors and start a business of her own. Her offer was enough to warrant my attention at just below half the appraised value. My stepmother though believed it could sell for eight times that value. But all over Bangkok family land lay locked up in such disputes. So what good was that? I didn't want to be such a road block. I accepted the offer and she took me to the bank to make a deposit into my brand new account. Then she handed me an envelope thick with cash.

"What's this for?" I asked her. She told me she wanted me to feel my money and get used to this new wealth, not hang on to it in fear like my stepmother.

Wow. No one in my frugal family had ever put such an idea into my head. But once in possession of this fat envelope of cash it did stir in me many new thoughts. I could buy three more tiny houses and put one in each country I wanted to visit, I thought, as I imagined living in England in one. But then that would just be more work to maintain it and to worry about when I wasn't there to take care of it. I already knew I had no real need for things. When my cousin asked if I'd like to buy a car to keep in Bangkok I just laughed. Who needs a car in Bangkok just to sit in traffic when the transit line came right to our lane. However I realized, I did have enough to buy land, not in Bangkok, of course, but outside of the city, a farm even. And then bam it hit me. I already knew someone with just such a plan.

I messaged Clasina. "How much is that farm you want to buy?" I asked without preamble. I hadn't been paying close attention, but she had talked about going to look at a farm while we were in the Pun Pun area.

"Good morning," she said reminding me of my manners. "I wouldn't want to pay more than two million for it," she said. Then she sent me a picture of the land. There were mountains in the background just as she had wanted—to remind her of her home in South Africa. In the foreground was a banana tree and a structure with a corrugated tin roof. The tin roof was my personal symbol of Thailand before globalization. I had used this same material in my tiny house to remind me of this humble past. It captured something this picture; something I longed for. Two million had sounded out of reach—a Bay Area price—but in American dollars it was a mere $64,000.

"You're serious," she said after I revealed my interest. "I thought you were pulling my leg."

"You better come over," I said.

Clasina lived near my family home in Bangkok. How perfect was that? She even spoke better Thai than me, having married a Thai husband who spoke no English. When I learned that she lived in Bangkok I had hoped to become friends with her, but her schedule kept her very busy. She tutored English for a living, going to the homes of her clients throughout our upscale neighborhood, Japanese families mostly. She was planning to eventually live on the farm she was looking to buy. She had a garden full of potted fruit trees waiting for that moment.

"Why me?" she asked as we stood on the grand patio of my Khun Ya's old house. She heard me out, telling her how I wanted to buy this farm she had looked at, help her develop it as a project and then leave it to her when I died. Being more cosmically inclined, I thought it was obvious why her. She had been the one person who was actively looking to buy a farm. And we had met at the women's build—an event sacred to me; thrown together for ten days to build a house so I could fully appreciate her work ethic, her friendly easy going personality and her determination sprinkled with visionary opinions she wasn't afraid to express. And like the rest of us she didn't mind getting muddy. She was at home with the mud and with hefting building materials. The dirt in every crevice of her hands didn't bother her. Nor did the composting toilets, though she did feel we could have had more comfortable beds and actual chairs in the dining hall.

One evening at the build Clasina and I had sat down at the same time at one of the long tables without chairs. We had got our meal ahead of everyone else. She asked me to explain what I had just learned about the micro biome. I had mentioned my enthusiasm for this new discovery in our group introduction on the first day. I felt that it fundamentally changed what we knew about health, cleanliness and the soil. I sought to boil it down for her.

"Well you know about the human genome project to identify all the genes in humans?"

"Yes."

"Well it turns out that humans have no more genes than a mouse. But they were able to use that same DNA identification technology to find out what creatures humans had living in the gut. And that's how we found out about beneficial bacteria helping us digest food, how that affects our moods, our health and that this same thing is happening in the soil with microbes breaking down nutrients so it can be used by plants. It just gave me a whole new appreciation for how we should be creating the best conditions both in the soil and in our bodies."

"I see," she said and I was pleased that I had managed to make this book length topic accessible in just a few sentences. I was glad to find that she wasn't a vegetarian, a philosophical stance I found troublesome in terms of health and later in terms of farming. I was firmly convinced that the key to rejuvenating the land was to use cattle and other domesticated animals to till it and in turn pay for themselves in meat, eggs and dairy products. She wasn't a picky eater, more of an adventurous one and a forager who knew her plants.

And then there was the outfit. She was the best dressed builder on the crew, sporting a pair of custom tailored blue jean overalls and rubber boots. None of us had boots; we just wore flip flops. A woman with serious work clothes was one committed to the idea of serious work even if just to look like she was, but Clasina clearly could work. She gamely carried iron beams to the worksite and thought our lunch breaks were too long. When I heard she had gotten a tailor to make her overalls I asked her why. She said she couldn't find any to fit her locally, not being as skinny as a Thai. No, she was definitely not shaped like a Thai; she was pleasantly plump with a mane of curly blond hair she tied up in a neck gator high on her head. Plus she was twenty years younger than me. Forty was exactly the perfect age for someone with a vision; seasoned enough to know how to get things done and still young enough to have the energy to do it.

I could also relate to her being a foreigner in my homeland where I felt somewhat of a foreigner too. She had an outsider's view of Americans which was always welcome. She had also lived in England as a young person seeking her future. So she had an idea of the culture of my birthplace. She was Dutch South African, known to be friendlier than the British kind, so I had heard from an American friend living in England. Like me, Clasina had a home country she loved that she did not live in where she still had family—her parents lived there. And like me she had made a home in her adopted country as a transplant. And there was no going back. She had married and settled here in Thailand.

I was also naturally intrigued by Clasina's South African heritage and what had befallen it. I already knew from reading Naomi Klein's Shock Doctrine that Mandela's South Africa had quickly succumbed to predatory corporate takeover by international interests leading to intense corruption and a deterioration of infrastructure still going on today.

Clasina had watched the white colonial culture give way to native power just as she was graduating high school. She had left South Africa as many of her generation had because new laws favored Black Africans being hired throughout the new government and schools. White South Africans could only be hired if no Blacks could be found to do the job, which was likely never since on-the-job training was preferred in order to hire Blacks in first. This experience of having already watched a society collapse was an added asset in my book. That she had survived such upheaval with such a sunny resilience was encouraging to me.

I mentioned briefly to her of my having gone to a protest against South African apartheid while in college at UC Santa Cruz (and hoping to get arrested just for the thrill of it). My mother had laughed at my participation and said that the same anti-apartheid protests had gone on when she was in college. Yes apartheid had gone on for a long time. Clasina was proud that the country still survived despite all the sanctions and withdrawal of investment money. She was pro Mandela, but told me how the process of restoring natives to power should have been done in stages so it could have gone more smoothly leaving infrastructure intact and less vulnerable to corruption.

I asked Clasina if she thought to return to South Africa. "No," she said, "it's just too sad."

I asked her why she came to Thailand. She told me that she had gone to England to study food service, but the English climate was depressing her so she had asked a travel agent where she could go that was warm. There were two choices Mexico and Thailand.

"Which one costs less to go to?" she asked. The haphazard chance of her destiny having been decided on such a whim struck me as poignant plus I appreciated how her frugality weighed in. And the adventure of throwing herself at a foreign place where she knew no one was ballsy. She had loved Thailand, loved how laid back the Thais were though their tendency to be late annoyed her work ethic, which was why she liked Japanese clients she told me. I too liked to be on time as did my Khun Ya who was somehow a carry over from her Chinese father when it came to time and productivity.

When I asked Clasina how she had learned Thai I was even more impressed. She told me she was the sort of person who just had to talk and she was not afraid of making a fool of herself by using the wrong words. So she had just asked all her Thai friends to teach her the correct words and how to say things. Strangely she did not see herself as very bright.

"Couldn't you tell?" she asked me. No it had not occurred to me to assess her intelligence as lacking. She may have suffered the same assessment of her intelligence as I had. We had simply attended schools that set the bar very high, giving us the sense that we would always struggle to make the grade while other classmates seemed to easily maintain top scores. She was clearly eager to learn and absorb information and could teach others. I had watched her during one of our lunch breaks teach a child at the build how to play Kim's game. I didn't have much experience with children and this was a skill Clasina was at ease with. I took a picture of her and the child intent in their game and sent it to a mentor back in the states with the words "A partner of a different sort" in the subject line and told her of our potential farm project.

She confirmed that Clasina's robust spirit was indeed obvious in the photo and how attractive such a vision of a farm in Thailand could be, but such a project so far from my base made her nervous. She reminded me of the cautionary tale of my experience in land investment in rental housing so fraught as it was with problems so far away. Would I be able to live on this farm as it was being developed? she asked. I could understand how jumping into something so suddenly would make people think I was being rash. I got a similar message from another elder I consulted who had a daughter in real estate. She asked me practical questions about whether the land would keep its value over time should I need to sell it and if I would have a way to back out should something come up in Clasina's life. But ultimately this friend saw this investment as a complication of my time, energy and finances. Why not keep things simple she said and just put the money in the bank so I could give it some more thought? Well what was the fun of that especially after being handed cash and told to feel my money.

Their sage words reminded me that I was not so much looking for a good return on a monetary investment. I was looking for something else.

A relationship perhaps, but not in the romantic way. More in an act of collaboration and a chance to build community. A project that would give my trips to Thailand meaning now that the family elders who loved me were dead. After all, my father had left me as an heir to the family compound in Bangkok so I would probably be involved as an owner for the rest of my life, which didn't seem like such a long time anymore. In the end, I was convinced that the timing of our meeting coming just before this money landed in my lap was a big sign from the universe for me to leap. Even the pendulum said so. I had brought it with me to Bangkok in case I needed to show my relatives I had spiritual juju.

Clasina had another question for me. "Am I a project then?" she asked me. The question surprised me as the idea of a person being a personal project had never occurred to me. I knew she meant someone I would wish to influence and shape into my own vision of a young person, possibly myself at a younger age.

"No," I said, "more like a niece who is an artist in need of a studio." This was a plot point of a Vita Sackville West novel I had read long ago in my youth. I was wishing that I had such a mentor to provide for me, if not a studio, then a mental artistic space to encourage my creative work.

Clasina seemed ok with this answer and we could go on to discuss why this particular farm. Why not a larger one closer to Bangkok that she had also considered. I could see the practical consideration. But I was most attracted to this particular location in Northern Thailand. A farm in the very area where Peggy and Jo had created a community seemed ideal for there were other mud hut sisters who had settled in the area. And Chiang Mai was a different kind of city than Bangkok. Much more low key in scale with an aesthetic that had aspired to be more European mountain town rather than the major metropolitan global capital that Bangkok had become.

While resting at my Bangkok home I spoke to Prayoon who lived on the family compound as staff as she had done since my childhood. She was now cooking my meals when I came back home. Her loyalty to caring for Khun Ya until her death carried over to me, and making sure I was not forgotten in Khun Ya's legacy. She thought the farm was a good idea. She understood my farming project, not so much as an investment, but as part of the small farm movement that the late King had promoted. It even had a name, Khrong Gahn Seta Pakit Por Piang, which translated to Project Farming Business For Enough. Enough being a concept of growing just what you needed to sustain yourself.

Prayoon urged me to meet Clasina's Thai husband and determine if he was a "good" person. So I asked Clasina if I could meet him and see how she lived with my practiced eye as an organizer. She invited me to lunch. She rarely had anyone over, she said, and served me a hearty soup in a house of a very similar vintage to the mid-century modern houses of my neighborhood. What was unusual about it was that it still contained the possessions of the long dead previous owners. The siblings who inherited this house couldn't get it together to agree to sell it or decide what price and who should get what percentage of that price. So they were renting it at a discount. Their indecisiveness had gone on for years. Some of those siblings had died and now their children were adding their opinions to the mix. This was so Thai I realized similar situations were happening all over Bangkok. I was glad I had agreed to sell my cousin my share of our business land for the price she offered. It had been her second offer. The first was so low I opted to wait to see if the property would sell. But the second was enough to take notice. When she couldn't persuade my stepmother to sell I asked her if she was sorry she had given me all that money.

"No," she said. "It was my mother's money and she would have wanted you to have it. She said that you were the only person who wasn't getting anything out of this property," she told me.

"Oh thank-you," I said looking heavenward at the dark wood ceiling of my Aunty Ah Pahdt's bedroom where we were going through her clothes. At least someone in the family recognized how I'd been sidestepped when my stepmother Ot inherited all the money my father had gotten from his mother. Khun Ya having only died a year before he had. And he had made Ot his executor and put her in charge of his house in Bangkok (not to mention leaving to her his house in Menlo Park). This family compound had been Khun Ya's vision. She had bought the land and developed it for all who lived there and I was her last remaining heir. That ought to be worth something..

After their initial surprise my family and friends in Thailand grasped the benefit of my farm project right away. They supported the plan because I was throwing in my lot with them in the country we loved.

I did meet Ya, Clasina's husband. He was very shy and low key, but so sweet it was hard to suspect him of any shenanigans or of hiding anything or trying to trick anyone. Between the class protocol and the limitations of the Thai language it was easy to read what people's intentions were and whether they were at peace with themselves. It was clear when a Thai thought I was beyond contempt, for they were usually so charming and friendly that refusing to be gracious was a big tell. They might ignore me or answer me curtly. In the States where no class protocol was really allowed people felt obliged to be friendly even in business transactions using a nuanced language of persuasion and friendship that might be true friendliness or just a bald face desire to win something from me. I was much more susceptible to con jobs from people in the States, especially men.

While Clasina attended to our lunch, Ya and I squatted by the tiny pond they had and talked about the large fish in it that were meant for eating. He told me how he was planning to make a pump to aerate the pond. I liked his earnestness and self confidence. He was an uncomplicated man. A good man in the sense that Prayoon meant. And I was grateful to him for letting me partner with his wife on the farm project. For Clasina and I would travel together to the farm when I came to visit every six months going forward.

Before I left Thailand, I gave Clasina a check to give to the farm owners for a deposit with the promise that I would be back in six months to pay the balance. Upon my return my partnership with Clasina paid off right away, as she took charge of booking train tickets and making all our travel arrangements.

We both loved these trips by overnight train to Chiang Mai and became very familiar with the government land transfer office in Mae Taeng, which was where the taxi let us off. The day I came to write my name on the deed (in Thai) I met the farm family that sold us the land. The old farmer spoke a northern Thai so thick I could hardly understand him. He sat at the counter first and signed off on the deed. He was selling the parcel that was the furthest away from home. He was old now. Too old to go out to this land and his family wanted to build him a nice house with all the amenities—two modern bathrooms with throne toilets and showers, glass windows, air conditioning and large screen TV. We were invited to the house warming party six months later.

The parcel of land itself had the unique feature of hosting a crematorium for a nearby temple in its far corner. This was probably what had made it a hard sell for Thai people who were famously afraid of ghosts. Ya did not like it at all and wanted us to build our adobe house as far away from it as possible. It was already well fenced off with a line of bamboo and trees up against the barbed wire fence on all sides.

Clasina and I went to check out the crematorium on its small pie shape plot of land. It had its own entrance and buildings consisting of a public toilet and open air shelter plus benches for outdoor seating. The crematorium itself sat across from these buildings at the narrow end of the lot. It was very small with three sets of stairs going up to the pavilion which bore the traditional orange tiled temple roof with the upturned corners. At the back was the windowless crematorium with its needle tall chimney. Once I'd seen it I rarely gave it another thought. It was hardly ever in use. I was somewhat proud of it; it probably counted for cosmic brownie points to be the land owner who offered this service to the temple and to the village.

On our second visit to the land we stayed at the lovely Thai style wooden house of a mud hut sister, one that had been brought to the site and assembled under her direction. We had some good fun hanging out with her. She also played a part in guiding us through our process. Jesse was a Canadian expat who had gone through a similar process of buying her land with Thai partners, since foreigners can only own land in Thailand if a Thai person owned a majority share of it. When Clasina asked me what my plan was in life I poetically said I wanted to be an Agent of the Goddess and do whatever was needed to better the planet. She was intimidated by such an altruistic statement. As Jesse listened to Clasina asking me these somewhat vague questions she gave me some sage advice.

"You have to tell her she is free to create whatever it is she wants on this land," she said. For while Clasina's head was full of practical concerns, I clearly did not have a clue. I was just enjoying the ride. So we decided to talk about what kind of house we would build with the help of our mud hut sisters. She brought up my having a room in this house. As I watched Clasina draw I realized she was envisioning her dream house, not a practical one room shack with outdoor kitchen as we had just seen that day at the home of a French expat with his Thai wife, but a serious house. Well why not? I asked myself. A woman needs to create her dream house. After all I had done my tiny house exactly as I had wanted it and it had been perfect suiting me to a T. So I began to contribute my ideas.

Then there was the matter of the lease. My cousins had all warned me severely that in Thailand you had to be very careful who you let use your land because you could lose it after seven years if they claimed squatters' rights. But this was not something I wanted to worry about. I wanted a hassle free lease, one that didn't require bookkeeping and workarounds to pay taxes that would be due on a supposed income I was receiving. I didn't want to charge Clasina rent. She would need her money to develop the farm. Clasina needed a lease to give her the right to be on the land, but she didn't want one that would be so restrictive that she would need permission to do every last thing. We asked people to show us their leases and passed them back and forth to each other, but none seemed quite to fit. Clasina then asked the land transfer office for advice and they said they had some leases they could show us. How helpful I thought. So on our next trip we sat down and spoke of our intentions to one of the officers. I explained that I didn't want to charge rent and I spoke of my desire to leave the land to Clasina. The officer reminded us that Clasina still didn't have a Thai I.D. so wouldn't be able to take ownership. As he came to understand our relationship of being unrelated yet friends, he said I could sign a lease that was usually signed between an elder family member and a younger one. It was called, in official terms, "a lease of affection." How perfect was that I thought. A lease of affection. A legal bond to a loved one. I felt as if I was about to get married.

It's a very generous thing to do, the officer said to us after we signed the lease. I nodded at his words without expression. Generous is what it might look like I thought. But what effort did it cost me? It was an inheritance. I'd already thrown away money I'd inherited before at a hot stock market a few months before it crashed spectacularly. That lesson made me feel such a fool I beat myself up for it for more than a year. But what I had learned was that it was not enough to just want to be rich. Money meant nothing unless it was grounded in vision. I bought an electric car with what I had left, which was loads of fun, but then it broke down indefinitely. I had invested my time in the rental property venture with people who screwed me in more ways than I could have imagined. A much needed lesson for a liberal to learn about one's best intentions with people who had not the best of intentions. I had no children so I hadn't had to sacrifice as a parent to raise them. No, this was my own lazy way of bringing a dream to fruition, get someone else to manifest it.

We were aiming to have our build with our team of friends as soon as possible, but there was so much to do to prepare. I could see Clasina would wear herself out trying to meet deadlines. She had already found someone who would teach us how to build these round houses. This teacher had built several such houses at the base of a spectacular mountain and had operated a successful bed and breakfast in them for years. She was also an expat, an English woman named Maggie. We went to stay at her Round House resort. I was already familiar with the technique she used to build these houses, for I had visited the center where the founder had built an entire compound of such houses in Southern California not far from my rental property. He was an Iranian and had adapted the indigenous house building methods of his country and modernized it. Maggie had adapted the technique to suit the tropical climate so it wouldn't feel damp inside. We stayed in one. The room was big and the walls made taller with the arc of the thatched roof.

In the morning Maggie made us a lovely breakfast of fresh fruit and home baked bread.

"What brought you to Thailand?" I asked her. She said she had come in her twenties to stay with her aunt, who was building a school in Bangkok for the children of English expats. When I asked her the name of the school I was astonished at the answer. It was Mrs Clayton's School, the very school I had gone to, and Mrs. Clayton was her aunt.

"I went there!" I exclaimed. This trail of serendipitous happenings just kept getting better. While we were still sitting at breakfast a Japanese man and his wife came down the path filled with words of admiration for what she had created. He said he was a landscape artist from Portland and had designed the Japanese gardens for the park there. "I've been there," I nearly shouted again. It was only meaningful to me for the Portland Japanese garden was famous and beautifully appointed, but it was unknown outside of Oregon. The spirits were working me now with all these serendipitous coincidences sent to wow me. I felt terrifically happy and confident that whatever befell us was meant to be.

But what to call the farm? Clasina wanted a working farm that would sell product so we needed a name. We brainstormed all sorts of ideas trying to find something that would say eco permaculture farm, wild weed products, barefoot farm, etc. Many such names were taken. Green Joy was one Clasina suggested.

Clasina always had things she planned to do on the farm whether to plant trees or meet with a consultant or farm hand. A pond had been dug first and during my next trip she wanted to add a piece of pipe to the pipe already installed as an outlet to empty the pond. The added pipe would stop the water from flowing out. This entailed going down to the waters edge and wading into the mud, trying to jam the pipe underwater to the end of the one installed. As I watched Clasina wading into the mud in her overalls and boots and start her attempt to connect the pipe I took photographs. But she couldn't manage it and I couldn't help because I had sprained my ankle the day before and was hobbling around with a stick. Eventually she gave it up, but as she turned to climb up the steep bank of the pond one of her boots was sucked back into the mud; she came out of it and was unable to rescue it. And she just laughed and laughed as she tried to make it up the bank slipping as she climbed.

This was such a funny story I posted about it on Facebook with the accompanying photos for my friends back home. Then we went back to brainstorming a name for the farm. As I checked back to see people laughing at Clasina's escapade a thought occurred to me.

"You know we could call it Lost Boots Farm" I said. Clasina liked it and told it to Ya who liked it better than any of the other names we'd come up with. It was easy to say for a Thai and they used the English word "boot" to identify footwear as a "boot shoe"— so they already knew what a boot was. I liked the carefree attitude the name implied as if this was where you came to lose your boots so you could be barefoot and free. Or where things went awry, but no one really worried about it. Clasina created a Facebook page for Lost Boots and we were launched.

Chapter 43

Pandemic Audit

I travelled back and forth to Thailand twice a year to meet Clasina for our Lost Boots Farm adventures. My last trip was scheduled when the pandemic hit Thailand. I went anyway.

Six months before that trip, my landlady told me she had decided to sell her house where I had so comfortably spent the first three years of my tiny house life in her backyard, hidden from view behind the line of bottle brush bushes tall enough to reach my roofline. The news hit me hard. I had been grateful to her for offering to host the tiny house and allowing me to practice my poop composting in her garden. Not many people would have welcomed such an experiment. Plus, the location was perfect just a short drive from Catherine's house where I went regularly to walk our dogs.

The Bay Area had not become any more tiny-house friendly in the three years I had been living in my tiny. In fact, because there were now 300 RVs parked on the streets all over Mountain View and Palo Alto residents had become even more resistant to any live aboard house on wheels. We had seen this housing crisis coming, but resident's resistance to increased density in these suburbs had now bloomed into the most obscene housing crisis in the nation, even as cities allowed Google and Facebook to add hundreds of thousands of jobs. We would never catch up to house them all.

The Bay Area was, for all intents and purposes, closed to tiny houses. And those people who had extended invitations to park on their property three years before now had thought better of it. It was all I could do to gather myself together and marshal enough personal courage to fight the overwhelming thought that it was hopeless. I told myself I was not just any homeless person living in an RV. I had skills to offer and I was a contributor. Look at all the things I could do! I duly listed them on my craigslist ad.

My plight prompted a friend to post my request to a group list where she and her wife lived. It was a 40 minutes drive over the Santa Cruz mountains, but it was a beautiful, meditative drive that did not involve bridge traffic or much traffic at all. I got two responses immediately. The first response was from a family 10 minutes further down the road in farm country. A bit too far and too remote, but I entertained the idea until the second offer, which was right down the street from my friends' house. Off I went to meet him.

Bob greeted me from his woodpile, where he cut up downed trees to heat his house. He was so chatty he made me feel at home right away. He offered me three different places where I could park. Across the street the resident lama and goat looked at us waiting for a treat of yard trimmings. Though I had long been an urban creature fond of public transport, I was warming to this rural town with its junked cars and casual live and let live DIY country sensibilities. It was horse country without the pretentiousness.

I showed him my photo album of my tiny house and disclosed how my composting toilet worked. He did not seem put off by it since I wouldn't be close enough to impact his garden. He asked $500 in rent with a work trade of 8 to 10 hours a month. I chose the upper pasture for my spot, the slope of the West facing hillside offering a splendid view of the Santa Cruz mountains. With Tim and his truck we began work to level and prepare the site, laying down the weed block fabric Bob offered me and a truck load of broken concrete I got free plus two loads of gravel to fashion a gopher resistant landing pad.

During this time PG&E, our utility company rolled out the first mandatory blackouts as fire season got underway. This prompted me to think of launching into solar, especially since Bob's property would require 250 feet of extension cords in order for me to plug into his house for power. The longest cord I could get was 100ft. Even I didn't like the idea of joining up so many cords. And the West facing hillside was ideal for solar.

As it turned out there was a man on craigslist selling a complete solar set-up that was just about the right size for a tiny house. He was offering a battery pack too. All for $1400. It was a risk to buy used equipment, but the set up had high grade components and I was being pulled by the serendipity of it all.

I had, for instance, exactly the right amount of cash on hand to finalize this deal on a bank holiday weekend. The size of the panels would just fit in my Prius. When I went to meet him he was Asian too and he took me into his backyard where I saw that he was also living in a tiny house—a converted garden shed. He had used his system very briefly for a grow project involving hydroponics, probably marijuana, but I didn't ask. He showed me how the components worked and how to hook them up. It all looked viable and I handed over the cash.

As I got up to leave I mentioned that my father had been an engineer and had taught me some things. He said his father had been in Vietnam in communications and had taught him a lot about components too.

"If your father was in Vietnam he must have spent some time in Thailand," I said.

"Yes," he said, "I am half Thai."

"So am I," I said. I was so bowled over by this serendipitous revelation I took this whole transaction as a blessing possibly arranged by my father himself from his heavenly perch. He smiled for the first time and gave me the traditional greeting of a wai with the words Sawadii Kup. I returned the greeting overcome by my good luck and drove away with my new solar system, tickled at how I was going to subvert the power company with all I needed fitting into my Prius.

Several you-tube tutorials later I was confident I could put the system together. I just needed a battery box. I dragged an old metal bathtub up to the site. It had been Bob's before he remodeled his bathroom and was just big enough to hold all four of the golf cart batteries. And the hole where the stopper lever was installed was perfect for the cables from the panels to enter into my bathtub battery cabinet. To make a cover for it I found two pieces of plywood and cut them to fit against the rim of the bathtub. Hinged in the middle like a dutch door it revealed the components while leaving the battery bank enclosed. I clamped the cover to the bathtub with wood working clamps and painted it a spritely green, feeling very satisfied with my low budget accomplishment.

Ironically, the house felt smaller in this big space, but once I had cooked a meal in it it was the same house it had always been only it wasn't at all the same experience. It was so quiet and the light coming through the windows was different, sunnier and vacation like. My view lay spread before me from my main window taking my eyes clear over the Santa Cruz mountains towards a sky populated with hawks. I felt different as if my identity had changed. I was now a country person. I belonged somewhere, to a community and a geography that had embraced me and made me feel like family just for settling there.

I had just settled in when it was time to fly back to Thailand, traveling through Taiwan where I saw all the masked precautions for COVID 19. Western travelers, including me, did not wear masks. In Thailand people were calm. It felt novel, but not panicky. There were no lines of shoppers trying to hoard every last item they might need. Clasina and I could travel about the country with little more than hand sanitizer being offered to us at the train station. And we went to an organic farm for a workshop specializing in bokashi technology with an international group of some 30 people all living in a dormitory for four days. Bokashi derived disinfectant was sprayed into the rooms at intervals. And Bokashi derived hand sanitizer was offered along with alcohol based sanitizer. We didn't worry much about catching the virus.

The day I left for home the airport was desolate; it felt eerie. I counted myself lucky to have nipped into Asia's coronavirus hotspot and gotten back before it hit the states. That glimpse into how Taiwan and Thailand handled the virus so competently would prove to be a mind saver as I watched things unfold not so competently from the White House.

As this unforeseen event flew into the world, rendering all that we were doing before COVID 19 somehow irrelevant, I felt incredibly fortunate to have so recently landed in a paradise of a spot. For the lockdown would test the tiny house for all it was worth. This wasn't the apocalypse I was expecting. Not one I had given any thought to; it didn't fit the model of collapse I had been occupying myself with for well over a decade. Normal life would resume shortly even if it took a couple of years I assured myself. This was just a temporary suspension of the frenetic energy of humans meddling with the natural environment all over the world. A nice respite for the planet, though as the U.S. response unfolded things looked precarious.

I was kept busy incessantly reading the news. The economic suffering due to the lockdown and related impact on families began to weigh on me. Those prone to depression and anxiety, those vulnerable to spousal abuse, parents now up against the double stress of working from home and taking care of kids, shut-in invalids unable to get deliveries. All this had me glued to Facebook making sure everyone on my feed was okay. I was a dedicated kollapsnik, but it had been just for fun. It was a world I created to escape from all that annoyed me about American consumer society. A psychological ruse to insure my own mental health. I never wanted it to happen for real.

The virus became an audit of the injustices of our social structures, our environmental hubris pushing ever further into wildlife habitat, our hyper consumption, the dysfunctional base of our government catering to corporate interests. So many things I had been trying to tell people now shouting from headlines. A meme popped up several times on my FB feed.

"I feel like we've been sent to our room to think about what we've done," it said. "And what did you come up with," I asked in the comments, but got no answer.

What I'd been perfecting within the frenetic bustle of the Bay Area for my own personal amusement was now considered a survivalist's solution to this end of civilization as we knew it scenario. I hadn't planned for that. Living in 130 square feet with no hot water on tap or flush toilet had been just a personal challenge to see what a minimal footprint lifestyle could teach me. I didn't want hoards of converts. I didn't even know if what I was doing was viable for such unforeseen circumstances. I was disoriented by my elevated status as a solution creator. I was unused to people actually listening to me.

"You were the go-to survivalist, but you were just running a sim," Tracy, my mud hut sister from England, wittily summed up from her expat home in Bangkok. I had met her at a build the year before I met Clasina. I laughed at the irony of this—me, playing a make-believe game in the comfort of suburbia with all it had to offer in ease of access to movie theaters, restaurants, public libraries and grocery stores. Plus, hot showers and laundry facilities at Catherine's house and the use of a full kitchen in which I cooked casseroles to share with her.

"Knowledge is knowledge though" she added. True that. When I saw that the seed rack at the hardware store had been decimated of the most popular vegetables, it made me wonder if people had any idea what they were doing. Likewise, when I heard that all of the chicks being bred for this Spring had already been bought in advance.

"Just food for hawks around here," Bob commented. But there was also the happy news that all the dogs and cats had been adopted out from the humane shelter to keep the humans company now they were in shelter. I bought some of the remaining seed packets, scarlet runner beans and sunflower seeds. I had books in my tiny home library with detailed instructions on growing plants from seed which I would now reread.

My home library in this internet age was an indulgence and a pointed statement on the fragility of our contemporary systems. My 18 feet of books took up valuable space in my tiny house. I had questioned every foot of my collection as I made my shelves the time consuming recycler's way—from used hollow core doors that had to be finished with cut to fit lumber squeezed into their cut open edges. The pandemic did not bring down the electrical grid, but it did slow the internet way down, and all those youtube videos took up too much of my data. I did not have unlimited data on my little wifi hotspot. But that was ok. Watching youtube took up way too much time and would just increase my screen time. I was glad I had the books.

"At least I've had time to practice living this lifestyle," I told Tracy, "I know what toys work and don't work". My homemade hot water heater only heated water when it was sunny and hot for instance. It was no better than a garden hose lying in the sun. In the end I just filled three discarded San Pellegrino bottles with water from my tap and put them in my solar oven. A few hours and I had boiling water which I then poured into a thermos for drinking and another larger one for dishwashing. The water stayed hot long into the evening.

It took longer to figure out laundry. Using a hand crank washing machine was time consuming and somehow ridiculous in the amount of work it took I told her. She laughed and said if she had just a t-shirt and three pairs of knickers she would have been tempted to buy a Scrubba. What was that? She gave me the link. It was a travel laundry washing device that was essentially a waterproof bag with a rubber washboard inside it. I was intrigued. Now that no one was traveling it was half off with free shipping. The bag also doubled as a day pack. I was very susceptible to things that had two uses. I ordered one.

"It's the missing link," I told Tracy. I could try it out to wash my socks and reusable cloth dish towels between laundry visits to my friends' house down the street. In the end I got a five gallon bucket and a plunger style washer. The challenge was in wringing wet laundry out. I ordered the old timer style hand crank wringer from eBay, but it was awkward to use, requiring two hands to feed each item into the double rollers and another hand to crank the item through. Finally, I ordered a spin dryer made for the Asian market of apartment dwellers. It had pulley ropes like an exercise machine. It did not require handling each item individually since you just stuffed as much as you could into the basket, shut the lid and pulled on the handles building up your biceps as you pulled. I could actually do laundry at my tiny house and hang it out to dry on collapsible drying racks I had as I had always done.

That night I turned on my HAM radio for the weekly check-in with local HAM enthusiasts. Nothing says survivalist like a HAM radio. That was the kind of town this was that it had volunteers offering to train people to get their license. Attending this two weekend class at the all volunteer fire station down the hill from me was the first community activity I participated in once I had moved in. "This is Kilo November Six ...." I transmitted proud of my snappy call number. People on the call talked about how nice it was to have the sun and what garden projects they were doing. It was really just transmission practice to create community so we could volunteer as a radio operator when phones stopped working during the power outages prompted by wildfires, or for outdoor events like bicycle races. Radio waves were free.

The radio would go down too without a charge though, so I was glad I had my solar powered battery bank. I had no business messing with a battery bank, as I found out when one of the wires started heating up because it wasn't bolted down tightly causing it to melt a hole in one of the batteries. I noticed this and touched the cable. I jumped when I saw the wire spark at the terminal as I moved the cable.

OMG I could have blown myself up, I realized as I frantically messaged a tiny house friend in Georgia for advice. He made me a video within the hour of how his battery pack was set up so I could troubleshoot what I'd done wrong.

The previous owner of my system had been using household wiring which was really too small for 12 volt batteries I learned. And in demonstrating the system to me he had only finger tightened the nuts not used a wrench to tighten the connection. Plus something about the way I configured the batteries differently from him had stretched the wires too tightly causing them to pull and rub together more. I had been lulled into a false sense of security by this fellow half Thai, DIYer.

I immediately carted the damaged lead acid battery off in a milk crate to a battery store where I got a new battery and had the man make me proper battery cables. I lugged it all back to my site swearing to be more careful and ask advice.

Bart comforted me telling me that many inventors had taken dangerous risks to discover important things so I was in good company. Then he advised me to ground all my gear in case of lightning, which could fry all my components and possibly start a fire. I promptly set out to do this.

The battery bank was not quite up to my needs I would find. After several days of rain I would be left in the dark, but that was only a day here and there in the rainy season. My landlord didn't mind if I strung extension cords down to his house on those occasions. This was cheating, but at least when the power was shut off during fire season the days would be long with no rain so I would have plenty of power when everyone else was running their gasoline powered generators. Off grid living was full of community relationships like this.

My electric kettle took up too much juice to use in the evenings so I just boiled water in a camping kettle on my stove. My one burner stove was non-electric at least, but required canisters of propane, for which I was constantly looking for refills. The price went up a dollar per can just before the lockdown I noted, as I ordered another case. I did not want to switch out the stove because it was just the right shape to fit in the drawer I had designed to pull out under the window I used for ventilation. I had a little fan sitting on the window sill to pull the steam out through the window. I also had a toaster oven I didn't try to use unless it had been sunny.

At least I was not cold. That's what my friends asked me about the most. I had neglected to install a heater in the tiny house. After all this was California and I was menopausal at the time. I was hot constantly. The year I moved into the tiny house was one of the coldest winters we'd had in years. Temperatures dipped to the freezing point. The tiny house was insulated enough to keep me ten degrees warmer than outside temperatures. I got myself down booties and wore coats and hats inside. Sheilagh, my Canadian girlfriend sent me long underwear and wool socks. I tried out various heaters both electrical and propane, plus the intriguing YouTube favorite of bolted together flowerpots turned upside down and suspended over candles. I grew so fond of my flowerpot heater that I started making my own candles so I could burn them through the night after I shut off my propane heater. It made a nice night light too. Clients often gave me old candles during a move, which I would melt down in the solar oven which didn't require tending like a double boiler of the stove would. And the jar candles I made were safest since the flame was inside the glass.

My new location was much colder than the fenced in backyard where I had cut my tiny house teeth. The house no longer offered me the 10° warmer inside temps. I suspected the wind coming up the hill was ripping under the house and pulling away the heat. I had to do what RV people do and install a skirt around the trailer to block the wind. I gave it a lot of thought. Over Thanksgiving weekend in defiance of the boycott of Black Friday sale, I just had to go down to Home Depot to see what they were selling at discounts. I stopped at a display of storage boxes so big they looked like coffins for short people. They had a 55 gallon capacity just like rain barrels. It dawned on me that these boxes might be just the thing to both block the wind and catch water. I bought six feeling slightly ridiculous as I loaded them into my Prius. What could a woman possibly have that she needed six body size storage boxes to contain? Shoes, bags?

The boxes did catch water and they did block the wind some. I put a few discarded pillows in black plastic bags and stuffed them in the cavities between the storage boxes. Still not enough. Finally I cut up a large cardboard box my freezer came in and wrapped the fiberfill from an old quilt around the plank width cardboard and then wrapped that whole package with one of the foil emergency blankets from a 12 pack that a friend had given me.

I crawled under the house and installed four of these wrapped cardboard units all around the perimeter of the trailer. It worked well enough. I raised the temp maybe 8° and I now had 330 gallons of water saved, plus assorted buckets and water containers I filled using an old gutter Bob had discarded. Having buckets of water was very handy to dilute the pee from my toilet tank before I poured the pee water around the house, watering my plants. I also hoped this would discourage mountain lions from camping out with me. Learning how much to dilute the pee so it wouldn't smell was another lesson I had learned in my first tiny house year when neighbors complained after I watered the sidewalk median strip plants with a particularly potent brew. Seven parts water to one parts pee was undetectable. But three parts to one part pee would keep from burning the plants. I had also dispensed with the chore of emptying my waste water tank and just routed my drain out into the garden filtered through a box of sand.

So yes all in all I had acquired valuable knowledge of use to nobody. Except marginally as entertainment for my FB feed. What it had done to my mind though was more interesting. When the pandemic hit in the U.S. it took me a month or so to separate myself from the feelings of chaos created by people who were suddenly thrown from their expectations. Expectations of life carrying on as they had planned. But my plans were all about things not going according to plan. In fact the plans I did have to travel to Thailand every six months was getting a little too hectic and I was somewhat relieved to take a break from this schedule.

In late February three weeks before the lockdown I was watching out for supply lines from China being cut off by the closing of their factories. At the market I saw small printed signs on the shelves. "Due to an unforeseen supply issue dried beans and rice are temporarily out of stock". I grabbed a five pound bag of pinto beans and bag of rice which I stashed at Catherine's house. The next week as people began their panic buying, I ordered her a chest freezer so we could all stock up on fresh foods. It allowed us all to shop less frequently, which was advisable to stay out of trouble.

The coronavirus required nothing more of us than masks. I had already outfitted both Catherine and myself with reusable N95 masks for the terrible air quality during the fires in the summer and for the air pollution in Bangkok. There wasn't anything else I really needed. Sheltering in place in my tiny house simply allowed me to continue the many projects of my off-grid pursuit full-time. In fact I needed such a sabbatical from others I realized as so much of my time had been taken up with helping people get their projects done. Life in this new normal had a less hectic, vintage feel to it as if I had stepped back in time before airplanes and industry. I could completely forget about the virus. It just gave me something fascinating to watch from afar. And I could still mail order items to further my efforts at problem solving.

"Can I bring you anything?" My friend Bart asked me before he drove up to join me for a social distance hike on one of the many trails into the foothills from my house.

"Do you have any movies on DVD?" I asked. He chuckled. This was not something he expected a tiny house survivalist to need. But I had made no contingencies for my appetite for moving pictures, or the closing of libraries and movie theaters. I was after all just running a sim.

Chapter 44

The Handmade Life

I had been raised in what was considered in Bangkok to be a wealthy family yet we did not own a great deal. One television, one telephone, a small fridge. We didn't have a big wardrobe or need to store a variety of gear so it didn't take a huge house to store it all in. We understood ourselves to be well off because my grandfather had a Merccdes Benz, my Khun Ya had a chauffeured Fiat, my father a sports car, and my mother her Morris Minor, and we lived on a large property across from members of the royal family. My Khun Ya had built a two story house that was relatively large compared to ordinary folk who lived in the country. And she provided housing for house staff and at one time a house and a livelihood for a school teacher to tutor the children in the family all living in the one house.

In contrast the poor, who lived with us had almost nothing at all. I saw what our house staff owned. I played in their rooms. Three girls would share a room just large enough for all of them to unfold a sleeping mattress each. They had one storage cabinet that also served as a dressing table. One of the doors was missing so I could see the contents of the three shelves within. One shelf for each of them for the neatly folded sarongs that they wore on a daily basis. On a clothes rack hung their blouses and skirts, mostly hand-me downs from my family members. Those were their dress-up outfits for outings beyond our compound walls.

The clapboard walls were covered with pictures from magazines to keep the mosquitos from entering the room. I learned how to make glue from rice flour and hot water the day I helped them to paste more pictures on the wall to cover new holes. A radio played in the kitchen and at night they could join my relatives in Khun Ya's living room to watch her TV. They sat quietly on the floor where I was apt to join them. This simplicity of material things became part of my memory of the country I loved.

I returned to Thailand a number of years after the room with the magazine covered walls had been replaced with three new rooms financed by my Aunty Lily, who had left her mid century modern stucco house to move to our compound to join forces with her oldest sister, my Khun Ya, so they would have company in their old age. Now their maids too would each have her own room to be shared with their husbands. The new housing was made from cinder blocks and had proper hand crank louvered windows with screens so no mosquitoes.

"Are these new rooms better than the old one?" I asked with a twinge of nostalgia.

"Of course they're better," said Prayoon who was now the head housekeeper. I could see she was slightly annoyed at such a question, that I couldn't see the substantial improvement. So seldom was this tone used with me that I realized I had no idea that the women who lived among us had wanted for themselves, how they might aspire to have things that were beyond their reach. How my projection of simplicity and nostalgia onto their humbleness was my own assumption that it was their wish to live this way and be an example to those better off, while I, whose life was filled with choices, was choosing this lifestyle. I who was freely able to choose how I lived. A crucial difference.

They made note of my choices too. They saw I was content to wear practical inexpensive clothes and did not aspire to expensive tastes. After spending a day shopping with me, Prayoon reported to the rest of the staff that I did not want to wear the latest linen outfits. She sounded proud of me as if some of her sensible peasant values had rubbed off on me. I was setting an example that my other relatives, who chased after the latest designer handbags, would not. Because it was more important how rich people chose to live than how poor people were forced to live. What rich people wore and what cars they drove would be looked up to and emulated.

Asian culture had not promoted this individualistic lifestyle until quite recently. Clothing had been prescribed by society as markers of professions and class status. The Thailand of my day revolved around uniforms and formalized dress for individuals according to rank and class status. The traditional sarong worn by the rural agricultural class, while those in the city really only adopted Western dress post World War II. The latest women's fashions came to us in Western fashion magazines and were faithfully copied by a community of neighborhood seamstresses.

The expensive designer labels of the West came decades later when import taxes changed and were immediately consumed as new markers of status, ones that could also be adopted by a rising middle class with knock offs, while corporate chains issued uniforms to their staff to match their logos. The seamstress shops gradually faded away save for a few custom men's suit tailors making suits for the tropical climate to fit petite Thai size men and butch women.

Asia, with all its new wealth riding the coattails of globalization, would take materialism into the stratosphere with cities that aspired to have the tallest skyscrapers, the most vertigo provoking rooftop swimming pools, the latest electronic gadgets and interactive entertainment. I realized how far we had gone down the consumer rabbit hole when I learned that in 2013 Instagram had recorded that the Siam Paragon, a popular shopping mall in Bangkok, had been the site of the most uploaded photos worldwide.

When I began to return to Thailand regularly for the mud hut building workshops I so enjoyed, I wore clothes I had sewn myself and handmade leather sandals I had designed and sewn together with a stitching awl, just the one pair which I wore everywhere. But even my cousins admired their stylishness and saw me as a designer.

My friend Bart told me that Tolstoy had also made shoes having decided that the peasants mental ease was a result of a life of toil and he hoped to counteract his despondency by taking up shoe making as well as scything his fields. I enjoyed thinking of Tolstoy with his aristocratic roots taking to the fields to toil alongside the peasants while making shoes in his leisure hours. That he was a writer doing this was also significant. I had taken up shoemaking as an intriguing practical hobby. Making shoes not only fulfilled my appetite to make things with my hands, but kept me in the mental flow state that is said to be the ideal for the creative brain. I felt it strengthened my mind against interruptions and distractions. It was meditative in the sense that thoughts could come and go without attachment.

Once I had my tiny house outfitted and moved in I showed my Thai family photos in an old style pocket size photo album, the kind no one bothered with any more. At lunch my cousins, Ah Neung and Nor, looked at my photos. Upon realizing I had no real bathroom Nor announced that I was crazy which I took as the highest compliment coming from one whose silver Prada sandals were so highly polished they looked like chrome.

I had also shown the photos to Prayoon along with Wel my Aunty Lily's maid. Their own rooms were bigger than the tiny house, though not by much; I wondered if they thought I had come so far down in the world I was now poor. But they could see I was so proud of my house they did not question why I lived there. Wel just asked if my stove being in a drawer could be closed when not in use. That was also one of my favorite features. Later she gifted me with a small enamel pot that I could easily store and use in my tiny house.

My Aunty Ah Pahdt's two children had both married and now had children of their own. Her daughter had married a man who worked for the World Bank. When I showed him the pictures of my tiny house, I explained that I was conducting an experiment to see just how little I needed to live. Framed in these terms he understood my motivation and concern for social problems in a world of diminishing resources. He gave me a little tour of the old style Thai house that belonged to his grandfather knowing that I would appreciate such history.

The house was set over the water on pilings attached to the seaside family restaurant where we had come for lunch following the ceremony to distribute Ah Pahdt's ashes. (Ah Pahdt's funeral had done us proud. So much loved was she in her community of women business owners that there were some 400 guests at her funeral, one of whom had arranged for royal patronage.)

The day after the cremation we had returned to the temple early in the morning for the ritual of the ashes. My aunt's ashes displayed on white cloth in the form of a doll size person startled me with this humbling vision; it made me feel naked to the bone looking at it. Monks came to chant and the family decorated the ash figure with flower petals. Then the attendants rolled the ashes up in a cloth and put the bundle in the urn for transport to the Gulf of Siam. There we boarded a hired boat to drop her ashes into the sea amidst a plume of flower petals and garlands swirling behind us just as we had done for Khun Ya 15 years before and my father a year after that when he died of cancer.

At the temple I had been pleased to see the two nuns who had been at the service the first evening of this three day funeral. One looked about my age and one younger. I knelt by them and asked if I could ask them some questions. They invited me to pull up a chair.

The eldest nun told me that the funeral ceremonies were more important even than the marriage ceremony, as it was a means to teach the people about impermanence and not to get too attached to things. It was also an opportunity to ask forgiveness of the deceased for any wrong doing, she said, in order to end any disputes. I began to see how this worked; that people were learning through death how to hold life with the wisdom of impermanence.

I saw the nuns again at the seaside restaurant at lunch, but they did not eat after the noon hour, as required by their vows, so I joined them later to show them my tiny house photos which they perused with interest.

"You are living like a hermit," pronounced the elder nun, "this is a good start for learning to let go of material things, plants, animals and people." I was so intrigued by this perspective I did not interrupt, though I had rather thought that the tiny house allowed me more time for plants, animals, and people.

I loved the vision of the Hermit, a familiar figure in Thai culture from childhood, since he appeared as a character in the alphabet and was depicted wearing a tiger skin, sporting a long white beard and a jaunty little tiger skin hat. I had often wondered if he was mad, touched in the head.

"It is very difficult to live as a hermit," she said. "It can be lonely and forces you into contemplation." Yes there was an element of that. I also needed this opportunity for retreat to calm my overstimulated mind.

The nuns asked me how many meters wide and long my house was and compared it to their own living quarters nodding their approval. Suddenly the elder nun poked my arm in a familiar way and said "Do you know how to leave your body?"

"No," I said thinking she was referring to an out of body experience. She explained that in meditation I could learn to leave my body which would make it easier to leave it when the body died. Then I would be reincarnated and each time it would be easier and easier to leave my body until finally I wouldn't need a body.

"Yes you get off the wheel of Samsara," I said recognizing this concept. The phrase was familiar as this was a goal many an ambitious American Buddhist would tell me they were aiming for in their practice.

When it came down to it I was in essence ascribing to a certain spiritual practice in using only as much as I needed. And more telling— disposing of my own bodily waste back to the land. Many thought I was touched in the head to want to do this part, even tiny house people. So yes—I was a slightly mad hermit by all accounts. Still my tiny house was a hermitage and most definitely a retreat space to contemplate my inner life, write down my revelations and dispense them to any who would listen. I was pleased by the nuns assessment of my hermit lifestyle and felt comforted to be so recognized by my home culture. But it was not quite accurate that I was centering my life around detachment to prepare for death as in this Buddhist teaching.

When I first started thinking about living in a tiny house, the idea was very trendy and was quickly being commodified as specialty housing or interim housing for those starting out. TV shows asked people what they most needed in order to live tiny; then a house would be built around these parameters to showcase the genius of the builders.

"All I want is a full size kitchen sink," some would say. While every tiny house show on these shows seemed to be sponsored by Moen faucets. One tiny house festival I attended showed a house with a full size bathtub; one with feet. The kind you used to find in Victorian houses.

"Is this a spec house?" I asked the builders. No, it was custom built the builder told me. Clearly for a man who had everything and this was his vacation tiny house. I just shook my head. What had started out as a revolutionary idea that promoted living with a smaller footprint had been commodified as an accessory for the rich, a novelty. This is how ideas are captured and tamed before they could do serious damage to the status quo.

Otherwise, tiny houses seemed to make people angry as if we were getting away with something and weren't upholding our duty to the middle class American dream. I asked a colleague who seemed to share this sentiment why people who embarked on an ocean voyage in similar sized sailboats were, in contrast, seen as heroic.

"Because it's temporary," she said. She seemed happier when I said living in my tiny house would likely be temporary too. After all, I would inherit my mother's house.

When my mother moved in with her boyfriend during the pandemic year, I had the option to move into her house, but I didn't want to. There were benefits to her larger house to be sure. The kitchen for one. It was much easier to cook complex meals in it—anything that required more than one pot and one burner. And I could have a sewing room where I could spread out my project and leave it for when I had a few minutes to work a seam. I also had a storage room in her garage where I had my workshop. But the house felt lonely without my mother in it. And it was bigger than I needed. There were also rats in the walls, squirrels in the attic, possibly mold and a lot of deferred maintenance.

So I let my steadfast handyman, Tim, move into the garage studio, the space where I had practiced my tiny house building skills aiming to make it into a viable living space. Tim caught the rats, cut the trees back to discourage the squirrels and continued work on the garage, finishing the windows and building a storage area underneath. He told me I was teaching him the benefits of living tiny. I enjoyed his company and support and counted him as a friend. We shared my mother's kitchen and TV room. I came down from my mountain paradise twice a week to work with clients, do jigsaw puzzles and watch streaming movies. But I was always relieved to get back to my efficient little house.

I lived alone in my tiny. I had never lived alone before. Being Thai, I was raised to live in community and thought it was essential to my well being to live with others. I did make sure my bed was big enough for two and had hosted two different girlfriends in it in the first few years. I had built my table to be accessible from both sides so I could sit across from my guest for a meal. I had added the privacy curtain around the toilet out of consideration for our being in this space together.

But in the end the tiny house saved me from myself in the romance department, for I had not designed it with two in mind. Nor did I need rescuing from my self imposed austerity. It was in this self isolation that I grew into a larger self, free to expand my vision of how one could live. I saw my tendency to fall for a romance that did not serve me. How willing I was, while in the throes of love, to sign up for someone else's plan, as if romantic love itself was a call to change my life as an act of fulfillment. In the gay community it had been a revolutionary act to live with a same sex partner. But now this single minded coupledom as the pinnacle of human relationships had eclipsed the possibility of other kinds of relationships including mentorship, intergenerational ones, and just plain friendships.

Being an independent entity had allowed me to make decisions for my own trajectory, even spur of the moment ones as I had done by securing land with Clasina. Our partnership inspired by her vision of a permaculture farm gave me a project that offered both her friendship and a connection to the land of my childhood. I benefitted from her youth and energy and could watch her goals unfold from afar. In this fashion I had extended my reach for I could not do everything in this one lifetime.

The tiny house and I had been on a journey and the house was now my primary relationship. When I was fitting her out I didn't think about what I most wanted a house to have. I wanted the house to teach me a different kind of living, a tiny house way of living. At first I thought the lesson was that living tiny meant having community to provide amenities like showering and laundering and a big kitchen to make casseroles. During the Covid 19 lockdown I learned that showering could be optional altogether and hand laundering on site meant more grey water for plants. I learned some tricks to cooking on one burner— how to keep cooked food warm for instance. And the nights that I cooked at my pod house with Catherine and her housemate were made more precious for the company and spaciousness.

John Jeavons, who developed the Grow Biointensive methods of sustainable agriculture, wanted to find out what was the smallest amount of land needed to feed one person. (5,000 square feet if you include the pathways between the 40 raised beds was what he came up with.) I wanted to find out what was the smallest space a person needs to live. It depends. 130 square feet has offered me basically everything I need efficiently and near to hand. But that wasn't all I had learned.

I centered myself differently than when I lived with indoor plumbing. To center myself around processing my own poop tied me to the earth in a unique way. The soil became an extension of myself when I added my fermented poop to it, and grew crops in it. The food scraps I generated could feed the two banana slugs who hung around my water catchment bins. This intimate relationship with my environment gave me a lot of satisfaction.

The tiny house life was not for everyone. Especially not as I had designed it. Possibly no one aspired to adopt such a life in so small a rig. Most tiny houses were bigger, some almost as big as a regular house. I could do with mine being a foot wider, but I did not aspire to it being longer. I saw a video of a man, Aaron Fletcher, who had a large following on YouTube; he had gone even smaller, sleeping in what was little more than a well designed cart pulled by his sheep, foraging and living on dairy he made from their milk. Now there was a life lived close to nature. He too was sharing his example on Facebook. He liked my scything video so I think we're friends.

Humans have been fond of choosing metaphors from every new technology that came available. From hydraulics to clocks to computers. My own father told me that humans could be thought of like computers. You had your hardware which was your body and then you had software which was what was in your mind. This metaphor leant itself to the idea that the mind—the brain itself—could be preserved, frozen at the point of death and dropped into an artificial entity that would support it and allow you to continue living, if you could call it living. The popularity of cryogenic technology, offering to freeze your body to await such technology coming down the pike, spoke to this vision. I did not wish to elevate myself to such a proposition of consumerism that surely required the maintenance service of IT staff, medical personal, biochemists and pharmaceuticals, not to mention a sizable budget.

Altering our bodies to improve performance or just to suit our idea of ourselves was a perpetual human endeavor. Tech magnates talked of trans humanism as a viable proposition that would allow one's brain to be uploaded into a robot or cybernetic organism. Such ideas were far from sustainable in practice unless you were a marketing guru, then it was the path to sustaining profit, by exploiting human flesh. But was the electrical workings of the brain really who we were? What if we had made a tactical error and had missed some essential connection to the body, just as we were missing essential connections to the land? And we ended up making ourselves into an AI—an artificial intelligence— unconnected to corporal meaning. It was the direction our high tech world wished to take us with its smart phones, smart houses, self driving cars, and chips embedded into our bodies to make us smarter. Fanciful moderations of the human body had long been the stuff of science fiction. This primed us for such high tech solutions blinding us to the wonders of our own body. I am convinced we are missing some amazing potential by neglecting to look at what we have.

In a biological metaphor, the human body is part of the living soil and the biosphere. It positions the mind to be a steward of this biological interrelationship. There is so much to explore in healing this connection. This handmade life, this off grid attempt to become self sufficient, I now realize is also a form of mental self-healing. The term emotional resiliency comes to mind. Tolstoy was onto something.

The journey to living in a tiny house was part of my integrating my past and honing my values in a world that reflected neither my values nor offered integration very often. The tiny house itself has taken me deeper into these values to a life I didn't know was possible. It had been a journey of discovery of what sustainable practices might feel like. I let my mind breathe in this resiliency as I contemplated a life prioritized around the things that nourish the soul and heal the body. What a different world that would be for both the planet and its humans. Amen to that.

Acknowledgements

So much gratitude goes to my beloved Sisters of the Holy Pen for receiving every tentative chapter I presented and guiding me, with their interest, toward the story I wanted to tell. You are my family, my refuge, my well of inspiration. Particular thanks to Wendy Craig for her invaluable story matrix and insights on story structure. To the sisters who went before me, raVen Lakin, Jeannie Goldman, and Trish Health, for inspiring me with the birthing of their own books. To Ellie Cypher, my first reader (and proofer), who assured me that our peers would relate to my story and that it had value for lesbian and gay history. To Kathy Carlson and Jan Edgerton for encouragement as beta readers and to our fearless leader, Pamela Eakins, for her vision and unconditional love.

Grateful thanks to my proof readers, Laura Neuman-Howe, Roberta Wentzel-Walter and Kathy McConnell for committing themselves to corralling my unruly sentence structure and comma deprived punctuation with enthusiasm. Thanks also to my book loving friend Jane Duffy, for catching missing continuity details, offering narrative advice and an intuitive sense of how the book should look.

To my mud hut sisters all over the world, especially Tracy Dumais, Clasina Erasmus, and Lisa Thom. You were often on my mind.

Finally kudos to my young self for persisting in the act of self preservation of putting pen to paper to carve out a space for herself and thus claim the right to witness and record whatever caught her fancy. Her do-it-yourself spirit lives on in this self-formatted, self-published book.

Bibliography

Brown, Azby, *Just Enough: Lessons in Living Green from Traditional Japan*, New York, Kodansha International, 2009.

Collen, Alanna, *10% Human: How Your Body's Microbes Hold The Key To Health And Happiness*, New York, Harper Collins, 2015.

Hamblin, James, *Clean: The New Science of Skin*, New York, Penguin Random House, 2020.

Edey, Anna, *Green Light At The End Of The Tunnel: Learning The Art of Living Well Without Causing Harm to Our Planet*, Massachusetts, Trailblazer Press, 2014.

George, Rose, *The Big Necessity: The Unmentionable World of Human Waste and Why It Matters*, London, Picador, 2014.

Heré-Gruyer, Perrine, Heré-Gruyer, Charles, *Miraculous Abundance: One Quarter Acre, Two French Farmers and Enough to Feed the World*, Vermont, Chelsea Green Publishing, 2016.

Jenkins, Joseph, *The Humanure Handbook: A Guide to Composting Human Manure*, 2nd Edition, Pennsylvania, Jenkins Publishing, 1999.

Kroon, Coen Van der, *The Golden Fountain: The Complete Guide to Urine Therapy*, Vermont, Echo Point Books & Media. LLC, 1993.

Lancaster, Brad, *Rainwater Harvesting for Drylands, Volume I: Guiding Principles to Welcome Rain into Your Life and Landscape*, Arizona, Rainsource Press, 2006.

Lengen, Johan van, *The Barefoot Architect: A Handbook for Green Building*, California, Shelter Publications Inc, 2008.

Steinfeld, Carol, *Liquid Gold: The Lore and Logic of Using Urine to Grow Plants*, United States, Ecowaters Books, 2004-2007.